GLEIM® | Aviation

FIRST EDITION

REMOTE PILOT

FAA Knowledge Test Prep

for the FAA Computer-Based Pilot Knowledge Test

Unmanned Aircraft - General

by

Irvin N. Gleim, Ph.D., CFII, and Garrett W. Gleim, CFII

Gleim Publications, Inc.
P.O. Box 12848 · University Station
Gainesville, Florida 32604

(352) 375-0772
(800) 87-GLEIM or (800) 874-5346
Website: www.GleimAviation.com
Email: admin@gleim.com

For updates to the first printing of the first edition of
Remote Pilot FAA Knowledge Test Prep

Go To: www.gleim.com/updates

Or: Email update@gleim.com with **RPKT 1-1** in the subject line. You will receive our current update as a reply.

Updates are available until the next edition is published.

ISSN Pending
ISBN 978-1-61854-111-6

YOU CAN HELP

This first edition is designed specifically for remote pilots. Please send any corrections and suggestions for subsequent editions to us via the feedback links within the online components or using the form at www.gleim.com/AviationQuestions.

Save time, money, and frustration--order online at www.GleimAviation.com today! Please bring Gleim books to the attention of flight instructors, fixed base operators, and others with a potential interest in flying. Wide distribution of these books and increased interest in flying depend on your assistance, good word, etc. Thank you.

Environmental Statement -- This book is printed on recyclable, environmentally friendly groundwood paper, sourced from certified sustainable forests and produced either TCF (totally chlorine-free) or ECF (elementally chlorine-free).

Our answers have been carefully researched and reviewed. Inevitably, there will be differences with competitors' books and even the FAA. If necessary, we will develop an UPDATE for **Remote Pilot FAA Knowledge Test Prep**. Visit our website or email update@gleim.com for the latest updates. Updates for this first edition will be available until the next edition is published. To continue providing our customers with first-rate service, we request that technical questions about our materials be sent to us via the feedback links within the online components. We will give each question thorough consideration and a prompt response. Questions concerning orders, prices, shipments, or payments will be handled via telephone by our competent and courteous customer service staff.

ABOUT THE AUTHORS

Irvin N. Gleim earned his private pilot certificate in 1965 from the Institute of Aviation at the University of Illinois, where he subsequently received his Ph.D. He is a commercial pilot and flight instructor (instrument) with multi-engine and seaplane ratings and is a member of the Aircraft Owners and Pilots Association, American Bonanza Society, Civil Air Patrol, Experimental Aircraft Association, National Association of Flight Instructors, and Seaplane Pilots Association. He is the author of flight maneuvers and practical test prep books for the sport, private, instrument, commercial, and flight instructor certificates/ratings and the author of study guides for the sport, private/recreational, instrument, commercial, flight/ground instructor, fundamentals of instructing, airline transport pilot, and flight engineer FAA knowledge tests. Three additional pilot training books are *Pilot Handbook*, *Aviation Weather and Weather Services*, and *FAR/AIM*.

Dr. Gleim has also written articles for professional accounting and business law journals and is the author of widely used review manuals for the CIA (Certified Internal Auditor) exam, the CMA (Certified Management Accountant) exam, the CPA (Certified Public Accountant) exam, and the EA (IRS Enrolled Agent) exam. He is Professor Emeritus, Fisher School of Accounting, University of Florida, and is a CFM, CIA, CMA, and CPA.

Garrett W. Gleim earned his private pilot certificate in 1997 in a Piper Super Cub. He is a commercial pilot (single- and multi-engine), ground instructor (advanced and instrument), and flight instructor (instrument and multi-engine), and he is a member of the Aircraft Owners and Pilots Association and the National Association of Flight Instructors. He is the author of study guides for the sport, private/recreational, instrument, commercial, flight/ground instructor, fundamentals of instructing, and airline transport pilot FAA knowledge tests. He received a Bachelor of Science in Economics from The Wharton School, University of Pennsylvania. Mr. Gleim is also a CPA (not in public practice).

REVIEWERS AND CONTRIBUTORS

Paul Duty, CFII, MEI, AGI, Remote Pilot, is a graduate of Embry-Riddle Aeronautical University with a Master of Business Administration-Aviation degree. He is our aviation marketing specialist and an aviation editor. Mr. Duty is an active flight instructor and has over 20 years of experience in remote control flight. He researched questions, wrote and edited answer explanations, and incorporated revisions into the text.

Char Marissa Gregg, CFII, ATP, Glider, ASES, LTA, Remote Pilot, is the Gleim Part 141 Chief Ground Instructor and one of our aviation editors. Ms. Gregg has over 16 years of aviation experience with a background in flight instruction and as a corporate pilot. She researched questions, wrote and edited answer explanations, and incorporated revisions into the text.

The CFIs who have worked with us throughout the years to develop and improve our pilot training materials.

The many FAA employees who helped, in person or by telephone, primarily in Gainesville; Orlando; Oklahoma City; and Washington, DC.

The many pilots who have provided comments and suggestions about *Remote Pilot FAA Knowledge Test Prep*.

A PERSONAL THANKS

This manual would not have been possible without the extraordinary effort and dedication of Julie Cutlip, Blaine Hatton, Belea Keeney, Kelsey Olson, Bree Rodriguez, Teresa Soard, Justin Stephenson, Joanne Strong, Elmer Tucker, and Candace Van Doren, who typed the entire manuscript and all revisions and drafted and laid out the diagrams, illustrations, and cover for this book.

The authors also appreciate the production and editorial assistance of Jacob Bennett, Melody Dalton, Jim Harvin, Jessica Hatker, Kristen Hennen, Katie Larson, Diana León, Jake Pettifor, Shane Rapp, Drew Sheppard, and Alyssa Thomas.

Finally, we appreciate the encouragement, support, and tolerance of our families throughout this project.

TABLE OF CONTENTS

NOTE: The FAA does not release its complete database of test questions to the public. Instead, sample questions are released on the Airman Testing page of the FAA website on a quarterly basis. These questions are similar to the actual test questions, but they are not exact matches.

Gleim utilizes customer feedback and FAA publications to create additional sample questions that closely represent the topical coverage of each FAA knowledge test. In order to do well on the knowledge test, you must study the Gleim outlines in this book, answer all the questions under exam conditions (i.e., without looking at the answers first), and develop an understanding of the topics addressed. You should not simply memorize questions and answers. This will not prepare you for your FAA knowledge test, and it will not help you develop the knowledge you need to safely operate an sUAS.

Always refer to the Gleim update service (www.gleim.com/updates) to ensure you have the latest information that is available. If you see topics covered on your FAA knowledge test that are not contained in this book, please contact us at www.gleim.com/AviationQuestions to report your experience and help us fine-tune our test preparation materials.

Thank you!

PREFACE

The primary purpose of this book is to provide you with the easiest, fastest, and least expensive means of passing the FAA knowledge test for the remote pilot certificate. The publicly released FAA knowledge test bank does **not** have questions grouped together by topic. We have organized them for you. We have

1. Reproduced all previously released knowledge test questions published by the FAA. We have also included many additional similar test questions, which we believe may appear in some form on your knowledge test.

2. Organized these topics into 9 study units.

3. Explained the answer immediately to the right of each question.

4. Provided an easy-to-study outline of exactly what you need to know (and no more) at the beginning of each study unit.

Accordingly, you can thoroughly prepare for the FAA pilot knowledge test by

1. Studying the brief outlines at the beginning of each study unit.

2. Answering the question on the left side of each page while covering up the answer explanations on the right side of each page.

3. Reading the answer explanation for each question that you answer incorrectly or have difficulty answering.

4. Facilitating this Gleim process with our **FAA Test Prep Online**. Our software allows you to emulate the FAA test (CATS or PSI). By practicing answering questions on a computer, you will become at ease with the computer testing process and have the confidence to PASS. Refer to pages 10 and 11.

Additionally, this book will introduce our entire series of pilot training texts, which use the same presentation method: outlines, illustrations, questions, and answer explanations. For example, *Pilot Handbook* is a textbook of aeronautical knowledge presented in easy-to-use outline format, with many charts, diagrams, figures, etc., included. While this book contains only the material needed to pass the FAA pilot knowledge test, *Pilot Handbook* contains the textbook knowledge required to be a safe and proficient pilot.

Many books create additional work for the user. In contrast, this book facilitates your effort. The outline/illustration format, type styles, and spacing are designed to improve readability. Concepts are often presented as phrases rather than as complete sentences – similar to notes that you would take in a class lecture.

We are confident this book and the **FAA Test Prep Online** will facilitate speedy completion of your knowledge test. We also wish you the very best as you complete your remote pilot certification and in related flying as the remote pilot in command.

Enjoy Flying Safely!

Irvin N. Gleim
Garrett W. Gleim
April 2017

INTRODUCTION: THE FAA REMOTE PILOT KNOWLEDGE TEST

WHAT IS A REMOTE PILOT CERTIFICATE?

A remote pilot certificate is much like a driver's license. A remote pilot certificate will allow you to operate a small unmanned aircraft system (sUAS) in accordance with the Small Unmanned Aircraft Regulations in 14 CFR Part 107. These regulations cover a broad spectrum of commercial uses for drones weighing less than 55 pounds. The certificate, which is plastic (similar to a driver's license), is sent to you by the FAA upon satisfactory completion of your pilot knowledge test and application for the certificate with the FAA. A sample remote pilot certificate is reproduced below.

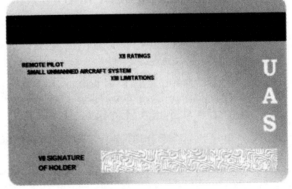

REQUIREMENTS TO OBTAIN A REMOTE PILOT CERTIFICATE

1. To operate the controls of an sUAS under Part 107, you must have a remote pilot airman certificate with an sUAS rating or you must be under the direct supervision of a person who holds such a certificate.
2. You must be at least 16 years old to qualify for a remote pilot certificate.

3. You must pass an initial aeronautical knowledge test with a score of 70% or better at an FAA-approved knowledge testing center.

    a. All FAA tests are administered at FAA-designated computer testing centers. The remote pilot knowledge test consists of 60 multiple-choice questions selected from the unmanned aircraft-related questions in the FAA's remote pilot test bank. The FAA's published unmanned aircraft-related questions, along with our own similar questions, are reproduced in this book with complete explanations.

4. If you already have a Part 61 pilot certificate, other than a student pilot certificate, you must have completed a flight review in the previous 24 months, and you must take an sUAS online training course provided by the FAA.

5. If you have a non-student pilot Part 61 certificate, you will immediately receive a temporary remote pilot certificate when you apply for a permanent certificate. Other applicants will obtain a temporary remote pilot certificate upon successful completion of a security background check. The FAA usually issues temporary certificates within 10 to 14 business days after receiving a completed application.

6. The knowledge test or online FAA course covers the following sUAS topics:

    a. Regulations
    b. Airspace Classification and Operating Requirements
    c. Meteorology
    d. Aircraft Performance
    e. Emergency Operations
    f. Crew Resource Management
    g. Radio Communication Procedures
    h. Human Factors
    i. Aeronautical Decision Making
    j. Airport Operations
    k. Maintenance
    l. Preflight Procedures

FAA PILOT KNOWLEDGE TEST AND TESTING SUPPLEMENT

1. This book is designed to help you prepare for and pass the following FAA knowledge test:

    a. Unmanned Aircraft General – Small (UAG), consisting of 60 questions. Time limit is 2 hours.

2. The FAA legends and figures are contained in a book titled *Airman Knowledge Testing Supplement for Sport Pilot, Recreational Pilot, and Private Pilot*, which you will be given to use at the time of your test.

    a. For the purpose of test preparation, the appropriate legends and figures are reproduced in color in this book.

As you practice answering questions, keep in mind that, on test day, you may need to refer to the legends in Appendix 1 of the testing supplement.

3. In an effort to develop better questions, the FAA frequently **pretests** questions on knowledge tests by adding up to five "pretest" questions. The pretest questions will not be graded.

    a. You will NOT know which questions are real and which are pretest, so you must attempt to answer all questions correctly.
    b. When you notice a question NOT covered by Gleim, it might be a pretest question.

        1) We want to know about each pretest question you see.

2) Please call 800-874-5346 or contact us at www.gleim.com/AviationQuestions with your recollection of any possible pretest questions so we may improve our efforts to prepare future pilots.

FAA'S KNOWLEDGE TESTS: CHEATING OR UNAUTHORIZED CONDUCT POLICY

To avoid test compromise, computer testing centers must follow strict security procedures established by the FAA and described in FAA Order 8080.6 (as amended), *Conduct of Airman Knowledge Tests.* The FAA has directed testing centers to terminate a test any time a test unit member suspects that a cheating incident has occurred.

The FAA will investigate, and if the agency determines that cheating or unauthorized conduct has occurred, any airman certificate or rating you hold may be revoked. You will also be prohibited from applying for or taking any test for a certificate or rating under 14 CFR 107.69 for a period of 1 year.

The following is taken verbatim from an FAA knowledge test. It is reproduced here to remind all test takers about the FAA's policy against cheating and unauthorized conduct, a policy that Gleim consistently supports and upholds. Test takers must click "Yes" to proceed from this page into the actual knowledge test.

14 CFR part 61, section 61.37 Knowledge tests: Cheating or other unauthorized conduct

(a) An applicant for a knowledge test may not:
(1) Copy or intentionally remove any knowledge test;
(2) Give to another applicant or receive from another applicant any part or copy of a knowledge test;
(3) Give assistance on, or receive assistance on, a knowledge test during the period that test is being given;
(4) Take any part of a knowledge test on behalf of another person;
(5) Be represented by, or represent, another person for a knowledge test;
(6) Use any material or aid during the period that the test is being given, unless specifically authorized to do so by the Administrator; and
(7) Intentionally cause, assist, or participate in any act prohibited by this paragraph.

(b) An applicant who the Administrator finds has committed an act prohibited by paragraph (a) of this section is prohibited, for 1 year after the date of committing that act, from:
(1) Applying for any certificate, rating, or authorization issued under this chapter; and
(2) Applying for and taking any test under this chapter.

(c) Any certificate or rating held by an applicant may be suspended or revoked if the Administrator finds that person has committed an act prohibited by paragraph (a) of this section.

FAA PILOT KNOWLEDGE TEST QUESTION BANK

In an effort to keep applicants from simply memorizing test questions, the FAA does not currently disclose all the questions you might see on your FAA knowledge test. We encourage you to take the time to fully learn and understand the concepts explained in the knowledge transfer outlines contained in this manual. **Using this book or other Gleim test preparation material to merely memorize the questions and answers is unwise and unproductive, and it will not ensure your success on your FAA knowledge test.** Memorization also greatly reduces the amount of information you will actually learn during your study.

The questions and answers provided in this book include questions developed from current FAA reference materials that closely approximate the types of questions you should see on your knowledge test. We are confident that by studying our knowledge transfer outlines, answering our questions under exam conditions, and not relying on rote memorization, you will be able to successfully pass your FAA knowledge test and begin learning to become a safe and competent pilot.

FAA QUESTIONS WITH TYPOGRAPHICAL ERRORS

Occasionally, FAA test questions contain typographical errors such that there is no correct answer. The FAA test development process involves many steps and people and, as you would expect, glitches occur in the system that are beyond the control of any one person. We indicate "best" rather than correct answers for some questions. Use these best answers for the indicated questions.

Note that the FAA corrects (rewrites) defective questions as they are discovered; these changes are explained in our updates. However, problems due to faulty or out-of-date figures printed in the FAA Airman Knowledge Testing Supplements are expensive to correct. Thus, it is important to carefully study questions that are noted to have a best answer in this book. Even though the best answer may not be completely correct, you should select it when taking your test.

HOW TO PREPARE FOR THE FAA PILOT KNOWLEDGE TEST

1. Begin by carefully reading the rest of this introduction. You need to have a complete understanding of the examination process prior to initiating your study. This knowledge will make your studying more efficient.

2. After you have spent an hour analyzing this introduction, set up a study schedule, including a target date for taking your knowledge test.

    a. Do not let the study process drag on and become discouraging; i.e., the quicker, the better.

    b. Determine where and when you are going to take your knowledge test.

3. Work through Study Units 1 through 9.

    Study Unit 1: Regulations
    Study Unit 2: Airspace Classification and Operating Requirements
    Study Unit 3: Aviation Weather Services
    Study Unit 4: Weather Effects on Performance
    Study Unit 5: Loading and Performance
    Study Unit 6: Radio Communications Procedures
    Study Unit 7: Airport Operations
    Study Unit 8: Aeronautical Decision-Making and Physiology
    Study Unit 9: Emergency Procedures, Maintenance, and Inspections

    a. Within each of the study units listed, questions relating to the same subtopic (e.g., thunderstorms, sectional charts, etc.) are grouped together to facilitate your study program. Each subtopic is called a subunit.

    b. For each question, we present

        1) The correct answer.

        2) The appropriate source document for the answer explanation. These publications can be obtained from the FAA (www.faa.gov) and aviation bookstores.

14 CFR	Federal Aviation Regulations	*AWS*	*Aviation Weather Services*
AC	Advisory Circular		Chart Supplement
ACL	Aeronautical Chart Legend	CRM	Crew Resource Management
ADM	Aeronautical Decision Making	*IFH*	*Instrument Flying Handbook*
	Aeronautical Charts	*PHAK*	*Pilot's Handbook of Aeronautical Knowledge*
AIM	*Aeronautical Information Manual*	SAFO	Safety Alert for Operators
AvW	*Aviation Weather*	sUASSG	Small Unmanned Aircraft Systems Study
AWBH	*Aircraft Weight and Balance Handbook*		Guide

        a) The codes may refer to an entire document, such as an advisory circular, or to a particular chapter or subsection of a larger document.

            i) See page 262 for a complete list of abbreviations and acronyms used in this book.

      3)   A comprehensive answer explanation, including

          a)   A discussion of the correct answer or concept and

          b)   An explanation of why the other two answer choices are incorrect.

4.   Begin by studying the outlines slowly and carefully. They are designed to help you pass the FAA knowledge test.

    a.   **CAUTION:** The **sole purpose** of this book is to expedite your passing the FAA knowledge test for the remote pilot certificate. Accordingly, all extraneous material (i.e., topics or regulations not directly tested on the FAA knowledge test) is omitted, even though much more knowledge is necessary to safely pilot unmanned aircraft.

5.   Next, answer the questions under exam conditions. Cover the answer explanations on the right side of each page with a piece of paper while you answer the questions.

> Remember, it is very important to the learning (and understanding) process that you honestly commit yourself to an answer. If you are wrong, your memory will be reinforced by having discovered your error. Therefore, it is crucial to cover up the answer and make an honest attempt to answer the question before reading the answer.

    a.   Study the answer explanation for each question that you answer incorrectly, do not understand, or have difficulty with.

    b.   Use our **FAA Test Prep Online** to ensure that you do not refer to answers before committing to one AND to simulate actual computer testing center exam conditions.

6.   Note that this manual contains questions grouped by topic. Thus, some questions may appear repetitive, while others may be duplicates or near-duplicates. Accordingly, do not work question after question (i.e., waste time and effort) if you are already conversant with a topic and the type of questions asked.

7.   As you move through study units, you may need further explanation or clarification of certain topics. You may wish to obtain and use the Gleim *Aviation Weather and Weather Services* book.

8.   Keep track of your work. As you complete a subunit, grade yourself with an A, B, C, or ? (use a ? if you need help on the subject).

    a.   The A, B, C, or ? is your self-evaluation of your comprehension of the material in that subunit and your ability to answer the questions.

        A   means a good understanding.
        B   means a fair understanding.
        C   means a shaky understanding.
        ?   means to ask others about the material and/or questions.

    b.   This procedure will provide you with the ability to quickly see how much studying you have done (and how much remains) and how well you have done.

    c.   This procedure will also facilitate review. You can spend more time on the subunits that were more difficult for you.

    d.   **FAA Test Prep Online** provides you with your historical performance data.

Follow the suggestions given throughout this introduction, and you will have no trouble passing the FAA knowledge test the first time you take it.

With this overview of exam requirements, you are ready to begin the easy-to-study outlines and rearranged questions with answers to build your knowledge and confidence and PASS THE FAA's REMOTE PILOT KNOWLEDGE TEST.

The feedback we receive from users indicates that our materials reduce anxiety, improve FAA test scores, and build knowledge. Studying for each test becomes a useful step toward advanced certificates and ratings.

MULTIPLE-CHOICE QUESTION-ANSWERING TECHNIQUE

Because the remote pilot knowledge test has a set number of questions (60) and a set time limit (2 hours), you can plan your test-taking session to ensure that you leave yourself enough time to answer each question with relative certainty. The following steps will help you move through the knowledge test efficiently and produce better test results.

1. **Budget your time.** We make this point with emphasis. Just as you would fill up your gas tank prior to reaching empty, so too should you finish your exam before time expires.

    a. If you utilize the entire time limit for the test, you will have about 2 minutes per question.

    b. If you are adequately prepared for the test, you should finish it well within the time limit.

        1) Use any extra time you have to review questions that you are not sure about and similar questions in your exam that may help you answer other questions.

    c. Time yourself when completing study sessions in this book and/or review your time investment reports from the Gleim **FAA Test Prep Online** to track your progress and adherence to the time limit and your own personal time allocation budget.

2. **Answer the questions in consecutive order.**

    a. Do **not** agonize over any one item. Stay within your time budget.

    b. Mark any questions you are unsure of and return to them later as time allows.

        1) Once you initiate test grading, you will no longer be able to review/change any answers.

    c. Never leave a multiple-choice question unanswered. Make your best educated guess in the time allowed. Remember, your score is based on the number of correct responses. You will not be penalized for guessing incorrectly.

3. **For each multiple-choice question,**

    a. **Try to ignore the answer choices.** Do not allow the answer choices to affect your reading of the question.

        1) If three answer choices are presented, two of them are incorrect. These choices are called **distractors** for good reason. Often, distractors are written to appear correct at first glance until further analysis.

        2) In computational items, the distractors are carefully calculated such that they are the result of making common mistakes. Be careful, and double-check your computations if time permits.

    b. **Read the question carefully** to determine the precise requirement.

        1) Focusing on what is required enables you to ignore extraneous information, to focus on the relevant facts, and to proceed directly to determining the correct answer.

            a) Be especially careful to note when the requirement is an **exception**; e.g., "Which of the following is **not** an operation allowed under Part 107?"

    c. **Determine the correct answer** before looking at the answer choices.

    d. **Read the answer choices carefully.**

        1) Even if the first answer appears to be the correct choice, do **not** skip the remaining answer choices. Questions often require the "best" answer of the choices provided. Thus, each choice requires your consideration.

        2) Treat each answer choice as a true/false question as you analyze it.

e. **Click on the best answer.**

  1) You have a 33% chance of answering the question correctly by blindly guessing; improve your odds with educated guessing.

  2) For many multiple-choice questions, at least one answer choice can be eliminated with minimal effort, thereby increasing your educated guess to a 50-50 proposition.

4. After you have been through all the questions in the test, consult the question status list to determine which questions are unanswered and which are marked for review.

   a. Go back to the marked questions and finalize your answer choices.
   b. Verify that all questions have been answered.

EDUCATED GUESSING

 The FAA knowledge test sometimes includes questions that are poorly worded or confusing. Expect the unexpected and move forward. Do not let confusing questions affect your concentration or take up too much time; make your best guess and move on.

1. If you don't know the answer, make an educated guess as follows:

   a. Rule out answers that you think are incorrect.
   b. Speculate on what the FAA is looking for and/or the rationale behind the question.
   c. Select the best answer or guess between equally appealing answers. Your first guess is usually the most intuitive. If you cannot make an educated guess, re-read the stem and each answer choice and pick the most intuitive answer. It's just a guess!

2. Avoid lingering on any question for too long. Remember your time budget and the overall test time limit.

SIMULATED FAA PRACTICE TEST

Appendix A, "Remote Pilot Practice Test," beginning on page 245, allows you to practice taking the FAA knowledge test without the answers next to the questions. This test has 60 questions randomly selected from the questions in our remote pilot knowledge test bank. Topical coverage in the practice test is similar to that of the FAA knowledge test.

It is very important that you answer all 60 questions in one sitting. You should not consult the answers, especially when being referred to figures (charts, tables, etc.) throughout this book where the questions are answered and explained. Analyze your performance based on the answer key that follows the practice test.

It is even better to practice with Test Sessions in the Gleim **FAA Test Prep Online**. These simulate actual computer testing conditions, including the screen layouts, instructions, etc., for CATS and PSI.

For more information on the Gleim **FAA Test Prep Online**, see pages 10 and 11.

WHEN TO TAKE THE FAA PILOT KNOWLEDGE TEST

1. You must be at least 14 years of age to take the remote pilot knowledge test.
2. Take the FAA knowledge test within 30 days of beginning your study.

   a. Get the knowledge test behind you.

WHAT TO TAKE TO THE FAA PILOT KNOWLEDGE TEST

1. A navigational plotter
2. A pocket calculator you are familiar with and have used before (no instructional material for the calculator is allowed)
3. Proper identification that contains your photograph, signature, date of birth, and actual residential address, if different from your mailing address.

NOTE: Paper and pencils are supplied at the examination site.

COMPUTER TESTING CENTERS

The FAA has contracted with two computer testing services to administer FAA knowledge tests. Both of these computer testing services have testing centers throughout the country. To register for the knowledge test, call one of the computer testing services listed below. More information can be found at www.gleim.com/testing_centers.

CATS   (800) 947-4228   PSI   (800) 211-2754

COMPUTER TESTING PROCEDURES

When you arrive at the testing center, you will be required to provide positive proof of identification and documentary evidence of your age. The identification must include your photograph, signature, and actual residential address if different from the mailing address. This information may be presented in more than one form of identification. Next, you will sign in on the testing center's daily log. Your signature on the logsheet certifies that, if this is a retest, you meet the applicable requirements (see "Failure on the FAA Pilot Knowledge Test" on page 10) and that you have not passed this test in the past 2 years.

Next, you will be taken into the testing room and seated at a computer terminal. A person from the testing center will assist you in logging onto the system, and you will be asked to confirm your personal data (e.g., name, Social Security number, etc.). Then you will be given an online introduction to the computer testing system, and you will take a sample test. If you have used our **FAA Test Prep Online**, you will be conversant with the computer testing methodology and environment and will breeze through the sample test. When you have completed your test, an Airman Computer Test Report will be printed out, validated (usually with an embossed seal), and given to you by a person from the testing center. Before you leave, you will be required to sign out on the testing center's daily log.

Each testing service has certain idiosyncrasies in its paperwork, scheduling, and telephone procedures as well as in its software. It is for this reason that our **FAA Test Prep Online** emulates both of the FAA-approved computer testing companies.

YOUR FAA PILOT KNOWLEDGE TEST REPORT

1. You will receive your FAA Pilot Knowledge Test Report upon completion of the test. An example test report is reproduced on the following page.

   a. Note that you will receive only one grade as illustrated.
   b. The expiration date is the date by which you must take your FAA practical test.
   c. The report lists the FAA learning statement codes of the questions you missed so you can review the topics you missed prior to your practical test.

Computer Test Report

U.S. DEPARTMENT OF TRANSPORTATION
Federal Aviation Administration

Airman Knowledge Test Report

NAME:

APPLICANT ID:　　　　　　　　　　　　EXAM ID:

EXAM: Unmanned Aircraft - General

EXAM DATE: 10/08/2016　　　　　　　EXAM SITE:

SCORE: 96　　　　GRADE: PASS　　　TAKE: 1

Learning statement codes listed below represent incorrectly answered questions. Learning statement codes and their associated statements can be found at **www.faa.gov/training_testing/testing/airmen**.

Reference material associated with the learning statement codes can be found in the appropriate knowledge test guide at **www.faa.gov/training_testing/testing/airmen/test_guides**.

A single code may represent more than one incorrect response.

PLT229 PLT306

EXPIRATION DATE:　10/31/2018　　　　　　CTD's Embossed Seal

DO NOT LOSE THIS REPORT

AUTHORIZED INSTRUCTOR'S STATEMENT: (If applicable)

On _____ (date) I gave the above named applicant ____ hours of additional instruction, covering each subject area shown to be deficient, and consider the applicant competent to pass the test.

Name _____ Initial____ Cert. No._____ Type_____
(Print clearly)

Signature _____

FRAUDULENT ALTERATION OF THIS FORM BY ANY PERSON IS A BASIS FOR SUSPENSION OR REVOCATION OF ANY CERTIFICATES OR RATINGS HELD BY THAT PERSON. THIS INFORMATION IS PROTECTED BY THE PRIVACY ACT. FOR OFFICIAL USE ONLY.

2. Use the FAA Listing of Learning Statement Codes on pages 253 through 258 to determine which topics you had difficulty with.

3. Keep your FAA Pilot Knowledge Test Report in a safe place because you must submit it to the FAA when you apply for the remote pilot certificate.

FAILURE ON THE FAA PILOT KNOWLEDGE TEST

1.   If you fail (score less than 70%) the knowledge test (which is virtually impossible if you follow the Gleim system), you may retake it after 14 days.

2.   Upon retaking the test, you will find that the procedure is the same except that you must also submit your FAA Pilot Knowledge Test Report indicating the previous failure to the computer testing center.

3.   Reasons for failure include

   a.   Failure to study the material tested and mere memorization of correct answers. (Relevant study material is contained in the outlines of Study Units 1 through 9 of this book.)

   b.   Failure to practice working through the questions under test conditions.

   c.   Poor examination technique, such as misreading questions and not understanding the requirements.

GLEIM FAA TEST PREP ONLINE

Computer testing is consistent with aviation's use of computers (e.g., DUATS, flight simulators, computerized cockpits, etc.). All FAA knowledge tests are administered by computer.

Computer testing is natural after computer study and computer-assisted instruction is a very efficient and effective method of study. The Gleim **FAA Test Prep Online** is designed to prepare you for computer testing because our software can simulate both CATS and PSI. We make you comfortable with computer testing!

FAA Test Prep Online contains all of the questions in our test bank, context-sensitive outline material, and on-screen charts and figures. It allows you to choose either Study Mode or Test Mode.

In Study Mode, the software provides you with an explanation of each answer you choose (correct or incorrect). You design each Study Session:

Topic(s) and/or FAA learning statement codes you wish to cover
Number of questions
Order of questions -- FAA, Gleim, or random
Order of answers to each question -- Gleim or random

Questions marked and/or missed from last session -- test, study, or both
Questions marked and/or missed from all sessions -- test, study, or both
Questions never seen, answered, or answered correctly

In Test Mode, you decide the format: CATS or PSI. When you finish your test, you can and should study the questions missed and access answer explanations. The software emulates the operation of FAA-approved computer testing companies. Thus, you have a complete understanding of how to take an FAA knowledge test and know exactly what to expect before you go to a computer testing center.

The Gleim **FAA Test Prep Online** is an all-in-one program designed to help anyone with Internet access and an interest in aviation pass the FAA knowledge tests.

Study Sessions and Test Sessions

Study Sessions give you immediate feedback on why your answer selection for a particular question is correct or incorrect and allow you to access the context-sensitive outline material that helps to explain concepts related to the question. Choose from several different question sources: all questions available for that library; questions from a certain topic (Gleim study units and subunits); questions that you missed or marked in the last sessions you created; questions that you have never seen, answered, or answered correctly; questions from certain FAA learning statement codes; etc. You can mix up the questions by selecting to randomize the question and/or answer order so that you do not memorize answer letters.

You may then grade your Study Sessions and track your study progress using the performance analysis charts and graphs. The Performance Analysis information helps you to focus on areas where you need the most improvement, saving you time in the overall study process. You may then want to go back and study questions that you missed in a previous session, or you may want to create a Study Session of questions that you marked in the previous session. All of these options are made easy with **FAA Test Prep Online**'s Study Sessions.

After studying the outlines and questions in a Study Session, you can further test your skills with a Test Session. These sessions allow you to answer questions under actual testing conditions using one of the simulations of the major testing services. In a Test Session, you will not know which questions you have answered correctly until the session is graded.

Recommended Study Program

1. Start with Study Unit 1 and proceed through study units in chronological order. Follow the three-step process below.

   a. First, carefully study the Gleim Outline.
   b. Second, create a Study Session of all questions in the study unit. Answer and study all questions in the Study Session.
   c. Third, create a Test Session of all questions in the study unit. Answer all questions in the Test Session.

2. After each Study Session and Test Session, create a new Study Session from questions answered incorrectly. This is of critical importance to allow you to learn from your mistakes.

Practice Test

Take an exam in the actual testing environment of either of the major testing centers: CATS or PSI. **FAA Test Prep Online** simulates the testing formats of these testing centers, making it easy for you to study questions under actual exam conditions. After studying with **FAA Test Prep Online**, you will know exactly what to expect when you go in to take your pilot knowledge test.

On-Screen Charts and Figures

One of the most convenient features of **FAA Test Prep Online** is the easily accessible on-screen charts and figures. Many of the questions refer to drawings, maps, charts, and other pictures that provide information to help answer the question. In **FAA Test Prep Online**, you can pull up any of these figures with the click of a button. You can increase or decrease the size of the images.

Free Updates and Technical Support

Gleim offers FREE technical support to all users of the current versions. Call (800) 874-5346, send an email to support@gleim.com, or fill out the technical support request form online (www.gleim.com/support/form.php). Additionally, Gleim **FAA Test Prep Online** is always up to date. The program is automatically updated when any changes are made, so you can be confident that Gleim will prepare you for your knowledge test. For more information on our email update service for books, turn to page ii.

STUDY UNIT ONE
REGULATIONS

(21 pages of outline)

1.1 GENERAL

1. **The applicant demonstrates understanding of the applicability of 14 CFR Part 107 to small unmanned aircraft operations.**

   a. Title 14 of the Code of Federal Regulations, Part 107, is Small Unmanned Aircraft Systems. 14 CFR Part 107 contains the operational rules for routine commercial use of small unmanned aircraft systems (sUAS or "drones").

      1) This rule includes operational limitations, requirements for certifications and responsibilities of the remote pilot in command (PIC), and aircraft requirements.

      2) Part 107 allows sUAS operations for many different non-hobby and nonrecreational purposes without requiring airworthiness certification, exemption, or a Certificate of Waiver (CoW) or Authorization (CoA).

         a) In addition, Part 107 applies to sUAS used for hobby or recreation that are not flown in accordance with Part 101, Subpart E.

   b. This section provides guidance regarding the applicability of Part 107 to civil sUAS operations conducted within the NAS. However, Part 107 does not apply to the following:

      1) Model aircraft that are operated in accordance with Part 101, Subpart E, Model Aircraft, which applies to model aircraft meeting all of the following criteria:

         a) The aircraft is flown strictly for hobby or recreational use;

         b) The aircraft is operated in accordance with a community-based set of safety guidelines and within the programming of a nationwide community-based organization;

         c) The aircraft is limited to no more than 55 pounds unless otherwise certified through a design, construction, inspection, flight test, and operational safety program administered by a community-based organization;

         d) The aircraft is operated in a manner that does not interfere with and gives way to any manned aircraft;

         e) When flown within 5 miles of an airport, the operator of the aircraft provides prior notice of the operation to the airport operator and the airport air traffic control (ATC) tower (when an air traffic facility is located at the airport);

         f) The aircraft is capable of sustained flight in the atmosphere; and

         g) The aircraft is flown within Visual Line of Sight (VLOS) of the person operating the aircraft.

      2) Operations conducted outside the United States;

      3) Amateur rockets;

      4) Moored balloons;

      5) Unmanned free balloons;

      6) Kites;

      7) Public aircraft operations;

      8) Military operations; and

      9) Air carrier operations.

2. **The applicant demonstrates understanding of definitions used in 14 CFR Part 107.**

    a. The following defined terms are used throughout Part 107.

        1) **Control station (CS)** is an interface used by the remote pilot or the person manipulating the controls to control the flight path of the sUA.

        2) **Corrective lenses** are spectacles or contact lenses.

        3) **Model aircraft** is a UA that is

            a) Capable of sustained flight in the atmosphere,
            b) Flown within VLOS of the person operating the aircraft, and
            c) Flown for hobby or recreational purposes.

        4) **Person manipulating the controls** is a person other than the remote PIC who is controlling the flight of an sUAS under the supervision of the remote PIC.

        5) **Remote pilot in command (PIC)** is a person who holds a remote pilot certificate with an sUAS rating and has the final authority and responsibility for the operation and safety of an sUAS operation conducted under Part 107.

        6) **Small unmanned aircraft (sUA)** is a UA weighing less than 55 pounds, including everything that is onboard or otherwise attached to the aircraft, and can be flown without the possibility of direct human intervention from within or on the aircraft.

        7) **Small unmanned aircraft system (sUAS)** is an sUA and its associated elements (including communication links and the components that control the sUA) that are required for the safe and efficient operation of the sUA in the NAS.

        8) **Unmanned aircraft (UA)** is an aircraft operated without the possibility of direct human intervention from within or on the aircraft.

        9) **Visual observer (VO)** is a person acting as a flightcrew member who assists the sUA remote PIC and the person manipulating the controls to see and avoid other air traffic or objects aloft or on the ground.

3. **The applicant demonstrates understanding of the ramification of falsification, reproduction, or alteration of a certificate, rating, authorization, record, or report.**

    a. The FAA relies on information provided by owners and remote pilots of sUAS when it authorizes operations or when it has to make a compliance determination.

        1) Accordingly, the FAA may take appropriate action against an sUAS owner, operator, remote PIC, or anyone else who fraudulently or knowingly provides false records or reports, or otherwise reproduces or alters any records, reports, or other information for fraudulent purposes.

        2) Such action could include civil sanctions and the suspension or revocation of a certificate or waiver.

4. **The applicant demonstrates understanding of accident reporting.**

    a. The remote PIC of the sUAS is required to report an accident to the FAA within 10 days if it meets any of the following thresholds:

        1) At least serious injury to any person or any loss of consciousness

            a) A serious injury is an injury that qualifies as Level 3 or higher on the Abbreviated Injury Scale (AIS) of the Association for the Advancement of Automotive Medicine (AAAM).

                i) The AIS is an anatomical scoring system that provides a means of ranking the severity of an injury and is widely used by emergency medical personnel.

                ii) Within the AIS system, injuries are ranked on a scale of 1 to 6, with Level 1 being a minor injury, Level 2 is moderate, Level 3 is serious, Level 4 is severe, Level 5 is critical, and Level 6 is a nonsurvivable injury.

iii) The FAA currently uses serious injury (AIS Level 3) as an injury threshold in other FAA regulations.

NOTE: It would be considered a "serious injury" if a person requires hospitalization but the injury is fully reversible [including head trauma, broken bone(s), laceration(s) to the skin that requires suturing, etc.].

2) Damage to any property, other than the sUA, if the cost is greater than $500 to repair or replace the property (whichever is lower)

NOTE: For example, an sUA damages a property whose fair market value is $200, and it would cost $600 to repair the damage. Because the fair market value is below $500, this accident is not required to be reported.

Similarly, if the aircraft causes $200 worth of damage to property whose fair market value is $600, that accident is also not required to be reported because the repair cost is below $500.

b. Submitting the Report

1) The accident report must be made within 10 calendar days of the operation that created the injury or damage.

2) The report may be submitted to the appropriate FAA Regional Operations Center (ROC) electronically or by telephone.

a) Electronic reporting can be completed at www.faa.gov/uas/.

b) To make a report by phone, see the FAA Regional Operations Centers Telephone List below.

3) Reports may also be made to the nearest jurisdictional FSDO (www.faa.gov/about/office_org/field_offices/fsdo/).

4) The report should include the following information:

a) sUAS remote PIC's name and contact information

b) sUAS remote PIC's FAA airman certificate number

c) sUAS registration number issued to the aircraft, if required (FAA registration number)

d) Location of the accident

e) Date of the accident

f) Time of the accident

g) Person(s) injured and extent of injury, if any or known

h) Property damaged and extent of damage, if any or known

i) Description of what happened

FAA Regional Operations Centers Telephone List

FAA REGIONAL OPERATIONS CENTERS	
LOCATION WHERE ACCIDENT OCCURRED:	TELEPHONE:
DC, DE, MD, NJ, NY, PA, WV, and VA	404-305-5150
AL, CT, FL, GA, KY, MA, ME, MS, NC, NH, PR, RI, SC, TN, VI, and VT	404-305-5156
AK, AS, AZ, CA, CO, GU, HI, ID, MP, MT, NV, OR, UT, WA, and WY	425-227-1999
AR, IA, IL, IN, KS, LA, MI, MN, MO, ND, NE, NM, OH, OK, SD, TX, and WI	817-222-5006

c. National Transportation Safety Board (NTSB) Reporting

1) In addition to the report submitted to the ROC, and in accordance with the criteria established by the NTSB, certain sUAS accidents must also be reported to the NTSB. For more information, visit www.ntsb.gov.

5. **The applicant demonstrates understanding of inspection, testing, and demonstration of compliance.**

    a. **Applicability.** 14 CFR 107.15 requires the remote PIC to perform checks of the UA prior to each flight to determine if the sUAS is in a condition for safe operation. This section provides guidance on how to inspect and maintain an sUAS.

        1) Additionally, Appendix C, sUAS Maintenance and Inspection Best Practices, contains expanded information and best practices for sUAS maintenance and inspection.

    b. **Inspection and testing.** Prior to flight, ensure that all control links between the CS and the sUA are working properly.

        1) For example, before each flight, the remote PIC must determine that the sUA flight control surfaces necessary for the safety of flight are moving correctly through the manipulation of the sUA CS.

        2) If the remote PIC observes that one or more of the control surfaces are not responding correctly to CS inputs, then the remote PIC may not conduct flight operations until correct movement of all flight control surface(s) is established.

        3) Ensure there is sufficient power to continue controlled flight operations to a normal landing. One of the ways this could be done is by following the sUAS manufacturer's operating manual power consumption tables.

           a) Another method would be to include a system on the sUAS that detects power levels and alerts the remote pilot when remaining aircraft power is diminishing to a level that is inadequate for continued flight operation.

        4) Ensure that any object attached or carried by the sUA is secure and does not adversely affect the flight characteristics or controllability of the aircraft.

    c. **Demonstration of compliance.** Ensure that all necessary documentation is available for inspection, including the remote PIC's remote pilot certificate, aircraft registration (if required), and Certificate of Waiver (CoW) (if applicable).

1.2 OPERATING RULES

1. **The applicant demonstrates understanding of registration requirements for sUAS.**

    a. An sUA must be registered, as provided for in 14 CFR Part 47 or Part 48 prior to operating under Part 107.

        1) As of December 21, 2015, the Federal Aviation Administration requires all owners of model aircraft, sUA or drones, or other RC aircraft weighing between 0.55 and 55 pounds to register online before taking to the skies.

        2) Part 48 is the regulation that establishes the streamlined online registration option for sUAS that will be operated only within the territorial limits of the United States.

        3) The online registration system requires drone owners 13 years and older to submit their name, email, and home address to receive a Certificate of Aircraft Registration/Proof of Ownership.

           a) This includes a unique identification number owners must affix to any drone they own and operate exclusively for recreation.

        4) As of March 31, 2016, public, commercial, and other non-model aircraft UAS operators may use the online registration system.

           a) During the registration process, users have to identify whether they are operating a model aircraft for recreational purposes or operating a UAS for business or government use.

    b.   Guidance regarding UAS registration and marking may be found at registermyuas.faa.gov.

        1)   Alternatively, sUAS operators can elect to register under Part 47 in the same manner as manned aircraft.

    c.   Registration of Foreign-Owned and Operated sUAS.

        1)   If sUAS operations involve the use of foreign civil aircraft, the operator needs to obtain a Foreign Aircraft Permit pursuant to 14 CFR 375.41 before conducting any commercial air operations under this authority.

        2)   Foreign civil aircraft is defined as

            a)   An aircraft of foreign registry that is not part of the armed forces of a foreign nation or

            b)   A U.S.-registered aircraft owned, controlled, or operated by persons who are not citizens or permanent residents of the United States.

    d.   Application instructions are specified in 14 CFR 375.43.

    e.   Applications should be submitted by electronic mail to the Department of Transportation (DOT) Office of International Aviation, Foreign Air Carrier Licensing Division.

    f.   Additional information can be obtained at cms.dot.gov/policy/aviation-policy/licensing/foreign-carriers.

    g.   The owner must use the traditional aircraft registration process under 14 CFR Part 47, (paper N-number), if any of the following apply:

        1)   His or her unmanned aircraft is 55 pounds or greater;

        2)   (S)he wants to qualify a small unmanned aircraft for operation outside the United States;

        3)   (S)he holds title to an aircraft in trust; or

        4)   (S)he uses a voting trust to meet U.S. citizenship requirements.

2.   **The applicant demonstrates understanding of the requirement for the sUAS to be in a condition for safe operation.**

    a.   The remote PIC must complete a preflight familiarization, inspection, and other actions, such as crewmember briefings, prior to beginning flight operations.

    b.   For more information, refer to item 20. on page 26.

3.   **The applicant demonstrates understanding of medical condition(s) that would interfere with safe operation of an sUAS.**

    a.   Medical condition. Being able to safely operate the sUAS relies on, among other things, the physical and mental capabilities of the remote PIC, person manipulating the controls, VO, and any other direct participant in the sUAS operation.

        1)   Though the person manipulating the controls of an sUAS and VO are not required to obtain an airman medical certificate, they may not participate in the operation of an sUAS if they know or have reason to know they have a physical or mental condition that could interfere with the safe operation of the sUAS.

    b.   Physical or mental incapacitations. Examples of physical or mental incapacitations that could render a remote PIC, person manipulating the controls, or VO incapable of performing their sUAS operational duties include

        1)   The temporary or permanent loss of the dexterity necessary to operate the CS to safely control the sUA

        2)   The inability to maintain the required "see and avoid" vigilance due to blurred vision

3) The inability to maintain proper situational awareness of the sUA operations due to illness and/or medication(s), such as after taking medications with cautions not to drive or operate heavy machinery

4) A debilitating physical condition, such as a migraine headache or moderate or severe body ache(s) or pain(s) that would render the remote PIC, person manipulating the controls, or VO unable to perform sUAS operational duties

5) A hearing or speaking impairment that would inhibit the remote PIC, person manipulating the controls, and VO from effectively communicating with each other

    a) In such a situation, the remote PIC must ensure that an alternative means of effective communication is implemented. For example, a person who is hearing impaired may be able to effectively use sign language to communicate.

4. **The applicant demonstrates understanding of the responsibility and authority of the remote PIC.**

    a. Allowing a person other than the remote PIC to manipulate the flight controls.

        1) A remote PIC must be designated before or during the flight of the sUA.

    b. The remote PIC is directly responsible for and is the final authority on the operation of the sUAS.

        1) The remote PIC must inform all participants about emergency procedures.

    c. The remote PIC must ensure that the sUA will pose no undue hazard to other people, other aircraft, or other property in the event of a loss of control (LOC) of the aircraft for any reason.

    d. The remote PIC must ensure that the sUAS operation complies with all applicable regulations.

    e. The remote PIC must have the ability to direct the sUA to ensure compliance with the applicable provisions of this chapter.

5. **The applicant demonstrates understanding of regulatory deviation and reporting requirements for in-flight emergencies.**

    a. An in-flight emergency is an unexpected and unforeseen serious occurrence or situation that requires urgent, prompt action.

    b. In case of an in-flight emergency, the remote PIC is permitted to deviate from any rule of Part 107 to the extent necessary to respond to that emergency.

        1) A remote PIC who exercises this emergency power to deviate from the rules of Part 107 is required, upon FAA request, to send a written report to the FAA explaining the deviation.

    c. Emergency action should be taken in such a way as to minimize injury or damage to property.

6. **The applicant demonstrates understanding of hazardous operations.**

    a. **Careless or reckless.** Similar to manned aircraft, Part 107 prohibits remote PICs from engaging in careless or reckless operation of an sUAS.

        1) Because sUAS have additional operating considerations that are not present in manned aircraft operations, additional activity may be careless or reckless if conducted using an sUAS.

            a) For example, failure to consider weather conditions near structures, trees, or rolling terrain when operating in a densely populated area could be determined as careless or reckless operation.

        b) Flying an sUAS while driving a moving vehicle is considered to be careless or reckless because the person's attention would be hazardously divided.

          i) Therefore, the remote PIC or person manipulating the controls cannot operate an sUAS and drive a moving vehicle in a safe manner and remain in compliance with Part 107.

    2) Applicable laws. Other laws, such as state and local traffic laws, may also apply to the conduct of a person driving a vehicle.

        a) Many states currently prohibit distracted driving; state or local laws also may be amended in the future to impose restrictions on how cars and public roads may be used with regard to an sUAS operation.

        b) The FAA emphasizes that people involved in an sUAS operation are responsible for complying with all applicable laws and not only the FAA's regulations.

  b. **Dropping an Object.**

    1) 14 CFR 91.15, Dropping Objects, states

        a) No pilot in command of a civil aircraft may allow any object to be dropped from that aircraft in flight that creates a hazard to persons or property. However, this section does not prohibit the dropping of any object if reasonable precautions are taken to avoid injury or damage to persons or property.

    2) Similarly, no items may be dropped from an sUA in a manner that creates an undue hazard to persons or property.

7. **The applicant demonstrates understanding of operating from a moving aircraft or moving land- or water-borne vehicle.**

  a. Operations from moving vehicles. Part 107 permits operation of an sUAS from a moving land or water-borne vehicle over a sparsely populated area. However, operation from a moving aircraft is prohibited.

    1) Additionally, sUA transporting another person's property for compensation or hire may not be operated from any moving vehicle.

  b. Waiving the sparsely-populated area provision. Although the regulation states that operations from a moving vehicle may only be conducted over a sparsely populated area, this provision may be waived.

    1) The operation is subject to the same restrictions that apply to all other Part 107 operations. For instance, the remote PIC operating from a moving vehicle is still required to maintain VLOS, and operations are still prohibited over persons not directly involved in the operation of the sUAS unless under safe cover.

    2) The remote PIC is also responsible for ensuring that no person is subject to undue risk as a result of LOC of the sUA for any reason. If a VO is not located in the same vehicle as the remote PIC, the VO and remote PIC must still maintain effective communication.

8. **The applicant demonstrates understanding of alcohol or drugs and the provisions on prohibition of use.**

  a. Operations while impaired. Part 107 does not allow operation of an sUAS if the remote PIC, person manipulating the controls, or VO is unable to safely carry out his or her responsibilities. It is the remote PIC's responsibility to ensure all crewmembers are not participating in the operation while impaired.

    1) While drug and alcohol use are known to impair judgment, certain over-the-counter medications and medical conditions could also affect the ability to safely operate an sUA. For example, certain antihistamines and decongestants may cause drowsiness.

2) Part 107 prohibits a person from serving as a remote PIC, person manipulating the controls, VO, or other crewmember if (s)he

    a) Consumed any alcoholic beverage within the preceding 8 hours,
    b) Is under the influence of alcohol,
    c) Has a blood alcohol concentration of .04% or greater, and/or
    d) Is using a drug that affects his or her mental or physical capabilities.

b. Medical conditions. Certain medical conditions, such as epilepsy, may also create a risk to operations. It is the remote PIC's responsibility to determine that his or her medical condition is under control and (s)he can safely conduct a UAS operation.

9. **The applicant demonstrates understanding of daylight operation.**

a. Daylight operations. Part 107 prohibits operation of an sUAS at night, which is defined in Part 1 as the time between the end of evening civil twilight and the beginning of morning civil twilight, as published in The Air Almanac, converted to local time.

1) In the continental United States (CONUS), evening civil twilight is the period of sunset until 30 minutes after sunset and morning civil twilight is the period of 30 minutes prior to sunrise until sunrise. In Alaska, the definition of civil twilight differs and is described in The Air Almanac.

2) The Air Almanac provides tables that are used to determine sunrise and sunset at various latitudes.

    a) These tables can also be downloaded from the Naval Observatory and customized for your location. The link for the Naval Observatory is aa.usno.navy.mil/publications/docs/aira.php.

b. Civil twilight operations. When sUAS operations are conducted during civil twilight, the sUA must be equipped with anticollision lights that are capable of being visible for at least 3 SM.

1) However, the remote PIC may reduce the visible distance of the lighting less than 3 SM during a given flight if (s)he has determined that it would be in the interest of safety to do so, for example if it impacts his or her night vision.

2) sUAS not operated during civil twilight are not required to be equipped with anti-collision lighting.

10. **The applicant demonstrates understanding of visual line of sight (VLOS) aircraft operations.**

a. VLOS aircraft operation. The remote PIC and person manipulating the controls must be able to see the sUA at all times during flight. Therefore, the sUA must be operated closely enough to the CS to ensure visibility requirements are met during sUA operations.

1) This requirement also applies to the VO, if used during the aircraft operation. However, the person maintaining VLOS may have brief moments in which (s)he is not looking directly at or cannot see the sUA but still retains the capability to see the UA or quickly maneuver it back to VLOS.

2) These moments can be for the safety of the operation (e.g., looking at the controller to see battery life remaining) or for operational necessity.

3) For operational necessity, the remote PIC or person manipulating the controls may intentionally maneuver the UA so that (s)he loses sight of it for brief periods of time. Should the remote PIC or person manipulating the controls lose VLOS of the sUAS, (s)he must regain VLOS as soon as practicable.

    a) For example, a remote PIC stationed on the ground utilizing an sUA to inspect a rooftop may lose sight of the aircraft for brief periods while inspecting the farthest point of the roof.

b) As another example, a remote PIC conducting a search operation aroun‹ a fire scene with an sUA may briefly lose sight of the aircraft while it is temporarily behind a dense column of smoke.

    i) However, it must be emphasized that even though the remote PIC may briefly lose sight of the sUA, (s)he always has the see-and-avoid responsibilities set out in 14 CFR 107.31 and 107.37.

    ii) The circumstances of what would prevent a remote PIC from fulfilling those responsibilities will vary, depending on factors such as the type of UAS, the operational environment, and distance between the remote PIC and the UA.

- For this reason, there is no specific time interval in which interruption of VLOS is permissible because it would have the effect of potentially allowing a hazardous interruption or prohibiting a reasonable one.

    iii) If VLOS cannot be regained, the remote PIC or person manipulating the controls should follow pre-determined procedures for a loss of VLOS.

    iv) These procedures are determined by the capabilities of the sUAS and may include immediately landing the UA, entering hover mode, or returning to home sequence.

- Thus, the VLOS requirement does not prohibit actions such as scanning the airspace or briefly looking down at the sUA CS.

b. Unaided vision. VLOS must be accomplished and maintained by unaided vision, except vision that is corrected by the use of eyeglasses (spectacles) or contact lenses.

1) Vision aids, such as binoculars, may be used only momentarily to enhance situational awareness. For example, the remote PIC, person manipulating the controls, or VO may use vision aids to avoid flying over persons or conflicting with other aircraft.

2) Similarly, first-person-view devices may be used during operations but do not satisfy the VLOS requirement.

    a) While the rule does not set specific vision standards, the FAA recommends remote PICs, persons manipulating the controls, and VOs maintain 20/20 distant vision acuity (corrected) and normal field of vision.

3) Limitations. As with other operations in Part 107, sUAS operations involving the transport of property must be conducted within VLOS of the remote pilot.

    a) While the VLOS limitation can be waived for some operations under the rule, it cannot be for transportation of property.

    b) Additionally, Part 107 does not allow the operation of an sUAS from a moving vehicle or aircraft if the sUA is being used to transport property for compensation or hire. This limitation cannot be waived.

    c) The maximum total weight of the sUA (including any property being transported) is limited to under 55 pounds.

        i) Additionally, other provisions of Part 107 require the remote pilot to know the UA's location; to determine the UA's attitude, altitude, and direction; to yield the right-of-way to other aircraft; and to maintain the ability to see and avoid other aircraft.

...licant demonstrates understanding of the requirements when a visual ...r is used.

...ual observer (VO) is a person acting as a flightcrew member who assists the sUA remote PIC and the person manipulating the controls to see and avoid other air traffic or objects aloft or on the ground.

b. The use of a VO is optional. The remote PIC may choose to use a VO to supplement situational awareness and VLOS.

  1) Although the remote PIC and person manipulating the controls must maintain the capability to see the UA, using one or more VOs allows the remote PIC and person manipulating the controls to conduct other mission-critical duties (such as checking displays) while still ensuring situational awareness of the UA.

  2) The VO must be able to effectively communicate

    a) The sUA location, attitude, altitude, and direction of flight;

    b) The position of other aircraft or hazards in the airspace; and

    c) The determination that the UA does not endanger the life or property of another.

  3) To ensure that the VO can carry out his or her duties, the remote PIC must ensure that the VO is positioned in a location where (s)he is able to see the sUA sufficiently to maintain VLOS. The remote PIC can do this by specifying the location of the VO. The FAA also requires that the remote PIC and VO coordinate to

    a) Scan the airspace where the sUA is operating for any potential collision hazard and

    b) Maintain awareness of the position of the sUA through direct visual observation.

      i) This is accomplished by the VO maintaining visual contact with the sUA and the surrounding airspace and then communicating to the remote PIC and person manipulating the controls the flight status of the sUA and any hazards that may enter the area of operation, so that the remote PIC or person manipulating the controls can take appropriate action.

  4) To make this communication possible, the remote PIC, person manipulating the controls, and VO must work out a method of effective communication that does not create a distraction and allows them to understand each other.

  5) The communication method must be determined prior to operation.

    a) This effective communication requirement would permit the use of communication-assisting devices, such as a hand-held radio, to facilitate communication from a distance.

12. **The applicant demonstrates understanding of the prohibition of operating multiple sUAS.**

a. A person may not operate or act as a remote PIC or VO in the operation of more than one unmanned aircraft at the same time.

13. **The applicant demonstrates understanding of the prohibition of carrying hazardous material.**

   a. Transportation of property. Part 107 permits transportation of property by sUAS for compensation or hire. These operations must be conducted within a confined area and in compliance with the operating restrictions of Part 107.

      1) When conducting the transportation of property, the transport must occur wholly within the bounds of a state. It may not involve transport between

         a) Hawaii and another place in Hawaii through airspace outside Hawaii,

         b) The District of Columbia (DC) and another place in DC, or

         c) A territory or possession of the United States and another place in the same territory or possession, as this is defined by statute as interstate air transportation.

   b. Hazardous materials. Part 107 does not allow the carriage of hazardous materials because the carriage of hazardous materials poses a higher level of risk.

14. **The applicant demonstrates understanding of staying safely away from other aircraft and right-of-way rules.**

   a. See and avoid other aircraft and other potential hazard considerations of the remote PIC.

      1) Remaining clear of other aircraft. A remote PIC has a responsibility to operate the sUA so it remains clear of and yields to all other aircraft.

         a) This is traditionally referred to as "see and avoid." To satisfy this responsibility, the remote PIC must know the location and flight path of his or her sUA at all times.

         b) The remote PIC must be aware of other aircraft, persons, and property in the vicinity of the operating area, and maneuver the sUA to avoid a collision as well as prevent other aircraft from having to take action to avoid the sUA.

      2) Each sUA must yield the right of way to all aircraft, airborne vehicles, and launch and reentry vehicles. Yielding the right of way means that the sUA must give way to the aircraft or vehicle and may not pass over, under, or ahead of it unless well clear.

      3) No person may operate an sUA so close to another aircraft that it creates a collision hazard.

15. **The applicant demonstrates understanding of operations over human beings.**

   a. Prohibited operation over persons. Part 107 prohibits a person from flying an sUAS directly over a person who is not under a safe cover, such as a protective structure or a stationary vehicle.

      1) However, an sUAS may be flown over a person who is directly participating in the operation of the sUAS, such as the remote PIC, other person manipulating the controls, a VO, or crewmembers necessary for the safety of the sUAS operation, as assigned and briefed by the remote PIC.

      2) There are several ways that the sUAS remote PIC can comply with these requirements, such as

         a) Selecting an operational area (site) that is clearly unpopulated/uninhabited;

            i) If selecting a site that is populated/inhabited, have a plan of action that ensures persons remain clear of the operating area, remain indoors, or remain under safe cover until such time that the sUAS flight has ended.

            ii) Safe cover is a structure or stationary vehicle that would protect a person from harm if the sUAS were to crash into that structure or vehicle.

b) Establishing an operational area in which the remote PIC has taken reasonable precautions to keep free of persons not directly participating in the operation of the sUAS;

c) Choosing an operating area that is sparsely populated, or, ideally, clear of persons if operating an sUAS from a moving vehicle;

d) Having a plan of action that ensures the sUAS remains clear of persons who may enter the operating area; or

e) Adopting an appropriate operating distance from persons not directly participating in the operation of the sUAS.

16. **The applicant demonstrates understanding of prior authorization required for operation in certain airspace.**

a. Though many sUAS operations will occur in uncontrolled airspace, there are some that may need to operate in controlled airspace.

1) Operations in Class B, Class C, or Class D airspace, or within the lateral boundaries of the surface area of Class E airspace designated for an airport, are not allowed unless that person has prior authorization from ATC.

2) The link to the current authorization process can be found at www.faa.gov/uas/request_waiver.

b. The sUAS remote PIC must understand airspace classifications and requirements. Failure to do so would be in violation of the Part 107 regulations and may adversely affect safety.

c. Although sUAS will not be subject to Part 91, the equipage and communications requirements outlined in Part 91 were designed to provide safety and efficiency in controlled airspace.

1) Accordingly, while sUAS operating under Part 107 are not subject to Part 91, as a practical matter, ATC authorization or clearance may depend on operational parameters similar to those found in Part 91.

d. The FAA has the authority to approve or deny aircraft operations based on traffic density, controller workload, communication issues, or any other type of operations that could potentially impact the safe and expeditious flow of air traffic in that airspace.

e. Those planning sUAS operations in controlled airspace are encouraged to contact the FAA at least 90 days in advance.

17. **The applicant demonstrates understanding of operating in the vicinity of airports.**

a. Unless the flight is conducted within controlled airspace, no notification or authorization is necessary to operate at or near an airport.

1) When operating in the vicinity of an airport, the remote PIC must be aware of all traffic patterns and approach corridors to runways and landing areas.

2) The remote PIC must avoid operating anywhere that the presence of the sUAS may interfere with operations at the airport, such as approach corridors, taxiways, runways, or helipads. Furthermore, the remote PIC must yield right-of-way to all other aircraft, including aircraft operating on the surface of the airport.

b. Remote PICs are prohibited from operating their sUA in a manner that interferes with operations and traffic patterns at airports, heliports, and seaplane bases.

1) While an sUA must always yield right-of-way to a manned aircraft, a manned aircraft may alter its flightpath, delay its landing, or take off in order to avoid an sUAS that may present a potential conflict or otherwise affect the safe outcome of the flight.

a) For example, a UA hovering 200 feet above a runway may cause a manned aircraft holding short of the runway to delay takeoff, or a manned aircraft on the downwind leg of the pattern to delay landing. While the UA in this scenario would not pose an immediate traffic conflict to the aircraft on the downwind leg of the traffic pattern or to the aircraft intending to take off, nor would it violate the right-of-way provision of 14 CFR 107.37(a), the sUA would have interfered with the operations of the traffic pattern at an airport.

c. In order to avoid interfering with operations in a traffic pattern, the remote PIC should avoid operating in the traffic pattern or published approach corridors used by manned aircraft.

1) When operational necessity requires the remote PIC to operate at an airport in uncontrolled airspace, the remote PIC should operate the sUA in such a way that the manned aircraft pilot does not need to alter his or her flightpath in the traffic pattern or on a published instrument approach in order to avoid a potential collision.

2) Because remote PICs have an obligation to yield right-of-way to all other aircraft and avoid interfering in traffic pattern operations, the FAA expects that most remote PICs will avoid operating in the vicinity of airports because their aircraft generally do not require airport infrastructure, and the concentration of other aircraft increases in the vicinity of airports.

18. **The applicant demonstrates understanding of operating in prohibited or restricted areas.**

a. No person may operate an sUAS in prohibited or restricted areas unless that person has permission from the using or controlling agency, as appropriate.

19. **The applicant demonstrates understanding of flight restrictions in the proximity of certain areas designated by notice to airmen (NOTAM).**

a. A person acting as a remote PIC must comply with the provisions of 14 CFR 91.137 through 91.145 and 99.7.

b. Certain temporary flight restrictions (tfr.faa.gov/tfr2/list.html) may be imposed by way of a NOTAM (pilotweb.nas.faa.gov/PilotWeb/). Therefore, it is necessary for the sUAS remote PIC to check for NOTAMs before each flight to determine if there are any applicable airspace restrictions.

1) According the 14 CFR 91.137, the Administrator will issue a NOTAM designating an area within which temporary flight restrictions apply and specifying the hazard or condition requiring their imposition, whenever (s)he determines it is necessary in order to

a) Protect persons and property on the surface or in the air from a hazard associated with an incident on the surface,

b) Provide a safe environment for the operation of disaster relief aircraft, or

c) Prevent an unsafe congestion of sightseeing and other aircraft above an incident or event which may generate a high degree of public interest.

2) The NOTAM will specify the hazard or condition that requires the imposition of temporary flight restrictions.

3) When a NOTAM has been issued for a temporary flight restriction, no person may operate an aircraft within the designated area unless that aircraft is participating in the hazard relief activities and is being operated under the direction of the official in charge of on scene emergency response activities.

4)   According to 14 CFR 91.145, the FAA will issue a NOTAM designating an area of airspace in which a temporary flight restriction applies when it determines that a temporary flight restriction is necessary to protect persons or property on the surface or in the air, to maintain air safety and efficiency, or to prevent the unsafe congestion of aircraft in the vicinity of an aerial demonstration or major sporting event.

20. **The applicant demonstrates understanding of preflight familiarization, inspection, and actions for aircraft operations.**

a.   The remote PIC must complete a preflight familiarization, inspection, and other actions, such as crewmember briefings, prior to beginning flight operations.

1)   The FAA has produced many publications providing in-depth information on topics such as aviation weather, aircraft loading and performance, emergency procedures, ADM, and airspace, which should all be considered prior to operations.

b.   Prior to flight, the remote PIC must

1)   Conduct an assessment of the operating environment. The assessment must include at least the following:

a)   Local weather conditions
b)   Local airspace and any flight restrictions
c)   The location of persons and property on the surface
d)   Other ground hazards

2)   Ensure that all persons directly participating in the sUA operation are informed about the following:

a)   Operating conditions
b)   Emergency procedures
c)   Contingency procedures
d)   Roles and responsibilities of each person involved in the operation
e)   Potential hazards

3)   Ensure that all control links between the CS and the sUA are working properly.

a)   For example, before each flight, the remote PIC must determine that the sUA flight control surfaces necessary for the safety of flight are moving correctly through the manipulation of the sUA CS.

b)   If the remote PIC observes that one or more of the control surfaces are not responding correctly to CS inputs, then the remote PIC may not conduct flight operations until correct movement of all flight control surface(s) is established.

4)   Ensure there is sufficient power to continue controlled flight operations to a normal landing.

a)   This can be done by following the sUAS manufacturer's operating manual power consumption tables.

b)   Another method would be to include a system on the sUAS that detects power levels and alerts the remote pilot when remaining aircraft power is diminishing to a level that is inadequate for continued flight operation.

5)   Ensure that any object attached or carried by the sUA is secure and does not adversely affect the flight characteristics or controllability of the aircraft.

6)   Ensure that all necessary documentation is available for inspection, including the remote PIC's remote pilot certificate, aircraft registration (if required), and Certificate of Waiver (CoW) (if applicable).

   c.   Safety Risk Assessment. These preflight familiarizations, inspections, and actions can be accomplished as part of an overall safety risk assessment.

       1)   The FAA encourages the remote PIC to conduct the overall safety risk assessment as a method of compliance with the prohibition on operations over certain persons and the requirement to remain clear of other aircraft.

       2)   Study Unit 8 provides additional guidance on how to conduct an overall safety risk assessment.

21. **The applicant demonstrates understanding of operating limitations for sUAS.**

   a.   The sUAS must be operated in accordance with the following limitations:

       1)   **Maximum groundspeed**

           a)   The sUAS cannot be flown faster than a groundspeed of 87 knots (100 miles per hour).

           b)   Determining groundspeed. There are many different types of sUAS and different ways to determine groundspeed. Therefore, this guidance will only touch on some of the possible ways for the remote PIC to ensure that the sUA does not exceed a groundspeed of 87 knots during flight operations. Some of the possible ways to ensure that 87 knots is not exceeded are as follows:

               i)   Installing a Global Positioning System (GPS) device on the sUA that reports groundspeed information to the remote pilot, wherein the remote pilot takes into account the wind direction and speed and calculates the sUA airspeed for a given direction of flight.

              ii)   Timing the groundspeed of the sUA when it is flown between two or more fixed points, taking into account wind speed and direction between each point, then noting the power settings of the sUA to operate at or less than 87 knots groundspeed.

             iii)   Using the sUA's manufacturer design limitations (e.g., installed groundspeed limiters).

       2)   **Altitude limitations**

           a)   The sUAS cannot be flown higher than 400 feet AGL, unless flown within a 400-foot radius of a structure and does not fly higher than 400 feet above the structure's immediate uppermost limit.

           b)   Determining altitude. In order to comply with the maximum altitude requirements of Part 107, as with determining groundspeed, there are multiple ways to determine an sUA's altitude above the ground or structure. Some possible ways for a remote pilot to determine altitude are as follows:

               i)   Installing a calibrated altitude reporting device on the sUA that reports the sUA altitude above mean sea level (MSL) to the remote pilot, wherein the remote pilot subtracts the MSL elevation of the CS from the sUA reported MSL altitude to determine the sUA AGL altitude above the terrain or structure.

              ii)   Installing a GPS device on the sUA that also has the capability of reporting MSL altitude to the remote pilot.

             iii)   With the sUA on the ground, having the remote pilot and VO pace off 400 feet from the sUA to get a visual perspective of the sUA at that distance, wherein the remote pilot and VO maintain that visual perspective or closer while the sUA is in flight.

             iv)   Using the known height of local rising terrain and/or structures as a reference.

3) **Minimum visibility**

a) Minimum visibility, as observed from the location of the CS, may not be less than 3 SM.

4) **Cloud clearance requirements**

a) The sUAS must have a minimum distance from clouds of no less than 500 feet below a cloud and no less than 2000 feet horizontally from the cloud.

NOTE: These operating limitations are intended, among other things, to support the remote pilot's ability to identify hazardous conditions relating to encroaching aircraft or persons on the ground, and to take the appropriate actions to maintain safety.

22. **The applicant demonstrates understanding of the requirements for a Remote Pilot Certificate with an sUAS rating.**

a. Remote pilot certification. A person exercising the authority of PIC in compliance with Part 107 is considered a "remote PIC." As such, prior to acting as remote PIC, (s)he must obtain a remote pilot certificate with an sUAS rating.

1.3 REMOTE PILOT CERTIFICATION WITH AN sUAS RATING

1. **The applicant demonstrates understanding of offenses involving alcohol or drugs.**

a. A conviction for the violation of any Federal or State statute relating to the growing, processing, manufacture, sale, disposition, possession, transportation, or importation of narcotic drugs, marijuana, or depressant or stimulant drugs or substances is grounds for

1) Denial of an application for a remote pilot certificate with an sUAS rating for a period of up to 1 year after the date of final conviction or

2) Suspension or revocation of a remote pilot certificate with an sUAS rating.

b. 14 CFR 91.17 states that no person may act or attempt to act as a crewmember of a civil aircraft within 8 hours after the consumption of any alcoholic beverage; while under the influence of alcohol; while using any drug that affects the person's faculties in any way contrary to safety; or with a blood-alcohol concentration of 0.04 or greater.

c. 14 CFR 91.19 states that no person may operate a civil aircraft within the United States with knowledge that narcotic drugs, marijuana, and depressant or stimulant drugs or substances as defined in federal or state statutes are carried in the aircraft.

d. Committing an act prohibited by 14 CFR 91.17(a) or 91.19(a) is grounds for

1) Denial of an application for a remote pilot certificate with an sUAS rating for a period of up to 1 year after the date of that act; or

2) Suspension or revocation of a remote pilot certificate with an sUAS rating.

2. **The applicant demonstrates understanding of the consequences of refusing to submit to a drug or alcohol test or to furnish test results.**

a. A refusal to submit to a test to indicate the percentage by weight of alcohol in the blood, when requested by a law enforcement officer in accordance with 14 CFR 91.17(c), or a refusal to furnish or authorize the release of the test results requested by the Administrator in accordance with 14 CFR 91.17(c) or (d) is grounds for

1) Denial of an application for a remote pilot certificate with an sUAS rating for a period of up to 1 year after the date of that refusal or

2) Suspension or revocation of a remote pilot certificate with an sUAS rating.

3. **The applicant demonstrates understanding of the eligibility requirements for a Remote Pilot Certificate with an sUAS rating.**

    a. A person applying for a remote pilot certificate with an sUAS rating must meet and maintain the following eligibility requirements, as applicable:

        1) Be at least 16 years of age.

        2) Be able to read, speak, write, and understand the English language. However, the FAA may make an exception if the person is unable to meet one of these requirements due to medical reasons, such as a hearing impairment.

        3) Be in a physical and mental condition that would not interfere with the safe operation of an sUAS.

        4) Pass the initial aeronautical knowledge test at an FAA-approved knowledge testing center (KTC).

          a) However, a person who already holds a pilot certificate issued under 14 CFR Part 61, except a student pilot certificate, and has successfully completed a flight review in accordance with Part 61 within the previous 24 calendar months is only required to successfully complete a Part 107 online training course, found at www.faasafety.gov.

          b) **Application process.** A person who does not have a Part 61 pilot certificate or a Part 61 certificate holder who has not completed a Part 61 flight review in the previous 24 calendar months must use the following process. A Part 61 pilot who has completed a flight review within the previous 24 calendar months may also elect to use this process.

            i) Pass an initial aeronautical knowledge test administered at an approved KTC.

            ii) Complete the Remote Pilot Certificate and/or Rating Application for a remote pilot certificate (FAA Form 8710-13).

              • **Option 1 (online form):** This is the fastest and simplest method. The FAA Form 8710-13 application should be completed online using the electronic FAA Integrated Airmen Certificate and/or Rating Application (IACRA) system (iacra.faa.gov/iacra/).

                ■ The applicant must have already passed the initial aeronautical knowledge test. Once registered with IACRA, (s)he will login with his or her username and password.

                ■ (S)he will click on "Start New Application" then select 1) "Pilot" under Application Type, 2) "Remote Pilot" under Certifications 3) "Other Path Information," and 4) "Start Application."

                ■ (S)he will continue through the application process, and, when prompted, enter the 17-digit Knowledge Test Exam ID from the knowledge test in IACRA.

                  • It may take up to 48 hours from the test date for the knowledge test to appear in IACRA. The KTC test proctor will be the one who verifies the identity of the applicant.

                  • Once the applicant completes the online application in IACRA, (s)he will sign the application electronically and submit it to the Airman Registry for processing. No FAA representative will be required to sign the application if the applicant was able to self-certify.

NOTE: When the applicant uses this online option, the application will be transmitted electronically from the applicant to the Airman Registry. The only electronic signature that will be reflected on the IACRA application will be the applicant's. The applicant will then receive a confirmation email once his or her application has completed the Transportation Security Administration (TSA) vetting process. The email will provide information that will allow the applicant to log into the IACRA system and print a copy of the temporary certificate.

- **Option 2 (paper application):** An applicant could also submit a paper application. If the applicant chooses the paper method, the original initial aeronautical knowledge test report must be mailed with the application to the following address:

> DOT/FAA
> Airmen Certification Branch (AFS-760)
> P.O. Box 25082
> Oklahoma City, OK 73125

NOTE: A temporary airman certificate will not be provided to the remote pilot applicant if (s)he does not hold a Part 61 certificate. For this reason, it would be of the applicant's best interest to utilize Option 1 (IACRA system) instead of the paper method in order to receive a temporary airman certificate once the application has completed the TSA vetting process.

iii) Receive permanent remote pilot certificate once all other FAA internal processing is complete.

c) **Applicants with Part 61 Certificates.** Instead of the process described above and on the previous page, a person who holds a Part 61 pilot certificate, except a student pilot certificate, and has completed a flight review within the previous 24 calendar months may elect to apply using the following process:

i) Complete the online course [Part 107 Small Unmanned Aircraft Systems (sUAS), ALC-451] located within the FAA Safety Team (FAASTeam) website (www.faasafety.gov) and receive a completion certificate.

ii) Complete the Remote Pilot Certificate and/or Rating Application for a remote pilot certificate (FAA Form 8710-13).

- **Option 1 (online application):** In almost all cases, the application should be completed online using the electronic FAA IACRA system (iacra.faa.gov/iacra/). The applicant must include verification that he or she completed the online course or passed an initial aeronautical knowledge test. The applicable official document(s) must be uploaded into IACRA either by the applicant or the certifying officer.

- **Option 2 (paper):** The application may be completed on paper. Using this method, the certificate of completion for the online course or original initial aeronautical knowledge test report must be included with the application. Please note that the processing time will be increased if a paper application is used.

iii) Contact an FSDO, a DPE, an ACR, or a CFI to make an appointment to validate the applicant's identification.

- The applicant must present the completed FAA Form 8710-13 along with the online course completion certificate or knowledge test report (as applicable) and proof of a current flight review.

- The FAA Form 8710-13 application will be signed by the applicant after the FSDO, DPE, ACR, or CFI examines the applicant's photo identification and verifies the applicant's identity. The identification presented must include a photograph of the applicant, the applicant's signature, and the applicant's actual residential address (if different from the mailing address).

    - This information may be presented in more than one form of identification. Acceptable methods of identification include, but are not limited to

        - U.S. drivers' licenses, government identification cards, passports, and military identification cards (refer to AC 61-65). If using paper or IACRA method, an appropriate FSDO representative, a DPE, or an ACR will issue the applicant a temporary airman certificate.

        NOTE: A CFI is not authorized to issue a temporary certificate. They can process applications for applicants who do not need a temporary certificate. If the applicant is using IACRA and utilizing a CFI as the FAA representative, the applicant can print his or her own temporary airman certificate after receiving an email from the FAA notifying them that it is available. If using the paper method and the applicant is utilizing a CFI as the FAA representative, the applicant will not be issued a temporary airman certificate. Once the FSDO has signed and approved the application, it will be mailed to the Registry for the issuance of the permanent certificate.

- The FAA representative will then sign the application.

iv) Receive permanent remote pilot certificate once all other FAA internal processing is complete.

d) **Security disqualification.** After the FAA receives the application, the TSA will automatically conduct a background security screening of the applicant prior to issuance of a remote pilot certificate. If the security screening is successful, the FAA will issue a permanent remote pilot certificate. If the security screening is not successful, the applicant will be disqualified and a temporary pilot certificate will not be issued.

i) Individuals who believe they improperly failed a security threat assessment may appeal the decision to the TSA.

4. **The applicant demonstrates understanding of aeronautical knowledge recency.**

    a. After a pilot receives a remote pilot certificate with an sUAS rating, that person must retain and periodically update the required aeronautical knowledge to continue to operate an sUA in the NAS.

    b. As a renewal process, the remote pilot must complete either a recurrent training course or a recurrent knowledge test within 24 calendar months of passing either an initial or recurrent aeronautical knowledge test. Recurrent Training Course Cycle Examples below illustrate an individual's possible renewal cycles.

Recurrent Training Course Cycle Examples

Person passes an initial aeronautical knowledge test on September 13, 2016.	then	Recurrent training course must be completed no later than September 30, 2018, which does not exceed 24 calendar months.
Person does not complete recurrent training course until October 5, 2018.	then	Person may not exercise the privileges of the remote pilot certificate between October 1, 2018, and October 5, 2018, when the course is completed. The next recurrent training course must be completed no later than October 31, 2020, which does not exceed 24 calendar months.
Person elects to complete recurrent training course prior to October 2020. The recurrent training course is taken and completed on July 15, 2020.	then	The next recurrent training course must be completed no later than July 31, 2022, which does not exceed 24 calendar months

    c. The recurrent aeronautical knowledge test areas are as follows:

        1) Applicable regulations relating to sUAS rating privileges, limitations, and flight operation

        2) Airspace classification and operating requirements and flight restrictions affecting sUA operation

        3) Emergency procedures

        4) Crew Resource Management (CRM)

        5) Aeronautical decision making (ADM) and judgment

        6) Airport operations

        7) Maintenance and preflight inspection procedures

    d. KTCs will administer initial and recurrent examinations provided by the FAA. In order to take an aeronautical knowledge test, an applicant will be required to schedule an appointment with the KTC providing proper government-issued photo identification to the KTC on the day of scheduled testing. The location of the closest KTC can be found at www.faa.gov/training_testing/testing/media/test_centers.pdf.

1.4 WAIVERS

1. **The applicant demonstrates understanding of the waiver policy and requirements.**

    a. The Administrator may issue a Certificate of Waiver (CoW) authorizing a deviation from any regulation specified in 14 CFR 107.205 if the Administrator finds that a proposed sUAS operation can safely be conducted under the terms of that CoW.

    b. A request for a CoW must contain a complete description of the proposed operation and justification that establishes that the operation can safely be conducted under the terms of a CoW.

c. The Administrator may prescribe additional limitations that the Administrator considers necessary.

d. A person who receives a CoW issued under this section

   1) May deviate from the regulations of this part to the extent specified in the CoW and

   2) Must comply with any conditions or limitations that are specified in the CoW.

e. Part 107 includes the option to apply for a CoW. A list of the waivable sections of Part 107 can be found in 14 CFR 107.205 and are listed below:

   1) 14 CFR 107.25, operation from a moving vehicle or aircraft. However, no waiver of this provision will be issued to allow the carriage of property of another by aircraft for compensation or hire.

   2) 14 CFR 107.29, daylight operation.

   3) 14 CFR 107.31, visual line of sight aircraft operation. However, no waiver of this provision will be issued to allow the carriage of property of another by aircraft for compensation or hire.

   4) 14 CFR 107.33, visual observer.

   5) 14 CFR 107.35, operation of multiple small unmanned aircraft systems.

   6) 14 CFR 107.37(a), yielding the right of way.

   7) 14 CFR 107.39, operation over people.

   8) 14 CFR 107.41, operation in certain airspace.

   9) 14 CFR 107.51, operating limitations for small unmanned aircraft.

f. **Applying for a CoW.** To apply for a CoW under 14 CFR 107.200, an applicant must go to www.faa.gov/uas/request_waiver/ and follow the instructions.

g. **Application process.** The application must contain a complete description of the proposed operation and a justification, including supporting data and documentation (as necessary), that establishes the proposed operation can safely be conducted under the terms of a CoW.

   1) Although not required by Part 107, the FAA encourages applicants to submit their application at least 90 days prior to the start of the proposed operation.

   2) The FAA will strive to complete review and adjudication of waivers within 90 days; however, the time required for the FAA to make a determination regarding waiver requests will vary based on the complexity of the request.

   3) The amount of data and analysis required as part of the application will be proportional to the specific relief that is requested.

      a) For example, a request to waive several sections of Part 107 for an operation that takes place in a congested metropolitan area with heavy air traffic will likely require significantly more data and analysis than a request to waive a single section for an operation that takes place in a sparsely populated area with minimal air traffic.

   4) If a CoW is granted, that certificate may include specific special provisions designed to ensure that the sUAS operation may be conducted as safely as one conducted under the provisions of Part 107. A listing of standard special provisions for Part 107 waivers will be available on the FAA's website at www.faa.gov/uas/beyond_the_basics/#waiver.

QUESTIONS

1.1   General

1. According to 14 CFR Part 107, what is required to operate a small UA within 30 minutes after official sunset?

    A. Use of anti-collision lights.

    B. Must be operated in a rural area.

    C. Use of a transponder.

Answer (A) is correct. *(14 CFR 107.29(b))*
    DISCUSSION: When sUAS operations are conducted during civil twilight or within 30 minutes after official sunset, the small UA must be equipped with anticollision lights that are capable of being visible for at least 3 statute miles.
    Answer (B) is incorrect. There is no requirement during civil twilight to operate a small UA in a rural area. Answer (C) is incorrect. There is no transponder requirement during civil twilight to operate a small UA.

2. To avoid a possible collision with a manned airplane, you estimate that your small UA climbed to an altitude greater than 600 feet AGL. To whom must you report the deviation?

    A. Air Traffic Control.

    B. The National Transportation Safety Board.

    C. Upon request of the Federal Aviation Administration.

Answer (C) is correct. *(14 CFR 107.21(b))*
    DISCUSSION: A remote PIC who exercises his or her emergency power to deviate from the rules of Part 107, upon FAA request, is required to send a written report to the FAA explaining the deviation.
    Answer (A) is incorrect. Upon request from the FAA, you must report a deviation to the FAA, not Air Traffic Control. Answer (B) is incorrect. Upon request from the FAA, you must report a deviation to the FAA, not the National Transportation Safety Board.

3. In accordance with 14 CFR Part 107, you may operate an sUAS from a moving vehicle when no property is carried for compensation of hire

    A. Over suburban areas.

    B. Over a sparsely populated area.

    C. Over a parade or other social events.

Answer (B) is correct. *(14 CFR 107.25; AC 107)*
    DISCUSSION: Part 107 permits operation of an sUAS from a moving land or water-borne vehicle over a sparsely populated area. Additionally, an sUAS transporting another person's property for compensation or hire may not be operated from any moving vehicle.
    Answer (A) is incorrect. Part 107 permits operation of an sUAS from a moving land or water-borne vehicle over a sparsely populated area, not over a suburban area. Answer (C) is incorrect. Part 107 permits operation of an sUAS from a moving land or water-borne vehicle over a sparsely populated area, not over a parade or other social events.

4. In accordance with 14 CFR Part 107, except when within a 400' radius of a structure, at what maximum altitude can you operate sUAS?

    A. 500 feet AGL.

    B. 400 feet AGL.

    C. 600 feet AGL.

Answer (B) is correct. *(14 CFR 107.51)*
    DISCUSSION: sUAS cannot be flown higher than 400 feet above ground level (AGL), unless flown within a 400-foot radius of a structure and does not fly higher than 400 feet above the structure's immediate uppermost limit.
    Answer (A) is incorrect. Except when within a 400-foot radius of a structure, the maximum altitude you can operate sUAS is 400 feet AGL, not 500 feet AGL. Answer (C) is incorrect. Except when within a 400-foot radius of a structure, the maximum altitude you can operate sUAS is 400 feet AGL, not 600 feet AGL.

5. According to 14 CFR Part 107, the remote pilot in command (PIC) of a small unmanned aircraft planning to operate within Class C airspace

    A. must use a visual observer.

    B. is required to file a flight plan.

    C. is required to receive ATC authorization.

Answer (C) is correct. *(14 CFR 107.41)*
    DISCUSSION: Operations in Class B, Class C, Class D airspace, or within the lateral boundaries of the surface area of Class E airspace designated for an airport are not allowed unless that person has prior authorization from ATC. It is the responsibility of the remote PIC of the sUAS to receive this prior authorization.
    Answer (A) is incorrect. The remote PIC of an sUAS planning to operate within Class C airspace is required to receive prior authorization from ATC, not use a visual observer. Answer (B) is incorrect. The remote PIC of an sUAS planning to operate within Class C airspace is required to receive prior authorization from ATC, not file a flight plan.

6. Which of the following operations would be regulated by 14 CFR 107?

    A. Flying for enjoyment with family and friends.

    B. Operating your sUAS for an imagery company.

    C. Conducting public operations during a search mission.

Answer (B) is correct. *(14 CFR 101.41, 107.1)*
    DISCUSSION: 14 CFR Part 107 include the rules for non-hobbyist small unmanned aircraft (sUAS) operations, which include a broad spectrum of commercial uses for drones weighing less than 55 pounds. Operating your sUAS for an imagery company would be a commercial operation and therefore would be regulated by Part 107.
    Answer (A) is incorrect. Flying for enjoyment with family and friends would not be a commercial operation; therefore, Part 107 would not apply. Answer (C) is incorrect. Part 107 does not apply to public aircraft operations; therefore, conducting public operations during a search mission would not be regulated by this Part.

7. Under what condition would a small UA not have to be registered before it is operated in the United States?

    A. When the aircraft weighs less than .55 pounds on takeoff, including everything that is on-board or attached to the aircraft.

    B. When the aircraft has a takeoff weight that is more than .55 pounds, but less than 55 pounds, not including fuel and necessary attachments.

    C. All small UAS need to be registered regardless of the weight of the aircraft before, during, or after the flight.

Answer (A) is correct. *(14 CFR 107.13)*
    DISCUSSION: You need to register your aircraft if it weighs between 0.55 lbs. and up to 55 lbs.
    Answer (B) is incorrect. Aircraft weighing between 0.55 lbs. and up to 55 lbs. must be registered. Answer (C) is incorrect. Small UAS do not need to be registered if they weigh less than .55 lbs.

8. Personnel at an outdoor concert venue use an sUAS to drop promotional t-shirts and CDs over the audience. Is this sUAS operation in compliance with 14 CFR Part 107?

    A. Compliant with Part 107.

    B. Not compliant with Part 107.

    C. Part 107 does not apply to this scenario.

Answer (B) is correct. *(14 CFR 107.39)*
    DISCUSSION: This sUAS operation is not in compliance with 14 CFR Part 107. Part 107 prohibits a person from flying an sUAS over anyone who is not directly participating in the operation, not under a covered structure, or not inside a covered stationary vehicle. In addition, no items may be dropped from an sUAS in a manner that creates an undue hazard to persons or property.
    Answer (A) is incorrect. This sUAS operation is not in compliance with 14 CFR Part 107. Answer (C) is incorrect. 14 CFR Part 107 includes the rules for non-hobbyist small unmanned aircraft (UAS) operations, which include a broad spectrum of commercial uses for drones weighing less than 55 pounds; therefore, this scenario would be regulated by Part 107.

9. A professional wildlife photographer operates an sUAS from a moving truck to capture aerial images of migrating birds in remote wetlands. The driver of the truck does not serve any crewmember role in the operation. Is this sUAS operation in compliance with 14 CFR Part 107?

    A. Compliant with Part 107.

    B. Not compliant with Part 107.

    C. Part 107 does not apply to this scenario.

Answer (A) is correct. *(14 CFR 107.25)*
    DISCUSSION: This sUAS operation is in compliance with 14 CFR Part 107. Part 107 permits operation of an sUAS from a moving land or water-borne vehicle over a sparsely populated area. In addition, this scenario is also compliant because the driver of truck does not serve any crewmember role in the sUAS operation.
    Answer (B) is incorrect. This operation is being conducted over a sparsely populated area, and the driver of the truck does not serve any crewmember role in the sUAS operation, therefore this operation is in compliance with Part 107. Answer (C) is incorrect. This is a commercial operation; therefore, Part 107 applies to this scenario.

10. You plan to operate a 33 lb. sUAS to capture aerial imagery over real estate for use in sales listings. Is this sUAS operation subject to 14 CFR Part 107?

    A.   Yes, this sUAS operation is subject to Part 107.

    B.   No, this sUAS operation is not subject to Part 107.

    C.   No, this sUAS operation requires a Section 333 exemption.

Answer (A) is correct. *(14 CFR 107.1)*
    DISCUSSION: Part 107 contain the rules for non-hobbyist small unmanned aircraft (sUAS) operations, which cover a broad spectrum of commercial uses for drones weighing less than 55 pounds. This scenario is a commercial operation, and the sUAS weighs less than 55 pounds; therefore, it is subject to Part 107.
    Answer (B) is incorrect. This sUAS operation is a commercial operation, and the sUAS weighs less than 55 pounds; therefore, it is subject to 14 CFR Part 107. Answer (C) is incorrect. This is a routine commercial sUAS operation that does not require an exemption or waiver.

11. You have accepted football tickets in exchange for using your sUAS to videotape the field before and after the game. Is this sUAS operation subject to 14 CFR Part 107?

    A.   Yes, this sUAS operation is subject to Part 107.

    B.   No, this sUAS operation is not subject to Part 107.

    C.   Yes, Part 107 allows flight directly over people to capture video.

Answer (A) is correct. *(14 CFR 107.1)*
    DISCUSSION: You have accepted football tickets as a form of compensation for sUAS services; therefore, this is a commercial operation and is subject to Part 107. Part 107 rules are for non-hobbyist small unmanned aircraft (sUAS) operations covering a broad spectrum of commercial uses.
    Answer (B) is incorrect. Compensation has been received for services; therefore, this scenario is a commercial operation and is subject to Part 107. Answer (C) is incorrect. Operations are prohibited over persons not directly involved in the operation of the sUAS unless under safe cover.

12. You are operating a 1280 g (2.8 lb.) quadcopter for your own enjoyment. Is this sUAS operation subject to 14 CFR Part 107?

    A.   Yes, this sUAS operation is subject to Part 107.

    B.   No, this sUAS operation is not subject to Part 107.

    C.   Yes, all sUAS aircraft weighing over .55 lbs. are subject to Part 107.

Answer (B) is correct. *(14 CFR 107.1)*
    DISCUSSION: This sUAS operation is not subject to Part 107 because it is being operated for recreational or hobby purposes. Part 107 rules are for non-hobbyist sUAS operations, and cover a broad spectrum of commercial uses for UAS weighing less than 55 pounds.
    Answer (A) is incorrect. 14 CFR Part 107 are the rules for non-hobbyist small unmanned aircraft operations and cover a broad spectrum of commercial uses for drones weighing less than 55 pounds; therefore, this operation is not subject to 14 CFR Part 107. Answer (C) is incorrect. An sUAS weighing over .55 lbs. must be registered, but it is not subject to Part 107 if operated for recreation or hobby.

13. According to 14 CFR Part 107, the responsibility to inspect the small UAS to ensure it is in a safe operating condition rests with the

    A.   remote pilot-in-command.

    B.   visual observer.

    C.   owner of the small UAS.

Answer (A) is correct. *(14 CFR 107.49)*
    DISCUSSION: The remote PIC has the final authority and responsibility for the operation and safety of an sUAS operation conducted under Part 107, which includes checks and inspection of the sUAS.
    Answer (B) is incorrect. It is the responsibility of the remote PIC (not the visual observer) to inspect the small UAS to ensure it is in a safe operating condition. Answer (C) is incorrect. It is the responsibility of the remote PIC (not the owner of the sUAS) to inspect the small UAS to ensure it is in a safe operating condition.

14. Who is responsible for ensuring that there are enough crewmembers for a given sUAS operation?

    A.   Remote Pilot in Command (Remote PIC).

    B.   Person manipulating the controls.

    C.   Visual observer.

Answer (A) is correct. *(14 CFR 107, AC 107-2)*
    DISCUSSION: The Remote PIC has the final authority and responsibility for the operation and safety of an sUAS operation conducted under Part 107, which includes ensuring that there are enough crewmembers for a given operation.
    Answer (B) is incorrect. The Remote PIC, not the person manipulating the controls, has the responsibility to ensure there are enough crewmembers for a given sUAS operation. The person manipulating the controls is under the supervision of the Remote PIC. Answer (C) is incorrect. The Remote PIC, not the visual observer, has the responsibility to ensure there are enough crewmembers for a given sUAS operation.

15. Unmanned aircraft means an aircraft operated

A. Without the possibility of direct human intervention from within or on the aircraft.

B. For hobby and recreational use when not certificated.

C. During search and rescue operations other than public.

Answer (A) is correct. *(14 CFR 107.1, 107.3; AC 107)*
DISCUSSION: The term unmanned aircraft means an aircraft operated without the possibility of direct human intervention from within or on the aircraft.
Answer (B) is incorrect. The type of operation for a UA does not determine whether or not the aircraft is a UA. Answer (C) is incorrect. The type of operation for a UA does not determine whether or not the aircraft is a UA.

16. While operating a small unmanned aircraft system (sUAS), you experience a flyaway and several people suffer injuries. Which of the following injuries requires reporting to the FAA?

A. Scrapes and cuts bandaged on site.

B. Minor bruises.

C. An injury requiring an overnight hospital stay.

Answer (C) is correct. *(14 CFR 107.9, 107(iii)9l)(2); AC 107)*
DISCUSSION: The remote PIC is required to report an accident if it is considered a serious injury; an example of "serious injury" is if a person required hospitalization.
Answer (A) is incorrect. Scrapes and cuts bandaged on site do not require the remote PIC to file an accident report to the FAA. Answer (B) is incorrect. Minor bruises do not require the remote PIC to file an accident report to the FAA.

17. According to 14 CFR Part 107, an sUAS is an unmanned aircraft system weighing

A. Less than 55 lbs.

B. 55 kg or less.

C. 55 lbs. or less.

Answer (A) is correct. *(14 CFR 107.1, 107.3; AC 107)*
DISCUSSION: Part 107 defines an sUAS as an unmanned aircraft system weighing less than 55 lbs., including everything that is onboard or otherwise attached to the aircraft.
Answer (B) is incorrect. Part 107 defines an sUAS as an unmanned aircraft system weighing less than 55 lbs., not 55 kg or less. Answer (C) is incorrect. Part 107 defines an sUAS as an unmanned aircraft system weighing less than 55 lbs., not 55 lbs. or less.

18. A person without a Part 107 remote pilot certificate may operate an sUAS for commercial operations:

A. Under the direct supervision of a Remote PIC.

B. Alone, if operating during daylight hours.

C. Only when visual observers participate in the operation.

Answer (A) is correct. *(AC 107)*
DISCUSSION: Under Part 107, which governs sUAS commercial operations, a person may operate an sUAS under the direct supervision of the remote PIC; this person is called the "person manipulating the controls."
Answer (B) is incorrect. A person without a remote pilot certificate may not operate an sUAS for commercial operations without direct supervision from a certificated remote PIC. Answer (C) is incorrect. A person without a remote pilot certificate may operate an sUAS for commercial operations only when a remote PIC is supervising the operation, not when visual observers participate.

19. Which of the following types of operations are excluded from the requirements in Part 107?

A. Quadcopter capturing a serial imagery for crop monitoring.

B. Model aircraft for hobby use.

C. UAS used for motion picture filming.

Answer (B) is correct. *(14 CFR 101.41, 107.1)*
DISCUSSION: Model aircraft for hobby use is excluded from the requirements in Part 107.
Answer (A) is incorrect. A quadcopter capturing imagery for crop monitoring is regulated by Part 107. Answer (C) is incorrect. UAS used for motion picture filming would be regulated by Part 107.

20. A person whose sole task is watching the sUAS to report hazards to the rest of the crew is called:

A. Remote PIC.

B. Visual observer.

C. Person manipulating the controls.

Answer (B) is correct. *(14 CFR 107.3; AC 107)*
DISCUSSION: The visual observer is defined as a person acting as a flightcrew member who assists the remote PIC and the person manipulating the controls to see and avoid other air traffic or objects aloft or on the ground.
Answer (A) is incorrect. The remote PIC is the person who holds a remote pilot certificate and has the final authority and responsibility for the operation, (s)he is not the visual observer. Answer (C) is incorrect. The person manipulating the controls is a person other than the remote PIC who is operating the control station, but is not a visual observer.

21. Who holds the responsibility to ensure all crewmembers who are participating in the operation are not impaired by drugs or alcohol?

    A. Remote Pilot in Command.

    B. Contractor.

    C. Site supervisor.

Answer (A) is correct. *(14 CFR 107.19(b), 107.19(d), and 107.57)*
    DISCUSSION: It is the remote PIC's responsibility to ensure all crewmembers are not participating in the operation while impaired.
    Answer (B) is incorrect. It is the responsibility of the remote PIC, not the contractor, to ensure crewmembers are not participating in the operation while impaired. Answer (C) is incorrect. It is the responsibility of the remote PIC, not a site supervisor, to ensure all crewmembers are not participating in the operation while impaired.

22. Power company employees use an sUAS to inspect a long stretch of high voltage powerlines. Due to muddy conditions, their vehicle must stay beside the road and the crew uses binoculars to maintain visual line of sight with the aircraft. Is this sUAS operation in compliance with 14 CFR Part 107?

    A. Compliant with Part 107.

    B. Not compliant with Part 107.

    C. Compliant with Part 107 when used with a first-person view (FPV) camera system.

Answer (B) is correct. *(14 CFR 107.31)*
    DISCUSSION: Visual line of sight (VLOS) must be accomplished and maintained by unaided vision, except vision that is corrected by the use of eyeglasses (spectacles) or contact lenses.
    Answer (A) is incorrect. Part 107 operations must be accomplished by unaided vision; therefore, binoculars cannot be used. Answer (C) is incorrect. An FPV camera system does not provide adequate see-and-avoid capabilities. VLOS must be accomplished and maintained by unaided vision.

23. Who is ultimately responsible for preventing a hazardous situation before an accident occurs?

    A. Remote Pilot in Command (Remote PIC).

    B. Person manipulating the controls.

    C. Visual observer.

Answer (A) is correct. *(14 CFR 107.19)*
    DISCUSSION: The remote PIC has the final authority and responsibility for the operation and safety of an sUAS operation conducted under Part 107.
    Answer (B) is incorrect. The remote PIC, not the person manipulating the controls, is responsible for preventing hazardous situations. Answer (C) is incorrect. The remote PIC, not the visual observer, is responsible for preventing hazardous situations.

24. Which crewmember is required to be under the direct supervision of the Remote PIC when operating an sUAS?

    A. Remote Pilot in Command (Remote PIC).

    B. Person manipulating the controls.

    C. Visual observer.

Answer (B) is correct. *(14 CFR 107.12)*
    DISCUSSION: The person manipulating the controls is a person other than the remote PIC who is controlling the flight of an sUAS and is under the direct supervision of the remote PIC when operating the sUAS.
    Answer (A) is incorrect. The person manipulating the controls is a person other than the remote PIC who is operating the control station. Answer (C) is incorrect. The visual observer does not have to be in direct supervision of the remote PIC if communication is maintained.

25. Which crewmember must hold a remote pilot certificate with an sUAS rating?

    A. Remote Pilot in Command (Remote PIC).

    B. Person manipulating the controls.

    C. Visual observer.

Answer (A) is correct. *(14 CFR 107.12)*
    DISCUSSION: The remote PIC must hold a remote pilot certificate with an sUAS rating.
    Answer (B) is incorrect. The remote PIC, not the person manipulating the controls, must hold a remote pilot certificate with an sUAS rating. Answer (C) is incorrect. The remote PIC, not the visual observer, must hold a remote pilot certificate with an sUAS rating.

26. According to 14 CFR Part 48, when would a small UA owner not be permitted to register it?

    A. If the owner is less than 13 years of age.

    B. All persons must register their small UA.

    C. If the owner does not have a valid United States driver's license.

Answer (A) is correct. *(14 CFR 48.25)*
    DISCUSSION: The owner must be at least 13 years of age to register a small UA.
    Answer (B) is incorrect. A small UA weighing less than .55 lbs. does not need registered. Answer (C) is incorrect. A driver's license is not required to register a small UA.

27. Whose sole task during an sUAS operation is to watch the sUAS and report potential hazards to the rest of the crew?

   A. Remote Pilot in Command (Remote PIC).

   B. Person manipulating the controls.

   C. Visual observer.

Answer (C) is correct. *(14 CFR 107.3)*
   DISCUSSION: The visual observer is a person acting as a flight crew member who sole task is to watch the sUAS and report potential hazards to the rest of the crew.
   Answer (A) is incorrect. The visual observer, not the remote PIC, has the sole task of watching the sUAS and reporting potential hazards to the rest of the crew. Answer (B) is incorrect. The visual observer, not the person manipulating the controls, has the sole task of watching the sUAS and reporting potential hazards to the rest of the crew.

28. Within how many days must an sUAS accident be reported to the FAA?

   A. 90 days.

   B. 30 days.

   C. 10 days.

Answer (C) is correct. *(14 CFR 107.9; AC 107)*
   DISCUSSION: The remote PIC of the sUAS is required to report an accident to the FAA within 10 days if it meets any of the required thresholds.
   Answer (A) is incorrect. An sUAS accident must be reported to the FAA in 10 days, not 90 days. Answer (B) is incorrect. An sUAS accident must be reported to the FAA in 10 days, not 30 days.

29. According to 14 CFR Part 48, when must a person register a small UA with the Federal Aviation Administration?

   A. All civilian small UAs weighing greater than .55 pounds must be registered regardless of its intended use.

   B. When the small UA is used for any purpose other than as a model aircraft.

   C. Only when the operator will be paid for commercial services.

Answer (A) is correct. *(14 CFR 107.13)*
   DISCUSSION: All civilian sUAS weighing more than 0.55 lbs. must be registered with the FAA regardless of its intended use.
   Answer (B) is incorrect. An sUAS weighing more than 0.55 lbs. must be registered even when used solely as a model aircraft. Answer (C) is incorrect. Weight of the sUAS, not the type of operation, determines if an sUAS must be registered.

30. You are part of a news crew, operating an sUAS to cover a breaking story. You experience a flyaway during landing. The unmanned aircraft strikes a vehicle, causing approximately $800 worth of damage. When must you report the accident to the FAA?

   A. Any time.

   B. Within 10 days.

   C. Not to exceed 30 days.

Answer (B) is correct. *(14 CFR 107.9)*
   DISCUSSION: An accident costing more than $500 to repair or replace damage to property, other than the sUAS, must be reported to the FAA within 10 days.
   Answer (A) is incorrect. The report must be made within 10 days, not any time. Answer (C) is incorrect. The report must be made within 10 days, not within 30 days.

31. Before each flight, the Remote PIC must ensure that

   A. Objects carried on the sUAS are secure.

   B. The site supervisor has approved the flight.

   C. ATC has granted clearance.

Answer (A) is correct. *(AC 107)*
   DISCUSSION: Ensure that any object attached or carried by the small UA is secure and does not adversely affect the flight characteristics or controllability of the aircraft.
   Answer (B) is incorrect. A site supervisor is not required under Part 107. Answer (C) is incorrect. ATC clearance is required before flights in controlled airspace, not before every flight.

32. Which operations must comply with 14 CFR Part 107?

   A. Civil and public aircraft operations.

   B. Public and military operations.

   C. Civil operations.

Answer (C) is correct. *(14 CFR 107.11)*
   DISCUSSION: According to 14 CFR 107.11, this subpart applies to the operation of all civil sUAS subject to this part.
   Answer (A) is incorrect. Part 107 applies to civil sUAS operations, not public aircraft operations. "Public" refers to aircraft used by the government. Answer (B) is incorrect. Part 107 applies to civil sUAS operations, not public or military aircraft operations.

1.2 Operating Rules

33. Responsibility for collision avoidance in an alert area rests with

    A. the controlling agency.

    B. the Remote PIC.

    C. Air Traffic Control.

Answer (B) is correct. *(AIM Para 3-4-6)*
    DISCUSSION: Alert areas may contain a high volume of pilot training or other unusual activity. The Remote PIC is responsible for collision avoidance.
    Answer (A) is incorrect. The remote PIC, not controlling agency, is responsible for collision avoidance. Answer (C) is incorrect. The remote PIC, not ATC, is responsible for collision avoidance.

34. Under what conditions may objects be dropped from an aircraft?

    A. Only in an emergency.

    B. If precautions are taken to avoid injury or damage to persons or property on the surface.

    C. If prior permission is received from the Federal Aviation Administration.

Answer (B) is correct. *(14 CFR 91.15)*
    DISCUSSION: No pilot in command of a civil aircraft may allow any object to be dropped from that aircraft in flight that creates a hazard to persons or property. However, this section does not prohibit the dropping of any object if reasonable precautions are taken to avoid injury or damage to persons or property.
    Answer (A) is incorrect. Objects may be dropped from an aircraft if precautions are taken to avoid injury or damage to persons or property on the surface, not only in an emergency. Answer (C) is incorrect. Objects may be dropped from an aircraft if precautions are taken to avoid injury or damage to persons or property on the surface. Prior permission from the FAA is not required.

35. No person may attempt to act as a crewmember of a civil aircraft with

    A. .008 percent by weight or more alcohol in the blood.

    B. .004 percent by weight or more alcohol in the blood.

    C. .04 percent by weight or more alcohol in the blood.

Answer (C) is correct. *(14 CFR 91.17)*
    DISCUSSION: No person may act or attempt to act as a crewmember of a civil aircraft while having a .04% by weight or more alcohol in the blood.
    Answer (A) is incorrect. No person may attempt to act as a crewmember of a civil aircraft with .04% (not .008%) by weight or more alcohol in the blood. Answer (B) is incorrect. No person may attempt to act as a crewmember of a civil aircraft with .04% (not .004%) by weight or more alcohol in the blood.

36. A person may not act as a crewmember of a civil aircraft if alcoholic beverages have been consumed by that person within the preceding

    A. 8 hours.

    B. 12 hours.

    C. 24 hours.

Answer (A) is correct. *(14 CFR 91.17)*
    DISCUSSION: No person may act as a crewmember of a civil aircraft if alcoholic beverages have been consumed by that person within the preceding 8 hours.
    Answer (B) is incorrect. No person may act as a crewmember of a civil aircraft within 8 hr. (not 12 hr.) after the consumption of any alcoholic beverage. Answer (C) is incorrect. No person may act as a crewmember of a civil aircraft within 8 hr. (not 24 hr.) after the consumption of any alcoholic beverage.

37. Under what condition, if any, may pilots fly through a restricted area?

    A. When flying on airways with an ATC clearance.

    B. With the controlling agency's authorization.

    C. Regulations do not allow this.

Answer (B) is correct. *(14 CFR 91.133)*
    DISCUSSION: An aircraft may not be operated within a restricted area unless permission has been obtained from the controlling agency. Frequently, the ATC within the area acts as the controlling agent's authorization; e.g., an approach control in a military restricted area can permit aircraft to enter it when the restricted area is not active.
    Answer (A) is incorrect. Airways do not penetrate restricted areas. Answer (C) is incorrect. Restricted areas may be entered with proper authorization.

38. According to 14 CFR Part 107, how may a remote pilot operate an unmanned aircraft in Class C airspace?

    A. The remote pilot must have prior authorization from the Air Traffic Control (ATC) facility having jurisdiction over that airspace.

    B. The remote pilot must monitor the Air Traffic Control (ATC) frequency from launch to recovery.

    C. The remote pilot must contact the Air Traffic Control (ATC) facility after launching the unmanned aircraft.

Answer (A) is correct. *(AIM Para 3-2-6)*
    DISCUSSION: Operations in controlled airspace designated for an airport are not allowed unless that person has prior authorization from Air Traffic Control (ATC).
    Answer (B) is incorrect. An ATC facility may require the remote pilot to monitor the ATC frequency, but only on a case by case basis. Answer (C) is incorrect. Prior authorization must be obtained from ATC prior to operating in the controlled airspace, not after launching the unmanned aircraft.

39. Flight through a restricted area should not be accomplished unless the pilot has

    A. filed a IFR flight plan.

    B. received prior authorization from the controlling agency.

    C. received prior permission from the commanding officer of the nearest military base.

Answer (B) is correct. *(AIM Para 3-4-3)*
    DISCUSSION: Before an aircraft penetrates a restricted area, authorization must be obtained from the controlling agency. Information pertaining to the agency controlling the restricted area may be found at the bottom of the En Route Chart appropriate to navigation.
    Answer (A) is incorrect. The restriction is to all flight, not just flights without an IFR flight plan. Answer (C) is incorrect. The commanding officer is not necessarily in charge (i.e., controlling agency) of nearby restricted areas.

40. When using a small unmanned aircraft in a commercial operation, who is responsible for informing the participants about emergency procedures?

    A. The Remote Pilot in Command.

    B. The FAA Inspector-in-Charge.

    C. The lead visual observer.

Answer (A) is correct. *(AC 107)*
    DISCUSSION: As part of the FAA requirement for the sUAS to be in a condition for safe operation, prior to flight, the remote PIC must ensure that all persons directly participating in the sUA operation are informed about emergency procedures.
    Answer (B) is incorrect. It is the responsibility of the remote PIC, not the FAA inspector-in-charge, to ensure that all persons directly participating in the sUA operation are informed about emergency procedures. Answer (C) is incorrect. It is the responsibility of the remote PIC, not the lead visual observer, to ensure that all persons directly participating in the sUA operation are informed about emergency procedures.

1.3 Remote Pilot Certification with an sUAS Rating

41. After receiving a Part 107 remote pilot certificate with an sUAS rating, how often must you satisfy recurrent training requirements?

    A. Every 12 months.

    B. Every 8 months.

    C. Every 24 months.

Answer (C) is correct. *(14 CFR 107.63, 107.65; AC 107)*
    DISCUSSION: A remote pilot must retain and update their aeronautical knowledge to operate in the NAS by completing either a recurrent training course or a recurrent knowledge test within 24 calendar months of passing either an initial or recurrent aeronautical knowledge test.
    Answer (A) is incorrect. A remote pilot must complete and satisfy recurrent training requirements every 24 calendar months, not 12 months. Answer (B) is incorrect. A remote pilot must complete and satisfy recurrent training requirements every 24 calendar months, not 8 months.

42. Which of the following individuals may process an application for a Part 107 remote pilot certificate with an sUAS rating?

    A. Remote Pilot in Command.

    B. Commercial Balloon pilot.

    C. Designated Pilot Examiner.

Answer (C) is correct. *(14 CFR 107.63, 61.56)*
    DISCUSSION: An FAA designated pilot examiner (DPE), an FSDO, an airmen certification representative (ACR), or an FAA certificated flight instructor (CFI), may process an application for a Part 107 remote pilot certificate with an sUAS rating.
    Answer (A) is incorrect. A Remote Pilot in Command is not authorized to process an application for a Part 107 remote pilot certificate with an sUAS rating. Answer (B) is incorrect. A commercial balloon pilot is not authorized to process an application for a Part 107 remote pilot certificate with an sUAS rating.

1.4 Waivers

43. When requesting a waiver, the required documents should be presented to the FAA at least how many days prior to the planned operation?

    A. 30 days.

    B. 10 days.

    C. 90 days.

Answer (C) is correct. *(AC 107)*
    DISCUSSION: Although not required by Part 107, the FAA encourages applicants to submit their application at least 90 days prior to the start of the proposed operation.
    Answer (A) is incorrect. When requesting a waiver, the required documents should be presented 90 days, not 30 days, prior to the planned operation. Answer (B) is incorrect. When requesting a waiver, the required documents should be presented 90 days, not 10 days, prior to the planned operation.

44. The FAA may approve your application for a waiver of provisions in Part 107 only when it has been determined that the proposed operation

    A. Involves public aircraft or air carrier operations.

    B. Will be conducted outside of the United States.

    C. Can be safely conducted under the terms of that certificate of waiver.

Answer (C) is correct. *(14 CFR 101.41, 107.1, 107.200, 107.205)*
    DISCUSSION: The Administrator may issue a certificate of waiver authorizing a deviation from any regulation specified in 14 CFR 107.205 if the Administrator finds that a proposed sUAS operation can safely be conducted under the terms of that certificate of waiver.
    Answer (A) is incorrect. Public aircraft or air carrier operations are not covered by Part 107. Answer (B) is incorrect. Operations outside the United States are not covered by Part 107.

STUDY UNIT TWO
AIRSPACE CLASSIFICATION AND OPERATING REQUIREMENTS

(17 pages of outline)

2.1 AIRSPACE CLASSIFICATION

1. **The applicant demonstrates understanding of general airspace.**

   a. Because of the nature of operations within certain airspace areas, restrictions are required for safety reasons.

      1) The complexity or density of aircraft movements in other airspace areas may result in additional aircraft and pilot requirements for operation within such airspace.

      2) It is important that you be familiar with the operational requirements for the various airspace segments.

      3) You must be familiar with aeronautical chart symbols. The chart legend is reproduced below and discussed in more detail in Study Unit 7.

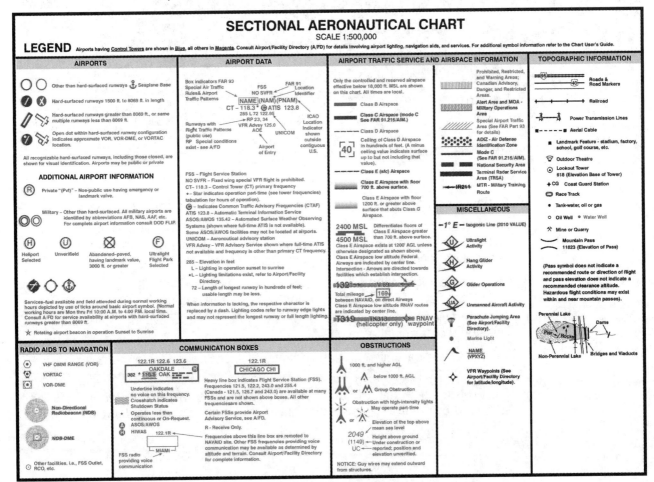

Legend 1. – Sectional Aeronautical Chart.

b. The federal airspace system is classified into six class designations.

1) The objectives of this airspace classification are to

a) Simplify the airspace designations

b) Increase standardization of equipment and pilot requirements for operations in various classes of airspace

c) Promote pilot understanding of ATC services available

d) Achieve international commonality and satisfy our responsibilities as a member state of ICAO (International Civil Aviation Organization)

2) The diagram below shows the airspace classification and summarizes the classifications with regard to the requirements and services available in each class of airspace.

3) Note that the airspace designated as Class F in the ICAO system is not used in the U.S.

4) This airspace classification conforms with the ICAO airspace system.

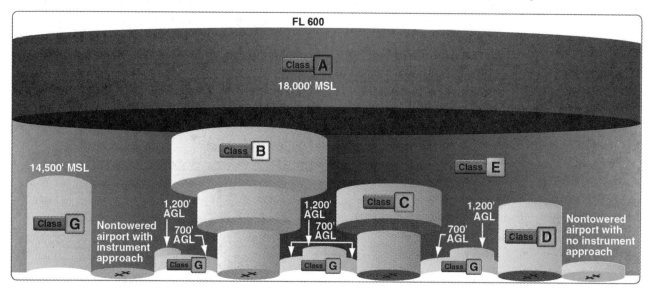

Airspace profile.

c. **The applicant demonstrates understanding of Class B controlled airspace.**

1) Class B airspace is generally the airspace from the surface to 10,000 ft. MSL surrounding the nation's busiest airports in terms of IFR operations or passenger enplanements (e.g., Atlanta, Chicago, etc.).

a) The configuration of each Class B airspace area is individually tailored and consists of a surface area and two or more layers.

2) The lateral limits of Class B airspace are depicted by heavy blue lines on a sectional or terminal area chart.

a) The vertical limits of each section of Class B airspace are shown in hundreds of feet MSL.

3) The 30-NM veil, within which an altitude-reporting transponder (Mode C) is required by manned aircraft regardless of aircraft altitude, is depicted by a thin magenta circle.

4) Class B airspace is shown on the sectional chart (below left) and on the diagram (below right).

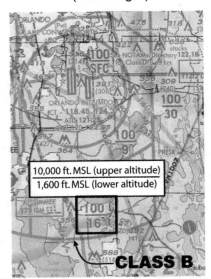

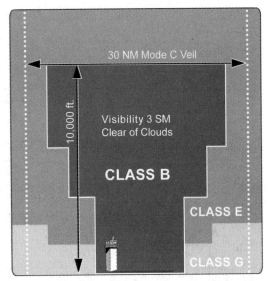

d. **The applicant demonstrates understanding of Class C controlled airspace.**

1) Class C airspace surrounds those airports that have an operational control tower, are serviced by a radar approach control, and have a certain number of IFR operations or passenger enplanements.

a) The lateral limits of Class C airspace are depicted by solid magenta lines on sectional and some terminal area charts.

i) The vertical limits of each circle are shown in hundreds of feet MSL.

ii) The inner surface area extends from the surface upward to the indicated altitude (usually 4,000 ft. above the airport elevation). It extends outward 5 NM from the primary airport.

iii) The shelf area extends from the indicated altitude (usually 1,200 ft. above the airport elevation) to the same upper altitude limit as the surface area.

b) Class C airspace is shown on the sectional chart (below left) and on the diagram (below right).

   i) Class C airspace vertical limits in the example extend

- From the surface (SFC) to 4,000 ft. MSL (40) in the surface area
- From 1,200 ft. MSL (12) to 4,000 ft. MSL in the shelf area

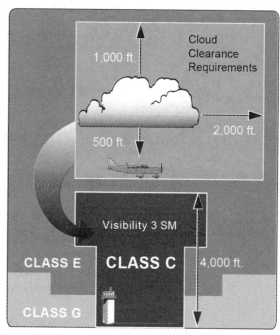

e. **The applicant demonstrates understanding of Class D controlled airspace.**

1) Class D airspace surrounds those airports that have both an operating control tower and weather services available and that are not associated with Class B or C airspace.

   a) Airspace at an airport with a part-time control tower is classified as Class D airspace only when the control tower is operating.

     i) When a tower ceases operation, the Class D airspace reverts to Class E or a combination of Class G and Class E airspace.

   b) Class D airspace is depicted by a blue segmented (dashed) circle on a sectional chart.

   c) Class D airspace normally extends from the surface up to and including 2,500 ft. AGL.

   d) The lateral limits of Class D airspace are depicted by dashed blue lines on a sectional or terminal area chart.

     i) The ceiling (usually 2,500 ft. above the airport elevation) is shown within the circle in hundreds of feet MSL.

     ii) The radius of airspace area is usually 5 NM.

     iii) The lateral dimensions of Class D airspace are based on the instrument procedures for which the controlled airspace is established.

e) Class D airspace is shown on the sectional chart (below left) and on the diagram (below right).

   i) The ceiling of Class D airspace in the examples is 2,700 ft. MSL.

   ii) If depicted, a dashed magenta line (see bottom left of sectional chart below) illustrates an area of Class E airspace extending upward from the surface.

 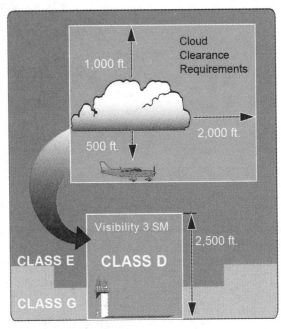

f. **The applicant demonstrates understanding of Class E controlled airspace.**

   1) Class E airspace is any controlled airspace that is not Class A, B, C, or D airspace.

      a) Except for 18,000 ft. MSL (the floor of Class A airspace), Class E airspace has no defined vertical limit but extends upward from either the surface or a designated altitude to the overlying or adjacent controlled airspace.

      b) In most areas, the Class E airspace base is 1,200 ft. AGL. In many other areas, the Class E airspace base is either the surface or 700 ft. AGL. Some Class E airspace begins at an MSL altitude depicted on the charts instead of an AGL altitude.

      c) A dashed magenta line around an airport indicates Class E airspace extending upward from the surface.

d)   A light magenta-shaded line indicates Class E airspace extending upward from 700 ft. AGL within the area enclosed by the line. Outside the line, Class E airspace begins at 1,200 ft. AGL.

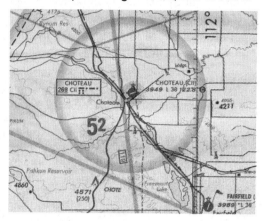

e)   The symbol shown below indicates Class E airspace extending upward from the indicated altitude. On sectional charts, it is illustrated in blue.

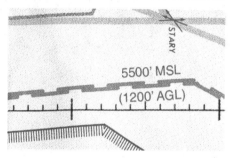

2)   Types of Class E Airspace

a)   Surface area designated for an airport

i)   When designated as a surface area for an airport, the Class E airspace will be configured to contain all instrument approach procedures (IAP).

b)   Extension to a surface area

i)   Some Class E airspace areas serve as extensions to Class B, Class C, and Class D surface areas designated for an airport.

ii) This Class E airspace provides controlled airspace to contain IAPs without imposing a communication requirement on pilots operating under VFR.

c)   Airspace used for transition

i)   This Class E airspace begins at either 700 ft. or 1,200 ft. AGL and is used to transition aircraft operating under IFR to/from the terminal or en route environment.

d)   Federal airways

i)   Federal airways (e.g., VOR or Victor airways) are Class E airspace areas and, unless otherwise specified, extend upward from 1,200 ft. AGL to, but not including, 18,000 ft. MSL.

e)   Offshore airspace areas

i)   This Class E airspace extends upward from a specified altitude to, but not including, 18,000 ft. MSL.

    ii)   Offshore airspace areas provide controlled airspace beyond 12 NM from the coast of the U.S. in those areas where there is a requirement to provide IFR en route ATC services and within which the U.S. is applying domestic ATC procedures.

    f)   Unless designated at a lower altitude, Class E airspace begins at 14,500 ft. MSL or 1,200 ft. AGL, whichever is higher, and extends to, but does not include, 18,000 ft. MSL. It includes the airspace overlying the waters within 12 NM of the coast of the 48 contiguous states and Alaska and that airspace above FL 600, but it excludes

        i)   The Alaskan peninsula west of 160° W longitude and

        ii)   The airspace below 1,500 ft. AGL unless specifically so designated.

g.   **The applicant demonstrates understanding of Class G uncontrolled airspace.**

    1)   Class G airspace is that airspace that has not been designated as Class A, Class B, Class C, Class D, or Class E airspace (i.e., it is uncontrolled airspace).

        a)   Class G airspace exists beneath the floor of controlled airspace in areas where the controlled airspace does not extend down to the surface.

        b)   Class G airspace vertical limit is up to, but not including, 14,500 ft. MSL.

    2)   Class G airspace is not shown. It is implied to exist everywhere controlled airspace does not exist.

        a)   Class G airspace extends upward from the surface to the floor of overlying controlled airspace.

2.   **The applicant demonstrates understanding of special-use airspace, such as prohibited, restricted, warning areas, military operations areas, alert areas, and controlled firing areas.**

    a.   **Prohibited areas** -- airspace within which flight is prohibited. Such areas are established for security or other reasons of national welfare.

        1)   Prohibited areas protect government interests as well as ecologically sensitive areas.

        2)   Prohibited areas are often surrounded by large Temporary Flight Restrictions (TFRs) when certain situations exist.

            a)   Because prohibited areas protect areas the President often visits, pilots must be aware that large TFRs will be implemented around those areas when the President is present.

        3)   Prohibited areas have varied ceilings but all begin at the surface. Depending on the area protected, prohibited area ceilings range from 1,000 feet MSL to 18,000 feet MSL.

        4)   Notices of new, uncharted prohibited areas are disseminated via the Notice to Airmen (NOTAM) system.

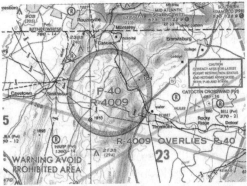

An example of a prohibited area, P-40 around Camp.

b. **Restricted areas** -- airspace within which flight, while not wholly prohibited, is subject to restrictions. Restricted areas denote the existence of unusual, often invisible hazards to aircraft, such as artillery firing, aerial gunnery, or guided missiles.

   1) The size and shape of restricted airspace areas vary based on the operation areas they restrict.

   2) Restricted areas are often placed next to, or stacked on top of, each other.

      a) The altitudes of restricted areas vary based on the operations conducted within them.

   3) If a restricted area is active, a pilot must receive prior permission of the controlling agency before attempting to fly through it.

      a) Times and altitudes of operation as well as the name of the controlling agency can be found on the sectional aeronautical chart.

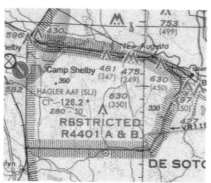

Restricted areas on a sectional chart.

c. **Warning areas** -- airspace of defined dimensions, extending from 3 NM outward from the coast of the U.S., that contains activity that may be hazardous to nonparticipating aircraft. The purpose of a warning area is to warn nonparticipating pilots of the potential danger (such as the hazards in restricted areas).

   1) A warning area may be located over domestic or international waters or both.

   2) Warning areas should be thought of exactly as restricted areas are.

      a) Because they are outside the 3 NM airspace boundary of U.S. airspace, they cannot be regulated as restricted areas are.

   3) Times and altitudes of operation can be found on the sectional aeronautical chart.

d. **Military operations areas (MOA)** -- airspace established to separate certain military training activities from IFR traffic.

   1) Pilots should exercise extreme caution while flying within an MOA when military activity is being conducted.

      a) Before beginning a flight that crosses an MOA, contact any FSS within 100 NM of the area to obtain accurate real-time information concerning the MOA hours of operation.

      b) Prior to entering an active MOA, contact the controlling agency for traffic advisories.

   2) MOAs are often placed next to, or stacked on top of, each other.

      a) The altitudes of MOAs vary based on the operations conducted within them.

      b) Times and altitudes of operation as well as the name of the controlling agency can be found on the sectional aeronautical chart.

        3) MOAs are often found in conjunction with restricted areas.

           a) Pay careful attention to such airspace when planning crossing flights to ensure you do not violate active restricted airspace.

    e. **Alert areas** -- areas depicted on aeronautical charts to inform nonparticipating pilots of areas that may contain a high volume of pilot training or an unusual type of aerial activity.

        1) All activity within an alert area is conducted in accordance with Federal Aviation Regulations.

           a) There is no specific controlling agency for an alert area, and crossing clearance is not required or given.

    f. **Controlled firing areas** -- areas containing activities that, if not conducted in a controlled environment, could be hazardous to nonparticipating aircraft.

        1) The activities are suspended immediately when spotter aircraft, radar, or ground lookout positions indicate an aircraft might be approaching the area.

        2) These areas are not depicted on charts because the pilot is not required to take action.

3. **The applicant demonstrates understanding of other airspace areas, such as Airport Advisory Services, Military Training Routes (MTRs), Temporary Flight Restrictions (TFRs), Parachute Jump Operations, Terminal Radar Service Areas (TRSAs), National Security Areas (NSAs), and Visual Flight Rules (VFR) routes.**

    a. **Airport advisory areas** encompass the areas within 10 SM of airports that have no operating control towers but where FSSs are located. At such locations, the FSS provides advisory service to arriving and departing aircraft. Participation in the Local Airport Advisory (LAA) program is recommended but not required.

    b. **Military training routes (MTRs)** are developed for use by the military for the purpose of conducting low-altitude (below 10,000 ft. MSL), high-speed training (more than 250 kt.).

        1) The routes above 1,500 ft. AGL are flown, to the maximum extent possible, under IFR.

           a) The routes at 1,500 ft. AGL and below are flown under VFR.

        2) Extreme vigilance should be exercised when flying through or near these routes.

        3) MTRs will be identified and charted as follows:

           a) MTRs with no segment above 1,500 ft. AGL must be identified by four-number characters, e.g., IR1206, VR1207.

           b) MTRs that include one or more segments above 1,500 ft. AGL must be identified by three-number characters, e.g., IR206, VR207.

           c) Alternate IR/VR routes or route segments are identified by using the basic/principal route designation followed by a letter suffix, e.g., IR008A, VR1007B, etc.

    c. **Temporary flight restrictions (TFRs)** contain airspace where the flight of aircraft is prohibited without advanced permission and/or an FAA waiver. This restriction exists because the area inside the TFR is often of key importance to national security or national welfare. TFRs may also be put into effect in the vicinity of any incident or event that by its nature may generate such a high degree of public interest that hazardous congestion of air traffic is likely.

        1) TFRs are very different from other forms of airspace because they are often created, canceled, moved, and/or changed.

           a) The temporary nature of TFRs can make keeping track of their locations and durations challenging.

2) TFRs protect government interests as well as the general public.

3) TFRs often surround other forms of airspace when extra security is necessary.

    a) Because TFRs protect the President, pilots must be aware that large TFRs will be implemented around any area where the President is present.

4) A NOTAM implementing temporary flight restrictions will contain a description of the area in which the restrictions apply.

    a) The size and shape of TFRs vary based on the areas they protect.

        i) Most TFRs are in the shape of a circle and are designed to protect the center of that circle.

        ii) TFRs always have defined vertical and lateral boundaries as indicated in the NOTAMs.

d. Flight limitations in the proximity of space flight operations are designated in a NOTAM.

e. Flight restrictions in the proximity of Presidential and other parties are put into effect by a regulatory NOTAM to establish flight restrictions.

1) Restrictions are required because numerous aircraft and large assemblies of persons may be attracted to areas to be visited or traveled by the President or Vice President, heads of foreign states, and other public figures.

    a) In addition, restrictions are imposed in the interest of providing protection to these public figures.

2) Presidential TFRs are issued with as much advanced notice as possible, given security concerns.

    a) The President is always surrounded by a 10-NM no-fly zone from the surface to 18,000 ft. MSL.

        i) No aircraft may operate in this area without a waiver or the advanced permission of the FAA.

    b) The President is also surrounded by a 30-NM TFR.

        i) Certain limited operations are allowed in this area.

f. Tabulations of **parachute jump areas** in the U.S. are contained in the Chart Supplement.

g. **VFR corridor** is airspace through Class B airspace, with defined vertical and lateral boundaries, in which aircraft may operate without an ATC clearance or communication with ATC. A VFR corridor is, in effect, a hole through the Class B airspace.

h. **Class B airspace VFR transition route** is a specific flight course depicted on a VFR terminal area chart for transiting a specific Class B airspace.

1) These routes include specific ATC-assigned altitudes, and pilots must obtain an ATC clearance prior to entering the Class B airspace.

i. **Terminal Radar Service Area (TRSA)**

1) TRSAs are not controlled airspace from a regulatory standpoint (i.e., they do not fit into any of the airspace classes) because TRSAs were never subject to the rulemaking process.

    a) TRSAs are areas where participating pilots can receive additional radar services known as TRSA Service.

2) The primary airport(s) within the TRSA are Class D airspace.

    a) The remaining portion of the TRSA normally overlies Class E airspace beginning at 700 or 1,200 ft. AGL.

j. **National security areas (NSAs)** are airspace established at locations where there is a requirement for increased security and safety of ground facilities.

    1) Pilots are requested to voluntarily avoid flying through the depicted NSA.

    2) When necessary, flight in a NSA may be prohibited, and this prohibition will be disseminated by a NOTAM.

k. Published VFR Routes

    1) Published VFR routes are for transitioning around, under, or through some complex airspace.

    2) Terms such as VFR flyway, VFR corridor, Class B airspace VFR transition route, and terminal area VFR route have been applied to such routes.

    3) These routes are generally found on VFR terminal area planning charts.

l. Wildlife Areas/Wilderness Areas/National Parks

    1) These are depicted as blue dotted outlined areas.

    2) Pilots of all aircraft are requested to operate above 2,000 ft. AGL in these areas.

    3) Because this altitude is above 400 ft. AGL, remote pilots should not consider operating in these areas.

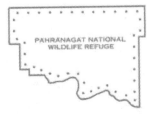

m. National Oceanic and Atmospheric Administration (NOAA) Marine Areas

    1) These are depicted off the coast as magenta dotted outlined areas.

    2) Pilots of all aircraft are required to operate above a minimum altitude as charted, usually 1,000 to 2,000 ft. AGL in these areas.

    3) Because this altitude is above 400 ft. AGL, remote pilots should not consider operating in these areas.

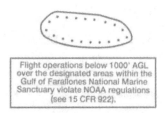

4. **The applicant demonstrates understanding of Air Traffic Control (ATC) and the NAS.**

a. The two categories of airspace are regulatory and nonregulatory.

    1) Within these two categories, there are four types:

        a) Controlled

        b) Uncontrolled

        c) Special use

        d) Other airspace

    2) The categories and types of airspace are dictated by the complexity or density of aircraft movements, nature of the operations conducted within the airspace, the level of safety required, and national and public interest.

b. Controlled airspace is defined as an area within which ATC service is provided to IFR and VFR flights in accordance with the airspace classification.

   1) Controlled airspace is designated as Class A, Class B, Class C, Class D, and Class E airspace.
   2) Uncontrolled airspace is designated as Class G airspace.

c. The distinction between uncontrolled airspace and the various types of controlled airspace relates to the following factors:

   1) ATC clearance requirements
   2) Pilot qualification requirements (as it relates to manned aircraft)
   3) VFR flight visibility and distance from clouds requirements

2.2 AIRSPACE OPERATIONAL REQUIREMENTS

1. **The applicant demonstrates understanding of basic weather minimums.**

   a. Minimum visibility, as observed from the location of the CS, may be no less than 3 SM.
   b. Minimum distance from clouds may be no less than 500 feet below a cloud and no less than 2000 feet horizontally from the cloud.
   c. One way to ensure adherence to the minimum visibility and cloud clearance requirements is to obtain local aviation weather reports that include current and forecast weather conditions.

      1) If there is more than one local aviation reporting station near the operating area, the remote pilot in command (PIC) should choose the closest one that is also the most representative of the terrain surrounding the operating area.
      2) If local aviation weather reports are not available, then the remote PIC may not operate the small unmanned aircraft (sUA) if (s)he is not able to determine the required visibility and cloud clearances by other reliable means.
      3) It is imperative that the UA not be operated above any cloud, and that there are no obstructions to visibility, such as smoke or a cloud, between the UA and the remote PIC.

   d. Manned aircraft are subject to the minimum visibility and cloud clearance requirements set forth in the table below.

Airspace	Flight Visibility	Distance from Clouds
Class A	Not Applicable	Not applicable
Class B	3 SM	Clear of Clouds
Class C	3 SM	500 ft. below 1,000 ft. above 2,000 ft. horiz.
Class D	3 SM	500 ft. below 1,000 ft. above 2,000 ft. horiz.
Class E:		
Less than 10,000 ft. MSL	3 SM	500 ft. below 1,000 ft. above 2,000 ft. horiz.
At or above 10,000 ft. MSL	5 SM	1,000 ft. below 1,000 ft. above 1 SM horiz.

Airspace	Flight Visibility	Distance from Clouds
Class G:		
1,200 ft. or less above the surface (regardless of MSL altitude)		
Day	1 SM	Clear of clouds
Night	3 SM	500 ft. below 1,000 ft. above 2,000 ft. horiz.
More than 1,200 ft. above the surface but less than 10,000 ft. MSL		
Day	1 SM	500 ft. below 1,000 ft. above 2,000 ft. horiz.
Night	3 SM	500 ft. below 1,000 ft. above 2,000 ft. horiz.
More than 1,200 ft. above the surface and at or above 10,000 ft. MSL	5 SM	1,000 ft. below 1,000 ft. above 1 SM horiz.

2. **The applicant demonstrates understanding of ATC authorizations and related operating limitations.**

   a. Although sUAS will not be subject to Part 91, the equipage and communications requirements outlined in Part 91 were designed to provide safety and efficiency in controlled airspace.

      1) Accordingly, although sUAS operating under Part 107 are not subject to Part 91, as a practical matter, ATC authorization or clearance may depend on operational parameters similar to those found in Part 91.

   b. The FAA has the authority to approve or deny aircraft operations based on traffic density, controller workload, communication issues, or any other type of operations that could potentially impact the safe and expeditious flow of air traffic in that airspace.

      1) Those planning sUAS operations in controlled airspace are encouraged to contact the FAA as early as possible.

3. **The applicant demonstrates understanding of operations near airports.**

   a. No person may operate an sUA in a manner that interferes with operations and traffic patterns at any airport, heliport, or seaplane base.

4. **The applicant demonstrates understanding of potential flight hazards.**

   a. **Common aircraft accident causal factors.**

      1) Common accident causal factors are often associated with pilot errors, lack of proficiency, and faulty knowledge.

      2) The 10 most frequent causal factors for general aviation accidents that involve the PIC are

         a) Inadequate preflight preparation and/or planning
         b) Failure to obtain and/or maintain flying speed
         c) Failure to maintain direction control
         d) Improper level off
         e) Failure to see and avoid objects or obstructions
         f) Mismanagement of fuel
         g) Improper inflight decisions or planning
         h) Misjudgment of distance and speed
         i) Selection of unsuitable terrain
         j) Improper operation of flight controls

      3) The PIC should be alert at all times. Strangely, air collisions almost invariably occur under ideal weather conditions. Unlimited visibility encourages a sense of security that is not at all justified.

      4) If another aircraft is too close, the PIC should give way instead of waiting for the other pilot.

   b. **Avoid flight beneath unmanned balloons.**

      1) The majority of unmanned free balloons currently being operated have, extending below them, either a suspension device to which the payload or instrument package is attached, or a trailing wire antenna, or both.

      2) In many instances these balloon subsystems may be invisible to the pilot until the sUAS is close to the balloon, thereby creating a potentially dangerous situation.

      3) Therefore, good judgment on the part of the remote pilot dictates that sUAS should remain well clear of all unmanned free balloons and flight below them should be avoided at all times.

c.   **Emergency airborne inspection of other aircraft.**

   1)   Providing airborne assistance to another aircraft may involve flying in very close proximity to that aircraft. Most pilots receive little, if any, formal training or instruction in this type of flying activity. Close proximity flying without sufficient time to plan (i.e., in an emergency situation), coupled with the stress involved in a perceived emergency, can be hazardous.

   2)   The pilot in the best position to assess the situation should take the responsibility of coordinating the airborne intercept and inspection and take into account the unique flight characteristics and differences of the category(s) of aircraft involved.

   3)   Some of the safety considerations are

   a)   Area, direction, and speed of the intercept

   b)   Aerodynamic effects (e.g., rotorcraft downwash)

   c)   Minimum safe separation distances

   d)   Communications requirements, lost communications procedures, and coordination with ATC

   e)   Suitability of diverting the distressed aircraft to the nearest safe airport

   f)   Emergency actions to terminate the intercept

   4)   Close proximity, in-flight inspection of another aircraft is uniquely hazardous. The PIC of the aircraft experiencing the emergency must not relinquish control of the situation and/or jeopardize the safety of his or her aircraft. The maneuver must be accomplished with minimum risk to both aircraft.

d.   **Precipitation static.**

   1)   Precipitation static (P-static) is caused by aircraft in flight coming in contact with uncharged particles. These particles can be rain, snow, fog, sleet, hail, volcanic ash, dust and any solid or liquid particles.

   a)   When the aircraft strikes these neutral particles the positive element of the particle is reflected away from the aircraft and the negative particle adheres to the skin of the aircraft. In a very short period of time, a substantial negative charge will develop on the skin of the aircraft.

   b)   If the aircraft is not equipped with static dischargers, or has an ineffective static discharger system, when a sufficient negative voltage level is reached, the aircraft may go into "CORONA." That is, it will discharge the static electricity from the extremities of the aircraft, such as the wing tips, horizontal stabilizer, vertical stabilizer, antenna, propeller tips, etc.

   c)   This discharge of static electricity can cause certain radio frequencies to become unreliable. This can lead to loss of control of the sUAS or interfere with other communication devices, such as first-person-view video systems or telemetry monitoring systems.

e.   **Light amplification by stimulated emission of radiation (laser) operations and reporting illumination of aircraft.**

   1)   Illumination from laser beam exposure can create significant hazards to pilots of manned aircraft resulting in temporary crewmember blindness.

   2)   For sUAS operators, lasers can interfere with camera operations and remote optical equipment used to monitor surroundings.

   3)   FAA regulations prohibit the disruption of aviation activity by any person on the ground or in the air. The FAA and the Food and Drug Administration (the federal agency that has the responsibility to enforce compliance with federal requirements for laser systems and laser light show products) are working together to ensure that operators of these devices do not pose a hazard to aircraft operators.

4) In cooperation with federal, state, and local law enforcement agencies, the FAA requests everyone's help in reporting laser incidents. If you are the victim of a laser incident or you witness a laser incident, please report it to the FAA.

    a) More information on reporting incidents can be found at www.faa.gov/aircraft/safety/report/laserinfo/.

f. **Avoiding flight in the vicinity of thermal plumes, such as smoke stacks and cooling towers.**

1) Thermal plumes are defined as visible or invisible emissions from power plants, industrial production facilities, or other industrial systems that release large amounts of vertically directed unstable gases.

    a) High-temperature exhaust plumes may cause significant air disturbances such as turbulence and vertical shear. Other identified potential hazards include, but are not necessarily limited to, reduced visibility, engine particulate contamination, and/or icing.

    b) Results of encountering a plume may include airframe damage, aircraft upset, and/or engine damage or failure.

    c) These hazards are most critical during low altitude flight, especially during takeoff and landing.

2) Thermal plumes may be associated with power plants or other sensitive properties and should be avoided. Failure to avoid these areas could be considered operating in a careless or reckless manner.

g. **Flying in the wire environment.**

1) Nearly all sUAS operations are conducted in the wire environment because of the altitudes flown.

    a) Below 1,000 ft. AGL, wires, towers, utility poles, guy wires, etc., create often invisible hazards to remote pilots.

    b) Many of the hazards are often visible to pilots; however, due to a focus on flying the sUAS and other distractions, the hazards can become invisible.

    c) Most skeletal structures are supported by guy wires that are very difficult to see in good weather and can be invisible at dusk or during periods of reduced visibility. These wires can extend about 1,500 ft. horizontally from a structure; therefore, all skeletal structures should be avoided horizontally by at least 2,000 ft.

    d) Overhead transmission and utility lines often span approaches to runways; natural flyways, such as lakes, rivers, gorges, and canyons; and cross other landmarks pilots frequently follow, such as highways, railroad tracks, etc.

        i) As with antenna towers, these high voltage/power lines or the supporting structures of these lines may not always be readily visible and the wires may be virtually impossible to see under certain conditions.

        ii) Many power lines do not require notice to the FAA and therefore are not marked and/or lighted. Many of those that do require notice do not exceed 200 ft. AGL or meet the Obstruction Standard of 14 CFR Part 77 and therefore are not marked and/or lighted.

        iii) All pilots are cautioned to remain extremely vigilant for these power lines or their supporting structures.

    e) Man-made obstacles and obstructions are typically depicted on sectional charts if they are over 200 ft. AGL. Consult the sectional chart legend presented in Subunit 2.1 for more details.

5.   **The applicant demonstrates understanding of the NOTAM system including how to obtain an established NOTAM through Flight Service.**

   a.   NOTAMs are time-critical aeronautical information either temporary in nature or not sufficiently known in advance to permit publication on aeronautical charts or in other operational publications.

   b.   The information receives immediate dissemination via the National NOTAM System.

   c.   NOTAMs contain current notices to airmen that are considered essential to the safety of flight, as well as supplemental data affecting other operational publications.

   d.   NOTAMs are grouped into five types:

      1)   **NOTAM (D)** includes information such as airport or primary runway closures; changes in the status of navigational aids, ILSs, and radar service availability; and other information essential to planned en route, terminal, or landing operations. Also included is information on airport taxiways, aprons, ramp areas, and associated lighting.

      2)   **FDC NOTAMs** are issued by the Flight Data Center and contain regulatory information such as amendments to published instrument approach charts and other current aeronautical charts.

      3)   **Pointer NOTAMs** reduce total NOTAM volume by pointing to other NOTAM (D) and FDC NOTAMs rather than duplicating potentially unnecessary information for an airport or NAVAID. They allow pilots to reference NOTAMs that might not be listed under a given airport or NAVAID identifier.

      4)   **SAA NOTAMs** are issued when Special Activity Airspace (SAA) will be active outside the published schedule times and when required by the published schedule, although pilots must still check published schedule times for SAA as well as any other NOTAMs for that airspace.

      5)   **Military NOTAMs** reference military airports and NAVAIDs and are rarely of any interest to civilian pilots.

   e.   NOTAMs should be checked prior to each flight. To check NOTAMs, the remote PIC should obtain a briefing.

   f.   There are several methods for checking NOTAMS.

      1)   FAA NOTAM retrieval: pilotweb.nas.faa.gov/PilotWeb/

         a)   This website allows the NOTAM database to be searched for a radius around a specific location(s), within a radius of a known latitude/longitude, or along a flight path.

      2)   Flight Service (online): www.1800wxbrief.com/

         a)   Leidos is the official Flight Service FAA contracted provider. Its services include answering flight service contacts from telephone, airborne, and online. According to their website, Leidos provides services to more than 80,000 general aviation community members weekly.

         b)   Many products can be accessed without signing up or logging in; however, official briefings may be accessed only after logging in to an account.

         c)   The main menu provides access to a pilot dashboard, weather, flight planning and briefing, airport information, UAS planning tools, account, links, and help information.

            i)   The UAS planning tools allow users to easily define UAS operating areas.

         d)   A user guide and videos with extensive instructions are available under the Help menu.

3) Flight Service (phone): 1-800-WX-BRIEF, (800-992-7433)

   a) A Leidos Flight Service Station specialist may be accessed by following the menu prompts to speak with a briefer.

   b) Identify yourself as a remote pilot and the area within which you are operating. You should reference an official aviation fix, such as an airport or navigational aid, if known. You can also identify your location using latitude and longitude.

      i) A standard briefing should be requested to obtain complete weather and NOTAMs for your area, for a flight within 8 hours.

      ii) An abbreviated briefing should be requested if only checking NOTAMs or obtaining an update following a previous briefing.

      iii) An outlook briefing should be requested for a flight more than 8 hours in the future.

4) DUATS: www.duats.com/

   a) The Direct User Access Terminal System (DUATS) is a computerized weather briefing and flight planning system that provides pilots with up-to-date and reliable briefing information.

   b) After creating an account and logging in, users have options to obtain aviation weather, charts, images, and preflight briefing tools.

   c) A user guide with extensive instructions is available under the Help menu.

g. The ***Notices to Airmen Publication (NTAP)*** is issued every 28 days and is an integral part of the NOTAM system. Once a NOTAM is published in the *NTAP*, the NOTAM is not provided during pilot weather briefings unless specifically requested.

   1) The *NTAP* contains (D) NOTAMs that are expected to remain in effect for an extended period and FDC NOTAMs that are current at the time of publication.

QUESTIONS

2.1 Airspace Classification

1. When a control tower located on an airport within Class D airspace ceases operation for the day, what happens to the airspace designation?

A. The airspace designation normally will not change.

B. The airspace remains Class D airspace as long as a weather observer or automated weather system is available.

C. The airspace reverts to Class E or a combination of Class E and G airspace during the hours the tower is not in operation.

Answer (C) is correct. *(AIM Para 3-2-5)*
   DISCUSSION: When a tower ceases operation, the Class D airspace reverts to Class E or a combination of Class G and Class E.
   Answer (A) is incorrect. Class D airspace is designated when there is an operating control tower. When the tower ceases operation for the day, the airspace reverts to Class E or a combination of Class G and Class E airspace. Answer (B) is incorrect. The airspace reverts to Class E, not Class D, when the tower ceases operation for the day and an approved weather observer or automated weather system is available.

2. Airspace at an airport with a part-time control tower is classified as Class D airspace only

A. when the weather minimums are below basic VFR.

B. when the associated control tower is in operation.

C. when the associated Flight Service Station is in operation.

Answer (B) is correct. *(AIM Para 3-2-5)*
   DISCUSSION: A Class D airspace area is automatically in effect when and only when the associated part-time control tower is in operation regardless of weather conditions, availability of radar services, or time of day. Airports with part-time operating towers only have a part-time Class D airspace area.
   Answer (A) is incorrect. A Class D airspace area is automatically in effect when the tower is in operation, regardless of the weather conditions. Answer (C) is incorrect. A Class D airspace area is in effect when the associated control tower, not FSS, is in operation.

3. The lateral dimensions of Class D airspace are based on

    A. the number of airports that lie within the Class D airspace.

    B. 5 statute miles from the geographical center of the primary airport.

    C. the instrument procedures for which the controlled airspace is established.

Answer (C) is correct. *(AIM Para 3-2-5)*
    DISCUSSION: The lateral dimensions of Class D airspace are based upon the instrument procedures for which the controlled airspace is established.
    Answer (A) is incorrect. While the FAA will attempt to exclude satellite airports as much as possible from Class D airspace, the major criteria for the lateral dimension will be based on the instrument procedures for which the controlled airspace is established. Answer (B) is incorrect. The lateral dimensions of Class D airspace are based on the instrument procedures for which the Class D airspace is established, not a specified radius from the primary airport.

4. A blue segmented circle on a Sectional Chart depicts which class airspace?

    A. Class B.

    B. Class C.

    C. Class D.

Answer (C) is correct. *(AIM Para 3-2-5)*
    DISCUSSION: A blue segmented circle on a sectional chart depicts Class D airspace.
    Answer (A) is incorrect. Class B airspace is depicted on a sectional chart by a solid, not segmented, blue circle. Answer (B) is incorrect. Class C airspace is depicted on a sectional chart by a solid magenta, not a blue segmented, circle.

5. (Refer to Figure 20 on page 61.) (Refer to area 5.) How would a remote PIC "CHECK NOTAMS" as noted in the CAUTION box regarding the unmarked balloon?

    A. By utilizing the B4UFLY mobile application.

    B. By contacting the FAA district office.

    C. By obtaining a briefing via an online source such as: 1800WXBrief.com.

Answer (C) is correct. *(AIM Para 5-1-3)*
    DISCUSSION: NOTAMs should be checked prior to each flight. To check NOTAMs, the remote PIC should obtain an official briefing online or over the phone.
    Answer (A) is incorrect. The B4UFLY mobile application does not provide NOTAMs. Answer (B) is incorrect. NOTAMs can be obtained from Flight Service or online sources, not the FAA district office.

6. (Refer to Figure 20 on page 61.) (Refer to area 1.) The NALF Fentress (NFE) Airport is in what type of airspace?

    A. Class C.

    B. Class E.

    C. Class G.

Answer (B) is correct. *(ACL)*
    DISCUSSION: The NALF Fentress (NFE) Airport is surrounded by a dashed magenta line, indicating Class E airspace from the surface.
    Answer (A) is incorrect. Class C airspace is surrounded by a solid magenta line. The line surrounding NFE airport is dashed magenta. Answer (C) is incorrect. The dashed magenta line surrounding NFE Airport indicates Class E begins at the surface. A shaded magenta line would be required to indicate Class G airspace from the surface up to 700 ft. AGL.

7. (Refer to Figure 20 on page 61.) (Refer to area 4.) What hazards to aircraft may exist in restricted areas such as R-5302A?

    A. Unusual, often invisible, hazards such as aerial gunnery or guided missiles.

    B. High volume of pilot training or an unusual type of aerial activity.

    C. Military training activities that necessitate acrobatic or abrupt flight maneuvers.

Answer (A) is correct. *(AIM Para 3-4-3)*
    DISCUSSION: See Fig. 20. Restricted areas denote the existence of unusual, often invisible, hazards to aircraft such as military firing, aerial gunnery, or guided missiles.
    Answer (B) is incorrect. A high volume of pilot training or an unusual type of aerial activity describes an alert area, not a warning area. Answer (C) is incorrect. Military training activities that necessitate acrobatic or abrupt flight maneuvers are characteristic of MOAs, not restricted areas.

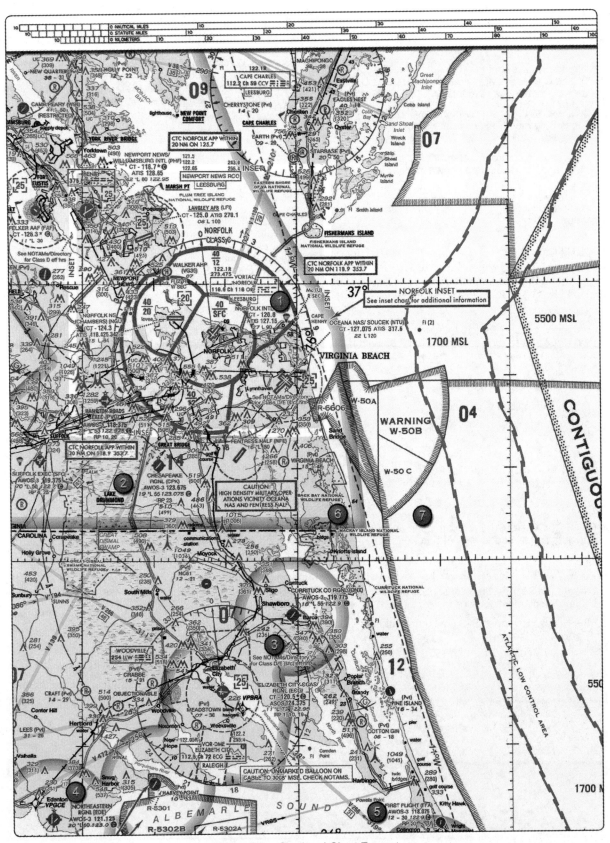

Figure 20. – Sectional Chart Excerpt.
NOTE: Chart is not to scale and should not be used for navigation. Use associated scale.

8. Which is true concerning the blue and magenta colors used to depict airports on Sectional Aeronautical Charts?

    A. Airports with control towers underlying Class A, B, and C airspace are shown in blue; Class D and E airspace are magenta.

    B. Airports with control towers underlying Class C, D, and E airspace are shown in magenta.

    C. Airports with control towers underlying Class B, C, D, and E airspace are shown in blue.

Answer (C) is correct. *(ACL)*
    DISCUSSION: On sectional charts, airports with control towers underlying Class B, C, D, E, or G airspace are shown in blue. Airports with no control towers are shown in magenta.
    Answer (A) is incorrect. There are no airports in Class A airspace. Airports with control towers are shown in blue, and all others are in magenta. Answer (B) is incorrect. Airports with control towers are shown in blue, not magenta.

9. Information concerning parachute jumping sites may be found in the

    A. NOTAMs.

    B. Chart Supplement.

    C. Graphic Notices and Supplemental Data.

Answer (B) is correct. *(Chart Supplement)*
    DISCUSSION: Information concerning parachute jump sites may be found in the Chart Supplement.
    Answer (A) is incorrect. NOTAMs are only issued for special situations, not routine jump sites. Answer (C) is incorrect. Graphic Notices and Supplemental Data are no longer published.

10. According to 14 CFR Part 107, the remote pilot in command (PIC) of a small unmanned aircraft planning to operate within Class C airspace

    A. must use a visual observer.

    B. is required to file a flight plan.

    C. is required to receive ATC authorization.

Answer (C) is correct. *(14 CFR 107.41)*
    DISCUSSION: Operations in Class B, Class C, Class D airspace, or within the lateral boundaries of the surface area of Class E airspace designated for an airport are not allowed unless that person has prior authorization from ATC. It is the responsibility of the remote PIC of the sUAS to receive this prior authorization.
    Answer (A) is incorrect. The remote PIC of an sUAS planning to operate within Class C airspace is required to receive prior authorization from ATC, not use a visual observer. Answer (B) is incorrect. The remote PIC of an sUAS planning to operate within Class C airspace is required to receive prior authorization from ATC, not file a flight plan.

11. (Refer to Figure 24 on page 63 and Legend 1 on page 65.) (Refer to area 1.) For information about the parachute jumping at Caddo Mills Airport, refer to

    A. notes on the border of the chart.

    B. the Airport/Facility Directory section of the Chart Supplement.

    C. the Notices to Airmen (NOTAM) publication.

Answer (B) is correct. *(ACL)*
    DISCUSSION: The miniature parachute near the Caddo Mills Airport (at 1 on Fig. 24) indicates a parachute jumping area. In Legend 1, the symbol for a parachute jumping area instructs you to see the Airport/Facility Directory section of the Chart Supplement for more information. Note, as of March 31, 2016, the *Airport/Facility Directory* book has been retitled to Chart Supplement.
    Answer (A) is incorrect. The sectional chart legend identifies symbols only. Answer (C) is incorrect. NOTAMs are issued only for hazards to flight.

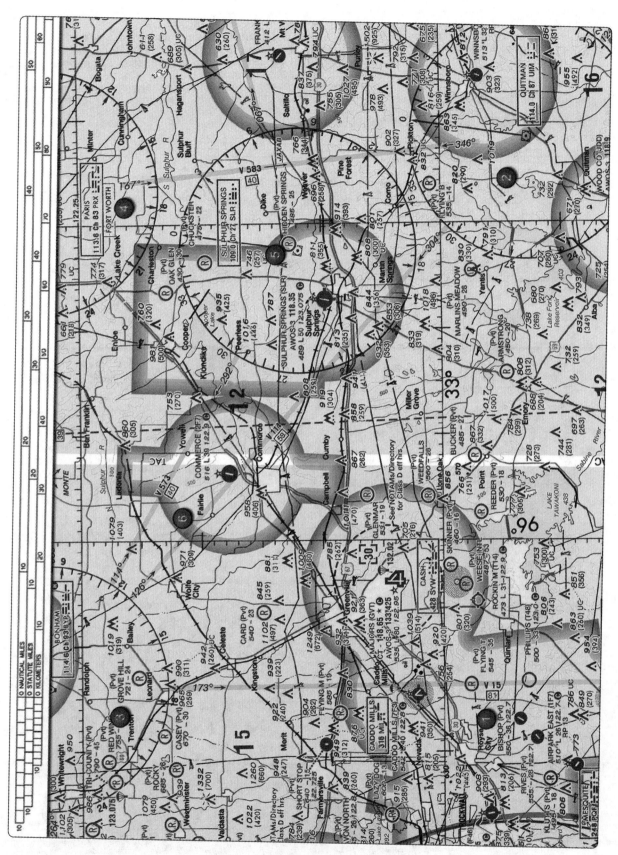

Figure 24. – Sectional Chart Excerpt.
NOTE: Chart is not to scale and should not be used for navigation. Use associated scale.

12. (Refer to Figure 23 below, and Legend 1 on page 65.) (Refer to area 3.) For information about glider operations at Ridgeland Airport, refer to

A. notes on the border of the chart.

B. the Chart Supplement.

C. the Notices to Airmen (NOTAM) publication.

Answer (B) is correct. *(ACL)*

DISCUSSION: The miniature glider near the Ridgeland Airport (at 3 on Fig. 23) indicates a glider operations area. The Chart Supplement will have information on the glider operations at Ridgeland Airport.

Answer (A) is incorrect. The sectional chart legend identifies symbols only. Answer (C) is incorrect. NOTAMs are issued only for hazards to flight.

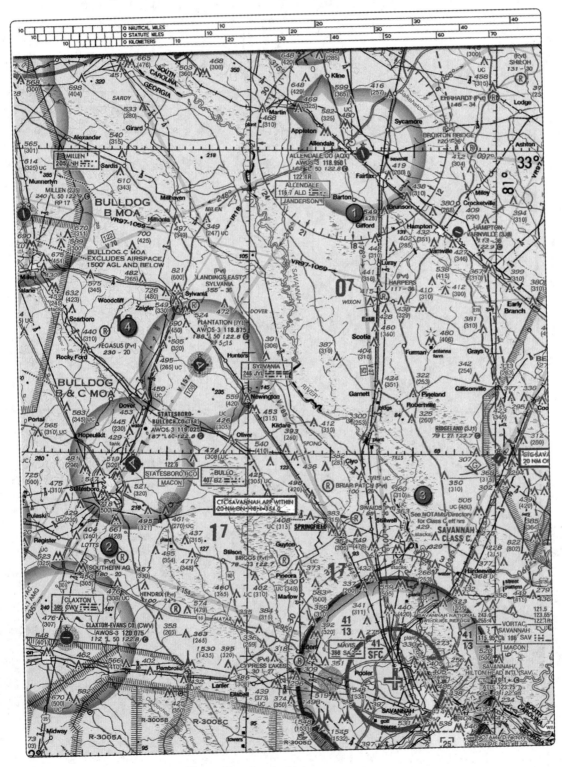

Figure 23. – Sectional Chart Excerpt.

NOTE: Chart is not to scale and should not be used for navigation. Use associated scale.

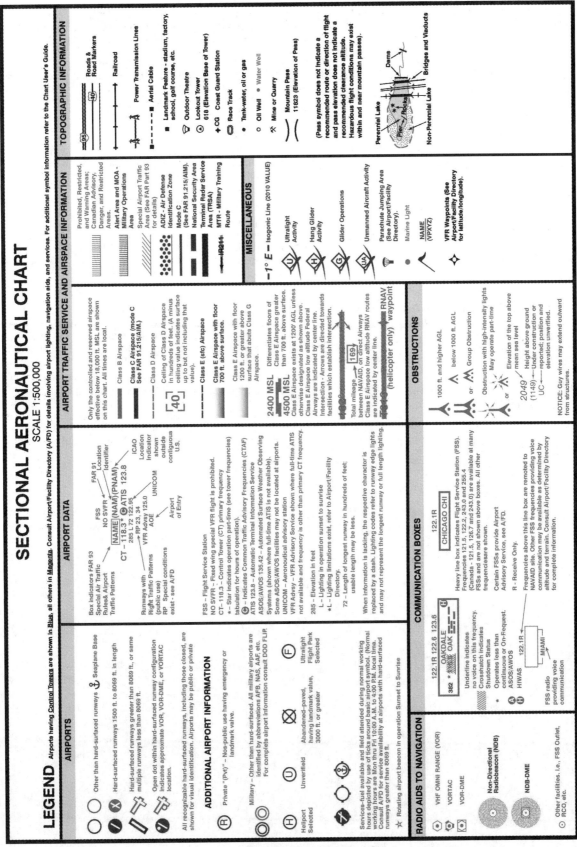

Legend 1. – Sectional Aeronautical Chart.

13. (Refer to Figure 25 on page 67.) What is the base of Class B airspace at Lakeview (30F) Airport (area 2)?

A. 4,000

B. 3,000

C. 1,700

Answer (B) is correct. *(AIM Chap 3)*
DISCUSSION: To the southwest of Lakeview Airport, there are numbers 110 over 30 in blue color. This indicates the base of Class B airspace between the blue airspace lines is 3,000 ft. MSL and the top is 11,000 ft. MSL.
Answer (A) is incorrect. The base is indicated at 4,000 ft. MSL beyond the blue line located north of Lakeview Airport. Answer (C) is incorrect. A base of 1,700 ft. would be below the maximum elevation figure in that quadrant.

14. (Refer to Figure 25 on page 67.) (Refer to area 4.) The airspace directly overlying Fort Worth Meacham is

A. Class B airspace to 10,000 feet MSL.

B. Class C airspace to 5,000 feet MSL.

C. Class D airspace to 3,200 feet MSL.

Answer (C) is correct. *(ACL)*
DISCUSSION: The airspace overlying Fort Worth Meacham (Fig. 25, southeast of 4) is Class D airspace as denoted by the segmented blue lines. The upper limit is depicted in a broken box in hundreds of feet MSL northeast of the airport. Thus, the Class D airspace extends from the surface to 3,200 ft. MSL.
Answer (A) is incorrect. Class D, not Class B, airspace extends from the surface of Ft. Worth Meacham. Class B airspace overlies the airport from 4,000 ft. MSL to 11,000 ft. MSL. Answer (B) is incorrect. Class D, not Class C, airspace directly overlies Ft. Worth Meacham from the surface to 3,200 ft. MSL, not 5,000 ft. MSL.

15. (Refer to Figure 25 on page 67.) (Refer to area 3.) The floor of Class B airspace at Dallas Executive Airport is

A. at the surface.

B. 3,000 feet MSL.

C. 3,100 feet MSL.

Answer (B) is correct. *(ACL, 14 CFR 71.9)*
DISCUSSION: Dallas Executive Airport (Fig. 25, area 3) has a segmented blue circle around it depicting Class D airspace. Dallas Executive Airport also underlies Class B airspace as depicted by solid blue lines. The altitudes of the Class B airspace are shown as $\frac{110}{30}$ to the southeast of the airport. The bottom number denotes the floor of the Class B airspace to be 3,000 ft. MSL.
Answer (A) is incorrect. The floor of Class D, not Class B, airspace is at the surface. Answer (C) is incorrect. This is not a defined limit of any airspace over Dallas Executive Airport.

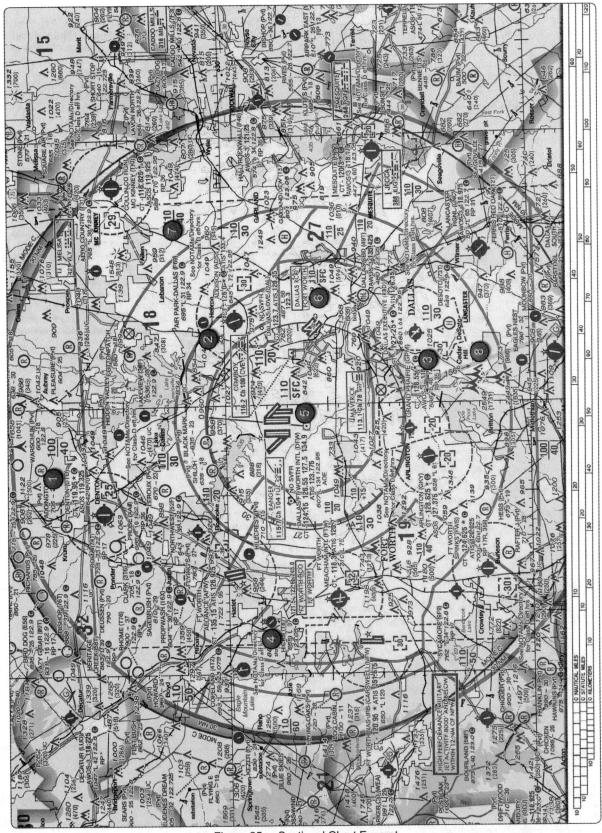

Figure 25. – Sectional Chart Excerpt.
NOTE: Chart is not to scale and should not be used for navigation. Use associated scale.

16. (Refer to Figure 26 on page 69.) (Refer to area 2.) What hazards to aircraft may exist in areas such as Devils Lake East MOA?

 A. Unusual, often invisible, hazards to aircraft such as artillery firing, aerial gunnery, or guided missiles.

 B. Military training activities that necessitate acrobatic or abrupt flight maneuvers.

 C. High volume of pilot training or an unusual type of aerial activity.

Answer (B) is correct. *(AIM Para 3-4-5)*
 DISCUSSION: Military Operations Areas (MOAs), such as Devils Lake East in Fig. 26 consist of defined lateral and vertical limits that are designated for the purpose of separating military training activities from IFR traffic. Most training activities necessitate acrobatic or abrupt flight maneuvers, i.e., air combat tactics, aerobatics, and formation training. Therefore, the likelihood of a collision is increased inside an MOA. VFR traffic is permitted, but extra vigilance should be exercised in seeing and avoiding military aircraft.
 Answer (A) is incorrect. Unusual, often invisible, hazards to aircraft, such as artillery firing, aerial gunnery, or guided missiles, are characteristic of restricted areas, not MOAs. Answer (C) is incorrect. A high volume of pilot training or an unusual type of aerial activity is characteristic of alert areas, not MOAs.

17. (Refer to Figure 26 on page 69.) (Refer to area 2.) Identify the airspace over Bryn Airport.

 A. Class G airspace -- surface up to but not including 1,200 feet AGL; Class E airspace -- 1,200 feet AGL up to but not including 18,000 feet MSL.

 B. Class G airspace -- surface up to but not including 18,000 feet MSL.

 C. Class G airspace -- surface up to but not including 700 feet MSL; Class E airspace -- 700 feet to 14,500 feet MSL.

Answer (A) is correct. *(ACL)*
 DISCUSSION: Bryn airport is the private airport located south of area 2. Due west of area 4, find the shaded blue markings that indicate Class E airspace with the floor 1,200 feet above the surface that abuts Class G airspace. The inside of the blue shaded area indicates that the regulations do not apply. The blue shading grading outward indicates the area of airspace that regulations do apply. Therefore, the airspace over Bryn airport is Class G airspace from the surface up to 1,200 feet AGL, then Class E airspace from 1,200 feet up to, but not including, 18,000 feet MSL.
 Answer (B) is incorrect. The Class G airspace above Bryn Airport ends at 1,200 ft. AGL (the beginning of Class E airspace), not 18,000 ft. MSL. Answer (C) is incorrect. Class G airspace above Bryn Airport extends to 1,200 ft. AGL, indicated by the shaded blue line in the bottom left corner of the chart excerpt. Class G airspace up to 700 ft. AGL (not MSL) would be indicated by magenta shading surrounding Bryn Airport. Additionally, Class E airspace above Bryn Airport extends to 18,000 ft. MSL, not 14,500 ft. MSL.

18. (Refer to Figure 26 on page 69.) (Refer to east of area 5.) The airspace overlying and within 5 miles of Barnes County Airport is

 A. Class D airspace from the surface to the floor of the overlying Class E airspace.

 B. Class E airspace from the surface to 1,200 feet MSL.

 C. Class G airspace from the surface to 700 feet AGL.

Answer (C) is correct. *(ACL)*
 DISCUSSION: The magenta band surrounding Barnes County Airport indicates that Class G airspace is from the surface to 700 ft. surrounding that 5 SM ring.
 Answer (A) is incorrect. Class D airspace requires a control tower. The Barnes County Airport does not have a control tower, since the airport identifier is magenta, not blue. Answer (B) is incorrect. An airport located in Class E airspace would be marked by magenta dashed lines, such as the ones surrounding Jamestown Airport to the left. Barnes has no such lines.

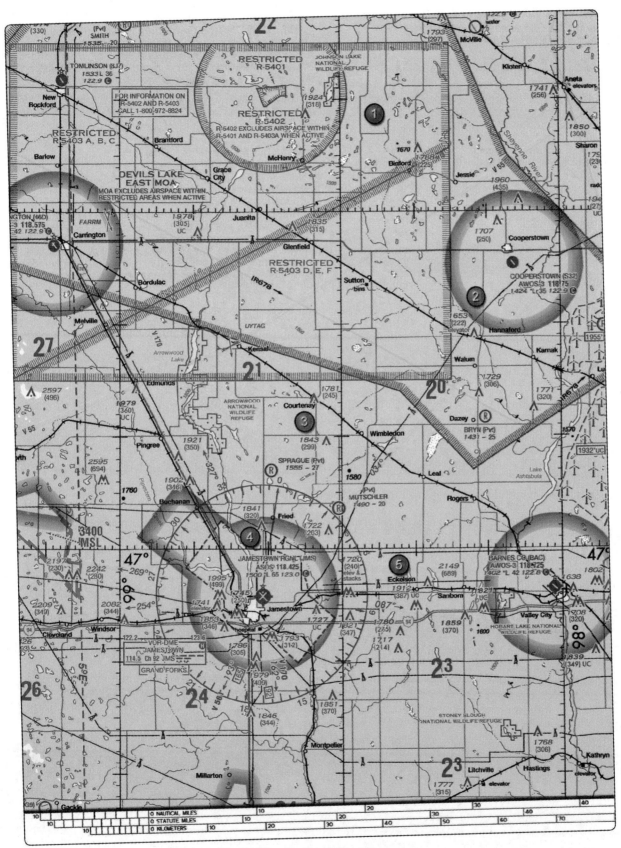

Figure 26. – Sectional Chart Excerpt.
NOTE: Chart is not to scale and should not be used for navigation. Use associated scale.

19. (Refer to Figure 75 on page 71.) The airspace surrounding the Gila Bend AF AUX Airport (GXF) (area 6) is classified as Class

A. B.

B. C.

C. D.

Answer (C) is correct. *(AIM Chap 3)*
    DISCUSSION: The GXF airport is surrounded by a dashed blue line, which indicates it is within Class D airspace.
    Answer (A) is incorrect. Class B airspace is surrounded by a solid blue line. Answer (B) is incorrect. Class C airspace is surrounded by a solid magenta line.

20. (Refer to Figure 75 on page 71.) What is the dotted outlined area northeast of Gila Bend Airport, near area 3?

A. Restricted airspace.

B. Military operations area.

C. Wilderness area.

Answer (C) is correct. *(PHAK Chap 16)*
    DISCUSSION: The area just to the west of area 3 represents an area that is a national park, wildlife refuge, primitive and wilderness area, etc. To the northwest of this area is the name, North Maricopa Mountains Wilderness Area.
    Answer (A) is incorrect. A restricted area on a sectional chart is outlined with a hashed blue border and labeled with an "R" followed by a numbered (e.g., R-1234). Answer (B) is incorrect. A military operations area (MOA) is outlined with a hashed magenta border. MOAs are named rather than numbered (e.g., Snowbird MOA) and further defined on the back of sectional charts.

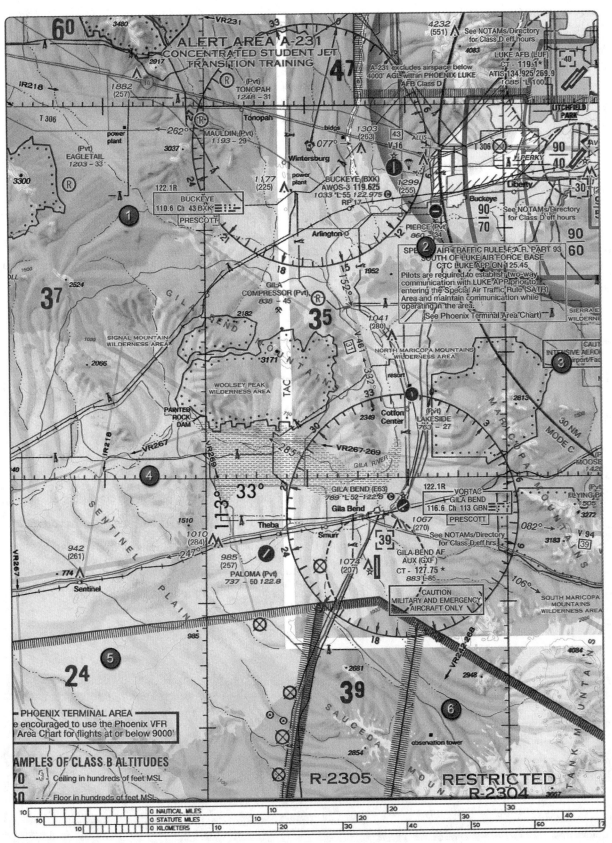

Figure 75. – Sectional Chart Excerpt.
NOTE: Chart is not to scale and should not be used for navigation. Use associated scale.

21. (Refer to Figure 59 on page 73.) (Refer to area 3.) What is the airspace classification around Findlay (FDY) airport?

   A. C.

   B. D.

   C. E.

Answer (C) is correct. *(PHAK Chap 16 and Sectional Chart)*
   DISCUSSION: A magenta dashed line surrounding an airport identifies it as Class E airspace that extends to the surface. The presence of this dashed magenta line indicates that this airport offers a precision instrument approach.
   Answer (A) is incorrect. Class C airspace is identified by two solid magenta lines surrounding the airport. Answer (B) is incorrect. Class D airspace is surrounded by dashed blue lines.

2.2 Airspace Operational Requirements

22. When NOTAMs are published in the *Notices to Airmen Publication (NTAP)*, they are

   A. Still a part of a standard weather briefing.

   B. Only available in a standard weather briefing if the pilot requests published NOTAMs.

   C. Canceled and are no longer valid.

Answer (B) is correct. *(AIM Para 5-1-3)*
   DISCUSSION: Once a NOTAM is published in the *NTAP*, the NOTAM is not provided during pilot weather briefings unless specifically requested.
   Answer (A) is incorrect. Published NOTAMs are only available in a pilot weather briefing if the pilot makes a specific request for them. NOTAMs that have not been published are a part of a standard weather briefing. Answer (C) is incorrect. A published NOTAM remains in effect until its expiration date or until an additional NOTAM is issued to cancel it.

23. What information is contained in the *Notices to Airmen Publication (NTAP)*?

   A. Current NOTAM (D) and FDC NOTAMs.

   B. All current NOTAMs only.

   C. Current Chart Supplement information and FDC NOTAMs.

Answer (A) is correct. *(AIM Para 5-1-3)*
   DISCUSSION: The *NTAP* contains (D) NOTAMs that are expected to remain in effect for an extended period and FDC NOTAMs that are current at the time of publication.
   Answer (B) is incorrect. Military NOTAMs are not published in the *NTAP*. Answer (C) is incorrect. While current FDC NOTAMs are published in the *NTAP*, current Chart Supplement information is not.

24. (Refer to Figure 59 on page 73.) (Refer to area 2.) The chart shows a gray line with "VR1667, VR1617, VR1638, and VR1668." Could this area present a hazard to the operations of a small UA?

   A. No, all operations will be above 400 feet.

   B. Yes, this is a Military Training Route from the surface to 1,500 feet AGL and below.

   C. Yes, the defined route provides traffic separation to manned aircraft.

Answer (B) is correct. *(AIM Para 3-5-2)*
   DISCUSSION: Military training routes (MTRs) are developed for use by the military for the purpose of conducting low-altitude (below 10,000 ft. MSL), high-speed training (more than 250 kt.). MTRs with no segment above 1,500 feet AGL must be identified by four number characters; e.g., IR1206, VR1207.
   Answer (A) is incorrect. Operations on these MTRs could also exist below 400 ft., not just above 400 ft. Answer (C) is incorrect. Manned aircraft operating in VFR conditions are expected to see-and-avoid to prevent collisions.

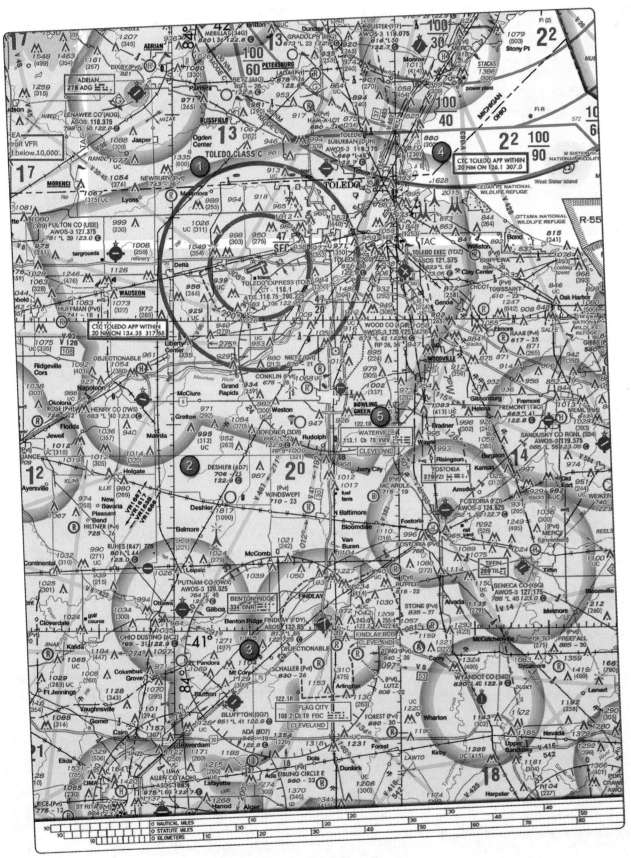

Figure 59. – Sectional Chart Excerpt.
NOTE: Chart is not to scale and should not be used for navigation. Use associated scale.

25. (Refer to Figure 20 on page 75.) (Refer to area 3.) With ATC authorization, you are operating your small unmanned aircraft approximately 4 SM southeast of Elizabeth City Regional Airport (ECG). What hazard is indicated to be in that area?

    A. High density military operations in the vicinity.

    B. Unmarked balloon on a cable up to 3,008 feet AGL.

    C. Unmarked balloon on a cable up to 3,008 feet MSL.

Answer (C) is correct. *(Aeronautical charts)*

    DISCUSSION: On Fig. 20, northwest of 5, find "CAUTION: UNMARKED BALLOON ON CABLE TO 3,008 MSL." This is self-explanatory.

    Answer (A) is incorrect. High density military operations are noted in the caution box south of Fentress NALF, not Elizabeth City. Answer (B) is incorrect. The balloon extends to 3,008 ft. MSL, not AGL.

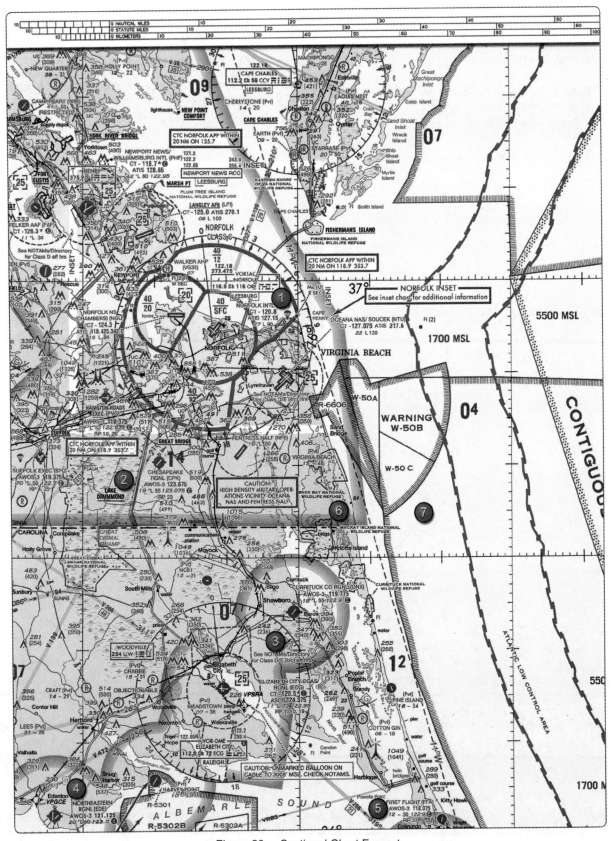

Figure 20. – Sectional Chart Excerpt.
NOTE: Chart is not to scale and should not be used for navigation. Use associated scale.

26. (Refer to Figure 21 on page 77.) You have been hired by a farmer to use your small UA to inspect his crops. The area that you are to survey is in the Devil's Lake West MOA, east of area 2. How would you find out if the MOA is active?

    A. Refer to the legend for special use airspace phone number.

    B. This information is available in the Small UAS database.

    C. Refer to the Military Operations Directory.

Answer (A) is correct. *(AIM Para 3-4-5)*
    DISCUSSION: Times and altitudes of operation as well as the name of the controlling agency can be found on the sectional aeronautical chart legend.
    Answer (B) is incorrect. MOA activity is found on the sectional chart legend, not a Small UAS database. Answer (C) is incorrect. MOA activity is found on the sectional chart legend, not the Military Operations Directory.

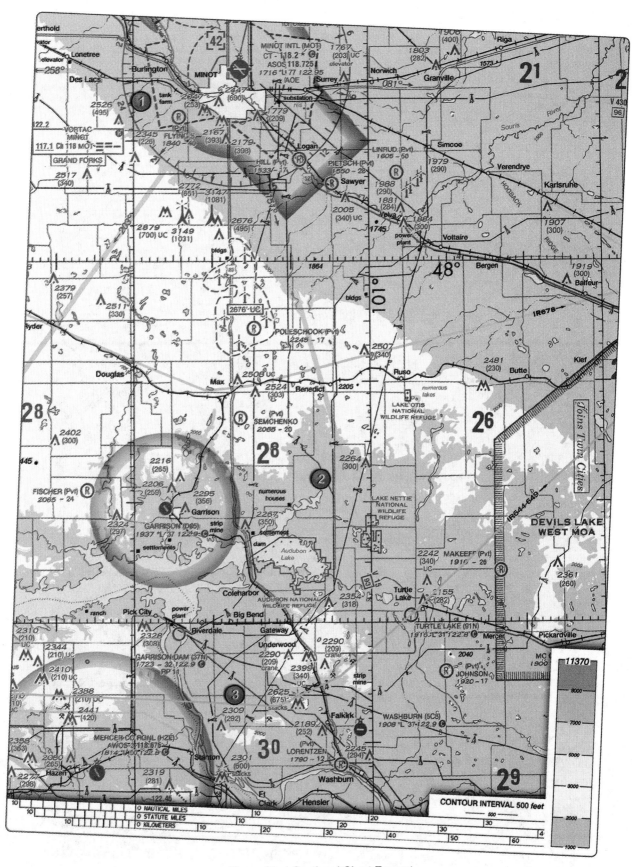

Figure 21. – Sectional Chart Excerpt.
NOTE: Chart is not to scale and should not be used for navigation. Use associated scale.

27. (Refer to Figure 23 below.) (Refer to area 3.) What is the floor of the Savannah Class C airspace at the shelf area (outer circle)?

A.   1,300 feet AGL.

B.   1,300 feet MSL.

C.   1,700 feet MSL.

Answer (B) is correct. *(AIM Para 3-2-4)*
   DISCUSSION: Savannah Class C (Fig. 23, area 3) has a magenta circle around it depicting Class C airspace. The altitudes of the Class C airspace shelf area are shown as 41/13 in the outer circle. The bottom number denotes the floor of the Class C airspace to be 1,300 ft. MSL
   Answer (A) is incorrect. The floor of the shelf area is charted in feet above MSL, not AGL. Answer (C) is incorrect. The floor of the shelf area is 1,300 ft. MSL, not 1,700 ft. MSL.

Figure 23. – Sectional Chart Excerpt.
NOTE: Chart is not to scale and should not be used for navigation. Use associated scale.

STUDY UNIT THREE
AVIATION WEATHER SERVICES

(23 pages of outline)

3.1 SOURCES OF WEATHER

1. **The applicant demonstrates understanding of internet weather briefing and sources of weather available for flight planning purposes.**

    a. Gleim recommends using official aviation weather sources, such as DUATS or Leidos Flight Service, to obtain your aviation weather information.

       1) **Flight Service (Online): www.1800wxbrief.com**

          a) Leidos is the official Flight Service FAA contracted provider. Its services include answering all types of flight service contacts through telephone, airborne, and online. According to its website, Leidos provides services to more than 80,000 general aviation community members weekly.

          b) Many products can be accessed without signing up or logging in; however, only official briefings may be accessed after logging in to an account.

          c) The main menu provides access to a pilot dashboard, weather, flight planning and briefing, airport information, UAS planning tools, account, links, and help information.

             i) The UAS planning tools allow users to easily define UAS operating areas.

          d) A user guide and helpful videos with extensive instructions are available under the Help menu.

       2) **Flight Service (Phone):** 1-800-WX-BRIEF (800-992-7433)

          a) A Leidos Flight Service Station specialist may be reached by following the menu prompts to speak with a briefer.

          b) Identify yourself as a remote pilot and the area you are operating in. You should reference an official aviation fix, such as an airport or navigational aid if known. You can also identify your location using latitude and longitude.

       3) **Direct User Access Terminal System (DUATS):** www.duats.com

          a) The DUATS is a computerized weather briefing and flight planning system that provides pilots with up-to-date and reliable briefing information.

          b) After creating an account and logging in, users have many options to obtain aviation weather, charts, images, and preflight briefing tools.

          c) A user guide with extensive instructions is available under the Help menu.

       4) **Types of Briefings**

          a) A standard briefing should be requested to obtain complete weather and NOTAMs for your area for a flight within 6 hours.

          b) An abbreviated briefing should be requested only if requesting specific information or obtaining an update following a previous briefing.

          c) An outlook briefing should be requested for a flight more than 6 hours in the future.

             i) Outlook briefings will usually not contain the same information as a standard briefing, such as current conditions.

b.   There are numerous sites on the Internet that distribute syndicated weather information or repackaged weather information derived from official sources.

1)   Although other sources may not be official, they are a convenient way to access a wide range of weather products quickly.

2)   Remember to always use official sources for navigation and flight planning. Most sites do not provide an official weather briefing and cannot be used to prove that you obtained sufficient weather information and NOTAMs pertinent to your flight.

3)   The following sites are popular weather resources for pilots.

a)   Gleim Aviation Weather: www.gleim.com/aviation/weather

i)   Links to National Weather Service radar images as well as METAR/ TAF reports by airport, winds aloft, and area forecast reports. An easy one-stop aviation weather information resource.

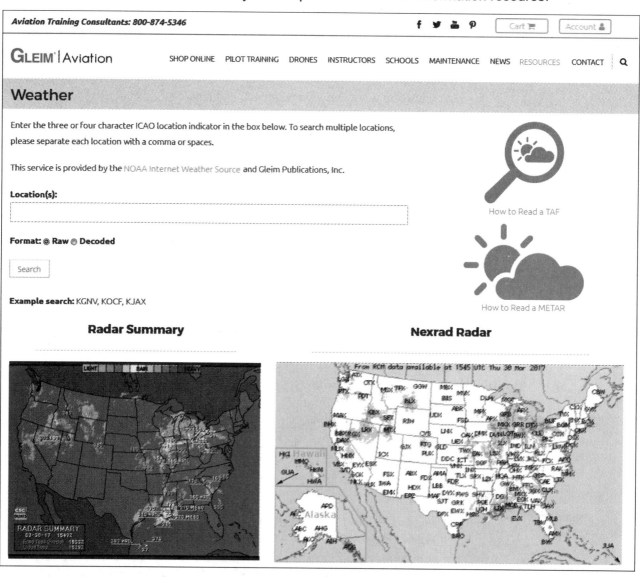

b)   Aviation Weather Center: www.aviationweather.gov

   i)   Official products, such as SIGMETs, AIRMETs, weather depiction, surface analysis, PROG Charts, METARS, TAFs, winds aloft forecasts, area forecasts, PIREPS, and excellent National Radar with tops and satellite imagery, etc. are available on this official government website.

   NOTE: Accessing this information does NOT constitute an official weather briefing.

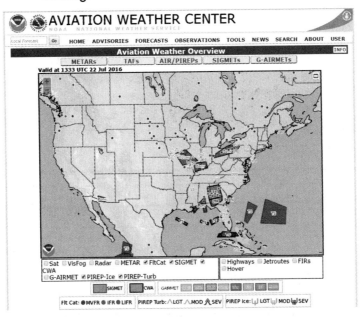

c)   National Weather Service: www.weather.gov

   i)   The official site of the National Weather Service contains local and national forecast products and full color maps.

   •   Many products are interactive, allowing the user to quickly zoom to specific regions and display a wide range of user-selected weather products including hazards, temperature, winds, sky cover, precipitation, etc.

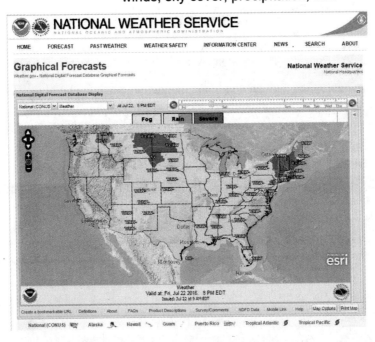

2.   **The applicant demonstrates understanding of aviation routine weather reports (METAR).**

   a.   **Elements.** A METAR report contains the following sequence of elements in the following order:

   1)   Type of report
   2)   ICAO station identifier
   3)   Date and time of report
   4)   Modifier (as required)
   5)   Wind
   6)   Visibility
   7)   Runway visual range (RVR)
   8)   Weather
   9)   Sky condition
   10)   Temperature/dew point
   11)   Altimeter
   12)   Remarks (RMK)

   > NOTE: The elements in the body of a METAR report are separated by a space, except temperature and dew point, which are separated by a solidus (/). When an element does not occur or cannot be observed, that element is omitted from that particular report.

   b.   **Example of a METAR Report**

METAR KGNV 201953Z 24015KT 3/4SM R28/2400FT + TSRA BKN008 OVC015CB 26/25 A2985 RMK TSB32RAB32

To aid in the discussion, we have divided the report into the 12 elements:

METAR	KGNV	201953Z	____	24015KT	3/4SM	R28/2400FT	+TSRA
1.	2.	3.	4.	5.	6.	7.	8.

BKN008 OVC015CB	26/25	A2985	RMK TSB32RAB32
9.	10.	11.	12.

   1)   Aviation routine weather report
   2)   Gainesville, FL
   3)   Observation taken on the 20th day at 1953 UTC (or Zulu)
   4)   Modifier omitted; i.e., not required for this report
   5)   Wind 240° true at 15 kt.
   6)   Visibility 3/4 statute miles
   7)   Runway 28, runway visual range 2,400 ft.
   8)   Thunderstorm with heavy rain
   9)   Ceiling 800 ft. broken, 1,500 ft. overcast, cumulonimbus clouds
   10)   Temperature 26°C, dew point 25°C
   11)   Altimeter 29.85
   12)   Remarks: Thunderstorm began at 32 min. past the hour; rain began at 32 min. past the hour.

---

   c.   **Type of Report** (element 1). The type of report will always appear as the lead element of the report. There are two types of reports:

   1)   **METAR** -- an aviation routine weather report
   2)   **SPECI** -- a nonroutine aviation weather report

   d.   **ICAO Station Identifier** (element 2). The METAR uses the ICAO four-letter station identifier.

   1)   In the contiguous 48 states, the three-letter domestic location identifier is prefixed with a "K."

      a)   EXAMPLE: The identifier for San Francisco, CA, is KSFO.

e. **Date and Time of Report** (element 3). The date and time the observation is taken are transmitted as a six-digit date/time group appended with the letter **Z** to denote Coordinated Universal Time (UTC).

   1) The first two digits are the date followed with two digits for the hour and two digits for minutes.

f. **Modifier** (element 4). There are two modifiers:

   1) **AUTO** -- identifies the report as an automated weather report with no human intervention.

      a) The type of sensor equipment used at the automated station will be encoded in the remarks section of the report.

   2) **COR** -- identifies the report as a corrected report to replace an earlier report with an error.

g. **Wind** (element 5). Wind follows the date/time or modifier element.

   1) The average 2-minute direction and speed are reported in a five- or six-digit format.

      a) The first three digits are the direction FROM which the wind is blowing. The direction is to the nearest 10-degree increment referenced to TRUE north.

      b) The last two or three digits are the wind speed in knots -- two digits for speeds less than 100 kt., three digits for speeds greater than 100 kt.

      c) The abbreviation **KT** is appended to denote the use of knots for wind speed.

   2) EXAMPLES:

      a) 24015KT means the wind is from 240° true at 15 kt.

      b) VRB04KT means the wind is variable in direction at 4 kt.

      c) 210103G130KT means the wind is from 210° true at 103 kt. with gusts to 130 kt.

      d) 00000KT means the wind is calm (i.e., less than 1 kt.).

h. **Visibility** (element 6).

   1) The visibility reported is called the prevailing visibility. **Prevailing visibility** is considered representative of the visibility conditions at the observing site. This representative visibility is the greatest distance at which objects can be seen and identified through at least 180° of the horizon circle, which need not be continuous.

   2) Visibility is reported in statute miles (SM) with a space and then fractions of statute miles, as needed, with **SM** appended to it.

      a) EXAMPLE: **1 1/2SM** means visibility is one and one-half statute miles.

   3) Automated reporting stations will show visibility less than 1/4 SM as **M1/4SM** and visibility of 10 SM and greater as **10SM**.

i. **Runway Visual Range (RVR)** (element 7).

   1) RVR is based on the measurement of a transmissometer made near the touchdown point of an instrument runway, which represents the horizontal distance a pilot will see down the runway from the approach end.

   2) RVR is reported whenever the prevailing visibility is 1 SM or less and/or the RVR for the designated instrument runway is 6,000 ft. or less.

      a) RVR is available only at airports equipped with a transmissometer.

   3) RVR is reported in the following format: **R** identifies the group, followed by the runway heading and parallel designator if needed, a solidus (/), and the visual range in feet (meters in other countries) followed with **FT**.

      a) EXAMPLE: **R28/1200FT** means runway 28 visual range is 1,200 ft.

j.   **Weather** (element 8). The weather groups are constructed by considering, in sequence, the intensity or proximity, followed by the descriptor and the weather phenomenon; e.g., heavy rain shower is coded as +SHRA. The weather phenomenon represented by UP means unknown precipitation (automated stations only).

1)   **Intensity or Proximity**

a)   Intensity may be shown with most precipitation types, including those of a showery nature.

Symbol	Meaning
+	Heavy
(no symbol)	Moderate
−	Light

i)   Intensity levels may be shown with obscurations, such as blowing dust, sand, or snow.

ii)   When more than one type of precipitation is present, the intensity refers to the first precipitation type (most predominant).

b)   Proximity is applied to and reported only for weather occurring in the vicinity of the airport (between 5 and 10 SM of the usual point of observation) and is denoted by **VC**.

i)   VC will replace the intensity symbol; i.e., intensity and VC will never be shown in the same group.

2)   **Descriptor.** The following eight descriptors further identify weather phenomena and are used with certain types of precipitation and obscurations.

Coded	Meaning	Coded	Meaning
TS	Thunderstorm	DR	Low drifting
SH	Showers	MI	Shallow
FZ	Freezing	BC	Patchy
BL	Blowing	PR	Partial

a)   Although **TS** and **SH** are used with precipitation and may be preceded with an intensity symbol, the intensity applies to the precipitation and not the descriptor.

i)   EXAMPLE: **+SHRA** means heavy rain showers.

3)   **Precipitation.** Precipitation is any form of water particles, whether solid or liquid, that fall from the atmosphere and reach the ground.

Coded	Meaning	Coded	Meaning
RA	Rain	GR	Hail (1/4 in. or greater)
DZ	Drizzle	GS	Small Hail/Snow Pellets
SN	Snow	PL	Ice Pellets
SG	Snow Grains	IC	Ice Crystals
UP	Unknown Precipitation		

a)   **UP** will be used only by automated weather reporting systems to indicate that the system cannot identify the precipitation with any degree of proficiency.

b)   **GS** is used to indicate hail less than 1/4 in. in diameter.

c)   For **IC** to be reported, the visibility must be reduced by ice crystals to 6 SM or less.

4) **Obscurations to visibility.** Obscurations are any phenomena in the atmosphere, other than precipitation, that reduce horizontal visibility.

Coded	Meaning	Coded	Meaning
FG	Fog (visibility less than 5/8 SM)	PY	Spray
BR	Mist (visibility 5/8 to 6 SM)	SA	Sand
FU	Smoke	DU	Dust
HZ	Haze	VA	Volcanic Ash

a) **FG** is used to indicate fog restricting visibility to less than 5/8 SM.

b) **BR** is used to indicate mist restricting visibility from 5/8 to 6 SM and is never coded with a descriptor.

c) **BCFG** and **PRFG** are used to indicate patchy fog or partial fog only if the prevailing visibility is 7 SM or greater.

5) **Other.** Six other weather phenomena are reported when they occur.

Coded	Meaning	Coded	Meaning
SQ	Squall	SS	Sandstorm
DS	Duststorm	PO	Well-Developed Dust/Sand Whirls
FC	Funnel Cloud	+FC	Tornado or Waterspout

a) A **squall** (**SQ**) is a sudden increase in wind speed of at least 16 kt., with the speed rising to 22 kt. or more and lasting at least 1 min.

b) **+FC** is used to denote a tornado, waterspout, or well-developed funnel cloud.

   i) The type will be indicated in the remarks.

6) **Examples of Reported Weather Phenomena**

   a) **TSRA** means thunderstorm with moderate rain.
   b) **+SN** means heavy snow.
   c) **–RA FG** means light rain and fog.
   d) **VCSH** means showers in the vicinity.

k. **Sky Condition** (element 9). The sky condition is reported in the following format:

1) **Amount.** The amount of sky cover is reported in eighths of sky cover, using the contractions shown below.

Contraction	Meaning	Summation Amount
SKC or CLR*	Clear	0 or 0 below 12,000 ft.
FEW	Few	>0 to 2/8
SCT	Scattered	3/8 to 4/8
BKN	Broken	5/8 to 7/8
OVC	Overcast	8/8
VV	Vertical Visibility (indefinite ceiling)	8/8
CB	Cumulonimbus	When present
TCU	Towering Cumulus	When present

* **SKC** will be reported at manual stations. **CLR** will be used at automated stations when no clouds below 12,000 ft. are reported.

a) A **ceiling** is defined as the lowest broken or overcast layer aloft or vertical visibility into a surface-based obstruction.

   i) The METAR code does not contain a provision for reporting a thin layer (i.e., a layer through which blue sky or higher sky cover is visible). A thin layer will be reported the same as if it were opaque.

2) **Height.** Cloud bases are reported with three digits in hundreds of feet above ground level (AGL).

    a) When more than one layer is reported, layers are given in ascending order of height. For each layer above a lower layer(s), the sky cover contraction for that layer will be the **total sky cover**, which includes that layer and all lower layers.

        i) EXAMPLE: **SCT010 BKN025 OVC080** reports three layers:

- A scattered layer at 1,000 ft.
- A broken layer (ceiling) at 2,500 ft.
- A top layer at 8,000 ft. In this case, it is assumed that the total sky covered by all the layers is 8/8. Thus, the upper layer is reported as overcast.

3) **Type or Vertical Visibility**

    a) If **towering cumulus clouds (TCU)** or cumulonimbus clouds **(CB)** are present, they are reported after the height that represents their base.

        i) EXAMPLES:

- **SCT025TCU BKN080 BKN250** means 2,500 ft. scattered towering cumulus, ceiling 8,000 ft. broken, 25,000 ft. broken.
- **SCT008 OVC012CB** means 800 ft. scattered, ceiling 1,200 ft. overcast cumulonimbus clouds.

    b) Height into an indefinite ceiling is preceded with **VV** (vertical visibility) followed by three digits indicating the vertical visibility in hundreds of feet.

        i) The layer is spoken of as an "indefinite ceiling" and indicates total obscuration.

        ii) EXAMPLE: **1/8SM FG VV006** means visibility 1/8 SM, fog, indefinite ceiling 600 ft.

l. **Temperature/Dew Point Group** (element 10)

1) Temperature and dew point are reported in a two-digit form in whole degrees Celsius (C) separated by a solidus (**/**).

    a) Temperatures below zero are prefixed with **M.**

2) EXAMPLES:

    a) **15/08** means temperature is 15°C and dew point is 8°C.
    b) **00/M02** means temperature is 0°C and dew point is –2°C.
    c) **M05/** means temperature is –5°C and dew point is missing.

3) An air mass with a 3°C or less temperature/dew point spread is considered saturated.

m. **Altimeter** (element 11)

1) The altimeter is reported in a four-digit format representing tens, units, tenths, and hundredths of inches of mercury prefixed with **A**. The decimal point is not reported.

    a) EXAMPLE: **A2995** means the altimeter setting is 29.95 inches of mercury.

n. **Remarks** (element 12)

1) Remarks will be included in all observations, when appropriate, and are preceded by the contraction **RMK.**

    a) Time entries are shown as minutes past the hour if the time reported occurs during the same hour the observation is taken.

   b)   Location of phenomena within 5 SM of the station will be reported as at the station.

   i)   Phenomena between 5 and 10 SM will be reported in the vicinity, **VC**.
   ii) Phenomena beyond 10 SM will be reported as distant, **DSNT**.

2) There are two categories of remarks:

   a) **Automated, manual, and plain language remarks category.** This category of remarks may be generated from either manual or automated weather reporting stations, and they generally elaborate on parameters reported in the body of the report. Some of these remarks include

      i)   **Station type.** This remark is shown only if the **AUTO** modifier was used.

         ● **AO1** means the automated weather station is without a precipitation discriminator.
         ● **AO2** means the automated weather station has a precipitation discriminator.
         ● A precipitation discriminator can determine the difference between liquid and frozen/freezing precipitation.

      ii) **Beginning and/or ending times for precipitation and thunderstorms.**

         ● When precipitation begins or ends, remarks will show the type of precipitation as well as the beginning and/or ending time(s) of occurrence.

            ■ Types of precipitation may be combined if beginning or ending at the same time.
            ■ EXAMPLE: **RAB05E30SNB20E55** means that rain began at 5 min. past the hour and ended at 30 min. past the hour, and snow began at 20 min. past the hour and ended at 55 min. past the hour.

         ● When thunderstorms begin or end, remarks will show the thunderstorm as well as the beginning and/or ending time(s) of occurrence.

            ■ EXAMPLE: **TSB05E40** means the thunderstorm began at 5 min. past the hour and ended at 40 min. past the hour.

   b) **Additive and maintenance data remarks category.** Additive data groups are reported only at designated stations, and the maintenance data groups are reported only from automated weather reporting stations. Some of these remarks include

      i)   **Sensor Status Indicators.**

         ● If automated weather reporting station sensors are not working, the following remarks will appear:

            ■ **PWINO** -- present weather identifier not available
            ■ **PNO** -- precipitation amount not available
            ■ **FZRANO** -- freezing rain information indicator not available
            ■ **TSNO** -- lightning information not available
            ■ **VISNO** -- visibility sensor information not available
            ■ **CHINO** -- cloud height indicator information not available

      ii) **Maintenance indicator.** A maintenance indicator (dollar) sign, **$**, is included when an automated weather reporting system detects that maintenance is needed on the system.

3.   **The applicant demonstrates understanding of terminal aerodrome forecasts (TAF).**

    a.   TAF is a concise statement of the expected weather at a specific airport during a 24- or 30-hour period.

        1)   The TAF covers an area within a 5-SM radius of the center of the airport and is prepared four times daily at 0000Z, 0600Z, 1200Z, and 1800Z.

        2)   Many of the weather codes used in the METAR are also used in the TAF.

        3)   The 32 largest airports in the U.S. offer 30-hour forecasts. Every other site provides a 24-hour forecast.

    b.   **Elements.** A TAF contains the following sequence of elements in the following order (items a-i). Forecast change indicators (items j-l) and probability forecast (item m) are used as appropriate.

Communications Header	Forecast of Meteorological Conditions	Time Elements
a. Type of report	e. Wind	j. Temporary (TEMPO)
b. ICAO station identifier	f. Visibility	k. From (FM)
c. Date and time of origin	g. Weather	l. Becoming (BECMG)
d. Valid period date and time	h. Sky condition	m. Probability (PROB)
	i. Wind shear (optional)	

    c.   **Example of a TAF:**

```
TAF
KOKC 051130Z 0512/0612 14008KT 5SM BR BKN030 WS018/32030KT
   TEMPO 0513/0516 1SM BR
   FM051600 16010KT P6SM SKC
   BECMG 0522/0624 20013G20KT 4SM SHRA OVC020
   PROB40 0600/0606 2SM TSRA OVC008CB=
```

To aid in the discussion, we have divided the TAF above into elements 1. – 13. as follows:

TAF	KOKC	051130Z	0512/0612	14008KT	5SM	BR	BKN030
1.	2.	3.	4.	5.	6.	7.	8.

WS018/32030KT	TEMPO 0513/0516 1SM BR	FM051600 16010KT P6SM SKC
9.	10.	11.

BECMG 0522/0624 20013G20KT 4SM SHRA OVC020
12.

PROB40 0600/0606 2SM TSRA OVC008CB=
13.

        1)   Routine terminal aerodrome forecast

        2)   Oklahoma City, OK

        3)   Forecast prepared on the 5th day at 1130 UTC (or Z)

        4)   Forecast valid from the 5th day at 1200 UTC until 1200 UTC on the 6th day

        5)   Wind 140° true at 8 kt.

        6)   Visibility 5 SM

        7)   Visibility obscured by mist

        8)   Ceiling 3,000 ft. broken

           a)   A vertical visibility (VV) may also be forecast as a sky condition when the sky is expected to be obscured by a surface-based phenomena.

        9)   Low-level wind shear at 1,800 ft., wind 320° true at 30 kt.

      10)   Temporary (spoken as occasional) visibility 1 SM in mist between 1300 UTC and 1600 UTC of the 5th day

      11)   From (or after) 1600 UTC on the 5th day, wind 160° true at 10 kt., visibility more than 6 SM, sky clear

Continued -- on next page

CONTINUED -- from previous page

12) Becoming (gradual change) wind 200° true at 13 kt., gusts to 20 kt., visibility 4 SM in moderate rain showers, ceiling 2,000 ft. overcast between 2200 UTC and 2400 UTC on the 5th and beginning the 6th day

13) Probability (40% chance) between 0000 UTC and 0600 UTC of the 6th day of visibility 2 SM, thunderstorm, moderate rain, ceiling 800 ft. overcast, cumulonimbus clouds (The = sign indicates end of forecast.)

---

d.   **Type of Report** (element 1). There are two types of TAF issuances:

   1) **TAF** means a routine forecast.
   2) **TAF AMD** means an amended forecast.

e.   **ICAO Station Identifier** (element 2). The TAF uses the ICAO four-letter station identifier.

f.   **Date and Time of Origin** (element 3). This element is the date and time (UTC) that the forecast is actually prepared. The format is a two-digit date and a four-digit time followed by the letter **Z.**

g.   **Valid Period Date and Time** (element 4). The UTC valid period of the forecast is a two-digit date followed by the two-digit beginning hour, a solidus, and the two-digit date and two-digit ending hour.

   1) Valid periods beginning at 0000 UTC will be indicated as **00**, and valid periods ending at 0000 UTC will be indicated as **24**.

h.   **Forecast Meteorological Conditions.** This element is the body of the TAF.

   1) The wind, visibility, and sky condition elements are always included in the initial date/time group of the forecast.

      a) Weather is included only if it is significant to aviation.

   2) If a significant, lasting change in any of the elements is expected during the valid period, a new date/time period with the changes is included.

      a) It should be noted that, with the exception of a From (FM) group, the new date/time period will include only those elements expected to change; i.e., if a lowering of the visibility is expected but the wind is expected to remain the same, the new period reflecting the lower visibility would not include a forecast wind.

         i) The forecast wind would remain the same as in the previous period.

   3) Any temporary conditions expected during a specific date/time period are included with that period.

i.   **Wind** (element 5). The wind element is a five- or six-digit group with the forecast surface wind direction (first three digits) referenced to true north and the speed (last two digits or three digits if 100 kt. or greater).

   1) The abbreviation **KT** is appended to denote the use of knots for wind speed.
   2) A calm wind (0 kt.) is forecast as **00000KT**.

j.   **Visibility** (element 6). The expected prevailing visibility is forecast in statute miles with a space and then fractions of statute miles, as needed, with **SM** appended to it.

   1) Forecast visibility greater than 6 SM is coded **P6SM**.

k. **Weather** (element 7). The expected weather phenomenon or phenomena are coded in TAF reports using the same format, qualifiers, and phenomena contractions as METAR reports, except **UP** (unknown precipitation).

   1) Obscurations to vision will be forecast whenever the prevailing visibility is forecast to be 6 SM or less.

   2) If no significant weather is expected to occur during a specific time period in the forecast, the weather group is omitted for that time period.

      a) If, after a time period in which significant weather has been forecast, a change to a forecast of no significant weather occurs, the contraction **NSW** (No Significant Weather) will appear as the weather included in becoming (BECMG) or temporary (TEMPO) groups.

         i) NSW will not be used in the initial time period of a TAF or in from (FM groups).

l. **Sky Conditions** (element 8). TAF sky conditions use the METAR format, except that cumulonimbus clouds (CB) are the only cloud type forecast in TAFs.

m. **Wind Shear** (element 9) (optional data). Wind shear is the forecast of nonconvective low-level winds (up to 2,000 ft. AGL) and is entered after the sky conditions when wind shear is expected. The wind shear element is omitted if not expected to occur.

   1) The forecast includes the height of the wind shear followed by the wind direction and wind speed at the indicated height.

   2) Wind shear is encoded with the contraction **WS**, followed by a three-digit height and winds at the height indicated in the same format as surface winds.

      a) Height is given in hundreds of feet AGL up to and including 2,000 ft.

n. There are three forecast change indicators used when either a rapid, a gradual, or a temporary change is expected in some or all of the forecast meteorological conditions.

   1) The change indicators are

      a) From (FM)
      b) Becoming (BECMG)
      c) Temporary (TEMPO)

   2) Each change indicator marks a time group within the TAF.

   3) The probability (PROB) forecast also indicates a time of forecast weather events.

o. **Temporary (TEMPO) Group** (element 10). The **TEMPO** group is used for any conditions in wind, visibility, weather, or sky condition expected to last for generally less than 1 hour at a time (occasional) and to occur during less than half the time period.

   1) The **TEMPO** indicator is followed by a four-digit group, a solidus, and another four-digit group giving the beginning day/hour and the ending day/hour of the time period during which the temporary conditions are expected.

   2) Only the changing forecast meteorological conditions are included in **TEMPO** groups.

      a) The omitted conditions are carried over from the previous time group.

p. **From (FM) Group** (element 11). The **FM** group is used when a rapid change, usually occurring in less than 1 hour, is expected.

1) Typically, a rapid change of prevailing conditions to a new set of conditions is associated with a synoptic feature (i.e., cold or warm front) passing through the terminal area.

2) Appended to the **FM** indicator is the two-digit date and the four-digit hour and minute when the change is expected to begin and continue until the next change group or until the end of the current forecast.

3) A **FM** group will always mark the beginning of a new line in a TAF report.

4) Each **FM** group contains all the required elements, i.e., wind, visibility, weather, and sky condition.

   a) Weather and wind shear will be omitted in **FM** groups when it is not significant to aviation.

   b) **FM** groups will not include the contraction **NSW**.

q. **Becoming (BECMG) Group** (element 12). The **BECMG** group is used when a gradual change in conditions is expected over a longer time period, but no longer than 2 hours.

1) Appended to the **BECMG** indicator is a four-digit group, a solidus, and another four-digit group with the beginning day/hour and the ending day/hour of the change period.

   a) The gradual change will occur within this time period.

2) Only the changing forecast meteorological conditions are included in **BECMG** groups.

   a) The omitted conditions are carried over from the previous time group.

r. **Probability (PROB) Forecast** (element 13). The **PROB** indicates the chance of thunderstorms or other precipitation events occurring, along with associated weather conditions (wind, visibility, and sky conditions).

1) A probability forecast will not be used during the first 6 hr. of a TAF.

2) Appended to the **PROB** contraction is the probability value.

   a) EXAMPLES:

   i) **PROB40** means there is a 40-49% probability.
   ii) **PROB30** means there is a 30-39% probability.

3) Appended to the **PROB** indicator is a four-digit group giving the beginning day/hour and another four-digit group giving the ending day/hour of the time period during which the precipitation or thunderstorms are expected.

4. **The applicant demonstrates understanding of weather charts.**

a. The surface analysis chart is a computer-prepared report showing areas of high and low pressure, fronts, temperatures, dew points, wind directions and speeds, local weather, and visual obstructions.

1) This chart is transmitted every 3 hours and covers the contiguous 48 states and adjacent areas.

b.   Surface weather observations for reporting points are also depicted on this chart.

1)   Each reporting point is illustrated by a station model, which includes the following: Type of Observation, Sky Cover, Clouds, Sea Level Pressure, Pressure Change/Tendency, Precipitation, Dew Point, Present Weather, Temperature, and Wind.

2)   The figure below shows weather chart symbols for a sample station model.

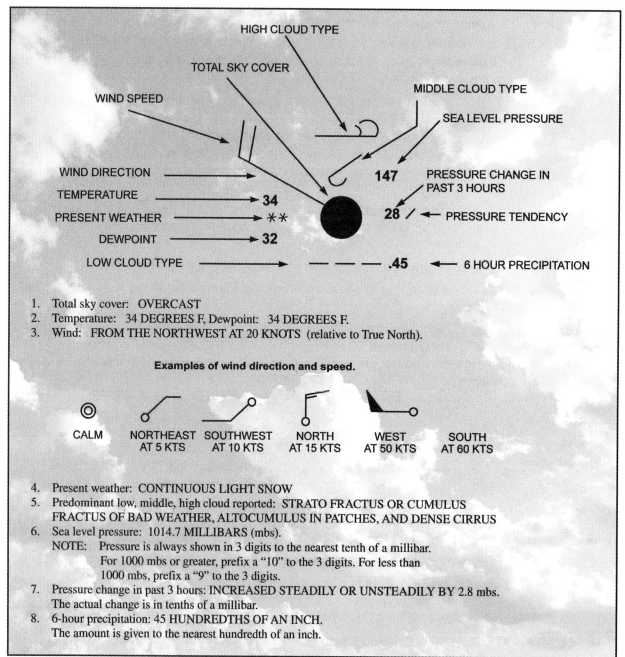

1.   Total sky cover: OVERCAST
2.   Temperature: 34 DEGREES F, Dewpoint: 34 DEGREES F.
3.   Wind: FROM THE NORTHWEST AT 20 KNOTS (relative to True North).

Examples of wind direction and speed.

CALM   NORTHEAST AT 5 KTS   SOUTHWEST AT 10 KTS   NORTH AT 15 KTS   WEST AT 50 KTS   SOUTH AT 60 KTS

4.   Present weather: CONTINUOUS LIGHT SNOW
5.   Predominant low, middle, high cloud reported: STRATO FRACTUS OR CUMULUS FRACTUS OF BAD WEATHER, ALTOCUMULUS IN PATCHES, AND DENSE CIRRUS
6.   Sea level pressure: 1014.7 MILLIBARS (mbs).
      NOTE: Pressure is always shown in 3 digits to the nearest tenth of a millibar. For 1000 mbs or greater, prefix a "10" to the 3 digits. For less than 1000 mbs, prefix a "9" to the 3 digits.
7.   Pressure change in past 3 hours: INCREASED STEADILY OR UNSTEADILY BY 2.8 mbs. The actual change is in tenths of a millibar.
8.   6-hour precipitation: 45 HUNDREDTHS OF AN INCH. The amount is given to the nearest hundredth of an inch.

c.   The weather depiction chart is computer-prepared from METAR reports.

1)   The weather depiction chart gives a broad overview of the observed flying category conditions at the valid time of the chart.

2)   This chart begins at 01Z (0100Z) each day, is transmitted at 3-hr. intervals, and is valid at the time of the plotted data.

3) A sample weather depiction chart is presented below.

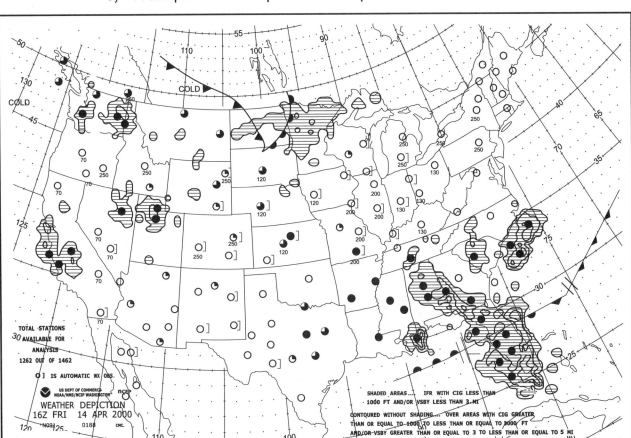

d. **Plotted Data.** Data for the chart come from the observations reported by both manual and automated observation stations. The automated stations are denoted by a bracket (]) plotted to the right of the station circle. The plotted data for each station includes the following:

1) **Total sky cover.** The amount of sky cover is shown by the shading of the station circle.

2) **Cloud height or ceiling.** Cloud height above ground level is entered under the station circle in hundreds of feet, the same as coded in the METAR.

   a) If total sky cover is scattered, the cloud height entered is the base of the lowest layer.

   b) If total sky cover is broken or greater, the cloud height entered is the ceiling.

   c) A totally obscured sky is shown by the sky cover symbol "X."

      i) A totally obscured sky always has a height entry of the ceiling (vertical visibility into the obscuration).

3) **Weather and obstructions to vision.** Weather and obstructions-to-vision symbols are entered to the left of the station circle.

   a) When a remark in a METAR reports clouds topping ridges, a symbol unique to the weather depiction chart is entered to the left of the station circle:

b) When several types of weather and/or obstructions to visibility are reported at a station, only the most significant one is entered.

4) **Visibility.** When visibility is 5 SM or less, it is entered to the left of the weather or obstruction-to-vision symbol.

a) Visibility is entered in statute miles and fractions of a mile.

5) Examples of plotted data are shown below.

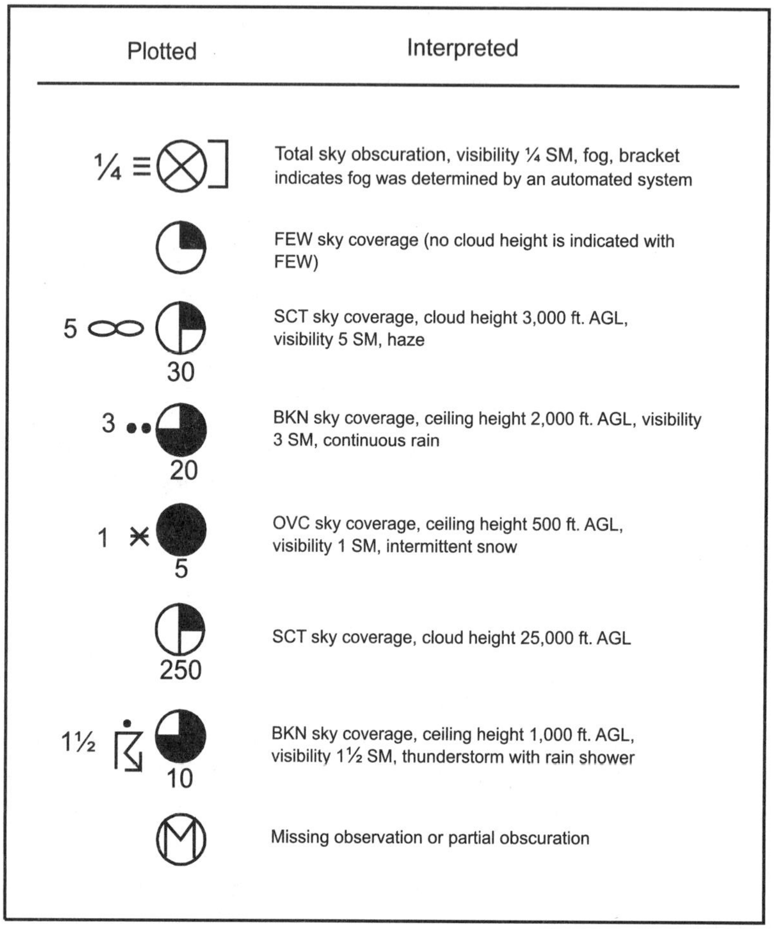

e. **Analysis**

1) The chart shows observed ceiling and visibility by categories as follows:

a) IFR -- ceiling less than 1,000 ft. and/or visibility less than 3 SM; hatched area outlined by a smooth line

b) MVFR (marginal VFR) -- ceiling 1,000 to 3,000 ft. inclusive and/or visibility 3 to 5 SM inclusive; non-hatched area outlined by a smooth line

c) VFR -- no ceiling or ceiling greater than 3,000 ft., and visibility greater than 5 SM; not outlined

2) The chart also shows fronts and troughs from the surface analysis for the preceding hour.

f. The weather depiction chart is an ideal place to begin preparing for a weather briefing and flight planning. From this chart, you can get a bird's-eye view of areas of favorable and adverse weather conditions for chart time.

1) This chart may not completely represent the en route conditions because of variations in terrain and possible weather occurring between reporting stations.

2) Due to the delay between data and transmission time, changes in the weather could occur. After initially sizing up the general weather picture, final flight planning must consider forecasts, prognostic charts (PROGs), and the latest pilot, radar, and METAR reports.

g. Short-Range Surface Prognostic (PROG) Charts provide a forecast of surface pressure systems, fronts, and precipitation for a 2-day period.

    1) The forecast area covers the 48-contiguous states, the coastal waters, and portions of Canada and Mexico.

    2) The forecasted conditions are divided into four forecast periods: 12, 24, 36, and 48 hours.

        a) Each chart depicts a "snapshot" of weather elements expected at the specified valid time.

h. PROGs are very similar to surface analysis charts.

    1) All of the symbols depicted on both charts are the same.

    2) The primary difference between the two charts is that PROGs are forecast charts, whereas the surface analysis chart is a "current conditions" chart.

        a) Additionally, PROG charts do not feature station model plots.

    3) Think of the PROG as a "future" version of the surface analysis chart.

i. Issuance

    1) The 12- and 24-hour charts are issued four times a day and are termed "Day 1" PROGs.

    2) The 36- and 48-hour charts are issued twice daily and are termed "Day 2" PROGs.

j. A PROG is reproduced below.

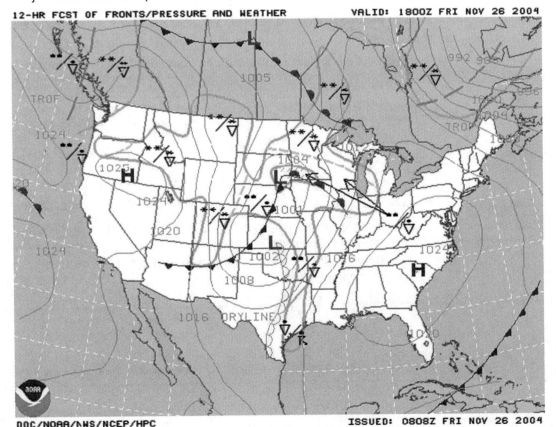

k.   Plotted Data

1)   Pressure Systems

a)   Pressure systems are depicted by pressure centers, troughs, isobars, drylines, tropical waves, tropical storms, and hurricanes using standard symbols.

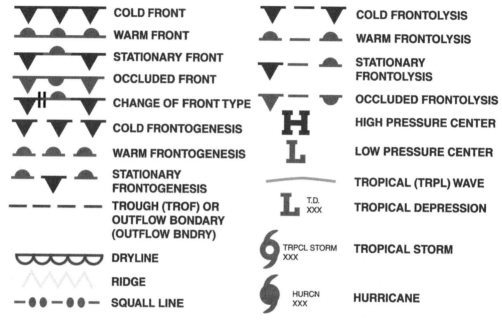

b)   Isobars are denoted by solid, thin gray lines and labeled with the appropriate pressure in millibars.

c)   The central pressure is plotted near the respective pressure center.

2)   Fronts

a)   Fronts are depicted to show their forecast position at the chart valid time.

i)   Again, standard chart symbols are used (see image above).

b)   Because frontal movement causes significant changes in weather, pressure, and wind, pilots should carefully consider the forecasted frontal depictions and plan their flight accordingly.

3)   Precipitation

a)   Precipitation areas are enclosed by thick, solid green lines.

b)   Standard precipitation symbols are used to identify precipitation types.

i)   These symbols are positioned within or adjacent to the associated area of precipitation.

ii)   If adjacent to the area, an arrow will point to the area with which they are associated.

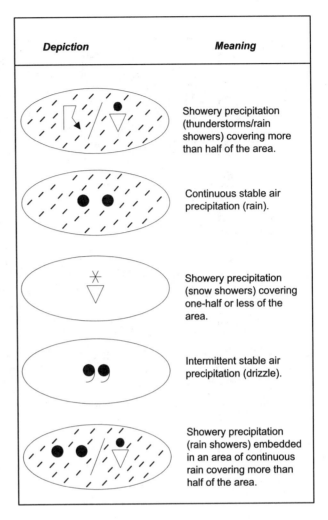

Symbol	Meaning	Symbol	Meaning
‾⋀‾	Moderate Turbulence	● ▽	Rain Shower
‾⋀̸‾	Severe Turbulence	✳ ▽	Snow Shower
⊍	Moderate Icing	⌐↘	Thunderstorm
⊍̸	Severe Icing	∿	Freezing Rain
●●	Rain	ϛ	Tropical Storm
✕ ✕	Snow	ϛ●	Hurricane (typhoon)
●, ●,	Drizzle		

Depiction	Meaning
(shaded ellipse with ⌐↘ / ● ▽)	Showery precipitation (thunderstorms/rain showers) covering more than half of the area.
(shaded ellipse with ●●)	Continuous stable air precipitation (rain).
(ellipse with ✳ ▽)	Showery precipitation (snow showers) covering one-half or less of the area.
(ellipse with ●●)	Intermittent stable air precipitation (drizzle).
(shaded ellipse with ●●● / ● ▽)	Showery precipitation (rain showers) embedded in an area of continuous rain covering more than half of the area.

  c) A mix of precipitation is indicated by the use of two pertinent symbols separated by a slash.

  d) A bold, dashed gray line is used to separate precipitation within an outlined area with contrasting characteristics.

    i) EXAMPLE: A dashed line would be used to separate an area of snow from an area of rain.

  e) Precipitation characteristics are further described by the use of shading.

    i) Shading or lack of shading indicates the expected coverage of the precipitation.

     • Shaded areas indicate the precipitation is expected to have more than 50% (broken) coverage.

     • Unshaded areas indicate 30-50% (scattered) coverage.

 4) The Low-Level Significant Weather (SIGWX) Chart provides a forecast of aviation weather hazards.

  a) The charts are primarily intended to be used as guidance products for preflight briefings.

  b) Each chart depicts a "snapshot" of weather expected at the specified valid time.

 5) The forecast domain covers the 48 contiguous states and the coastal waters for altitudes 24,000 ft. MSL (FL240 or 400 millibars) and below.

6) The figure below is an example of this product.

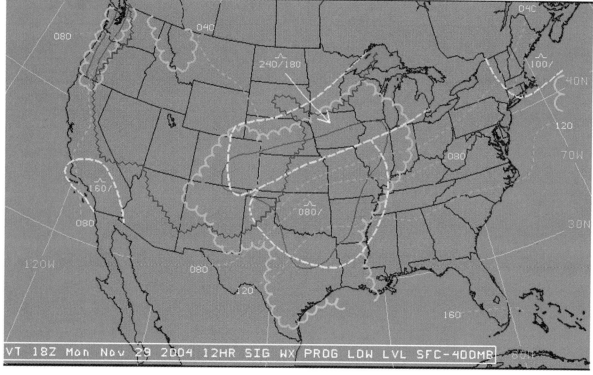

VT 18Z Mon Nov 29 2004 12HR SIG WX PROG LOW LVL SFC-400MB

7) SIGWX charts are issued four times per day by the Aviation Weather Center (AWC).

   a) Two charts are issued: a 12-hour and a 24-hour chart.

8) Low-Level SIGWX Charts depict weather flying categories (VFR, IFR, etc.), turbulence, and freezing levels. Icing is not specifically forecast.

   a) See the chart symbol legend below.

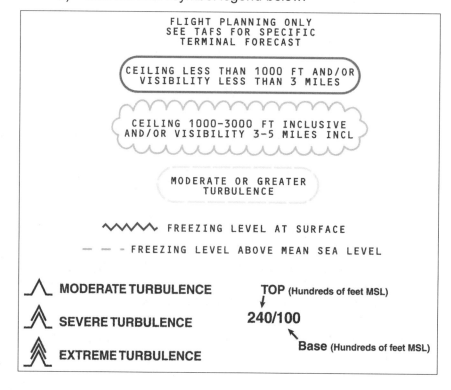

9) **Flying Categories**

    a) Instrument Flight Rules (IFR) areas are outlined with a solid red line.

    b) Marginal Visual Flight Rules (MVFR) areas are outlined with a scalloped blue line.

    c) Visual Flight Rules (VFR) areas are implied and therefore not depicted.

10) **Turbulence**

    a) Areas of moderate or greater turbulence are enclosed by bold, dashed yellow lines.

    b) Turbulence intensities are identified by standard symbols, as shown in the turbulence figure on the previous page.

    c) Turbulence height is depicted by two numbers separated by a solidus (/).

        i) EXAMPLE: An area on the chart with turbulence indicated as **240/100** indicates the turbulence can be expected from the top at FL240 to the base at 10,000 feet MSL.

        ii) When the base height is omitted, the turbulence is forecast to reach the surface.

            • EXAMPLE: An indication of **080/** identifies a turbulence layer from the surface to 8,000 feet MSL.

        iii) Turbulence associated with thunderstorms is not depicted on the chart.

    d) The intensity symbols and height information may be located within or adjacent to the forecast areas of turbulence.

        i) If located adjacent to an area, an arrow will point to the associated area.

11) **Freezing Levels**

    a) If the freezing level is at the surface, it is depicted by a blue saw-toothed symbol.

    b) Freezing levels above the surface are depicted by fine, green dashed lines labeled in hundreds of feet MSL beginning at 4,000 feet using 4,000 foot intervals.

        i) If multiple freezing levels exist, these lines are drawn to the highest freezing level.

            • For example, **80** identifies the 8,000-foot freezing level contour.
            • The lines are discontinued where they intersect the surface.

    c) The freezing level for locations between lines is determined by interpolation.

        i) EXAMPLE: The freezing level midway between the 4,000- and 8,000-foot lines is 6,000 feet.

l. Radar Observations

    1) Radar observations provide information about the location and intensity of precipitation.

        a) NEXRAD (**Nex**t Generation **Rad**ar) obtains weather information based upon returned energy. The radar emits a burst of energy. If the energy strikes an object, such as precipitation, the energy is scattered in all directions. A small fraction of that scattered energy is directed back toward the radar.

2) There are three types of land-based radars that provide information about precipitation and wind:

   a) **WSR-88D NEXRAD**, commonly called Doppler radar, provides in-depth observations that inform surrounding communities of impending weather.

      i) Doppler radar has two operational modes: clear air and precipitation.

- In clear air mode, the radar is in its most sensitive operational mode because a slow antenna rotation allows the radar to sample the atmosphere longer.
  - Images are updated about every 10 minutes in this mode.
- Precipitation mode is used when precipitation is present. These images update approximately every 4 to 6 minutes.
- Intensity values are measured in dBZ (decibels of Z) and are depicted in color on the radar image.
- Intensities are correlated to intensity terminology (phraseology) for ATC purposes.

Example of a weather radar scope.

Clean Air Mode	Precipitation Mode
DBZ	DBZ
+28	75
+24	70
+20	65
+16	60
+12	55
+8	50
+4	45
0	40
-4	35
-8	30
-12	25
-16	20
-20	15
-24	10
-28	5
ND	ND

WSR-88D Weather Radar Echo Intensity Legend.

Reflectivity (dBZ) Ranges	Weather Radar Echo Intensity
<30 dBZ	Light
30–40 dBZ	Moderate
>40–50 dBZ	Heavy
50+ dBZ	Extreme

WSR-88D Weather Radar Precipitation Intensity Terminology.

   b) **FAA terminal Doppler weather radar**, installed at some major airports around the country, also aids in providing severe weather alerts and warnings to ATC. Terminal radar ensures pilots are aware of wind shear, gust fronts, and heavy precipitation, all of which are dangerous to arriving and departing aircraft.

   c) **Airport surveillance radar** is used primarily to detect aircraft, but it also detects the location and intensity of precipitation, which is used to route aircraft traffic around severe weather in an airport environment.

5. **The applicant demonstrates understanding of automated surface observing systems (ASOS) and automated weather observing systems (AWOS).**

   a. Automated weather reporting systems are increasingly being installed at airports. These systems consist of various sensors, a processor, a computer-generated voice subsystem, and a transmitter to broadcast local, minute-by-minute weather data directly to the pilot.

      1) These systems provide information that can be used by flight crews to make approach decisions and by the National Weather Service to generate METARs.

   b. Two common types of automated systems are used throughout the country:

      1) **Automated Weather Observing System (AWOS)**

         a) Transmits on a discrete VHF radio frequency

         b) Engineered to be receivable to a maximum of 25 NM from the site and a maximum altitude of 10,000 feet above ground level

            i) At many locations, AWOS signals may be received on the surface of the airport, but local conditions may limit the maximum AWOS reception distance and/or altitude.

         c) Transmits a 20 to 30 second weather message updated each minute

            i) Pilots monitor the designated frequency for the automated weather broadcast.

            ii) There is no two-way communication capability.

      2) **Automated Surface Observing System (ASOS)/Automated Weather Sensor System (AWSS)**

         a) Primary surface weather observing system of the U.S.

            i) AWSS is a follow-on program that provides identical data as ASOS.

            ii) ASOS/AWSS is more sensitive and provides more information than AWOS.

         b) Designed to support aviation operations and weather forecast activities

            i) ASOS/AWSS will provide continuous minute-by-minute observations and perform the basic observing functions necessary to generate a METAR and other aviation weather information.

         c) Transmitted and received by the pilot in exactly the same way as AWOS

   c. The following table explains what information is provided by each automated weather reporting system type:

WEATHER REPORTING SYSTEMS					
Element Reported	**AWOS-A**	**AWOS-1**	**AWOS-2**	**AWOS-3**	**ASOS**
Altimeter	X	X	X	X	X
Wind		X	X	X	X
Temperature/ Dew Point		X	X	X	X
Density Altitude		X	X	X	X
Visibility			X	X	X
Clouds/Ceiling				X	X
Precipitation					X
Remarks					X

QUESTIONS

3.1 Sources of Weather

1. (Refer to Figure 12 below.) Which of the reporting stations have VFR weather?

    A. All.

    B. KINK, KBOI, and KJFK.

    C. KINK, KBOI, and KLAX.

Answer (C) is correct. *(AWS Sect 3)*
    DISCUSSION: KINK is reporting visibility of 15 SM and sky clear (15SM SKC); KBOI is reporting visibility of 30 SM and a scattered cloud layer base at 15,000 ft. (30SM SCT150); and KLAX is reporting visibility of 6SM in mist (foggy conditions > 5/8 SM visibility) with a scattered cloud layer at 700 ft. and another one at 25,000 ft. (6SM BR SCT007 SCT250). All of these conditions are above VFR weather minimums of 1,000-ft. ceiling and/or 3-SM visibility.
    Answer (A) is incorrect. KMDW is reporting a visibility of 1 1/2 SM in rain and a ceiling of 700 ft. overcast (1 1/2SM RA OVC007), and KJFK is reporting a visibility of 1/2SM in fog and a ceiling of 500 ft. overcast (1/2SM FG OVC005). Both of these are below VFR weather minimums of 1,000-ft. ceiling and/or 3-SM visibility. Answer (B) is incorrect. KJFK is reporting a visibility of 1/2 SM in fog and a ceiling of 500 ft. overcast (1/2SM FG OVC005), which is below the VFR weather minimums of 1,000-ft. ceiling and/or 3-SM visibility.

```
METAR KINK 121845Z 11012G18KT 15SM SKC 25/17 A3000

METAR KBOI 121854Z 13004KT 30SM SCT150 17/6 A3015

METAR KLAX 121852Z 25004KT 6SM BR SCT007 SCT250 16/15 A2991

SPECI KMDW 121856Z 32005KT 1 1/2SM RA OVC007 17/16 A2980 RMK RAB35

SPECI KJFK 121853Z 18004KT 1/2SM FG R04/2200 OVC005 20/18 A3006
```

Figure 12. – Aviation Routine Weather Reports (METAR).

2. (Refer to Figure 12 above.) What are the wind conditions at Wink, Texas (KINK)?

    A. Calm.

    B. 110° at 12 knots, gusts 18 knots.

    C. 111° at 2 knots, gusts 18 knots.

Answer (B) is correct. *(AWS Sect 3)*
    DISCUSSION: The wind group at KINK is coded as 11012G18KT. The first three digits are the direction the wind is blowing from referenced to true north. The next two digits are the wind speed in knots. If the wind is gusty, it is reported as a "G" after the speed followed by the highest (or peak) gust reported. Thus, the wind conditions at KINK are 110° true at 12 knots, peak gust at 18 knots.
    Answer (A) is incorrect. A calm wind would be reported as 00000KT, not 11012G18KT. Answer (C) is incorrect. The wind conditions at KINK are 110°, not 111°, at 12 knots, not 2 knots.

3. (Refer to Figure 12 above.) The remarks section for KMDW has RAB35 listed. This entry means

    A. blowing mist has reduced the visibility to 1-1/2 SM.

    B. rain began at 1835Z.

    C. the barometer has risen .35" Hg.

Answer (B) is correct. *(AWS Sect 3)*
    DISCUSSION: In the remarks (RMK) section for KMDW, RAB35 means that rain began at 35 min. past the hour. Since the report was taken at 1856Z, rain began at 35 min. past the hour, or 1835Z.
    Answer (A) is incorrect. RAB35 means that rain began at 35 min. past the hour, not that blowing mist has reduced the visibility to 1 1/2 statute miles. Answer (C) is incorrect. RAB35 means that rain began at 35 min. past the hour, not that the barometer has risen .35 in. Hg.

4. (Refer to Figure 12 above.) The wind direction and velocity at KJFK is from

    A. 180° true at 4 knots.

    B. 180° magnetic at 4 knots.

    C. 040° true at 18 knots.

Answer (A) is correct. *(PHAK Chap 3)*
    DISCUSSION: The wind group at KJFK is coded as 18004KT. The first three digits are the direction the wind is blowing from referenced to true north. The next two digits are the speed in knots. Thus, the wind direction and speed at KJFK are 180° true at 4 knots.
    Answer (B) is incorrect. Wind direction is referenced to true, not magnetic, north. Answer (C) is incorrect. The wind direction is 180° true at 4 knots, not 040° true at 18 knots.

5. (Refer to Figure 12 on page 102.) What are the current conditions for Chicago Midway Airport (KMDW)?

A. Sky 700 feet overcast, visibility 1-1/2SM, rain.

B. Sky 7000 feet overcast, visibility 1-1/2SM, heavy rain.

C. Sky 700 feet overcast, visibility 11, occasionally 2SM, with rain.

Answer (A) is correct. *(PHAK Chap 3)*
DISCUSSION: At KMDW, a special METAR (SPECI) taken at 1856Z reported wind 320° at 5 kt., visibility 1 1/2 SM in moderate rain, overcast clouds at 700 ft., temperature 17°C, dew point 16°C, altimeter 29.80" Hg, remarks follow, and rain began at 35 min. past the hour.
Answer (B) is incorrect. The intensity of the rain is moderate, not heavy. Heavy rain would be coded +RA. Answer (C) is incorrect. Visibility is 1 1/2 SM, not 11 SM with an occasional 2 SM.

6. To get a complete weather overview for the planned flight, the Remote Pilot in Command should obtain

A. an outlook briefing.

B. an abbreviated briefing.

C. a standard briefing.

Answer (C) is correct. *(AWS Sect 1)*
DISCUSSION: A standard briefing should be requested to obtain complete weather and NOTAMs for your area.
Answer (A) is incorrect. An outlook briefing should be requested for a flight more than 6 hours in the future. Answer (B) is incorrect. An abbreviated briefing should be requested when the user needs to supplement mass disseminated data, to update a previous briefing, or to obtain specific information.

7. To get a complete weather briefing for the planned flight, the pilot should request

A. a general briefing.

B. an abbreviated briefing.

C. a standard briefing.

Answer (C) is correct. *(AWS Sect 1)*
DISCUSSION: To get a complete briefing before a planned flight, the pilot should request a standard briefing. This will include all pertinent information needed for a safe flight.
Answer (A) is incorrect. A general briefing is not standard terminology for any type of weather briefing. Answer (B) is incorrect. An abbreviated briefing is provided as a supplement to mass disseminated data or a previous briefing. It can also be used to obtain specific information.

8. Which type of weather briefing should a pilot request to supplement mass disseminated data?

A. An outlook briefing.

B. A supplemental briefing.

C. An abbreviated briefing.

Answer (C) is correct. *(AWS Sect 1)*
DISCUSSION: An abbreviated briefing will be provided when the user requests information to supplement mass disseminated data, to update a previous briefing, or to obtain specific information.
Answer (A) is incorrect. An outlook briefing should be requested if the proposed departure time is 6 hr. or more in the future. Answer (B) is incorrect. A supplemental briefing is not a standard type of briefing.

9. A weather briefing that is provided when the information requested is 6 or more hours in advance of the proposed departure time is

A. an outlook briefing.

B. a forecast briefing.

C. a prognostic briefing.

Answer (A) is correct. *(AWS Sect 1)*
DISCUSSION: An outlook briefing is given when the briefing is 6 or more hours before the proposed departure time.
Answer (B) is incorrect. A forecast briefing is not a type of weather briefing. Answer (C) is incorrect. A prognostic briefing is not a type of weather briefing.

10. To update a previous weather briefing, a pilot should request

A. an abbreviated briefing.

B. a standard briefing.

C. an outlook briefing.

Answer (A) is correct. *(AWS Sect 1)*
DISCUSSION: An abbreviated briefing will be provided when the user requests information (1) to supplement mass disseminated data, (2) to update a previous briefing, or (3) to be limited to specific information.
Answer (B) is incorrect. A standard briefing is a complete preflight briefing to include all (not update) information pertinent to a safe flight. Answer (C) is incorrect. An outlook briefing is for a flight at least 6 hr. in the future.

11. (Refer to Figure 15 on page 105.) In the TAF for KMEM, what does "SHRA" stand for?

A. Rain showers.

B. A shift in wind direction is expected.

C. A significant change in precipitation is possible.

Answer (A) is correct. *(AWS Sect 7)*
DISCUSSION: SHRA is a coded group of forecast weather. SH is a descriptor that means showers. RA is a type of precipitation that means rain. Thus, SHRA means rain showers.
Answer (B) is incorrect. SHRA means rain showers, not that a shift in wind direction is expected. A change in wind direction would be reflected by a forecast wind. Answer (C) is incorrect. SHRA means rain showers, not that a significant change in precipitation is possible.

12. (Refer to Figure 15 on page 105.) During the time period from 0600Z to 0800Z, what visibility is forecast for KOKC?

A. Greater than 6 statute miles.

B. Possibly 6 statute miles.

C. Not forecasted.

Answer (A) is correct. *(AWS Sect 7)*
DISCUSSION: At KOKC, between 0600Z and 0800Z, conditions are forecast to become wind 210° at 15 kt., visibility greater than 6 SM (P6SM), scattered clouds at 4,000 ft. with conditions continuing until the end of the forecast (1200Z).
Answer (B) is incorrect. Between 0600Z and 0800Z, the visibility is forecast to be greater than, not possibly, 6 statute miles. Answer (C) is incorrect. Between 0600Z and 0800Z, the visibility is forecast to be greater than 6 statute miles (P6SM).

13. (Refer to Figure 15 on page 105.) In the TAF from KOKC, the clear sky becomes

A. overcast at 2,000 feet during the forecast period between 2200Z and 2400Z.

B. overcast at 200 feet with a 40 percent probability of becoming overcast at 600 feet during the forecast period between 2200Z and 2400Z.

C. overcast at 200 feet with the probability of becoming overcast at 400 feet during the forecast period between 2200Z and 2400Z.

Answer (A) is correct. *(AWS Sect 7)*
DISCUSSION: In the TAF for KOKC, from 2200Z to 2400Z, the conditions are forecast to gradually become wind 200° at 13 kt. with gusts to 20 kt., visibility 4 SM in moderate rain showers, overcast clouds at 2,000 feet. Between the hours of 0000Z and 0600Z, a chance (40 percent) exists of visibility 2 SM in thunderstorm with moderate rain, and 800 ft. overcast, cumulus clouds.
Answer (B) is incorrect. Between 2200Z and 2400Z, the coded sky condition of OVC020 means overcast clouds at 2,000 ft., not 200 feet. Answer (C) is incorrect. Between 2200Z and 2400Z, the coded sky condition of OVC020 means overcast clouds at 2,000 ft., not 200 feet.

14. (Refer to Figure 15 on page 105.) What is the valid period for the TAF for KMEM?

A. 1200Z to 1800Z.

B. 1200Z to 2400Z.

C. 1800Z to 2400Z.

Answer (C) is correct. *(AWS Sect 7)*
DISCUSSION: The valid period of a TAF follows the four-letter location identifier and the six-digit issuance date/time. The valid period group is a two-digit date followed by the two-digit beginning hour and the two-digit ending hour. The valid period of the TAF for KMEM is 1218/1324, which means the forecast is valid from the 12th day at 1800Z until the 13th at 2400Z.
Answer (A) is incorrect. The valid period of the TAF for KOKC, not KMEM, is from 1200Z to 1800Z. Answer (B) is incorrect. The valid period of the TAF for KMEM is from the 12th day, not 1200Z, at 1800Z until the 13th at 2400Z.

15. (Refer to Figure 15 on page 105.) Between 1000Z and 1200Z the visibility at KMEM is forecast to be?

A. 1/2 statute mile.

B. 3 statute miles.

C. 6 statute miles.

Answer (B) is correct. *(AWS Sect 7)*
DISCUSSION: Between 1000Z and 1200Z, the conditions at KMEM are forecast to gradually become wind calm, visibility 3 SM in mist, sky clear with temporary (occasional) visibility 1/2 SM in fog between 1200Z and 1400Z. Conditions are expected to continue until 1600Z.
Answer (A) is incorrect. Between the hours of 1200Z and 1400Z, not between 1000Z and 1200Z, the forecast is for temporary (occasional) visibility of 1/2 SM in fog. Answer (C) is incorrect. Between 1000Z and 1200Z, the forecast visibility for KMEM is 3 SM, not 6 SM.

16. (Refer to Figure 15 on page 105.) In the TAF from KOKC, the "FM (FROM) Group" is forecast for the hours from 1600Z to 2200Z with the wind from

A. 160° at 10 knots.

B. 180° at 10 knots.

C. 180° at 10 knots, becoming 200° at 13 knots.

Answer (B) is correct. *(AWS Sect 7)*
DISCUSSION: The FM group states that, from 1600Z until 2200Z (time of next change group), the forecast wind is 180° at 10 knots.
Answer (A) is incorrect. The forecast wind is 180°, not 160°, at 10 knots. Answer (C) is incorrect. The BECMG (becoming) group is a change group and is not part of the FM forecast group. The wind will gradually become 200° at 13 kt. with gusts to 20 kt., between 2200Z and 2400Z.

17. (Refer to Figure 15 below.) The only cloud type forecast in TAF reports is

A. nimbostratus.

B. cumulonimbus.

C. scattered cumulus.

Answer (B) is correct. *(AWS Sect 7)*
 DISCUSSION: Cumulonimbus clouds are the only cloud type forecast in TAFs. If cumulonimbus clouds are expected at the airport, the contraction CB is appended to the cloud layer that represents the base of the cumulonimbus cloud(s).
 Answer (A) is incorrect. The only cloud type forecast in TAFs is cumulonimbus, not nimbostratus, clouds. Answer (C) is incorrect. The only cloud type forecast in TAFs is cumulonimbus, not scattered cumulus, clouds.

TAF

KMEM 121720Z 1218/1324 20012KT 5SM HZ BKN030 PROB40 2022 1SM TSRA OVC008CB
 FM2200 33015G20KT P6SM BKN015 OVC025 PROB40 2202 3SM SHRA
 FM0200 35012KT OVC008 PROB40 0205 2SM-RASN BECMG 0608 02008KT BKN012
 BECMG 1310/1312 00000KT 3SM BR SKC TEMPO 1212/1214 1/2SM FG
 FM131600 VRB06KT P6SM SKC=

KOKC 051130Z 0512/0618 14008KT 5SM BR BKN030 TEMPO 0513/0516 1 1/2SM BR
 FM051600 18010KT P6SM SKC BECMG 0522/0524 20013G20KT 4SM SHRA OVC020
 PROB40 0600/0606 2SM TSRA OVC008CB BECMG 0606/0608 21015KT P6SM SCT040=

Figure 15. – Terminal Aerodrome Forecasts (TAF).

18. Of what value is the Weather depiction chart to the pilot?

A. For determining general weather conditions on which to base flight planning.

B. For a forecast of cloud coverage, visibilities, and frontal activity.

C. For determining frontal trends and air mass characteristics.

Answer (A) is correct. *(AWS Sect 5)*
 DISCUSSION: The Weather depiction chart is prepared from surface aviation weather reports giving a quick picture of weather conditions as of the time stated on the chart. Thus, it presents general weather conditions on which to base flight planning.
 Answer (B) is incorrect. A significant weather prognostic chart can provide a forecast of cloud coverage, visibilities, and frontal activity. A weather depiction chart shows actual, not forecast, conditions. Answer (C) is incorrect. A lifted index chart would be used to determine the characteristics of an air mass.

19. For aviation purposes, ceiling is defined as the height above the Earth's surface of the

A. lowest reported obscuration and the highest layer of clouds reported as overcast.

B. lowest broken or overcast layer or vertical visibility into an obscuration.

C. lowest layer of clouds reported as scattered, broken, or thin.

Answer (B) is correct. *(AWS Sect 3)*
 DISCUSSION: A ceiling layer is not designated in the METAR code. For aviation purposes, the ceiling is the lowest broken or overcast layer, or vertical visibility into an obscuration.
 Answer (A) is incorrect. A ceiling is the lowest, not highest, broken or overcast layer, or the vertical visibility into an obscuration, not the lowest obscuration. Answer (C) is incorrect. A ceiling is the lowest broken or overcast, not scattered, layer. Also, there is no provision for reporting thin layers in the METAR code.

20. When requesting weather information for the following morning, a pilot should request

A. an outlook briefing.

B. a standard briefing.

C. an abbreviated briefing.

Answer (A) is correct. *(AWS Sect 1)*
 DISCUSSION: An outlook briefing should be requested when the briefing is 6 or more hours in advance of the proposed departure.
 Answer (B) is incorrect. A standard briefing should be requested if the proposed departure time is less than 6 hr. in the future and if you have not received a previous briefing or have received information through mass dissemination media. Answer (C) is incorrect. An abbreviated briefing is provided as a supplement to mass disseminated data, to update a previous briefing, or to obtain specific information.

21. Radar weather reports are of special interest to pilots because they indicate

    A. large areas of low ceilings and fog.

    B. location of precipitation along with type, intensity, and cell movement of precipitation.

    C. location of precipitation along with type, intensity, and trend.

Answer (B) is correct. *(AWS Sect 3)*
    DISCUSSION: Radar weather reports are of special interest to pilots because they report the location of precipitation along with type, intensity, and cell movement.
    Answer (A) is incorrect. Weather radar cannot detect clouds or fog, only precipitation size particles. Answer (C) is incorrect. Radar weather reports no longer include trend information.

22. (Refer to Figure 18 on page 107.) What is the status of the front that extends from Nebraska through Minnesota?

    A. Cold.

    B. Stationary.

    C. Warm.

Answer (A) is correct. *(AWS Sect 5)*
    DISCUSSION: Refer to the Weather depiction chart in Fig. 18. The front that extends from Nebraska through Minnesota is a cold front, as shown by the pointed scallops on the southern side of the frontal line.
    Answer (B) is incorrect. A stationary front has pointed scallops on one side of the frontal line and rounded scallops on the other. Answer (C) is incorrect. A warm front has rounded scallops, not pointed scallops.

23. (Refer to Figure 18 on page 107.) According to the weather depiction chart, the weather for a flight from southern Michigan to north Indiana is ceilings

    A. 1,000 to 3,000 feet and/or visibility 3 to 5 miles.

    B. less than 1,000 feet and/or visibility less than 3 miles.

    C. greater than 3,000 feet and visibility greater than 5 miles.

Answer (C) is correct. *(AWS Sect 5)*
    DISCUSSION: Refer to the Weather depiction chart in Fig. 18. The weather from southern Michigan to north Indiana is shown by the lack of shading or contours to have ceilings greater than 3,000 ft. and visibilities greater than 5 miles.
    Answer (A) is incorrect. Ceilings from 1,000 to 3,000 ft. and/or visibilities between 3 and 5 statute miles (MVFR conditions) are indicated on Weather depiction charts by an unshaded area surrounded by a contour. Answer (B) is incorrect. Ceilings less than 1,000 ft. and/or visibilities less than 3 statute miles (IFR conditions) are indicated on Weather depiction charts by a shaded area surrounded by a contour.

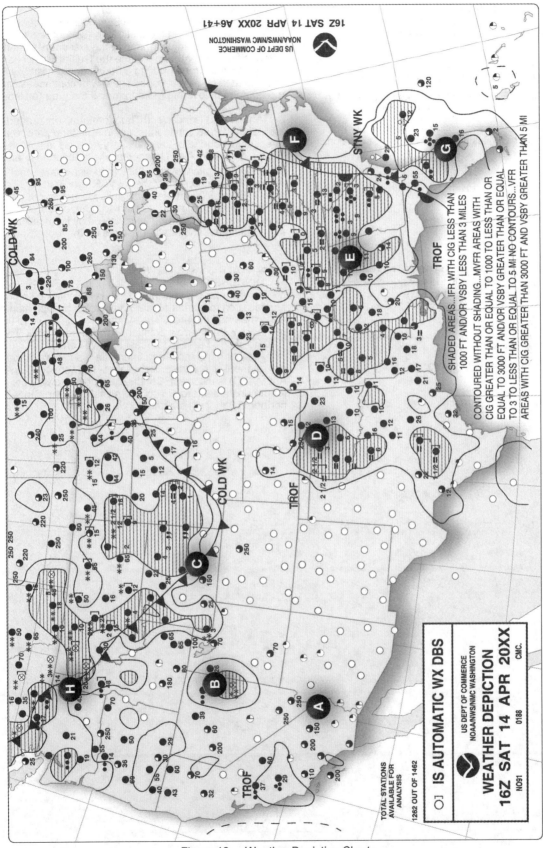

Figure 18. — Weather Depiction Chart.

24. (Refer to Figure 19 on page 109.) What weather is forecast for the Florida area just ahead of the stationary front during the first 12 hours?

   A.   Ceiling 1,000 to 3,000 feet and/or visibility 3 to 5 miles with intermittent precipitation.

   B.   Ceiling 1,000 to 3,000 feet and/or visibility 3 to 5 miles with continuous precipitation.

   C.   Ceiling less than 1,000 feet and/or visibility less than 3 miles with continuous precipitation.

Answer (B) is correct. *(AWS Sect 8)*
   DISCUSSION: Refer to the Significant weather prognostic chart in Fig. 19. During the first 12 hr. (bottom and top left panels), the weather just ahead of the stationary front that extends from coastal Virginia into the Gulf of Mexico is forecast to have ceilings from 1,000 to 3,000 ft. and/or visibility 3 to 5 SM (as indicated by the scalloped lines) with continuous light to moderate rain covering more than half the area (as indicated by the shading).
   Answer (A) is incorrect. Thunderstorms embedded in an area of moderate continuous, not intermittent, precipitation are forecast just ahead of the stationary front, as indicated by the following symbol: ⚡ . Thunderstorms embedded in an area of intermittent rain would be indicated with this symbol: ⚡ . Answer (C) is incorrect. Marginal VFR conditions (ceilings from 1,000 to 3,000 ft. and/or visibility from 3 to 5 SM), not IFR conditions (ceilings less than 1,000 ft. and/or visibility less than 3 miles) are forecast, as indicated by the scalloped line surrounding the southeastern states on the top left panel.

25. (Refer to Figure 19 on page 109.) The enclosed shaded area associated with the low pressure system over northern Utah is forecast to have

   A.   continuous snow.

   B.   intermittent snow.

   C.   continuous snow showers.

Answer (A) is correct. *(AWS Sect 8)*
   DISCUSSION: In the lower left panel of Fig. 19, the low pressure center over northern Utah is indicated by a bold "L." The shaded area to the left of the "L" indicates precipitation covering more than half the area. The symbol ∗∗/∗∗ is just to the right of the "L" with an arrow pointing to the shaded area. This means that the shaded area is forecast to have continuous light snow.
   Answer (B) is incorrect. Intermittent snow would be indicated by a symbol with vertical snowflakes, not horizontal ones. Answer (C) is incorrect. Continuous snow showers are indicated for the unshaded area in southern Utah, not the shaded area in northern Utah, by the symbol ∗∗/∗ .

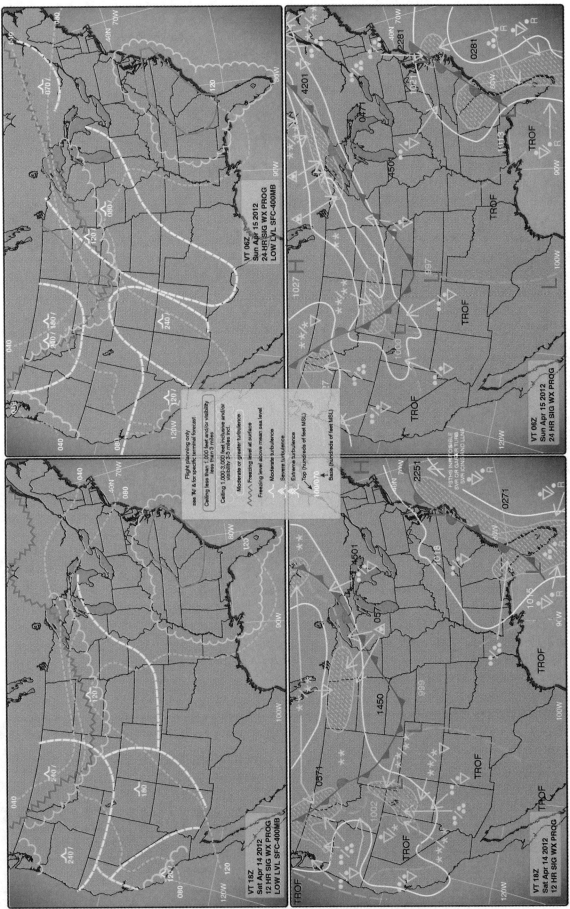

Figure 19. – Low-Level Significant Weather (SIGWX) Prognostic Charts.

STUDY UNIT FOUR
WEATHER EFFECTS ON PERFORMANCE

(21 pages of outline)

4.1 EFFECTS OF WEATHER ON PERFORMANCE

1. **The applicant demonstrates understanding of weather factors and their effects on performance.**

    a. Effects of Weather on Performance

        1) Even though sUAS operations are often conducted at very low altitudes, weather factors can greatly influence performance and safety of flight.

        2) Specifically, factors that affect sUAS performance and risk management include

            a) Atmospheric pressure and stability
            b) Wind and currents
            c) Uneven surface heating
            d) Visibility and cloud clearance

        3) As with any flight, the Remote PIC should check and consider the weather conditions prior to and during every sUAS flight.

    b. **Density altitude**

        1) Density altitude is a measurement of the density of the air.

            a) Density altitude accounts for variations in non-standard pressures and non-standard temperature in the atmosphere.

                i)   As air density decreases, density altitude is said to increase.

            b) Density altitude is used in determining an airplane's performance capabilities.

        2) Because of the inescapable influence density altitude has on an aircraft and performance, every pilot should understand its effects. Air density is affected by pressure, temperature, and humidity.

            a) The density of air is directly proportional to pressure.

                i)   Since air is a gas, it can be compressed or expanded.

                    • When air is compressed (resulting in increased pressure), a greater amount of air occupies a given volume; thus, the density of air is increased.

                    • When pressure is decreased on a given volume of air, the air expands and occupies a greater space; thus, the density of air is decreased.

            b) The density of air varies inversely with temperature.

                i)   As the temperature of the air increases, the air expands, occupying more volume.

                    • Thus, a given volume holds less air, and air density is decreased.

                ii) As air temperature decreases, the air contracts and density is increased.

    c)   Humidity is the amount of water vapor in the air and is not generally considered a major factor in density altitude computation because the effect of humidity is related more to engine power than to aerodynamic efficiency.

        i)   Because water vapor weighs less than dry air, any given volume of moist air weighs less (i.e., is less dense) than an equal volume of dry air.

            ●   Warm, moist air is less dense (i.e., has a higher density altitude) than cold, dry air.

        ii)   Humidity affects engine power because the water vapor uses airspace that is available for vaporized fuel.

            ●   As humidity increases, less air enters the cylinders, causing a slight increase in density altitude.

    d)   In the atmosphere, both temperature and pressure decrease with altitude and have conflicting effects on density. However, the fairly rapid drop in pressure as altitude is increased usually has a dominating effect over the decrease in temperature.

        i)   Thus, we can expect the air density to decrease with altitude.

    e)   At airports of higher elevations, such as those in the western U.S., high temperatures sometimes have such an effect on density altitude that safe operations may be impossible.

        i)   Even at lower elevations with excessively high temperature or humidity, airplane performance can become marginal, and it may be necessary to reduce the airplane's weight for safe operations.

3)   Density altitude is determined by finding the pressure altitude and adjusting for the temperature.

    a)   This adjustment is made using a density altitude chart or a flight computer.

4)   Density Altitude Chart

    a)   Adjust the airport elevation to pressure altitude based upon the actual altimeter setting.

        i)   On the chart on the following page, the conversion in feet is provided for different altimeter settings.

    b)   Plot the intersection of the actual air temperature (listed on the horizontal axis of the chart) with the pressure altitude (indicated by the diagonal lines).

    c)   Move straight across to the vertical column. This is the density altitude.

    d)   EXAMPLE:

        Outside air temperature   90°F
        Altimeter setting   30.20" Hg
        Airport elevation   4,725 ft.

        i)   Note that the altimeter setting of 30.20" Hg requires a −257-ft. correction factor.

        ii)   Subtract 257 ft. from field elevation of 4,725 ft. to obtain pressure altitude of 4,468 ft.

        iii)   Locate 90°F on the bottom axis of the chart, and move up vertically to intersect the diagonal pressure altitude line of 4,468 ft.

        iv)   Move horizontally to the left axis of the chart to obtain the density altitude of 7,400 ft.

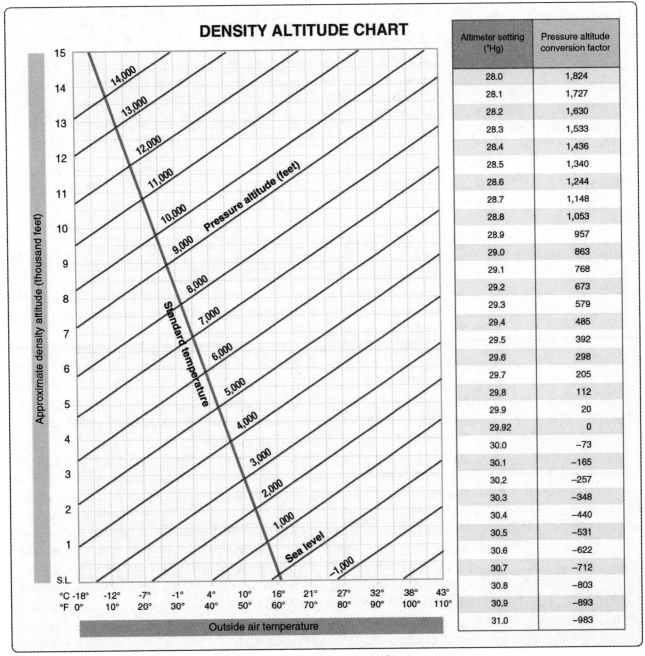

Figure 8. – Density Altitude Chart.

c. **Wind and currents**

   1) Differences in temperature create differences in pressure. These pressure differences cause the movement of air masses.

      a) The horizontal movement of air is called wind, and the vertical movement of air is called convection.

      b) A cooler surface area would create a high-pressure area, while a warmer surface area would create a low-pressure area. (Recall the effect of temperature on air pressure.)

2) Whenever a pressure difference develops, a force is created that moves the air from the higher pressure to the lower pressure. This force is called the **pressure gradient force**.

   a) The strength of the pressure gradient force is determined by the amount of pressure difference and the distance between the high- and low-pressure areas. (See the isobar image under item 1.d.8.a.)

      i)   The pressure gradient force increases as the pressure difference increases and/or the distance between the two pressure areas decreases.

3) Since the Earth rotates, the air does not flow directly from high- to low-pressure areas. In the Northern Hemisphere, it is deflected to the right by what is called the **Coriolis Force**.

   a) In the Northern Hemisphere, the wind blows clockwise around a high and counterclockwise around a low due to the Coriolis Force.

   b) The strength of the Coriolis Force is directly proportional to wind speed. The faster the wind, the stronger the Coriolis Force.

4) At approximately 3,000 ft. AGL and below, friction between the wind and the Earth's surface slows the wind. This reduces the Coriolis Force but does not affect the pressure gradient force.

5) Since friction does not affect upper-level winds, the pressure gradient force and the Coriolis Force are equal, which causes the wind to flow around, but not into, the low-pressure area.

   a) Near the surface, friction slows the wind speed, reducing the Coriolis Force but not the pressure gradient force. Thus, the wind flows into the low-pressure area.

      i)   Surface winds are slower and from a different direction than upper-level winds.

6) At the surface when air converges into a low, it cannot go outward against the pressure gradient nor can it go downward into the ground. It must go upward. Therefore, a low or a trough is an area of rising air.

   a) Rising air is conducive to cloud development and precipitation. Thus, low-pressure areas are generally associated with bad weather.

   b) Conversely, air moving out from a high or a ridge depletes the quantity of air and is an area of descending air.

      i)   Descending air tends to dissipate clouds, so highs are usually associated with good weather.

7) Wind and currents can affect sUAS performance and maneuverability during all phases of flight. Be vigilant when operating sUAS at low altitudes, in confined areas, near buildings or other man-made structures, and near natural obstructions (such as mountains, bluffs, or canyons).

    a) Consider the following effects of wind on performance:

        i) Obstructions on the ground affect the flow of wind, may create rapidly changing wind gusts, and can be an unseen danger.

        ii) The intensity of the turbulence associated with ground obstructions depends on the size of the obstacle and the primary velocity of the wind.

        iii) Even when operating in an open field, wind blowing against surrounding trees can create significant low-level turbulence.

    b) High winds may make it difficult to maintain a geographical position in flight and may consume more battery power.

    c) Remember that local conditions, geological features, and other anomalies can change the wind direction and speed close to the Earth's surface.

        i) For example, when operating close to a building, winds blowing against the building could cause strong updrafts that can result in ballooning or a loss of positive control. On the other hand, winds blowing over the building from the opposite side can cause significant downdrafts that can have a dramatic sinking effect on the unmanned aircraft.

    d) Different surfaces radiate heat in varying amounts. The resulting uneven heating of the air creates small areas of local circulation called convective currents.

        i) Convective currents can cause bumpy, turbulent air that can dramatically affect the Remote PIC's ability to control unmanned aircraft at lower altitudes. For example,

- Plowed ground, rocks, sand, and barren land give off a large amount of heat and are likely to result in updrafts.
- Water, trees, and other areas of vegetation tend to absorb and retain heat and are likely to result in downdrafts.

8) **Types of Wind**

    a) A **jet stream** is a narrow band of strong winds (50 kt. or more) moving generally from west to east at a level near the tropopause.

    b) A **valley wind** occurs when colder, denser air in the surroundings settles downward and forces the warmer air near the ground up the mountain slope.

    c) A **mountain wind** occurs at night when the air near the mountain slope is cooled by terrestrial radiation, becomes heavier than the surrounding air, and sinks along the slope.

    d) A **katabatic wind** is a wind blowing down an incline, where the incline itself has been a factor in causing the wind. A mountain wind is a good example of a katabatic wind.

e) **Sea and land breezes**

   i) During the day, the land is warmer than the sea.

- Sea breezes are caused by cooler and denser air moving inland off the water.
- Once over the warmer land, the air heats up and rises.
- Currents push the air out over the water where it cools and descends, starting the process over again.

   ii) At night, the wind reverses from the cool land to the warmer water.

- This is called a land breeze.

   iii) These breezes occur only when the overall pressure gradient is weak.

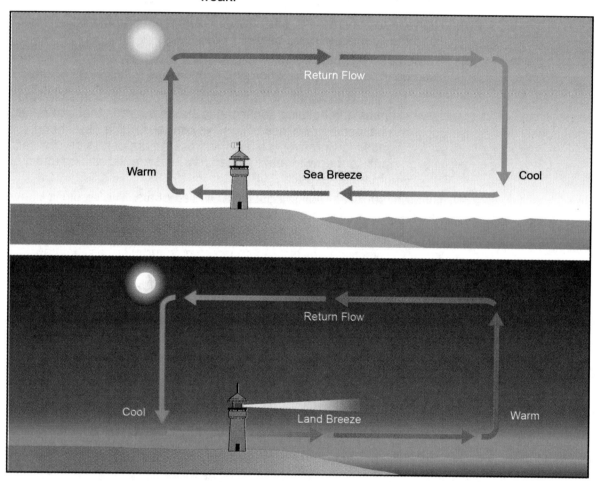

d. **Atmospheric stability, pressure, and temperature**

   1) Stability of air masses.

     a) Stable air characteristics

       i) Stratiform clouds
       ii) Smooth air
       iii) Fair-to-poor visibility in haze and smoke
       iv) Continuous precipitation

     b) Unstable air characteristics

       i) Cumuliform clouds
       ii) Turbulent air
       iii) Good visibility
       iv) Showery precipitation

    c)   When air is warmed from below, it rises and causes instability.

    d)   The lapse rate is the decrease in temperature with increase in altitude. As the lapse rate increases (i.e., air cools more with increases in altitude), air is more unstable.

        i)   The lapse rate can be used to determine the stability of air masses.

    e)   Moist, stable air moving up a mountain slope produces stratus type clouds as it cools.

    f)   Turbulence and clouds with extensive vertical development result when unstable air rises.

    g)   Steady precipitation preceding a front is usually an indication of a warm front, which results from warm air being cooled from the bottom by colder air.

        i)   This results in stable air with stratiform clouds and little or no turbulence.

2)   Temperature Inversions.

    a)   Normally, temperature decreases as altitude increases. A temperature inversion occurs when temperature increases as altitude increases.

    b)   Temperature inversions usually result in a stable layer of air.

    c)   A temperature inversion often develops near the ground on clear, cool nights when the wind is light.

        i)   It is caused by terrestrial radiation.

    d)   Smooth air with restricted visibility is usually found beneath a low-level temperature inversion.

3)   Temperature Scales. Two commonly used temperature scales are Celsius (C) and Fahrenheit (F).

    a)   The Celsius scale is used in most aviation weather reports, forecasts, and charts.

    b)   Two common temperature references are the melting point of pure ice and the boiling point of pure water at sea level.

        i)   The boiling point of water is 100°C or 212°F.
        ii)   The melting point of ice is 0°C or 32°F.

    c)   Most flight computers provide for direct conversion of temperature from one scale to the other.

    d)   The simple formulas below demonstrate how to mathematically convert from one unit of measure to the other.

$$°C = \frac{5}{9}(F - 32) \quad or \quad °F = \frac{9}{5}C + 32$$

4)   Heat is a form of energy. When a substance contains heat, it exhibits the property we measure as temperature, which is the degree of a substance's warmth or coldness.

    a)   A specific amount of heat added to or removed from a substance will raise or lower its temperature a definite amount. Each substance has a unique temperature change per specific change in heat.

        i)   EXAMPLE: If a land surface and a water surface have the same temperature and an equal amount of heat is added, the land surface becomes hotter than the water surface. Conversely, with equal heat loss, the land becomes colder than the water.

    b)   Every physical process of weather either is accompanied by or is the result of heat exchanges.

5) Temperature Variations. Five main types of temperature variations affect weather:

    a) **Diurnal variation.** This change in temperature from day to night and night to day is brought about by the rotation of the Earth.

    b) **Seasonal variation.** Since the Earth's axis is tilted with respect to its orbit, the angle at which a particular spot or region receives solar radiation varies throughout the year. This phenomenon accounts for the temperature variations of the four seasons.

    c) **Variation with latitude.** The sun is nearly overhead in the equatorial regions. Since the Earth is spherical, the sun's rays reach the higher latitudes at an angle. For this reason, the equatorial regions receive the most radiant energy and are the warmest.

    d) **Variations with topography.** Since land heats and cools at a faster rate than water, air temperatures over land vary more widely than those over large bodies of water, which tend to have more minimal temperature changes. Wet soil, swamps, and thick vegetation also help to control temperature fluctuations.

    e) **Temperature variation with altitude.** The amount of temperature decrease with increases in altitude is defined as the **lapse rate**.

        i) Standard sea level temperature is 15°C.

        ii) The average standard lapse rate in the troposphere is 2°C per 1,000 ft.

        iii) An increase in temperature with an increase in altitude is called an **inversion** because the lapse rate is inverted.

          • An inversion may occur when the ground cools faster than the air over it. Air in contact with the ground becomes cold, while only a few hundred feet higher, the temperature has changed very little. Thus, the temperature increases with altitude.

          • Inversions may occur at any altitude.

6) Atmospheric pressure is the force per unit area exerted by the weight of the atmosphere. It is measured per unit area, e.g., pounds per square inch (psi).

    a) The instrument designed for measuring atmospheric pressure is the barometer, with the aneroid barometer being the most common.

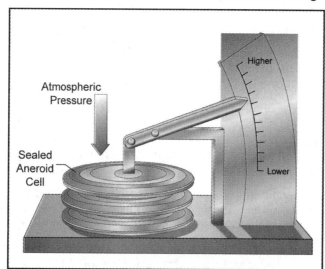

        i) The aneroid barometer consists of a partially evacuated flexible metal cell connected to a registering mechanism. As the atmospheric pressure changes, the metal cell expands or contracts, which drives a needle along a scale calibrated in pressure units.

    b)   The commonly used pressure units are inches of mercury (in. Hg.), millibars (mb), and hectoPascal (hPa).

       i)   Inches of mercury notation is used in automated weather report broadcasts, and millibar notation is commonly used (interchangeably with hectoPascal notation) on weather charts.

    c)   The pressure measured at a station is called the **station pressure**.

    d)   Standard atmospheric pressure at sea level is 29.92 in. Hg.

7) **Pressure Variation**

    a)   Pressure varies with changes in altitude and temperature of the air. Other factors also affect pressure, but their effects are negligible.

       i)   **Altitude.** At higher altitudes, the weight of the air above decreases.

          •   This decrease in pressure from air above results in a lower atmospheric pressure.

             ▪   The amount of air remains constant as altitude increases, but the pressure exerted on it is less.

             ▪   A volume of air at 18,000 ft. above the surface weighs only half of the same volume at sea level.

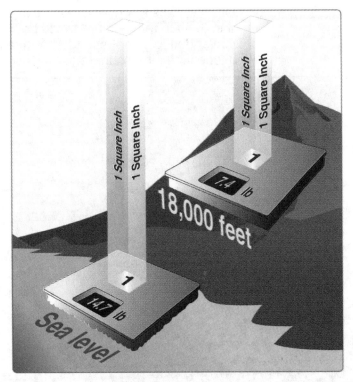

          •   Within the lower few thousand feet of the troposphere (i.e., near the Earth's surface), pressure decreases at a rate of roughly 1 in. Hg per 1,000 ft. of altitude. As one goes higher, this rate of decrease slows.

       ii)   **Temperature.** Like most substances, air expands as it becomes warmer and shrinks as it cools.

          •   When air is warm and expands, pressure decreases because the same amount of air exists in a larger area.

          •   When air is cooled, it contracts. The pressure is greater than that of the warm air because the same amount of air takes up a smaller area.

b)   **Sea-level pressure.** Since pressure varies with altitude, you cannot accurately compare pressures between airports or weather stations at different altitudes unless you adjust those pressures to a common reference point. The standardized measurement used in aviation is mean sea level (MSL).

i)   EXAMPLE:

- Denver, CO, is approximately 5,000 ft. above sea level. If the station pressure in Denver is 24.92 in. Hg, you can determine the sea level pressure with a simple calculation.

- The standard pressure lapse rate is 1 in. Hg per 1,000 ft. of altitude. Denver is approximately 5,000 ft. above sea level, which equates to a correction factor of 5 in. Hg.

- Add 5 in. Hg to the Denver station pressure to determine the approximate sea-level pressure is 29.92 in. Hg.

- The weather observer takes temperature and other factors into account, but this simplified example explains the basic principle of sea-level pressure.

- The following image graphically explains the pressure variation changes by showing that a "standard atmosphere" day in Denver occurs when the pressure is 24.92 in. Hg. (Bear in mind that the temperature would be 5°C on a standard day in Denver due to a corresponding temperature lapse rate with altitude in the troposphere.)

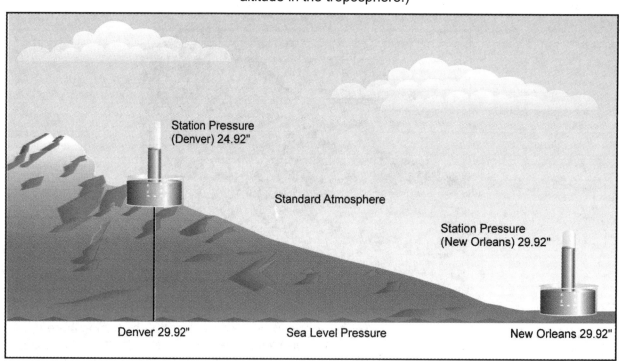

8) **Pressure analyses.** Various weather charts depict lines that connect points of equal pressure. These lines are called **isobars**.

a) Weather charts depicting isobars allow you to see identifiable, organized pressure patterns.

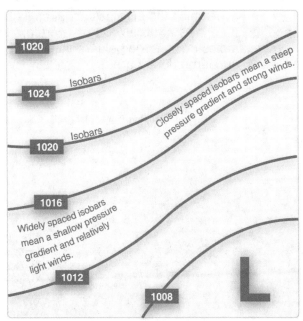

b) The five pressure systems shown on these charts are defined as follows:

i) **Low** -- an area of pressure surrounded on all sides by higher pressure, also called a cyclone. In the Northern Hemisphere, a cyclone, or low pressure system, is a mass of air that rotates counterclockwise when viewed from above.

ii) **High** -- a center of pressure surrounded on all sides by lower pressure, also called an anticyclone. In the Northern Hemisphere, an anticyclone, or high-pressure system, is a mass of air that rotates clockwise when viewed from above.

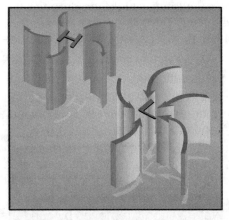

iii) **Trough** -- an elongated area of low pressure, with the lowest pressure along a line marking maximum cyclonic curvature.

iv) **Ridge** -- an elongated area of high pressure, with the highest pressure along a line marking maximum anticyclonic curvature.

v) **Col** -- the neutral area between two highs or two lows. It also is the intersection of a trough and a ridge. The col on a pressure surface is analogous to a mountain pass on a topographic surface.

e.   **Air masses and fronts**

1)   **Air masses.** When a body of air comes to rest or moves slowly over an extensive area having uniform properties of temperature and moisture, the body of air takes on the same properties.

a)   The area over which the air mass acquires its properties of temperature and moisture is its **source region**. There are many source regions, the best examples being large polar regions, cold northern and warm tropical oceans, and large desert areas.

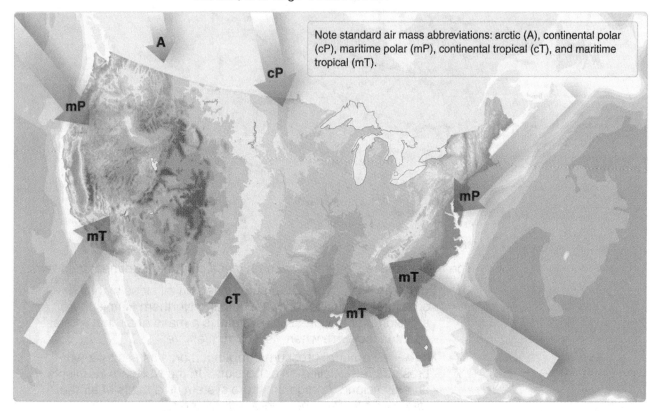

Note standard air mass abbreviations: arctic (A), continental polar (cP), maritime polar (mP), continental tropical (cT), and maritime tropical (mT).

b)   An air mass tends to take on properties of the underlying surface when it moves away from its source region, thus becoming modified. Some ways in which air masses are modified include the following:

i)   Cool air moving over a warm surface is heated from below, generating instability and increasing the possibility of showers.

ii)   Warm air moving over a cool surface is cooled from below, increasing stability. If air is cooled to its dew point, stratus clouds and/or fog forms.

iii)   Evaporation from water surfaces and falling precipitation adds water vapor to the air. When the water is warmer than the air, evaporation can raise the dew point sufficiently to saturate the air and form stratus clouds or fog.

iv)   Water vapor is removed by condensation and precipitation.

2)   **Fronts.** The zone between two different air masses is a frontal zone or front. Across this zone, temperature, humidity, and wind often change rapidly over short distances.

a)   Discontinuities. When you pass through a frontal zone, these changes may be abrupt, indicating a narrow front. A more subtle change indicates a broad and diffused front.

      i)   The most easily recognizable indication that you are passing through a front will be a temperature change.

      ii)   Temperature-dew point spread usually differs across a front.

      iii) Wind always changes across a front. Direction, speed, or both will change.

      iv) Pressure may change abruptly as you move from one air mass to another. It is important to keep a current altimeter setting when in the vicinity of a front.

  b)   Types of fronts. There are four principal types of fronts:

      i)   Cold front -- the leading edge of an advancing cold air mass. At the surface, cold air overtakes and replaces warm air. Cold fronts tend to precede high-pressure systems.

      ii)   Warm front -- the leading edge of an advancing mass of warm air. Since cold air is more dense, it hugs the ground. Warm air slides up and over the cold mass. This elongates the frontal zone making it more diffuse. Warm fronts generally move about half as fast as cold fronts under the same wind conditions. Warm fronts tend to precede low-pressure systems.

      iii) Stationary front -- occurs when neither air mass is replacing the other and there is little or no movement. Surface winds tend to blow parallel to the front.

      iv) Occluded front -- occurs when a fast-moving cold front catches up with a slow-moving warm front. The difference in temperature within each frontal system is a major factor in determining whether a cold or warm front occlusion (i.e., which will be dominant) occurs.

  c)   Frontolysis and Frontogenesis

      i)   As adjacent air masses converge and as temperature and pressure differences equalize, the front dissipates. This dissipation is called frontolysis.

      ii)   When two air masses come together and form a front, the process is called frontogenesis.

  d)   Weather occurring with a front depends on the

      i)   Amount of moisture available
      ii)   Degree of stability of the air that is forced upward
      iii) Slope of the front
      iv) Speed of the frontal movement
      v)   Upper wind flow

f. **Moisture, cloud formation, and precipitation**

  1)   Water vapor is invisible, like the other atmospheric gases, but its quantity in the air can still be measured. It is generally expressed as

    a)   Relative humidity -- a ratio of how much actual water vapor is present to the amount that could be present. At 100% relative humidity, the air is saturated.

    b)   Dew point -- the temperature to which air must be cooled to become saturated by the water vapor that is already present in that air.

      i)   Dew point is compared to air temperature to determine how close the air is to saturation. This difference is referred to as the temperature-dew point spread.

      ii)   As the temperature and dew point converge, fog, clouds, or rain should be anticipated.

c)   The following image explains relative humidity and dew point:

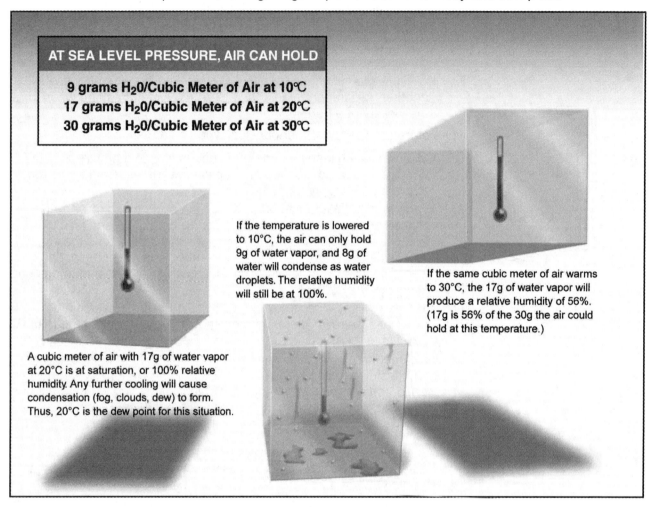

AT SEA LEVEL PRESSURE, AIR CAN HOLD

9 grams H₂0/Cubic Meter of Air at 10°C
17 grams H₂0/Cubic Meter of Air at 20°C
30 grams H₂0/Cubic Meter of Air at 30°C

If the temperature is lowered to 10°C, the air can only hold 9g of water vapor, and 8g of water will condense as water droplets. The relative humidity will still be at 100%.

If the same cubic meter of air warms to 30°C, the 17g of water vapor will produce a relative humidity of 56%. (17g is 56% of the 30g the air could hold at this temperature.)

A cubic meter of air with 17g of water vapor at 20°C is at saturation, or 100% relative humidity. Any further cooling will cause condensation (fog, clouds, dew) to form. Thus, 20°C is the dew point for this situation.

2)   The six possible transformations of water are designated by the following terms:

a)   **Condensation** -- the change of water vapor to liquid water
b)   **Evaporation** -- the change of liquid water to water vapor
c)   **Freezing** -- the change of liquid water to ice
d)   **Melting** -- the change of ice to liquid water
e)   **Sublimation** -- the change of ice to water vapor
f)   **Deposition** -- the change of water vapor to ice

3)   Supercooled water consists of water droplets existing at temperatures below freezing.

a)   Supercooled water is dangerous because it immediately forms into heavy, clear ice when it strikes an airplane's surface.

4)   Dew forms when the Earth's surface cools to below the dew point of adjacent air as a result of heat radiation. Moisture forms (condenses) on leaves, grass, and exposed objects. This is the same process that causes a cold glass of water to "sweat" in warm, humid weather.

5)   Frost forms in much the same way as dew. The difference is that the dew point of surrounding air must be colder than freezing. Water vapor changes directly to ice crystals or frost (deposition) rather than condensing as dew.

6) Clouds are a visible collection of minute water or ice particles suspended in air. A cloud may be composed entirely of liquid water, ice crystals, or a mixture of the two.

   a) Cloud formation. Normally, air must become saturated for condensation to occur. Saturation may result from cooling the temperature, increasing the dew point, or both. Cooling is far more predominant. There are three ways to cool air to saturation:

      i)   Air moving over a colder surface
      ii) Stagnant air lying over a cooling surface
      iii) Expansional cooling in upward-moving air (the major cause of cloud formation)

   b) If the cloud is on the ground, it is fog.

   c) When entire layers of air cool to the point of saturation, fog or sheet-like stratus clouds result.

   d) Saturation of a localized updraft produces a towering cumulus cloud.

7) Precipitation is an all-inclusive term denoting drizzle, rain, snow, ice pellets, hail, and ice crystals. Precipitation occurs when any of these particles grow in size and weight until the atmosphere can no longer suspend them, and they fall.

   a) Precipitation can change its state as the temperature of its environment changes.

      i) Falling snow may melt to form rain in warmer layers of air at lower altitudes.

      ii) Rain falling through colder air may become supercooled, freezing on impact as freezing rain.

         • Freezing rain always indicates warmer air at higher altitudes.
         • It may freeze during its descent, falling as ice pellets.

            ▪ Ice pellets always indicate freezing rain at higher altitudes.

      iii) Hailstones form when water droplets are lifted above the freezing level by updrafts of a thunderstorm, where they freeze solid. They may be circulated up and down within the storm, increasing in size and weight until they become too heavy to remain aloft and fall to the surface or are ejected through the anvil.

         • Hail may be encountered up to 20 miles from a strong thunderstorm cell.

   b) To produce significant precipitation, clouds must be at least 4,000 ft. thick.

g. **Thunderstorms and microbursts**

   1) For a thunderstorm to form, the air must have

      a) Sufficient water vapor
      b) An unstable lapse rate
      c) An initial upward boost (lifting) to start the storm process in motion

         i) Surface heating, converging winds, sloping terrain, a frontal surface, or any combination of these can provide the necessary lifting.

2)   A thunderstorm cell progresses through three stages during its life cycle:

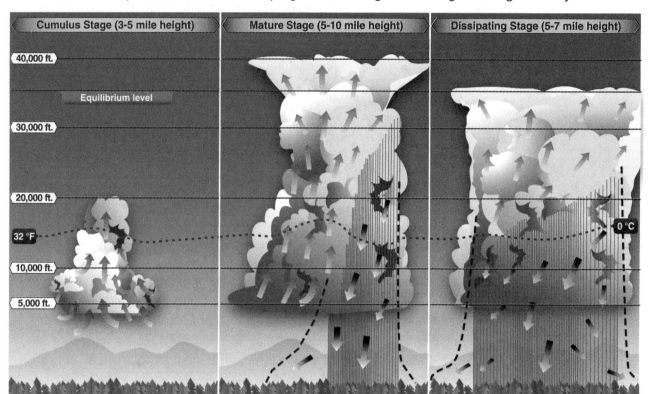

a)   The **cumulus stage**. Although most cumulus clouds do not grow into thunderstorms, every thunderstorm begins as a cumulus. The key feature in the cumulus stage is the updraft.

    i)   Early during the cumulus stage, water droplets are quite small but grow to raindrop size as the cloud grows.

        •   As the raindrops grow still heavier, they fall. This cold rain drags air with it, creating a cold downdraft coexisting with the updraft.

b)   The **mature stage**. Precipitation beginning to fall from the cloud base is the sign that a downdraft has developed and a cell has entered the mature stage.

    i)   Cold rain in the downdraft retards compressional (adiabatic) heating, and the downdraft remains cooler than the surrounding air. Thus, its downward speed is accelerated.

    ii)   The downrushing air spreads outward at the surface, producing strong gusty surface winds, a sharp temperature drop, and a rapid rise in pressure.

    iii)   Updrafts and downdrafts in close proximity create strong vertical shear and a very turbulent environment.

    iv)   All thunderstorm hazards reach their greatest intensity during the mature stage.

        •   Hazards include tornadoes, turbulence, icing, hail, lightning, low visibility and ceiling, and effects on an airplane's altimeter.

c)   The **dissipating stage**. Downdrafts characterize the dissipating stage of the thunderstorm cell, and the storm dies.

3) **Types of Thunderstorms**

    a) Air mass thunderstorms most often result from surface heating and last only about 20 to 90 min.

    b) Steady state thunderstorms are usually associated with weather systems.

        i) Fronts, converging winds, and troughs aloft force air upwards to initiate the storms.

        ii) They may last for several hours.

4) A **squall line** is a nonfrontal narrow band of steady state thunderstorms.

    a) Squall lines often form in front of cold fronts in moist unstable air, but they may also develop in unstable air far removed from any fronts.

    b) Squall lines generally produce the most severe thunderstorm conditions (e.g., heavy hail, destructive winds, tornadoes, etc.).

h. **Tornadoes**

1) The most violent thunderstorms draw air into their cloud bases with great vigor. If the incoming air has any initial rotating motion, it often forms an extremely concentrated vortex from the surface well into the cloud. Meteorologists have estimated that wind in such a vortex can exceed 200 knots with quite low pressure inside the vortex.

    a) The strong winds gather dust and debris and the low pressure generates a funnel-shaped cloud extending downward from the cumulonimbus base.

        i) If the cloud does not reach the surface, it is a funnel cloud.

        ii) If the cloud touches a land surface, it is a tornado.

        iii) If the cloud touches water, it is a waterspout.

    b) Tornadoes occur with both isolated and squall-line thunderstorms.

        i) Reports for forecasts of tornadoes indicate that atmospheric conditions are favorable for violent turbulence.

        ii) An aircraft entering a tornado vortex is almost certain to suffer loss of control and structural damage.

        iii) Since the vortex extends well into the cloud, any aircraft inadvertently caught in a severe thunderstorm could encounter a hidden vortex.

    c) Families of tornadoes have been observed as appendages of the main cloud extending several miles outward from the area of lightning and precipitation. Thus, any cloud connected to a severe thunderstorm carries a threat of violence.

i.   **Icing**

    1)   Icing is a cumulative hazard to aircraft. When ice builds up on the surface of an aircraft, it increases weight and drag while reducing lift and thrust. These factors tend to slow the aircraft and/or force it to descend. Icing can also seriously impair engine performance and instruments.

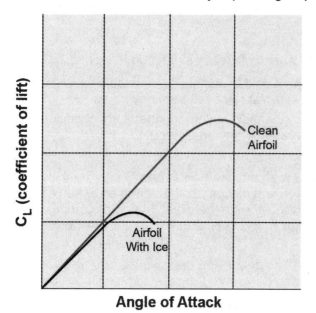

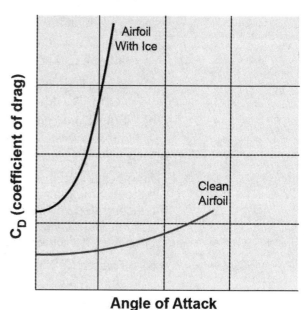

    2)   Structural icing will occur if two conditions are met:

      a)   The aircraft is flying through visible moisture, such as rain or cloud droplets.

      b)   The air temperature where the moisture strikes the aircraft is 0°C or cooler.

        i)   Aerodynamic cooling can lower the temperature of an airfoil to 0°C even though ambient temperature is slightly higher.

    3)   Three types of ice can form on an airplane:

      a)   **Clear ice** forms when water droplets that touch the airplane flow across the surface before freezing. Clear ice will accumulate as a smooth sheet. This type of ice forms when the water droplets are large, such as in rain or cumuliform clouds.

        i)   Clear ice is very heavy and difficult to remove.
        ii) It can substantially increase the gross weight of an airplane.

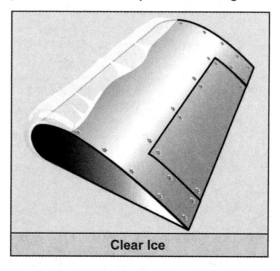

Clear Ice

b) **Rime ice** forms when water droplets are small, such as those in stratiform clouds or light drizzle, and freeze on impact without spreading. Rime ice is rough and opaque, similar to frost in your home freezer.

i) Its irregular shape and rough surface greatly decrease the aerodynamic efficiency of an airplane's wings, thus reducing lift and increasing drag.

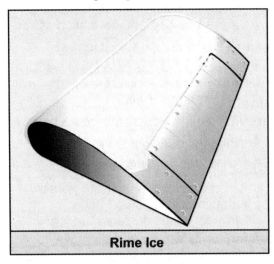

Rime Ice

c) **Mixed ice** is a combination of clear and rime ice. It forms when water droplets vary in size. Some freeze on impact and some spread before freezing. Mixed ice is opaque and has a very rough surface.

4) Frost, ice, and/or snow may accumulate on parked airplanes. All frost, ice, and/or snow should be removed before takeoff.

j. **Hail**

1) Hail competes with turbulence as the greatest thunderstorm hazard to aircraft. Supercooled drops above the freezing level begin to freeze.

a) Once a drop has frozen, other drops latch on and freeze to it, so the hailstone grows—sometimes into a huge ice ball.

b) Large hail occurs with severe thunderstorms with strong updrafts that have built to great heights. Eventually, the hailstones fall, possibly some distance from the storm core.

i) Hail may be encountered in clear air several miles from thunderstorm clouds.

2) As hailstones fall through air whose temperature is above 0 °C, they begin to melt and precipitation may reach the ground as either hail or rain.

a) Rain at the surface does not mean the absence of hail aloft.

b) Possible hail should be anticipated with any thunderstorm, especially beneath the anvil of a large cumulonimbus.

i) Hailstones larger than one-half inch in diameter can significantly damage larger aircraft in a few seconds.

ii) Hailstones of any size should be considered a significant hazard to sUAS.

k. **Fog**

1) Fog is a surface-based cloud composed of either water droplets or ice crystals.

   a) It is the most frequent cause of IFR conditions and is one of the most persistent weather hazards encountered in aviation.

   b) A small temperature-dew point spread is essential for fog to form.

      i) Abundant condensation nuclei, such as may be found in industrial areas, enhance the formation of fog.

   c) Fog is classified by the way it forms.

2) **Radiation fog**, or ground fog, is relatively shallow. It forms almost exclusively at night or near daybreak under a clear sky, with little or no wind, and with a small temperature-dew point spread.

   a) Terrestrial radiation cools the ground, which cools the air in contact with it.

      i) When the air is cooled to its dew point, fog forms.

   b) Radiation fog is restricted to land because water cools little at night.

      i) It is shallow when the wind is calm.
      ii) It deepens in wind up to 5 kt.
      iii) Stronger winds disperse the fog.

3) **Advection fog** forms when moist air moves over colder ground or water. At sea, it is called sea fog.

   a) Advection fog deepens in wind speeds up to 15 kt.

   b) Wind much stronger than 15 kt. lifts the fog into a layer of low clouds.

   c) Advection fog is more persistent and extensive than radiation fog and can appear during day or night.

4) **Upslope fog** forms as a result of moist, stable air being cooled adiabatically as it moves up sloping terrain.

   a) Once the upslope wind ceases, the fog dissipates.
   b) Upslope fog is often quite dense and extends to high altitudes.

5) **Precipitation-induced fog** forms when relatively warm rain falls through cool air; evaporation from the precipitation saturates the cool air and forms fog.

   a) Precipitation-induced fog can become quite dense and continue for a long time.

   b) It is most commonly associated with warm fronts.

   c) It occurs near other possible hazards, such as icing, turbulence, and thunderstorms.

6) **Steam fog** forms in winter when cold, dry air passes from land areas over comparatively warm ocean waters.

   a) It is composed entirely of water droplets that often freeze quickly.
   b) Low-level turbulence and hazardous icing can occur.

7) Be especially alert for development of fog when

   a) The following morning when at dusk temperature-dew point spread is 10°C (15°F) or less, skies are clear, and winds are light

   b) When moist air is flowing from a relatively warm surface to a colder surface

   c) When temperature-dew point spread is 3°C (5°F) or less and decreasing

   d) When a moderate or stronger moist wind is blowing over an extended upslope

      i) Temperature and dew point converge at about 2°C (4°F) for every 1,000 ft. the air is lifted.

e) When air is blowing from a cold surface (either land or water) over warmer water

    i) This would produce steam fog.

f) When rain or drizzle falls through cool air

    i) This is especially prevalent during winter ahead of a warm front and behind a stationary front or stagnating cold front.

l. **Ceiling and visibility**

1) Cloud height above ground level is entered under the station circle in hundreds of feet, the same as coded in the METAR.

    a) If total sky cover is scattered, the cloud height entered is the base of the lowest layer.

    b) If total sky cover is broken or greater, the cloud height entered is the ceiling.

    c) A totally obscured sky is shown by the sky cover symbol "X."

        i) A totally obscured sky always has a height entry of the ceiling (vertical visibility into the obscuration).

m. **Lightning**

1) NEVER operate sUAS when lightning is in the area.

    a) NO PLACE outside is safe when thunderstorms are in the area!

    b) If you hear thunder, lightning is close enough to strike you.

    c) When you hear thunder, immediately move to safe shelter. A safe shelter is a substantial building with electricity or plumbing or an enclosed, metal-topped vehicle with windows up.

    d) Stay in a safe shelter at least 30 minutes after you hear the last sound of thunder.

2) Lightning strikes the United States about 25 million times a year. Although most lightning occurs in the summer, people can be struck at any time of year.

    a) According to the National Weather Service, lightning kills an average of 49 people in the United States each year, and hundreds more are severely injured.

3) Lightning strikes can destroy an sUAS and interfere with communications and electronic navigational equipment.

4) Lightning discharges, even distant ones, can disrupt radio communications on low and medium frequencies.

5) Though lightning intensity and frequency have no simple relationship to other storm parameters, severe storms, as a rule, have a high frequency of lightning.

QUESTIONS

4.1 Effects of Weather on Performance

1. How would high density altitude affect the performance of a small unmanned aircraft?

A. Decreased performance.

B. No change in performance.

C. Increased performance.

Answer (A) is correct. *(PHAK Chap 10)*
    DISCUSSION: Takeoff and climb performance are reduced by high density altitude. High density altitude is a result of high temperatures and high relative humidity.
    Answer (B) is incorrect. High density altitude decreases performance. Answer (C) is incorrect. High density altitude decreases performance.

2. (Refer to Figure 8 on page 133.) Determine the density altitude for these conditions:

Altimeter setting   30.35
Runway temperature   +25°F
Airport elevation   3,894 ft. MSL

   A.   2,000 feet MSL.

   B.   2,900 feet MSL.

   C.   3,500 feet MSL.

Answer (A) is correct. *(PHAK Chap 11)*
   DISCUSSION: With an altimeter setting of 30.35" Hg, 394 ft. must be subtracted from a field elevation of 3,894 to obtain a pressure altitude of 3,500 feet. Note that the higher-than-normal pressure of 30.35 means the pressure altitude will be less than true altitude. The 394 ft. was found by interpolation: 30.3 on the graph is –348, and 30.4 was –440 feet. Adding one-half the –92 ft. difference (–46 ft.) to –348 ft. results in –394 feet. Once you have found the pressure altitude, use the chart to plot 3,500 ft. pressure altitude at 25°F, to reach 2,000 ft. density altitude. Note that since the temperature is lower than standard, the density altitude is lower than the pressure altitude.
   Answer (B) is incorrect. This would be the density altitude if you added (not subtracted) 394 ft. to 3,894 feet. Answer (C) is incorrect. This is pressure (not density) altitude.

3. (Refer to Figure 8 on page 133.) Determine the pressure altitude at an airport that is 3,563 feet MSL with an altimeter setting of 29.96.

   A.   3,527 feet MSL.

   B.   3,556 feet MSL.

   C.   3,639 feet MSL.

Answer (A) is correct. *(PHAK Chap 11)*
   DISCUSSION: Note that the question asks only for pressure altitude, not density altitude. Pressure altitude is determined by adjusting the altimeter setting to 29.92" Hg, i.e., adjusting for nonstandard pressure. This is the true altitude plus or minus the pressure altitude conversion factor (based on current altimeter setting). On the chart, an altimeter setting of 30.0 requires you to subtract 73 ft. to determine pressure altitude (note that at 29.92, nothing is subtracted because that is pressure altitude). Since 29.96 is halfway between 29.92 and 30.0, you need only subtract 36 (–73/2) from 3,563 ft. to obtain a pressure altitude of 3,527 ft. (3,563 – 36). Note that a higher-than-standard barometric pressure means pressure altitude is lower than true altitude.
   Answer (B) is incorrect. You must subtract 36 (not 7) from 3,563 ft. to obtain the correct pressure altitude. Answer (C) is incorrect. You must subtract 36 (not add 76) from 3,563 ft. to obtain the correct pressure altitude.

4. (Refer to Figure 8 on page 133.) Determine the pressure altitude at an airport that is 1,386 feet MSL with an altimeter setting of 29.97.

   A.   1,341 feet MSL.

   B.   1,451 feet MSL.

   C.   1,562 feet MSL.

Answer (A) is correct. *(PHAK Chap 11)*
   DISCUSSION: Pressure altitude is determined by adjusting the altimeter setting to 29.92" Hg. This is the true altitude plus or minus the pressure altitude conversion factor (based on current altimeter setting). Since 29.97 is not a number given on the conversion chart, you must interpolate. Compute 5/8 of –73 (since 29.97 is 5/8 of the way between 29.92 and 30.0), which is 45. Subtract 45 ft. from 1,386 ft. to obtain a pressure altitude of 1,341 feet. Note that if the altimeter setting is greater than standard (e.g., 29.97), the pressure altitude (i.e., altimeter set to 29.92) will be less than true altitude.
   Answer (B) is incorrect. You must subtract 45 ft. (not add 65) from 1,386 ft. to obtain the correct pressure altitude. Answer (C) is incorrect. You must subtract 45 ft. (not add 176) from 1,386 ft. to obtain the correct pressure altitude.

5. (Refer to Figure 8 on page 133.) Determine the density altitude for these conditions:

Altimeter setting   29.25
Runway temperature   +81°F
Airport elevation   5,250 ft MSL

   A.   4,600 feet MSL.

   B.   5,877 feet MSL.

   C.   8,500 feet MSL.

Answer (C) is correct. *(PHAK Chap 11)*
   DISCUSSION: With an altimeter setting of 29.25" Hg, about 626 ft. (579 plus 1/2 the 94-ft. pressure altitude conversion factor difference between 29.2 and 29.3) must be added to the field elevation of 5,250 ft. to obtain the pressure altitude, or 5,876 feet. Note that barometric pressure is less than standard and pressure altitude is greater than true altitude. Next, convert pressure altitude to density altitude. On the chart, find the point at which the pressure altitude line for 5,876 ft. crosses the 81°F line. The density altitude at that spot shows somewhere in the mid-8,000s of feet. The closest answer choice is 8,500 feet. Note that, when temperature is higher than standard, density altitude exceeds pressure altitude.
   Answer (A) is incorrect. This would be pressure altitude if 650 ft. were subtracted from, not added to, 5,250 ft. MSL. Answer (B) is incorrect. This is pressure altitude, not density altitude.

6. (Refer to Figure 8 below.) What is the effect of a temperature increase from 25 to 50° F on the density altitude if the pressure altitude remains at 5,000 feet?

A. 1,200-foot increase.

B. 1,400-foot increase.

C. 1,650-foot increase.

Answer (C) is the best answer. *(PHAK Chap 11)*
DISCUSSION: Increasing the temperature from 25°F to 50°F, given a pressure altitude of 5,000 feet, requires you to find the 5,000-foot line on the density altitude chart at the 25°F level. At this point, the density altitude is approximately 3,800 feet. Then move up the 5,000-foot line to 50°F, where the density altitude is approximately 5,400 feet. There is about a 1,600-foot increase (5,400 – 3,800 feet). As temperature increases, so does density altitude; i.e., the atmosphere becomes thinner (less dense). Because 1,600-foot increase is not an answer choice, 1,650-foot increase would be the best answer.

Answer (A) is incorrect. A 1,200-foot increase would result from a temperature increase of 18°F (not 25°F). Answer (B) is incorrect. A 1,400-foot increase would result from a temperature increase of 20°F (not 25°F).

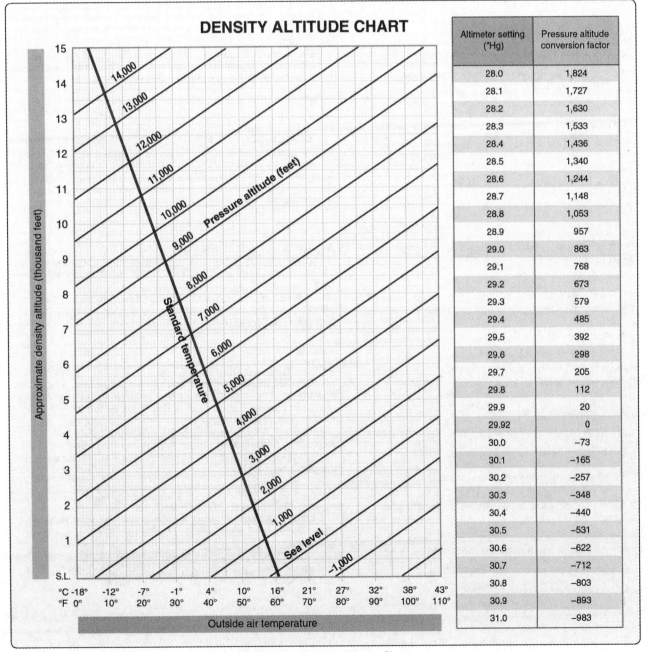

Figure 8. – Density Altitude Chart.

7. You have received an outlook briefing from flight service through 1800wxbrief.com. The briefing indicates you can expect a low-level temperature inversion with high relative humidity. What weather conditions would you expect?

    A. Smooth air, poor visibility, fog, haze, or low clouds.

    B. Light wind shear, poor visibility, haze, and light rain.

    C. Turbulent air, poor visibility, fog, low stratus type clouds, and showery precipitation.

Answer (A) is correct. *(PHAK Chap 4)*
    DISCUSSION: A low-level inversion is usually associated with stable air. Characteristics of a stable air mass include stratiform clouds, continuous precipitation, smooth air, and fair to poor visibility in haze and smoke.
    Answer (B) is incorrect. Smooth air, not light wind shear is a characteristic of stable (not unstable) air. Answer (C) is incorrect. Smooth air and steady precipitation, not turbulence and showery precipitation, is a characteristic of stable (not unstable) air.

8. What effect does high density altitude have on the efficiency of a UA propeller?

    A. Propeller efficiency is increased.

    B. Propeller efficiency is decreased.

    C. Density altitude does not affect propeller efficiency.

Answer (B) is correct. *(PHAK Chap 4)*
    DISCUSSION: The propeller produces thrust in proportion to the mass of air being accelerated through the rotating propeller. If the air is less dense, the propeller efficiency is decreased. A higher density altitude means less dense air.
    Answer (A) is incorrect. Propeller efficiency is decreased, not increased. Answer (C) is incorrect. The propeller exerts less force on the air at higher density altitudes.

9. An air mass moving inland from the coast in winter is likely to result in

    A. rain.

    B. fog.

    C. frost.

Answer (B) is correct. *(PHAK Chap 12)*
    DISCUSSION: Advection fog forms when moist air moves over colder ground or water. It is most common in coastal areas.
    Answer (A) is incorrect. Fog (not rain) is most likely to result from an air mass moving inland from the coast in the winter. Answer (C) is incorrect. Frost additionally requires freezing temperatures.

10. What are the standard temperature and pressure values for sea level?

    A. 15°C and 29.92" Hg.

    B. 59°C and 1013.2 millibars.

    C. 59°F and 29.92 millibars.

Answer (A) is correct. *(PHAK Chap 12)*
    DISCUSSION: The standard temperature and pressure values for sea level are 15°C and 29.92" Hg. This is equivalent to 59°F and 1013.2 millibars of mercury.
    Answer (B) is incorrect. Standard temperature is 59°F (not 59°C). Answer (C) is incorrect. Standard pressure is 29.92" Hg (not 29.92 millibars).

11. What effect, if any, does high humidity have on aircraft performance?

    A. It increases performance.

    B. It decreases performance.

    C. It has no effect on performance.

Answer (B) is correct. *(PHAK Chap 11)*
    DISCUSSION: As the air becomes more humid, it becomes less dense. This is because a given volume of moist air weighs less than the same volume of dry air. Less dense air reduces aircraft performance.
    Answer (A) is incorrect. High humidity reduces (not increases) performance. Answer (C) is incorrect. The three factors that affect aircraft performance are pressure, temperature, and humidity.

12. Which factor would tend to increase the density altitude at a given airport?

    A. An increase in barometric pressure.

    B. An increase in ambient temperature.

    C. A decrease in relative humidity.

Answer (B) is correct. *(AvW Chap 3)*
    DISCUSSION: When air temperature increases, density altitude increases because, at a higher temperature, the air is less dense.
    Answer (A) is incorrect. Density altitude decreases as barometric pressure increases. Answer (C) is incorrect. Density altitude decreases as relative humidity decreases.

13. What effect does high density altitude, as compared to low density altitude, have on propeller efficiency and why?

    A. Efficiency is increased due to less friction on the propeller blades.

    B. Efficiency is reduced because the propeller exerts less force at high density altitudes than at low density altitudes.

    C. Efficiency is reduced due to the increased force of the propeller in the thinner air.

Answer (B) is correct. *(AvW Chap 3)*

    DISCUSSION: The propeller produces thrust in proportion to the mass of air being accelerated through the rotating propeller. If the air is less dense, the propeller efficiency is decreased. Remember, higher density altitude refers to less dense air.

    Answer (A) is incorrect. There is decreased, not increased, efficiency. Answer (C) is incorrect. The propeller exerts less (not more) force on the air when the air is thinner, i.e., at higher density altitudes.

14. Which combination of atmospheric conditions will reduce aircraft takeoff and climb performance?

    A. Low temperature, low relative humidity, and low density altitude.

    B. High temperature, low relative humidity, and low density altitude.

    C. High temperature, high relative humidity, and high density altitude.

Answer (C) is correct. *(PHAK Chap 11)*

    DISCUSSION: Takeoff and climb performance are reduced by high density altitude. High density altitude is a result of high temperatures and high relative humidity.

    Answer (A) is incorrect. Low temperature, low relative humidity, and low density altitude all improve airplane performance. Answer (B) is incorrect. Low relative humidity and low density altitude both improve airplane performance.

15. Every physical process of weather is accompanied by, or is the result of, a

    A. movement of air.

    B. pressure differential.

    C. heat exchange.

Answer (C) is correct. *(AvW Chap 2)*

    DISCUSSION: Every physical process of weather is accompanied by, or is the result of, a heat exchange. A heat differential (difference between the temperatures of two air masses) causes a differential in pressure, which in turn causes movement of air. Heat exchanges occur constantly, e.g., melting, cooling, updrafts, downdrafts, wind, etc.

    Answer (A) is incorrect. Movement of air is a result of heat exchange. Answer (B) is incorrect. Pressure differential is a result of heat exchange.

16. What causes variations in altimeter settings between weather reporting points?

    A. Unequal heating of the Earth's surface.

    B. Variation of terrain elevation.

    C. Coriolis force.

Answer (A) is correct. *(AvW Chap 3)*

    DISCUSSION: Unequal heating of the Earth's surface causes differences in air pressure, which is reflected in differences in altimeter settings between weather reporting points.

    Answer (B) is incorrect. Variations in altimeter settings between stations is a result of unequal heating of the Earth's surface, not variations of terrain elevations. Answer (C) is incorrect. Variations in altimeter settings between stations is a result of unequal heating of the Earth's surface, not the Coriolis force.

17. The wind at 5,000 feet AGL is southwesterly while the surface wind is southerly. This difference in direction is primarily due to

    A. stronger pressure gradient at higher altitudes.

    B. friction between the wind and the surface.

    C. stronger Coriolis force at the surface.

Answer (B) is correct. *(AvW Chap 4)*

    DISCUSSION: Winds aloft at 5,000 ft. are largely affected by Coriolis force, which deflects wind to the right, in the Northern Hemisphere. But at the surface, the winds will be more southerly (they were southwesterly aloft) because Coriolis force has less effect at the surface where the wind speed is slower. The wind speed is slower at the surface due to the friction between the wind and the surface.

    Answer (A) is incorrect. Pressure gradient is a force that causes wind, not the reason for wind direction differences. Answer (C) is incorrect. The Coriolis force at the surface is weaker (not stronger) with slower wind speed.

18. The development of thermals depends upon

    A. a counterclockwise circulation of air.

    B. temperature inversions.

    C. solar heating.

Answer (C) is correct. *(AvW Chap 4)*
    DISCUSSION: Thermals are updrafts in small-scale convective currents. Convective currents are caused by uneven heating of the Earth's surface. Solar heating is the means of heating the Earth's surface.
    Answer (A) is incorrect. A counterclockwise circulation describes an area of low pressure in the Northern Hemisphere. Answer (B) is incorrect. A temperature inversion is an increase in temperature with height, which hinders the development of thermals.

19. Convective circulation patterns associated with sea breezes are caused by

    A. warm, dense air moving inland from over the water.

    B. water absorbing and radiating heat faster than the land.

    C. cool, dense air moving inland from over the water.

Answer (C) is correct. *(AvW Chap 4)*
    DISCUSSION: Sea breezes are caused by cool and more dense air moving inland off the water. Once over the warmer land, the air heats up and rises. Thus the cooler, more dense air from the sea forces the warmer air up. Currents push the hot air over the water where it cools and descends, starting the cycle over again. This process is caused by land heating faster than water.
    Answer (A) is incorrect. The air over the water is cooler (not warmer). Answer (B) is incorrect. Water absorbs and radiates heat slower (not faster) than land.

20. The boundary between two different air masses is referred to as a

    A. frontolysis.

    B. frontogenesis.

    C. front.

Answer (C) is correct. *(AvW Chap 8)*
    DISCUSSION: A front is a surface, interface, or transition zone of discontinuity between two adjacent air masses of different densities. It is the boundary between two different air masses.
    Answer (A) is incorrect. Frontolysis is the dissipation of a front. Answer (B) is incorrect. Frontogenesis is the initial formation of a front or frontal zone.

21. One weather phenomenon which will always occur when flying across a front is a change in the

    A. wind direction.

    B. type of precipitation.

    C. stability of the air mass.

Answer (A) is correct. *(AvW Chap 8)*
    DISCUSSION: The definition of a front is the zone of transition between two air masses of different air pressure or density, e.g., the area separating high and low pressure systems. Due to the difference in changes in pressure systems, there will be a change in wind.
    Answer (B) is incorrect. Frequently, precipitation will exist or not exist for both sides of the front: rain showers before and after or no precipitation before and after a dry front. Answer (C) is incorrect. Fronts separate air masses with different pressures, not stabilities; e.g., both air masses could be either stable or unstable.

22. One of the most easily recognized discontinuities across a front is

    A. a change in temperature.

    B. an increase in cloud coverage.

    C. an increase in relative humidity.

Answer (A) is correct. *(AvW Chap 8)*
    DISCUSSION: Of the many changes that take place across a front, the most easily recognized is the change in temperature. When flying through a front, you will notice a significant change in temperature, especially at low altitudes.
    Answer (B) is incorrect. Although cloud formations may indicate a frontal system, they may not be present or easily recognized across the front. Answer (C) is incorrect. Precipitation is not always associated with a front.

23. If there is thunderstorm activity in the vicinity of an airport at which you plan to land, which hazardous atmospheric phenomenon might be expected on the landing approach?

    A. Precipitation static.

    B. Wind-shear turbulence.

    C. Steady rain.

Answer (B) is correct. *(AvW Chap 11)*
    DISCUSSION: The most hazardous atmospheric phenomenon near thunderstorms is wind shear turbulence.
    Answer (A) is incorrect. Precipitation static is a steady, high level of noise in radio receivers, which is caused by intense corona discharges from sharp metallic points and edges of flying aircraft. This discharge may be seen at night and is also called St. Elmo's fire. Answer (C) is incorrect. Thunderstorms are usually associated with unstable air, which would produce rain showers (not steady rain).

24. A nonfrontal, narrow band of active thunderstorms that often develop ahead of a cold front is known as a

    A. prefrontal system.

    B. squall line.

    C. dry line.

Answer (B) is correct. *(AvW Chap 11)*
    DISCUSSION: A nonfrontal, narrow band of active thunderstorms that often develops ahead of a cold front is known as a squall line.
    Answer (A) is incorrect. A prefrontal system is a term that has no meaning. Answer (C) is incorrect. A dry line is a front that seldom has any significant air mass contrast except for moisture.

25. What conditions are necessary for the formation of thunderstorms?

    A. High humidity, lifting force, and unstable conditions.

    B. High humidity, high temperature, and cumulus clouds.

    C. Lifting force, moist air, and extensive cloud cover.

Answer (A) is correct. *(AvW Chap 11)*
    DISCUSSION: Thunderstorms form when there is sufficient water vapor, an unstable lapse rate, and an initial upward boost (lifting) to start the storm process.
    Answer (B) is incorrect. A high temperature is not required for the formation of thunderstorms. Answer (C) is incorrect. Extensive cloud cover is not necessary for the formation of thunderstorms.

26. During the life cycle of a thunderstorm, which stage is characterized predominately by downdrafts?

    A. Cumulus.

    B. Dissipating.

    C. Mature.

Answer (B) is correct. *(AvW Chap 11)*
    DISCUSSION: Thunderstorms have three life cycles: cumulus, mature, and dissipating. It is in the dissipating stage that the storm is characterized by downdrafts as the storm rains itself out.
    Answer (A) is incorrect. Cumulus is the building stage when there are updrafts. Answer (C) is incorrect. The mature stage is when there are both updrafts and downdrafts, which create dangerous wind shears.

27. Thunderstorms reach their greatest intensity during the

    A. mature stage.

    B. downdraft stage.

    C. cumulus stage.

Answer (A) is correct. *(AvW Chap 11)*
    DISCUSSION: Thunderstorms reach their greatest intensity during the mature stage, where updrafts and downdrafts cause a high level of wind shear.
    Answer (B) is incorrect. The downdraft stage is known as the dissipating stage, which is when the thunderstorm rains itself out. Answer (C) is incorrect. The cumulus stage is characterized by continuous updrafts and is not the most intense stage of a thunderstorm.

28. What feature is normally associated with the cumulus stage of a thunderstorm?

    A. Roll cloud.

    B. Continuous updraft.

    C. Frequent lightning.

Answer (B) is correct. *(AvW Chap 11)*
    DISCUSSION: The cumulus stage of a thunderstorm has continuous updrafts that build the storm. The water droplets are carried up until they become too heavy. Once they begin falling and creating downdrafts, the storm changes from the cumulus to the mature stage.
    Answer (A) is incorrect. The roll cloud is the cloud on the ground, which is formed by the downrushing cold air pushing out from underneath the bottom of the thunderstorm. Answer (C) is incorrect. Frequent lightning is associated with the mature stage, where there is a considerable amount of wind shear and static electricity.

29. Which weather phenomenon signals the beginning of the mature stage of a thunderstorm?

    A. The appearance of an anvil top.

    B. Precipitation beginning to fall.

    C. Maximum growth rate of the clouds.

Answer (B) is correct. *(AvW Chap 11)*
    DISCUSSION: The mature stage of a thunderstorm begins when rain begins falling. This means that the downdrafts are occurring sufficiently to carry water all the way through the thunderstorm.
    Answer (A) is incorrect. The appearance of an anvil top normally occurs during the dissipating stage when the upper winds blow the top of the cloud downwind. Answer (C) is incorrect. The maximum growth rate of clouds is later in the mature stage and does not necessarily mark the start of the mature stage.

30. Which weather phenomenon is always associated with a thunderstorm?

    A. Lightning.

    B. Heavy rain.

    C. Hail.

Answer (A) is correct. *(AvW Chap 11)*
    DISCUSSION: A thunderstorm, by definition, has lightning because lightning causes the thunder.
    Answer (B) is incorrect. Although heavy rain showers usually occur, hail may occur instead. Answer (C) is incorrect. Hail is produced only when the lifting action extends above the freezing level and the supercooled water begins to freeze.

31. One in-flight condition necessary for structural icing to form is

    A. small temperature/dewpoint spread.

    B. stratiform clouds.

    C. visible moisture.

Answer (C) is correct. *(AvW Chap 10)*
    DISCUSSION: Two conditions are necessary for structural icing while in flight. First, the airplane must be flying through visible moisture, such as rain or cloud droplets. Second, the temperature at the point where the moisture strikes the airplane must be freezing or below.
    Answer (A) is incorrect. The temperature dew point spread is not a factor in icing as it is in the formation of fog or clouds. Answer (B) is incorrect. No special cloud formation is necessary for icing as long as visible moisture is present.

32. In which environment is aircraft structural ice most likely to have the highest accumulation rate?

    A. Cumulus clouds with below freezing temperatures.

    B. Freezing drizzle.

    C. Freezing rain.

Answer (C) is correct. *(AvW Chap 10)*
    DISCUSSION: Freezing rain usually causes the highest accumulation rate of structural icing because of the nature of the supercooled water striking the airplane.
    Answer (A) is incorrect. While icing potential is great in cumulus clouds with below freezing temperatures, the highest accumulation rate is in an area with large, supercooled water drops (i.e., freezing rain). Answer (B) is incorrect. Freezing drizzle will not build up ice as quickly as freezing rain.

33. The presence of ice pellets at the surface is evidence that there

    A. are thunderstorms in the area.

    B. has been cold frontal passage.

    C. is a temperature inversion with freezing rain at a higher altitude.

Answer (C) is correct. *(AvW Chap 5)*
    DISCUSSION: Rain falling through colder air may freeze during its descent, falling as ice pellets. Ice pellets always indicate freezing rain at a higher altitude.
    Answer (A) is incorrect. Ice pellets form when rain freezes during its descent, which may or may not be as a result of a thunderstorm. Answer (B) is incorrect. Ice pellets only indicate that rain is freezing at a higher altitude, not that a cold front has passed through an area.

34. Where does wind shear occur?

    A. Only at higher altitudes.

    B. Only at lower altitudes.

    C. At all altitudes, in all directions.

Answer (C) is correct. *(AvW Chap 9)*
    DISCUSSION: Wind shear is the eddies in between two wind currents of differing velocities, direction, or both. Wind shear may be associated with either a wind shift or a wind speed gradient at any level in the atmosphere.
    Answer (A) is incorrect. A wind shear may occur at any (not only higher) altitudes. Answer (B) is incorrect. A wind shear may occur at any (not only lower) altitudes.

35. When may hazardous wind shear be expected?

    A. When stable air crosses a mountain barrier where it tends to flow in layers forming lenticular clouds.

    B. In areas of low-level temperature inversion, frontal zones, and clear air turbulence.

    C. Following frontal passage when stratocumulus clouds form indicating mechanical mixing.

Answer (B) is correct. *(AvW Chap 9)*
    DISCUSSION: Wind shear is the abrupt rate of change of wind velocity (direction and/or speed) per unit of distance and is normally expressed as vertical or horizontal wind shear. Hazardous wind shear may be expected in areas of low-level temperature inversion, frontal zones, and clear air turbulence.
    Answer (A) is incorrect. A mountain wave forms when stable air crosses a mountain barrier where it tends to flow in layers forming lenticular clouds. Turbulence, not wind shear, is expected in this area. Answer (C) is incorrect. Mechanical turbulence (not wind shear) may be expected following frontal passage when clouds form, indicating mechanical mixing.

36. If the temperature/dewpoint spread is small and decreasing, and the temperature is 62°F, what type weather is most likely to develop?

   A. Freezing precipitation.

   B. Thunderstorms.

   C. Fog or low clouds.

Answer (C) is correct. *(AvW Chap 5)*
   DISCUSSION: The difference between the air temperature and dew point is the temperature/dew point spread. As the temperature/dew point spread decreases, fog or low clouds tend to develop.
   Answer (A) is incorrect. There cannot be freezing precipitation if the temperature is 62°F. Answer (B) is incorrect. Thunderstorms have to do with unstable lapse rates, not temperature/dew point spreads.

37. What is meant by the term "dewpoint"?

   A. The temperature at which condensation and evaporation are equal.

   B. The temperature at which dew will always form.

   C. The temperature to which air must be cooled to become saturated.

Answer (C) is correct. *(AvW Chap 5)*
   DISCUSSION: Dew point is the temperature to which air must be cooled to become saturated or have 100% humidity.
   Answer (A) is incorrect. Evaporation is the change from water to water vapor and is not directly related to the dew point. Answer (B) is incorrect. Dew forms only when heat radiates from an object whose temperature lowers below the dew point of the adjacent air.

38. The amount of water vapor which air can hold depends on the

   A. dewpoint.

   B. air temperature.

   C. stability of the air.

Answer (B) is correct. *(AvW Chap 5)*
   DISCUSSION: Air temperature largely determines how much water vapor can be held by the air. Warm air can hold more water vapor than cool air.
   Answer (A) is incorrect. Dew point is the temperature at which air must be cooled to become saturated by the water vapor already present in the air. Answer (C) is incorrect. Air stability is the state of the atmosphere at which vertical distribution of temperature is such that air particles will resist displacement from their initial level.

39. What are the processes by which moisture is added to unsaturated air?

   A. Evaporation and sublimation.

   B. Heating and condensation.

   C. Supersaturation and evaporation.

Answer (A) is correct. *(AvW Chap 5)*
   DISCUSSION: Evaporation is the process of converting a liquid to water vapor, and sublimation is the process of converting ice to water vapor.
   Answer (B) is incorrect. Heating alone does not add moisture. Condensation is the change of water vapor to liquid water. Answer (C) is incorrect. Supersaturation is a nonsense term in this context.

40. Which conditions result in the formation of frost?

   A. The temperature of the collecting surface is at or below freezing when small droplets of moisture fall on the surface.

   B. The temperature of the collecting surface is at or below the dewpoint of the adjacent air and the dewpoint is below freezing.

   C. The temperature of the surrounding air is at or below freezing when small drops of moisture fall on the collecting surface.

Answer (B) is correct. *(AvW Chap 5)*
   DISCUSSION: Frost forms when both the collecting surface is below the dew point of the adjacent air and the dew point is below freezing. Frost is the deposition of water vapor to ice crystals.
   Answer (A) is incorrect. If small droplets of water fall on the collecting surface, which is at or below freezing, ice (not frost) will form. Answer (C) is incorrect. If small droplets of water fall while the surrounding air is at or below freezing, ice (not frost) will form.

41. Clouds, fog, or dew will always form when

   A. water vapor condenses.

   B. water vapor is present.

   C. relative humidity reaches 100 percent.

Answer (A) is correct. *(AvW Chap 5)*
   DISCUSSION: As water vapor condenses, it becomes visible as clouds, fog, or dew.
   Answer (B) is incorrect. Water vapor is usually always present but does not form clouds, fog, or dew without condensation. Answer (C) is incorrect. Even at 100% humidity, water vapor may not condense, e.g., sufficient condensation nuclei may not be present.

42. Low-level turbulence can occur and icing can become hazardous in which type of fog?

    A. Rain-induced fog.

    B. Upslope fog.

    C. Steam fog.

Answer (C) is correct. *(AvW Chap 14)*
    DISCUSSION: Steam fog forms in winter when cold, dry air passes from land areas over comparatively warm ocean waters and is composed entirely of water droplets that often freeze quickly. Low-level turbulence can occur, and icing can become hazardous.
    Answer (A) is incorrect. Precipitation- (rain-) induced fog is formed when relatively warm rain or drizzle falls through cool air and evaporation from the precipitation saturates the cool air and forms fog. While the hazards of turbulence and icing may occur in the proximity of rain-induced fog, these hazards occur as a result of the steam fog formation process. Answer (B) is incorrect. Upslope fog forms when moist, stable air is cooled as it moves up sloping terrain.

43. In which situation is advection fog most likely to form?

    A. A warm, moist air mass on the windward side of mountains.

    B. An air mass moving inland from the coast in winter.

    C. A light breeze blowing colder air out to sea.

Answer (B) is correct. *(AvW Chap 12)*
    DISCUSSION: Advection fog forms when moist air moves over colder ground or water. It is most common in coastal areas.
    Answer (A) is incorrect. A warm, moist air mass on the windward side of mountains produces rain or upslope fog as it blows upward and cools. Answer (C) is incorrect. A light breeze blowing colder air out to sea causes steam fog.

44. What situation is most conducive to the formation of radiation fog?

    A. Warm, moist air over low, flatland areas on clear, calm nights.

    B. Moist, tropical air moving over cold, offshore water.

    C. The movement of cold air over much warmer water.

Answer (A) is correct. *(AvW Chap 12)*
    DISCUSSION: Radiation fog is shallow fog of which ground fog is one form. It occurs under conditions of clear skies, little or no wind, and a small temperature/dew point spread. The fog forms almost exclusively at night or near dawn as a result of terrestrial radiation cooling the ground and the ground cooling the air on contact with it.
    Answer (B) is incorrect. Moist, tropical air moving over cold, offshore water causes advection fog, not radiation fog. Answer (C) is incorrect. Movement of cold, dry air over much warmer water results in steam fog.

45. What types of fog depend upon wind in order to exist?

    A. Radiation fog and ice fog.

    B. Steam fog and ground fog.

    C. Advection fog and upslope fog.

Answer (C) is correct. *(AvW Chap 14)*
    DISCUSSION: Advection fog forms when moist air moves over colder ground or water. It is most common in coastal areas. Upslope fog forms when wind blows moist air upward over rising terrain and the air cools below its dew point. Both advection fog and upslope fog require wind to move air masses.
    Answer (A) is incorrect. No wind is required for the formation of either radiation (ground) or ice fog. Answer (B) is incorrect. No wind is required for the formation of ground (radiation) fog.

46. The suffix "nimbus," used in naming clouds, means

    A. a cloud with extensive vertical development.

    B. a rain cloud.

    C. a middle cloud containing ice pellets.

Answer (B) is correct. *(AvW Chap 7)*
    DISCUSSION: The suffix "nimbus" or the prefix "nimbo" means a rain cloud.
    Answer (A) is incorrect. Clouds with extensive vertical development are called either towering cumulus or cumulonimbus. Answer (C) is incorrect. A middle cloud has the prefix "alto."

47. The conditions necessary for the formation of cumulonimbus clouds are a lifting action and

    A. unstable air containing an excess of condensation nuclei.

    B. unstable, moist air.

    C. either stable or unstable air.

Answer (B) is correct. *(AvW Chap 11)*
    DISCUSSION: Unstable, moist air, in addition to a lifting action, i.e., convective activity, is needed to form cumulonimbus clouds.
    Answer (A) is incorrect. There must be moisture available to produce the clouds and rain; e.g., in a hot, dry dust storm, there would be no thunderstorm. Answer (C) is incorrect. The air must be unstable or there will be no lifting action.

48. What clouds have the greatest turbulence?

   A. Towering cumulus.

   B. Cumulonimbus.

   C. Nimbostratus.

Answer (B) is correct. *(AvW Chap 7)*
   DISCUSSION: The greatest turbulence occurs in cumulonimbus clouds, which are thunderstorm clouds.
   Answer (A) is incorrect. Towering cumulus clouds are an earlier stage of cumulonimbus clouds. Answer (C) is incorrect. Nimbostratus is a gray or dark, massive cloud layer diffused by continuous rain or ice pellets. It is a middle cloud with very little turbulence but may pose serious icing problems.

49. What cloud types would indicate convective turbulence?

   A. Cirrus clouds.

   B. Nimbostratus clouds.

   C. Towering cumulus clouds.

Answer (C) is correct. *(AvW Chap 7)*
   DISCUSSION: Towering cumulus clouds are an early stage of cumulonimbus clouds, or thunderstorms, that are based on convective turbulence, i.e., an unstable lapse rate.
   Answer (A) is incorrect. Cirrus clouds are high, thin, featherlike ice crystal clouds in patches and narrow bands that are not based on any convective activity. Answer (B) is incorrect. Nimbostratus are gray or dark, massive clouds diffused by continuous rain or ice pellets with very little turbulence.

50. What is a characteristic of stable air?

   A. Stratiform clouds.

   B. Unlimited visibility.

   C. Cumulus clouds.

Answer (A) is correct. *(AvW Chap 8)*
   DISCUSSION: Characteristics of a stable air mass include stratiform clouds, continuous precipitation, smooth air, and fair to poor visibility in haze and smoke.
   Answer (B) is incorrect. Restricted, not unlimited, visibility is an indication of stable air. Answer (C) is incorrect. Fair weather cumulus clouds indicate unstable conditions, not stable conditions.

51. What are characteristics of unstable air?

   A. Turbulence and good surface visibility.

   B. Turbulence and poor surface visibility.

   C. Nimbostratus clouds and good surface visibility.

Answer (A) is correct. *(AvW Chap 8)*
   DISCUSSION: Characteristics of an unstable air mass include cumuliform clouds, showery precipitation, turbulence, and good visibility, except in blowing obstructions.
   Answer (B) is incorrect. Poor surface visibility is a characteristic of stable (not unstable) air. Answer (C) is incorrect. Stratus clouds are characteristic of stable (not unstable) air.

52. A stable air mass is most likely to have which characteristic?

   A. Showery precipitation.

   B. Turbulent air.

   C. Poor surface visibility.

Answer (C) is correct. *(AvW Chap 8)*
   DISCUSSION: Characteristics of a stable air mass include stratiform clouds and fog, continuous precipitation, smooth air, and fair to poor visibility in haze and smoke.
   Answer (A) is incorrect. Showery precipitation is a characteristic of an unstable (not stable) air mass. Answer (B) is incorrect. Turbulent air is a characteristic of an unstable (not stable) air mass.

53. What are characteristics of a moist, unstable air mass?

   A. Cumuliform clouds and showery precipitation.

   B. Poor visibility and smooth air.

   C. Stratiform clouds and showery precipitation.

Answer (A) is correct. *(AvW Chap 8)*
   DISCUSSION: Characteristics of an unstable air mass include cumuliform clouds, showery precipitation, turbulence, and good visibility, except in blowing obstructions.
   Answer (B) is incorrect. Poor visibility and smooth air are characteristics of stable (not unstable) air. Answer (C) is incorrect. Stratiform clouds and continuous precipitation are characteristics of stable (not unstable) air.

54. What measurement can be used to determine the stability of the atmosphere?

A. Atmospheric pressure.

B. Actual lapse rate.

C. Surface temperature.

Answer (B) is correct. *(AvW Chap 6)*
DISCUSSION: The stability of the atmosphere is determined by vertical movements of air. Warm air rises when the air above is cooler. The actual lapse rate, which is the decrease of temperature with altitude, is therefore a measure of stability.
Answer (A) is incorrect. Atmospheric pressure is the pressure exerted by the atmosphere as a consequence of gravitational attraction exerted upon the "column" of air lying directly above the point in question. It cannot be used to determine stability. Answer (C) is incorrect. While the surface temperature may have some effect on temperature changes and air movements, it is the actual lapse rate that determines the stability of the atmosphere.

55. What would decrease the stability of an air mass?

A. Warming from below.

B. Cooling from below.

C. Decrease in water vapor.

Answer (A) is correct. *(AvW Chap 6)*
DISCUSSION: When air is warmed from below, even though cooling adiabatically, it remains warmer than the surrounding air. The colder, more dense surrounding air forces the warmer air upward, and an unstable condition develops.
Answer (B) is incorrect. Cooling from below means the surrounding air is warmer, which would increase (not decrease) the stability of an air mass. Answer (C) is incorrect. As water vapor in air decreases, the air mass tends to increase (not decrease) stability.

56. What are characteristics of a moist, unstable air mass?

A. Turbulence and showery precipitation.

B. Poor visibility and smooth air.

C. Haze and smoke.

Answer (A) is correct. *(AC 00-6)*
DISCUSSION: Characteristics of an unstable air mass include cumuliform clouds, showery precipitation, turbulence, and good visibility, except in blowing obstructions.
Answer (B) is incorrect. Poor visibility and smooth air are characteristics of stable (not unstable) air. Answer (C) is incorrect. Haze and smoke are characteristics of stable (not unstable) air.

57. What are the characteristics of stable air?

A. Good visibility and steady precipitation.

B. Poor visibility and steady precipitation.

C. Poor visibility and intermittent precipitation.

Answer (B) is correct. *(PHAK Chap 12)*
DISCUSSION: Characteristics of a stable air mass include stratiform clouds, continuous precipitation, smooth air, and fair to poor visibility in haze and smoke
Answer (A) is incorrect. Good visibility is a characteristic of unstable (not stable) air. Answer (C) is incorrect. Intermittent precipitation is a characteristic of unstable (not stable) air.

58. Which of the following considerations is more relevant to a Remote PIC when evaluating unmanned aircraft performance?

A. Current weather conditions.

B. The number of available ground crew.

C. The type of the sUAS operation.

Answer (A) is correct. *(PHAK Chap 11)*
DISCUSSION: Even though sUAS operations are often conducted at very low altitudes, weather factors can greatly influence performance and safety of flight. As with any flight, the Remote PIC should check and consider the weather conditions prior to and during every sUAS flight.
Answer (B) is incorrect. The number of available ground crew is not relevant to the evaluating performance. Answer (C) is incorrect. Weather conditions, not the type of sUAS operation, is the most relevant factor affecting performance.

59. While operating around buildings, the Remote Pilot in Command should be aware of the creation of wind gusts that

A. increase performance of an aircraft.

B. change rapidly in direction and speed causing turbulence.

C. enhance stability and imagery.

Answer (B) is correct. *(sUASSG Chap 3)*
DISCUSSION: Wind and currents can affect sUAS performance and maneuverability during all phases of flight. Be vigilant when operating sUAS at low altitudes, in confined areas, near buildings or other man-made structures, and near natural obstructions (such as mountains, bluffs, or canyons).
Answer (A) is incorrect. Wind gusts require more extensive control inputs to counter its effects. This decreases performance and maneuverability. Answer (C) is incorrect. Rapidly changing wind gusts can be an unseen danger causing significant low-level turbulence that adversely affects stability and imagery.

STUDY UNIT FIVE
LOADING AND PERFORMANCE

(8 pages of outline)

5.1 LOADING AND PERFORMANCE

1.   **The applicant demonstrates understanding of general loading and performance.**

   a.   **Effects of Loading Changes**

   1)   As with any aircraft, compliance with weight and balance limits is critical to the safety of flight for sUAS. An unmanned aircraft that is loaded out of balance may exhibit unexpected and unsafe flight characteristics.

   2)   Before any flight, verify that the unmanned aircraft is correctly loaded by determining the weight and balance condition.

   3)   An aircraft's weight and balance restrictions established by the manufacturer or the builder should be closely followed.

   a)   Compliance with the manufacturer's weight and balance limits is critical to flight safety. The remote PIC must consider the consequences of an overweight aircraft if an emergency condition arises.

   4)   Although a maximum gross takeoff weight may be specified, the aircraft may not always safely take off with this load under all conditions.

   a)   Conditions that affect takeoff and climb performance, such as high elevations, high air temperatures, and high humidity (high density altitudes), may require a reduction in weight before flight is attempted.

   b)   Other factors to consider prior to takeoff are runway/launch area length, surface, slope, surface wind, and the presence of obstacles. These factors may require a reduction in weight prior to flight.

   5)   Weight changes during flight also have a direct effect on aircraft performance.

   a)   Fuel burn is the most common weight change during flight. As fuel is used, the aircraft becomes lighter and performance is improved, but this could have a negative effect on balance.

   b)   In UAS operations, weight change during flight may occur when expendable items are used on board (e.g., a jettisonable load).

   b.   **Balance, Stability, and Center of Gravity (CG)**

   1)   Adverse balance conditions (i.e., weight distribution) may affect flight characteristics in much the same manner as excess weight conditions.

   2)   Review any available manufacturer weight and balance data and follow all restrictions and limitations.

   a)   The CG is a point at which the unmanned aircraft would balance if it were suspended at that point.

   b)   The CG is not a fixed point marked on the aircraft; its location depends on the distribution of aircraft weight.

   c)   As variable load items are shifted or expended, there may be a resultant shift in CG location.

   d)   The remote PIC should determine how the CG will shift and the resultant effects on the aircraft.

   e)   If the CG is not within the allowable limits after loading or does not remain within the allowable limits for safe flight, it will be necessary to relocate or shed some weight before flight is attempted.

3)   If the manufacturer does not provide specific weight and balance data, apply general weight and balance principals to determine limits for a given flight.

a)   For example, add weight to the unmanned aircraft in a manner that does not adversely affect the aircraft's CG location.

c.   **Stalls**

1)   A stall is a loss of lift and an increase in drag occurring when an aircraft is flown at an angle of attack greater than the angle for maximum lift. The angle of attack for maximum lift is also called the critical angle of attack.

a)   Thus, a stall occurs whenever the critical angle of attack is exceeded.

2)   To understand the stall phenomenon, some basic factors affecting aerodynamics and flight should be reviewed with particular emphasis on their relation to stall speeds. The stall speed is the speed at which the critical angle of attack is exceeded.

a)   When the angle of attack is increased to approximately 18° to 20° on most airfoils, the airstream can no longer follow the upper curvature of the wing because of the excessive change in direction. This is the critical angle of attack.

i)   As the critical angle of attack is approached, the airstream begins separating from the rear of the upper wing surface. As the angle of attack is further increased, the airstream is forced to flow straight back, away from the top surface of the wing and from the area of highest camber. See the figure on the following page.

ii)   This causes a swirling or burbling of the air as it attempts to follow the upper surface of the wing. When the critical angle of attack is reached, the turbulent airflow, which appeared near the trailing edge of the wing at lower angles of attack, quickly spreads forward over the entire upper wing surface.

iii)   This results in a sudden increase in pressure on the upper wing surface and a considerable loss of lift. Due to both this loss of lift and the increase in form drag (a larger area of the wing and fuselage is exposed to the airstream), the remaining lift is insufficient to support the airplane, and the wing stalls.

iv)   To recover from a stall, the angle of attack must be decreased so that the airstream can once again flow smoothly over the wing surface.

• Remember that the angle of attack is the angle between the chord line and the relative wind, not between the chord line and the horizon.

• An airplane can be stalled in any attitude of flight with respect to the horizon, at any airspeed, and at any power setting, if the critical angle of attack is exceeded.

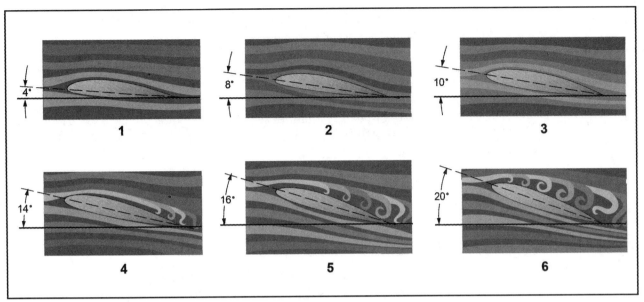

Airflow at various angles of attack.

2. **The applicant demonstrates understanding of the importance and use of performance data to predict the effect on the aircraft's performance of an sUAS.**

    a. Although a maximum gross takeoff weight is normally specified for a given unmanned aircraft, the aircraft may not be able to launch with this load under all conditions.

        1) Or if it does become airborne, the unmanned aircraft may exhibit unexpected and unusually poor flight characteristics.

    b. Gross weight of an aircraft is the empty weight of the aircraft (sUAS), plus the weight of any fuel, batteries, and payload, i.e., the aircraft and everything it is carrying.

        1) Payload usually refers to the weight of optional components or accessories carried by the sUAS that are not required for flight.

            a) Examples of payload equipment may include electro-optical equipment, mounting hardware, and electronics such as

                i) Camera(s) and associated controls, gimbals, and equipment
                ii) Direct mapping equipment, such as LIDAR
                iii) Georeferencing equipment
                iv) See and avoid sensors
                v) Optional batteries
                vi) Data link systems (nonessential)

        2) The empty weight provided for an sUAS may or may not include the weight of the battery or fuel source.

            a) The empty weight will be provided by the manufacturer in the operating handbook or flight manual.

            b) Verify which components are included in the empty weight by studying the notes in the manufacturer's manuals and by weighing the sUAS.

3) Factors that may require a reduction in weight prior to flight include:

    a) High density altitude conditions

        i) High elevations.

        ii) High air temperatures.

        iii) High humidity.

        iv) At higher density altitudes, air density actually decreases. Air that is less dense has fewer air molecules and decreases performance.

    b) Runway/launch area length

    c) Surface

    d) Slope

    e) Surface wind

    f) Presence of obstacles

c. Common Performance Deficiencies of Overloaded Aircraft

1) Excessive weight reduces the flight performance in almost every respect. In addition, operating above the maximum weight limitation can compromise the structural integrity of an unmanned aircraft.

2) The most common performance deficiencies of an overloaded aircraft are

    a) Reduced rate of climb

    b) Lower maximum altitude

    c) Shorter endurance

    d) Reduced maneuverability

d. Effects of Weight Changes

1) Weight changes have a direct effect on aircraft performance.

2) Fuel burn is the most common weight change that takes place during flight.

3) For battery-powered unmanned aircraft, weight change during flight may occur when expendable items are used on board (e.g., agricultural use).

    a) Changes of mounted equipment between flights, such as the installation of cameras, battery packs, or other instruments, may also affect the weight and balance and performance of an sUAS.

e. Effects of Load Factor

1) Load factor is the ratio of the amount of lift generated to the weight of the aircraft.

    a) In a level turn, the wings must produce additional lift because both a vertical and horizontal component of lift is being generated by the wings.

2) Unmanned airplane performance can be decreased due to an increase in load factor when the airplane is operated in maneuvers other than straight-and-level flight.

3) The load factor increases at a terrific rate after a bank has reached 45° or 50°.

    a) The load factor for any aircraft in a coordinated level turn at 60° bank is 2 Gs.

    b) The load factor in an 80° bank is 5.76 Gs.

    c) The wing must produce lift equal to these load factors if altitude is to be maintained.

4) The remote PIC should be mindful of the increased load factor and its possible effects on the aircraft's structural integrity and the results of an increase in stall speed.

   a) As with manned aircraft, an unmanned airplane will stall when critical angle of attack is exceeded.

      i) Due to the low altitude operating environment, consideration should be given to ensure aircraft control is maintained and the aircraft is not operated outside its performance limits.

5) A load factor chart like the one below is given with the amount of bank on the horizontal axis (along the bottom of the graph), and the load factor on the vertical axis (up the left side of the graph). Additionally, a table that provides the load factor corresponding to specific bank angles is found on the left side of the chart. Use this table to answer load factor questions.

   a) Compute the load factor by multiplying the airplane's weight by the load factor that corresponds to the given angle of bank. For example, the wings of a 33-lb. airplane in a 60° bank must support 66 lb. (33 lb. × 2.000).

   b) Example load factor chart:

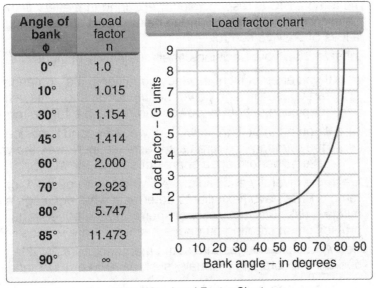

Figure 2. – Load Factor Chart.

f. Performance or operational information may be provided by the manufacturer in the form of an Aircraft Flight Manual (AFM), Pilot's Operating Handbook (POH), or owner's manual. Follow all manufacturer recommendations for evaluating performance to ensure safe and efficient operation.

1) These charts usually require cross-referencing two or more variables to determine allowable gross weight.

2) For example, cross reference a given pressure altitude with a known temperature to determine the maximum weight limitation.

   a) Performance tables usually list limitations according to specific temperature or altitude increments, e.g., 0°C, 10°C, 20°C, 30°C, etc. and S.L. (sea level), 1000', 2000', 3000, etc.

b) Performance limitations can be estimated by using the increments closest to actual conditions but should be interpolated when exact limitations must be known.

   i) EXAMPLE: If the temperature is 25°C, the limitation would be halfway between the limits listed for 20°C and 30°C.

c) Pay attention to the unit of measurement. If the temperature on the performance charts is listed in Celsius, but the known temperature for your area is reported in Fahrenheit, you will need to convert.

d) Remember to convert the altitude above sea level to pressure altitude by using the pressure altitude conversion factor on the density altitude chart in Study Unit 4, "Weather Effects on Performance."

   i) You will also need to know the local altimeter setting for this conversion.

   ii) This is obtained from a nearby aviation routine weather report (METAR).

g. Even when specific performance data is not provided, the remote PIC should be familiar with the operating environment and all available information regarding the safe and recommended operation of the sUAS.

   1) The remote PIC is responsible for ensuring that every flight can be accomplished safely, does not pose an undue hazard, and does not increase the likelihood of a loss of positive control.

   2) Consider how your decisions affect the safety of flight.

      a) If you attempt flight in windy conditions, the unmanned aircraft may require an unusually high power setting to ascend. This action may cause a rapid depletion of battery power and result in a failure mode.

      b) If you attempt flight in wintery weather conditions, ice may accumulate on the unmanned aircraft's surface. Ice increases the weight and adversely affects performance characteristics of the sUAS.

   3) Due to the diversity and rapidly-evolving nature of sUAS operations, individual remote PICs have flexibility to determine what equipage methods, if any, mitigate risk sufficiently to meet performance-based requirements, such as the prohibition on creating an undue hazard if there is a loss of aircraft control.

   4) The FAA acknowledges that some manufacturers provide comprehensive operational data and manuals, such as AFM or POH, and others do not.

      a) When operational data is provided, follow the manufacturer's instructions and recommendations.

         i) The chart below shows the effect of higher density altitude on allowable gross weight for the Freefly Alta 8.

         ii) EXAMPLE: At sea level, 10 degrees C, the allowable gross weight is 40.0 lbs. At a 10,000 ft. pressure altitude and 30 degrees C, the allowable gross weight is 26.1 lbs., a 35% decrease in performance.

Press Alt Ft	0°C		10°C		20°C		30°C		40°C	
	Maximum Gross Weight (lb)	Maximum Gross Weight (kg)	Maximum Gross Weight (lb)	Maximum Gross Weight (kg)	Maximum Gross Weight (lb)	Maximum Gross Weight (kg)	Maximum Gross Weight (lb)	Maximum Gross Weight (kg)	Maximum Gross Weight (lb)	Maximum Gross Weight (kg)
S.L.	40.0	18.1	40.0	18.1	39.3	17.8	38.0	17.2	36.8	16.7
1000	40.0	18.1	39.3	17.8	37.9	17.2	36.7	16.6	35.5	16.1
2000	39.2	17.8	37.8	17.2	36.6	16.6	35.4	16.0	34.2	15.5
3000	37.8	17.2	36.5	16.5	35.2	16.0	34.1	15.5	33.0	15.0
4000	36.4	16.5	35.2	15.9	34.0	15.4	32.8	14.9	31.8	14.4
5000	35.1	15.9	33.9	15.4	32.7	14.8	31.6	14.3	30.6	13.9
6000	33.8	15.3	32.6	14.8	31.5	14.3	30.5	13.8	29.5	13.4
7000	32.6	14.8	31.4	14.2	30.3	13.8	29.3	13.3	28.4	12.9
8000	31.3	14.2	30.2	13.7	29.2	13.2	28.2	12.8	27.3	12.4
9000	30.2	13.7	29.1	13.2	28.1	12.7	27.2	12.3	26.3	11.9
10000	29.0	13.2	28.0	12.7	27.0	12.3	26.1	11.9	25.3	11.5

This chart is from an Alta 8 and was used with permission from Freefly Systems.

    b)   Even when operational data is not supplied by the manufacturer, the remote PIC can better understand the unmanned aircraft's capabilities and limitations by establishing a process for tracking malfunctions, defects, and flight characteristics in various environments and conditions.

        i)   Use this operational data to establish a baseline for determining performance, reliability, and risk assessment for your particular system.

h.   Endurance is the approximate flight time before the energy source (fuel or battery power) is depleted.

    1)   Any operation or factor requiring more use of power reduces endurance times.

        a)   Factors affecting endurance include

            i)   Gross weight. A higher gross weight requires increased power settings to lift the sUAS and maneuver.

            ii)   Extensive maneuvering. Constant and abrupt control movements such as quick turns and variations in altitude require higher power consumption.

            iii)   Wind and gusty conditions require increased power settings to sustain flight. A 10-kt. wind will cause the sUAS to move with the air unless controls are inputted to counter the effects of the wind.

                •   If the mission requires extensive hovering, wind in one direction requires control inputs nearly equal forward flight at the same speed as the wind.

2) Performance tables, charts, or graphs may be given to approximate flight times versus payload.

    a) Using the performance data requires cross referencing factors such as payload and battery or fuel capacity to determine the approximate flight time for a specified period of time.

        i) Performance tables may include more than one variable for battery capacity. For comparison, a 16Ah battery lasts longer than a 10Ah battery.

        ii) The chart below shows the effect carrying a heavier payload has on endurance for the Freefly Alta 8.

        iii) EXAMPLE: For a given sUAS make and model, a 10-lb. payload using a 16Ah battery may allow approximately 19-min. of endurance. The same 10-lb. payload using a 10Ah battery may only have a 12-min. endurance.

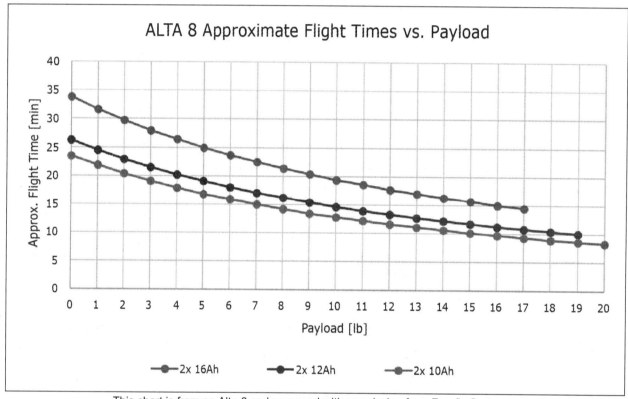

This chart is from an Alta 8 and was used with permission from Freefly Systems.

3) Ensure sufficient reserve power is available to safely operate the sUAS.

    a) As reserve power is depleted, there may not be sufficient power to perform abrupt maneuvers or return the sUAS to the home location.

    b) Voltage by itself is not adequate to determine remaining endurance.

    c) Unlike engines powered by liquid fuel, a minimum voltage is necessary to provide power to all sUAS components.

        i) EXAMPLE: A full charge of 4.2 volts for a specific sUAS may provide 100% power. The same battery at 3.7 volts might only provide 20% of the remaining usable capacity. This is only a 0.5 volt reduction but is an 80% reduction in remaining capacity.

QUESTIONS

5.1 Loading and Performance

1. To ensure that the unmanned aircraft center of gravity (CG) limits are not exceeded, follow the aircraft loading instructions specified in the

A. Pilot's Operating Handbook or UAS Flight Manual.

B. Aeronautical Information Manual (AIM).

C. Aircraft Weight and Balance Handbook.

Answer (A) is correct. *(AWBH 4-4-5)*
   DISCUSSION: Performance or operational information may be provided by the manufacturer in the form of an Aircraft Flight Manual, Pilot's Operating Handbook, or owner's manual. Follow all manufacturer recommendations for evaluating performance to ensure safe and efficient operation.
   Answer (B) is incorrect. The AIM is a guide to basic flight information and ATC procedures. Answer (C) is incorrect. The Aircraft Weight and Balance Handbook does not contain the limitations for a specific aircraft.

2. According to 14 CFR part 107, who is responsible for determining the performance of a small unmanned aircraft?

A. Remote pilot-in-command.

B. Manufacturer.

C. Owner or operator.

Answer (A) is correct. *(14 CFR 107.49)*
   DISCUSSION: Even when specific performance data is not provided, the remote PIC should be familiar with the operating environment and all available information regarding the safe and recommended operation of the sUAS.
   Answer (B) is incorrect. Manufacturers do not always provide specific performance data. Answer (C) is incorrect. The remote PIC, not the owner or operator, is responsible for determining performance. Note that the operator may refer to someone other than the remote PIC.

3. When operating an unmanned airplane, the remote pilot should consider that the load factor on the wings may be increased anytime

A. the CG is shifted rearward to the aft CG limit.

B. the airplane is subjected to maneuvers other than straight and level flight.

C. the gross weight is reduced.

Answer (B) is correct. *(PHAK Chap 5)*
   DISCUSSION: Load factor is the ratio of the amount of lift generated to the weight of the aircraft. In a level turn, the wings must produce additional lift because both a vertical and horizontal component of lift is being generated by the wings.
   Answer (A) is incorrect. An aft CG may affect the handling characteristics, not the load factor. Answer (C) is incorrect. Load factor is a ratio that is increased by maneuvers other than straight-and-level flight, not changes in weight.

4. A stall occurs when the smooth airflow over the unmanned airplane's wing is disrupted and the lift degenerates rapidly. This is caused when the wing

A. exceeds the maximum speed.

B. exceeds maximum allowable operating weight.

C. exceeds its critical angle of attack.

Answer (C) is correct. *(PHAK Chap 5)*
   DISCUSSION: A stall is a loss of lift and an increase in drag that occurs when an aircraft is flown at an angle of attack greater than the angle for maximum lift. The angle of attack for maximum lift is also called the critical angle of attack.
   Answer (A) is incorrect. Exceeding the maximum speed may cause structural damage, but the critical angle of attack must be exceeded in order to stall. Answer (B) is incorrect. Exceeding the maximum allowable operating weight may adversely affect performance, but the critical angle of attack must be exceeded in order to stall.

5. What could be a consequence of operating a small unmanned aircraft above its maximum allowable weight?

A. Faster speed.

B. Shorter endurance.

C. Increased maneuverability.

Answer (B) is correct. *(PHAK Chap 10)*
   DISCUSSION: Excessive weight reduces flight performance in almost every respect. In addition, operating above the maximum weight limitation can compromise the structural integrity of an unmanned aircraft.
   Answer (A) is incorrect. Speed will be slower when operating above the maximum allowable weight. Answer (C) is incorrect. Maneuverability will be reduced when operating above the maximum allowable weight.

6. When loading cameras or other equipment on an sUAS, mount the items in a manner that

A. is visible to the visual observer or other crewmembers.

B. does not adversely affect the center of gravity.

C. can be easily removed without the use of tools.

Answer (B) is correct. *(14 CFR 107.49)*
DISCUSSION: Adverse balance conditions (i.e., weight distribution) may affect flight characteristics in much the same manner as an excess weight condition. Weight should be added to the unmanned aircraft in a manner that does not adversely affect the aircraft's center of gravity (CG).
Answer (A) is incorrect. The entire sUAS must be visible to visual observers or other crewmembers, not necessarily external equipment. Answer (C) is incorrect. External equipment should be securely attached, but it does not need to be easily removable without the use of tools.

7. (Refer to Figure 2 below.) If an unmanned airplane weighs 33 pounds, what approximate weight would the airplane structure be required to support during a 30° banked turn while maintaining altitude?

A. 34 pounds.

B. 47 pounds.

C. 38 pounds.

Answer (C) is correct. *(PHAK Chap 5)*
DISCUSSION: Look on the left side of the chart in Fig. 2 to extrapolate that at a 30° bank angle, the load factor is 1.154. Thus, a 33-lb. airplane in a 30° bank would require its wings to support 38 lb. (33 lb. × 1.154).
Answer (A) is incorrect. An airplane supporting a load of 34 lb. in a 30° banked turn would weigh 29.5 lb., not 33 lb. Answer (B) is incorrect. A 33-lb. airplane supporting a load of 47 lb. would require a 45° banked turn, not a 30° banked turn.

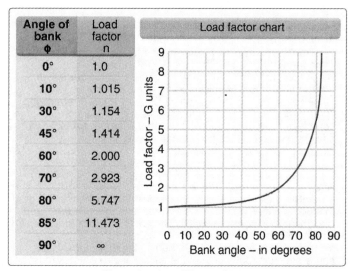

Figure 2. – Load Factor Chart.

8. The term "angle of attack" is defined as the angle between the

A. chord line of the wing and the relative wind.

B. airplane's longitudinal axis and that of the air striking the airfoil.

C. airplane's center line and the relative wind.

Answer (A) is correct. *(PHAK Chap 4)*
DISCUSSION: The angle of attack is the angle between the wing chord line and the direction of the relative wind. The wing chord line is a straight line from the leading edge to the trailing edge of the wing. The relative wind is the direction of the airflow relative to the wing when the wing is moving through the air.
Answer (B) is incorrect. Angle of attack is the angle between the wing chord line and the relative wind, not the airplane's longitudinal axis. Answer (C) is incorrect. The centerline of the airplane and its relationship to the relative wind is not a factor in defining angle of attack. Angle of attack is the relationship between the wing chord line and the relative wind.

9. The angle of attack at which an airplane wing stalls will

    A. increase if the CG is moved forward.

    B. change with an increase in gross weight.

    C. remain the same regardless of gross weight.

Answer (C) is correct. *(PHAK Chap 5)*
    DISCUSSION: A given airplane wing will always stall at the same angle of attack regardless of airspeed, weight, load factor, or density altitude. Each wing has a particular angle of attack (the critical angle of attack) at which the airflow separates from the upper surface of the wing and the stall occurs.
    Answer (A) is incorrect. A change in CG will not change the wing's critical angle of attack. Answer (B) is incorrect. The critical angle of attack does not change when gross weight changes.

10. (Refer to Figure 1 below.) The acute angle A is the angle of

    A. incidence.

    B. attack.

    C. dihedral.

Answer (B) is correct. *(PHAK Chap 4)*
    DISCUSSION: The angle between the relative wind and the wing chord line is the angle of attack. The wing chord line is a straight line from the leading edge to the trailing edge of the wing.
    Answer (A) is incorrect. The angle of incidence is the acute angle formed by the chord line of the wing and the longitudinal axis of the airplane. Answer (C) is incorrect. The dihedral is the angle at which the wings are slanted upward from the wing root to the wingtip.

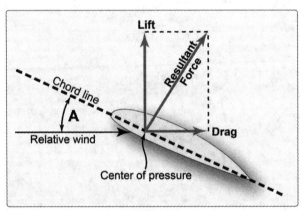

Figure 1. – Lift Vector.

154

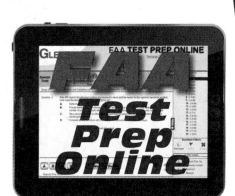

STUDY UNIT SIX
RADIO COMMUNICATIONS PROCEDURES

(7 pages of outline)

6.1 RADIO COMMUNICATIONS PROCEDURES

1. **The applicant demonstrates understanding of airport operations with and without an operating control tower.**

   a. An airport with an operating control tower normally has the following:

      1) Ground control for control of aircraft taxiing on the surface of the airport (except the runway)

      2) Tower control for control of aircraft on the active runway and in the vicinity of the airport

      3) Many busy airports also have approach control and departure control.

         a) The approach or departure controller coordinates arriving and departing traffic, usually for a busy airport with a control tower.

      4) Automatic Terminal Information Service (ATIS) is a continuous airport advisory service also provided at busy airports.

      5) Clearance delivery is a required communication at very busy and medium-density airports. It is used before contacting ground control to obtain departure instructions.

   b. At an airport that does not have an operating control tower, there is no air traffic control over movements of aircraft on the ground or around the airport in the air. The term "uncontrolled airport" is also used to mean an airport without an operating control tower.

      1) It is essential that pilots be alert, look for other traffic, and exchange information when approaching or departing an airport without an operating control tower.

         a) This is of particular importance since other aircraft may not have communication capability, or pilots may not communicate their presence or intentions.

      2) To achieve the greatest degree of safety, it is essential that all radio-equipped aircraft transmit/receive on a common frequency identified for the purpose of airport advisories.

      3) Observing and avoiding other aircraft at an airport without an operating control tower is of paramount importance.

         a) Relatedly, being considerate to the other pilots should have high priority both in the air and on the ground.

         b) Finally, do not assume absence of traffic because few airplanes use an airport.

2. **The applicant demonstrates understanding of the description and use of a Common Traffic Advisory Frequency (CTAF) to monitor manned aircraft communications.**

   a. The key to communicating at an airport without an operating control tower is the selection of the correct frequency. The term **CTAF** is synonymous with this program.

      1) CTAF is a frequency designated for the purpose of carrying out airport advisory practices while operating to or from an airport without an operating control tower.

         a) CTAF may be a UNICOM, MULTICOM, FSS, or tower frequency.

   b)   The CTAF at an airport is indicated on the sectional chart by a © next to the appropriate frequency.

2)   Pilots of inbound aircraft should monitor and communicate as appropriate on the CTAF 10 NM from the airport.

   a)   Pilots of departing aircraft should monitor and communicate on the CTAF from start-up, during taxi, and until 10 NM from the airport unless the FARs or local procedures require otherwise.

3)   Pilots of aircraft conducting other than arriving or departing operations at altitudes normally used by arriving and departing aircraft should monitor/ communicate on the CTAF while within 10 NM of the airport unless the FARs or local procedures require otherwise.

4)   **MULTICOM** is a frequency (122.9 MHz) used for self-announced procedures at airports without operating control towers that are not served by an FSS or UNICOM.

   a)   At such an airport, the MULTICOM frequency will be identified on charts as the CTAF.
   b)   Use the same phraseology as explained for UNICOM.

3.   **The applicant demonstrates understanding of recommended traffic advisory procedures used by manned aircraft pilots, such as self-announcing of position and intentions.**

   a.   Pilots use radios to

   1)   Obtain air traffic control (ATC) clearances

      a)   Ground control
      b)   Tower control, e.g., takeoffs and landings
      c)   Approach and departure control (in the vicinity of the airport)
      d)   En route control

   2)   Obtain weather briefings, file flight plans, etc., with Flight Service Stations (FSSs)

   3)   Communicate with FBOs and each other on CTAF, UNICOM, and MULTICOM frequencies

   b.   Airplane communication radios operate on the VHF (very high frequency) band between 118.000 MHz and 136.975 MHz.

   1)   VHF radios are limited to line-of-sight transmissions; thus, aircraft at higher altitudes are able to transmit and receive at greater distances.

   c.   Radio communications are a critical link in the ATC system. The link can be a strong bond between pilots and controllers, or it can be broken with surprising speed and disastrous results.

   1)   The single most important factor in pilot-controller communications is understanding.

      a)   Good phraseology enhances safety and is a mark of a professional pilot.
      b)   Jargon, chatter, and "CB" slang have no place in ATC communications.

   d.   In virtually all situations, pilot radio broadcasts can be thought of as

   1)   To whom they are talking
   2)   Who they are
   3)   Where they are
   4)   What they want to do
   5)   To whom they are talking (when making common traffic advisories in uncontrolled airport areas)

e. Summary of Recommended Communication Procedures

	FACILITY AT AIRPORT	FREQUENCY USE	COMMUNICATION/ BROADCAST PROCEDURES	
			OUTBOUND	INBOUND
1.	UNICOM (no tower or FSS)	Communicate with UNICOM station on published CTAF frequency (122.7, 122.8, 122.725, 122.975, or 123.0). If unable to contact UNICOM station, use self-announced procedures on CTAF.	Before taxiing and before taxiing on the runway for departure.	10 NM out. Entering downwind, base, and final. Leaving the runway.
2.	No tower, FSS, or UNICOM	Self-announce on MULTICOM frequency 122.9.	Before taxiing and before taxiing on the runway for departure.	10 NM out. Entering downwind, base, and final. Leaving the runway.

4. **The applicant demonstrates understanding of aeronautical advisory communications station (UNICOM) and associated communication procedures used by manned aircraft pilots.**

   a. UNICOM is a nongovernment air/ground radio communication station that may provide airport advisories at airports where there is no tower or FSS. UNICOM stations may provide pilots with weather information, wind direction, the recommended runway, or other necessary information.

      1) If the UNICOM frequency is designated as the CTAF, it will be identified on aeronautical charts and the Chart Supplement.

         a) UNICOM frequencies include 122.8, 122.7, 122.725, 122.975, and 123.0 MHz.

      2) The following practices help identify the location of aircraft in the traffic pattern and enhance safety of flight.

         a) Select the correct UNICOM/CTAF frequency.

         b) Monitor the frequency for these types of communications.

         c) Approximately 10 NM from the airport, pilots report altitude; state the airplane type, airplane identification, location relative to the airport, and the decision to land or overfly; and request wind information and runway in use.

         d) Report on downwind, base, and final approach.

         e) Report leaving the runway.

      3) Example of UNICOM phraseologies:

         a) Inbound examples

            i) Pilot: JONESVILLE UNICOM CESSNA ONE ZERO TWO FOXTROT, 10 MILES NORTH DESCENDING THROUGH (ALTITUDE) LANDING JONESVILLE, REQUEST WIND AND RUNWAY INFORMATION JONESVILLE.

               • Response from FBO: CESSNA CALLING JONESVILLE, WIND THREE FOUR ZERO AT SEVEN, RUNWAY THREE SIX IN USE WITH TWO AIRCRAFT IN THE PATTERN.

            ii) Pilot: JONESVILLE TRAFFIC CESSNA ONE ZERO TWO FOXTROT ENTERING (DOWNWIND/BASE/FINAL) FOR RUNWAY THREE SIX (FULL STOP/TOUCH-AND-GO) JONESVILLE.

            iii) Pilot: JONESVILLE TRAFFIC CESSNA ONE ZERO TWO FOXTROT CLEAR OF RUNWAY THREE SIX JONESVILLE.

b) Outbound examples

   i) Pilot: JONESVILLE UNICOM CESSNA ONE ZERO TWO FOXTROT (LOCATION ON AIRPORT) TAXIING TO RUNWAY THREE SIX, REQUEST WIND AND TRAFFIC INFORMATION JONESVILLE.

   ii) Pilot: JONESVILLE TRAFFIC CESSNA ONE ZERO TWO FOXTROT DEPARTING RUNWAY THREE SIX. REMAINING IN THE PATTERN/ DEPARTING THE PATTERN TO THE (DIRECTION) (AS APPROPRIATE) JONESVILLE.

5. **The applicant demonstrates understanding of automatic Terminal Information Service (ATIS).**

   a. If available, the ATIS frequency is listed on the sectional chart just under the tower control frequency for the airport, e.g., ATIS 125.05. ATIS provides a continuous transmission that provides information for arriving and departing aircraft, including

      1) Time of the latest weather report

      2) Sky conditions, visibility, and obstructions to visibility

         a) The absence of a sky condition or ceiling and/or visibility and obstructions to visibility on ATIS indicates a sky condition of 5,000 ft. or above and visibility of 5 SM or more.

            i) A remark on the broadcast may state, "The weather is better than 5,000 and 5," or the existing weather may be broadcast.

      3) Temperature and dewpoint (degrees Celsius)

      4) Wind direction (magnetic) and velocity

      5) Altimeter

      6) Other pertinent remarks, instrument approach, and runway in use

         a) The departure runway will be given only if it is different from the landing runway, except at locations having a separate ATIS for departure.

   b. The purpose of ATIS is to relieve the ground controllers' and approach controllers' workload. They need not repeat the same information.

   c. The ATIS broadcast is updated whenever any official weather is received, regardless of content or changes, or when a change is made in other pertinent data, such as a runway change. Each new broadcast is labeled with a letter of the alphabet at the beginning of the broadcast; e.g., "This is information alpha" or "information bravo."

6. **The applicant demonstrates understanding of aircraft call signs and registration numbers.**

   a. Pilots and controllers use aircraft call signs to direct communication with specific aircraft.

      1) Call signs may consist of an aircraft type and registration number, airline and flight number, and some other call sign and designated number.

         a) EXAMPLES: Bonanza six-six-four-two-one, Delta two-three-eight, Angel flight seven-five-five.

         b) Improper use of call signs can result in pilots executing a clearance intended for another aircraft.

         c) ATC specialists will not abbreviate call signs of air carrier or other civil aircraft having authorized call signs.

            i) ATC specialists may initiate abbreviated call signs of other aircraft by using the prefix and the last three digits/letters of the aircraft identification after communications are established.

            ii) Pilots may use the abbreviated call sign in subsequent contacts with the ATC specialist.

7. **The applicant demonstrates understanding of the phonetic alphabet.**

    a. Phonetic Alphabet

        1) Pilots and ATC use the phonetic alphabet to help differentiate between similar sounding identifications.

A	.-	Alpha	(AL-FAH)	T	-	Tango	(TANG-GO)
B	-...	Bravo	(BRAH-VOH)	U	..-	Uniform	(YOU-NEE-FORM)
C	-.-.	Charlie	(CHAR-LEE) or (SHAR-LEE)	V	...-	Victor	(VIK-TAH)
D	-..	Delta	(DELL-TAH)	W	.--	Whiskey	(WISS-KEY)
E	.	Echo	(ECK-OH)	X	-..-	Xray	(ECKS-RAY)
F	..-.	Foxtrot	(FOKS-TROT)	Y	-.--	Yankee	(YANG-KEY)
G	--.	Golf	(GOLF)	Z	--..	Zulu	(ZOO-LOO)
H	....	Hotel	(HOH-TEL)				
I	..	India	(IN-DEE-AH)				
J	.---	Juliett	(JEW-LEE-ETT)	1	.----	One	(WUN)
K	-.-	Kilo	(KEY-LOH)	2	..---	Two	(TOO)
L	.-..	Lima	(LEE-MAH)	3	...--	Three	(TREE)
M	--	Mike	(MIKE)	4	....-	Four	(FOW-ER)
N	-.	November	(NO-VEM-BER)	5	.....	Five	(FIFE)
O	---	Oscar	(OSS-CAH)	6	-....	Six	(SIX)
P	.--.	Papa	(PAH-PAH)	7	--...	Seven	(SEV-EN)
Q	--.-	Quebec	(KEH-BECK)	8	---..	Eight	(AIT)
R	.-.	Romeo	(ROW-ME-OH)	9	----.	Nine	(NIN-ER)
S	...	Sierra	(SEE-AIR-RAH)	0	-----	Zero	(ZEE-RO)

        2) The phonetic equivalents is used for single letters and for spelling out groups of letters or difficult words.

        3) Work through the listing of alphabetic phonetic equivalents, saying each out loud to learn it.

            a) Note that the Morse code is also provided, although it is not used as frequently as it once was. You need not learn the Morse code; just keep it handy.

8. **The applicant demonstrates understanding of phraseology: altitudes, directions, speed, and time.**

    a. **Figures**

        1) Figures indicating hundreds and thousands in round numbers, as for ceiling heights and upper wind levels up to 9,900, are spoken in accordance with the following:

            a) EXAMPLES: 500 is "FIVE HUNDRED"
                4,500 is "FOUR THOUSAND FIVE HUNDRED"

        2) Numbers above 9,900 are spoken by separating the digits preceding the word "thousand."

            a) EXAMPLES: 10,000 is "ONE ZERO THOUSAND"
                13,500 is "ONE THREE THOUSAND FIVE HUNDRED"

        3) Airway numbers. Airways are routes between navigational aids, such as VORs (i.e., airways are highways in the sky).

            a) EXAMPLE: V12 is "VICTOR TWELVE"

        4) All other numbers are spoken by pronouncing each digit.

            a) EXAMPLE: 10 is "ONE ZERO"

        5) When a radio frequency contains a decimal point, the decimal point is spoken as "POINT."

            a) EXAMPLE: 122.1 is "ONE TWO TWO POINT ONE"

b. **Altitudes and Flight Levels**

   1) Up to but not including 18,000 ft. MSL, state the separate digits of the thousands, plus the hundreds, if appropriate.

      a) EXAMPLES: 12,000 is "ONE TWO THOUSAND"
            12,500 is "ONE TWO THOUSAND FIVE HUNDRED"

   2) At and above 18,000 ft. MSL (FL 180), state the words "flight level" followed by the separate digits of the flight level.

      a) EXAMPLE: FL 190 is "FLIGHT LEVEL ONE NINER ZERO" (19,000 ft. MSL).

c. **Directions.** The three digits of bearing, course, heading, and wind direction should always be magnetic. The word "TRUE" must be added when it applies.

   1) EXAMPLES:

      a) (Magnetic course) 005 is "ZERO ZERO FIVE"
      b) (True course) 050 is "ZERO FIVE ZERO TRUE"
      c) (Magnetic bearing) 360 is "THREE SIX ZERO"
      d) (Magnetic heading) 100 is "ONE ZERO ZERO"
      e) (Wind direction) 220 is "TWO TWO ZERO"

   2) Wind velocity (speed) is always included with wind direction, e.g., "THREE FOUR ZERO AT ONE ZERO."

      a) ATC gives winds in magnetic direction.
      b) FSS gives winds in true direction from weather reports and forecasts.

d. **Speeds**

   1) Say the separate digits of the speed followed by the word "knots."

      a) EXAMPLES: 250 is "TWO FIVE ZERO KNOTS"
            185 is "ONE EIGHT FIVE KNOTS"

   2) The controller may omit the word "knots" when using speed adjustment procedures, e.g., "INCREASE SPEED TO ONE FIVE ZERO."

e. **Time**

   1) Aviation uses an international standard time with a 24-hour clock system to establish a common time.

   2) The international standard time is called Coordinated Universal Time (UTC). The term "Zulu" (Z) may be used to denote UTC. This used to be referred to as Greenwich Mean Time (GMT).

      a) UTC is actually the time at the 0° meridian, which passes through the Royal Observatory in Greenwich, England.

   3) The FAA uses UTC or Zulu time for all operations. Use the time conversion table below to find UTC. For daylight savings time, subtract 1 hour.

      a) When converting from UTC or Zulu time to local time, subtract the hours.

Time Zone	UTC
Eastern Standard Time	+5 hr.
Central Standard Time	+6 hr.
Mountain Standard Time	+7 hr.
Pacific Standard Time	+8 hr.
Alaska Standard Time	+9 hr.
Hawaii Standard Time	+10 hr.

4)   The 24-hr. clock system is used in radio transmissions. The hour is indicated by the first two figures and the minutes by the last two figures.

a)   EXAMPLES: 0000 is "ZERO ZERO ZERO ZERO" (midnight)
0920 is "ZERO NINER TWO ZERO" (9:20 a.m.)
1850 is "ONE EIGHT FIVE ZERO" (6:50 p.m.)

QUESTIONS

6.1   Radio Communications Procedures

1. Automatic Terminal Information Service (ATIS) is the continuous broadcast of recorded information concerning

A.   pilots of radar-identified aircraft whose aircraft is in dangerous proximity to terrain or to an obstruction.

B.   nonessential information to reduce frequency congestion.

C.   noncontrol information in selected high-activity terminal areas.

Answer (C) is correct. *(AIM Para 4-1-13)*
DISCUSSION: The continuous broadcast of recorded noncontrol information is known as the ATIS. ATIS includes weather, active runway, and other information that arriving and departing pilots need to know.
Answer (A) is incorrect. A controller who has a radar-identified aircraft under his or her control will issue a terrain or obstruction alert to an aircraft that is in dangerous proximity to terrain or to an obstruction. Answer (B) is incorrect. ATIS is considered essential (not nonessential) information, but routine, i.e., noncontrol.

2. Absence of the sky condition and visibility on an ATIS broadcast indicates that

A.   weather conditions are at or above VFR minimums.

B.   the sky condition is clear and visibility is unrestricted.

C.   the ceiling is at least 5,000 feet and visibility is 5 miles or more.

Answer (C) is correct. *(AIM Para 4-1-13)*
DISCUSSION: The ceiling/sky condition, visibility, and obstructions to vision may be omitted from the ATIS broadcast if the ceiling is above 5,000 ft. with visibility more than 5 statute miles.
Answer (A) is incorrect. The absence of the sky condition and visibility on an ATIS broadcast implies that the ceiling is above 5,000 ft. and the visibility is more than 5 statute miles. Answer (B) is incorrect. The absence of the sky condition and visibility on an ATIS broadcast implies that the ceiling is above 5,000 ft., not clear, and the visibility is more than 5 SM, not unrestricted.

3. The correct method of stating 4,500 feet MSL to ATC is

A.   "FOUR THOUSAND FIVE HUNDRED."

B.   "FOUR POINT FIVE."

C.   "FORTY-FIVE HUNDRED FEET MSL."

Answer (A) is correct. *(AIM Para 4-2-9)*
DISCUSSION: The proper phraseology for altitudes up to but not including 18,000 ft. MSL is to state the separate digits of the thousands, plus the hundreds, if appropriate. It would be "four thousand, five hundred."
Answer (B) is incorrect. Four point five is slang (not correct) phraseology. Answer (C) is incorrect. The thousand is spoken separately from the hundreds and not together. A stated altitude is understood to be MSL, unless otherwise stated.

4. The correct method of stating 10,500 feet MSL to ATC is

A.   "TEN THOUSAND, FIVE HUNDRED FEET."

B.   "TEN POINT FIVE."

C.   "ONE ZERO THOUSAND, FIVE HUNDRED."

Answer (C) is correct. *(AIM Para 4-2-9)*
DISCUSSION: The proper phraseology for altitudes up to but not including 18,000 ft. MSL is to state the separate digits of the thousands, plus the hundreds, if appropriate. It would be one zero thousand, five hundred.
Answer (A) is incorrect. It is one zero, not ten. Answer (B) is incorrect. Ten point five is slang (not correct) phraseology.

5. An ATC radar facility issues the following advisory to a pilot flying on a heading of 090°:

"TRAFFIC 3 O'CLOCK, 2 MILES, WESTBOUND..."

Where should the pilot look for this traffic?

    A. East.

    B. South.

    C. West.

Answer (B) is correct. *(AIM Para 4-1-14)*
    DISCUSSION: If you receive traffic information service from radar and are told you have traffic at the 3 o'clock position, traffic is in the direction of the right wingtip, or to the south.
    Answer (A) is incorrect. East is the 12 o'clock position. Answer (C) is incorrect. West is the 6 o'clock position.

6. An ATC radar facility issues the following advisory to a pilot flying on a heading of 360°:

"TRAFFIC 10 O'CLOCK, 2 MILES, SOUTHBOUND..."

Where should the pilot look for this traffic?

    A. Northwest.

    B. Northeast.

    C. Southwest.

Answer (A) is correct. *(AIM Para 4-1-14)*
    DISCUSSION: The controller is telling you that traffic is at 10 o'clock and 2 mi. 9 o'clock is the left wingtip, and 10 o'clock is 2/3 of the way from the nose of the airplane (12 o'clock) to the left wingtip. Thus, you are looking northwest.
    Answer (B) is incorrect. Northeast would be in the 1 to 2 o'clock position. Answer (C) is incorrect. Southwest would be in the 7 to 8 o'clock position.

7. An ATC radar facility issues the following advisory to a pilot flying north in a calm wind:

"TRAFFIC 9 O'CLOCK, 2 MILES, SOUTHBOUND..."

Where should the pilot look for this traffic?

    A. South.

    B. North.

    C. West.

Answer (C) is correct. *(AIM Para 4-1-14)*
    DISCUSSION: Traffic at 9 o'clock is off the left wingtip. The nose of the airplane is 12 o'clock, the left wingtip is 9 o'clock, the tail is 6 o'clock, and the right wingtip is 3 o'clock. With a north heading, the aircraft at 9 o'clock would be west of you.
    Answer (A) is incorrect. South would be the 6 o'clock position. Answer (B) is incorrect. North would be the 12 o'clock position.

8. (Refer to Figure 22 on page 163 and Figure 31 on page 164.) (Refer to area 2 in Figure 22.) At Coeur D`Alene which frequency should be used as a Common Traffic Advisory Frequency (CTAF) to monitor airport traffic?

    A. 122.05 MHz.

    B. 135.075 MHz.

    C. 122.8 MHz.

Answer (C) is correct. *(AIM Para 4-1-9)*
    DISCUSSION: The common traffic advisory frequency is 122.8. It is given in Fig. 22, after "L74" in the airport information on the sectional chart. Radio frequencies are also given in Fig. 31, the Chart Supplement, under "Communications."
    Answer (A) is incorrect. This is the remote communication outlet (RCO) frequency to contact Boise FSS in the vicinity of Coeur D'Alene, not the CTAF. Answer (B) is incorrect. This is the AWOS frequency, not the CTAF.

9. (Refer to Figure 22 on page 163 and Figure 31 on page 164.) (Refer to area 2 in Figure 22.) At Coeur D'Alene, which frequency should be used as a Common Traffic Advisory Frequency (CTAF) to self-announce position and intentions?

    A. 122.05 MHz.

    B. 122.1/108.8 MHz.

    C. 122.8 MHz.

Answer (C) is correct. *(Chart Supplement)*
    DISCUSSION: Fig. 31 is the Chart Supplement excerpt for Coeur D'Alene Air Terminal. Look for the section titled **Communications**. On that same line, it states the CTAF (and UNICOM) frequency is 122.8 MHz.
    Answer (A) is incorrect. This is the remote communications outlet (RCO) frequency to contact Boise FSS in the vicinity of Coeur D'Alene, not the CTAF. Answer (B) is incorrect. The COE VOR/DME frequency, not the CTAF, is 108.8 MHz.

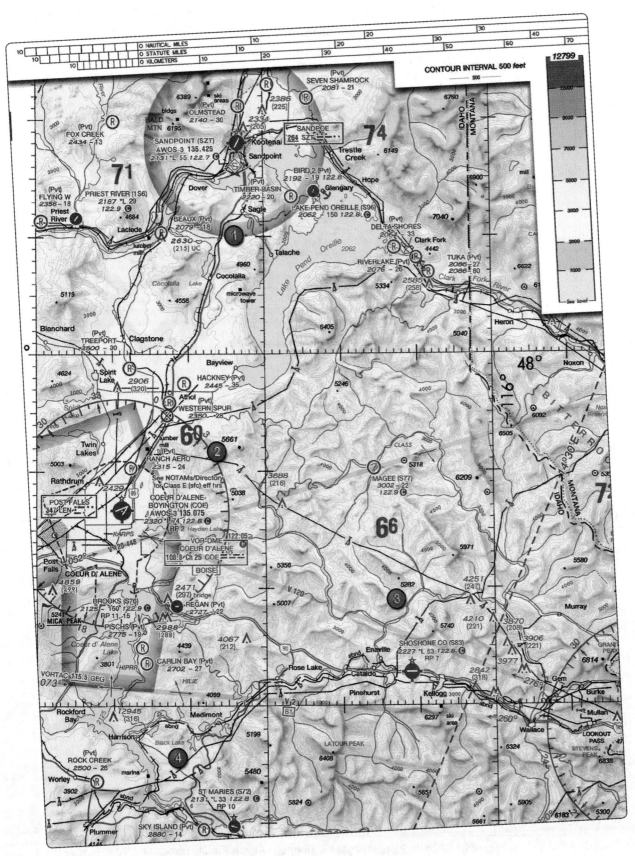

Figure 22. – Sectional Chart Excerpt.
NOTE: Chart is not to scale and should not be used for navigation. Use associated scale.

IDAHO   31

- -

COEUR D'ALENE–PAPPY BOYINGTON FLD   (COE)   9 NW   UTC–8(–7DT)
    N47°46.46' W116°49.18'   **GREAT FALLS**
  2320   B   S4   **FUEL** 100, JET A   OX 1, 2, 3, 4   Class IV, ARFF Index A   NOTAM FILE COE   **H–1C, L–13B**
  RWY 05–23: H7400X100 (ASPH–GRVD)   S–57, D–95, 2S–121, 2D–165   HIRL   0.6% up NE   **IAP**
    RWY 05: MALSR (NSTD). PAPI(P4R)—GA 3.0° TCH 56'.
    RWY 23: REIL. PAPI(P4R)—GA 3.0° TCH 50'.
  RWY 01–19: H5400X75 (ASPH)   S–50, D–83, 2S–105, 2D–150
    MIRL   0.3% up N
    RWY 01: REIL. PAPI(P2L)—GA 3.0° TCH 39'. Rgt tfc.
    RWY 19: PAPI(P2L)—GA 3.0° TCH 41'.
  RUNWAY DECLARED DISTANCE INFORMATION

RWY 01:	TORA–5400	TODA–5400	ASDA–5400	LDA–5400
RWY 05:	TORA–7400	TODA–7400	ASDA–7400	LDA–7400
RWY 19:	TORA–5400	TODA–5400	ASDA–5400	LDA–5400
RWY 23:	TORA–7400	TODA–7400	ASDA–7400	LDA–7400

AIRPORT REMARKS: Attended Mon–Fri 1500–0100Z‡. For after hrs
  fuel-self svc avbl or call 208–772–6404, 208–661–4174,
  208–661–7449, 208–699–5433. Self svc fuel avbl with credit
  card. 48 hr PPR for unscheduled ops with more than 30
  passenger seats call arpt manager 208–446–1860. Migratory
  birds on and invof arpt Oct–Nov. Remote cntl airstrip is 2.3 miles
  west AER 05. Arpt conditions avbl on AWOS. Rwy 05 NSTD
  MALSR, thld bar extends 5' byd rwy edge lgts each side. ACTIVATE
  MIRL Rwy 01–19, HIRL Rwy 05–23, REIL Rwy 01 and Rwy 23, MALSR Rwy 05—CTAF. PAPI Rwy 01, Rwy 19, Rwy
  05, and Rwy 23 opr continuously.
WEATHER DATA SOURCES: AWOS-3 135.075 (208) 772–8215.
  HIWAS 108.8 COE.
COMMUNICATIONS: CTAF/UNICOM 122.8
  RCO 122.05 (BOISE RADIO)
® SPOKANE APP/DEP CON 132.1
AIRSPACE: CLASS E svc continuous.
RADIO AIDS TO NAVIGATION: NOTAM FILE COE.
  (T) **VORW/DME** 108.8   COE   Chan 25   N47°46.42' W116°49.24'   at fld. 2320/19E.   **HIWAS.**
    DME portion unusable:
      220°–240° byd 15 NM   280°–315° byd 15 NM blo 11,000'.
  POST FALLS NDB (MHW) 347   LEN   N47°44.57' W116°57.66'   053° 6.0 NM to fld.
  ILS 110.7   I–COE   Rwy 05   Class ID.   Localizer unusable 25° left and right of course.

- -

Figure 31. – Chart Supplements U.S. (formerly Airport/Facility Directory).

10. (Refer to Figure 21 below.) (Refer to area 2.) The CTAF/MULTICOM frequency for Garrison Airport is

A. 122.8 MHz.

B. 122.9 MHz.

C. 123.0 MHz.

Answer (B) is correct. *(ACL)*

DISCUSSION: The CTAF for Garrison Municipal Airport (west of area 2 in Fig. 21) is 122.9 MHz, because that frequency is marked with a C.

Answer (A) is incorrect. There is no indication of 122.8 MHz at Garrison. Answer (C) is incorrect. There is no indication of 123.0 MHz at Garrison.

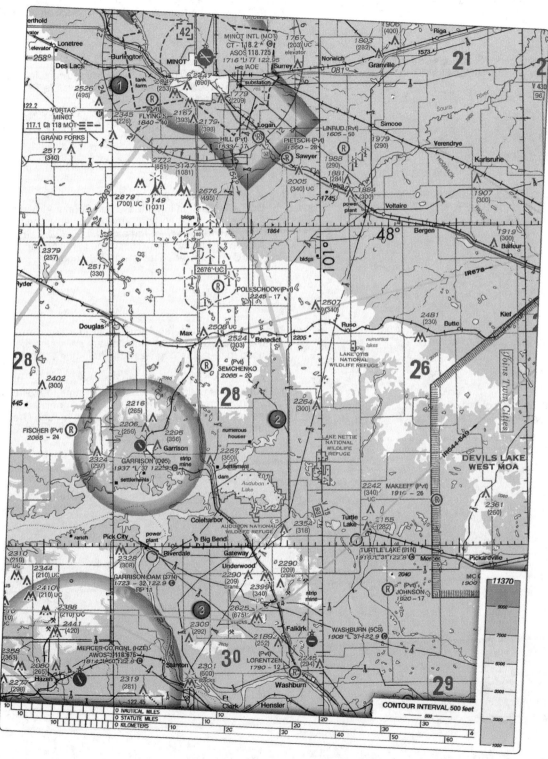

Figure 21. – Sectional Chart Excerpt.
NOTE: Chart is not to scale and should not be used for navigation. Use associated scale.

11. (Refer to Figure 26 on page 167.) (Refer to area 2.) While monitoring the Cooperstown CTAF you hear an aircraft announce that they are midfield left downwind to RWY 13. Where would the aircraft be relative to the runway?

    A.   The aircraft is East.

    B.   The aircraft is South.

    C.   The aircraft is West.

Answer (A) is correct. *(AIM Para 4-1-5)*
    DISCUSSION: Cooperstown Airport shows one runway. Runway numbers and letters are determined from the approach direction. A runway designated at 13 has a magnetic direction of 130°. An aircraft on the midfield left downwind is at the midpoint of the left side of the runway, heading in the opposite direction (310°). This places the aircraft to the east of the runway.
    Answer (B) is incorrect. An aircraft south of the runway would be on the left base leg for RWY 31. Answer (C) is incorrect. An aircraft west of the runway would be midfield left downwind to RWY 31.

12. (Refer to Figure 26 on page 167.) (Refer to area 4.) The CTAF/UNICOM frequency at Jamestown Airport is

    A.   122.2 MHz.

    B.   123.0 MHz.

    C.   123.6 MHz.

Answer (B) is correct. *(ACL)*
    DISCUSSION: The UNICOM frequency is printed in bold italics in the airport identifier. At Jamestown it is 123.0 MHz. The C next to it indicates it as the CTAF.
    Answer (A) is incorrect. This is the Flight Service frequency, not UNICOM. Answer (C) is incorrect. This is an FSS frequency, not UNICOM.

13. (Refer to Figure 26 on page 167.) (Refer to area 5.) What is the CTAF/UNICOM frequency at Barnes County Airport?

    A.   122.2 MHz.

    B.   122.8 MHz.

    C.   123.6 MHz.

Answer (B) is correct. *(ACL)*
    DISCUSSION: In Fig. 26, Barnes County Airport is to the west of area 5. The CTAF at Barnes County Airport is marked as the UNICOM frequency for the airport, i.e., 122.8 MHz.
    Answer (A) is incorrect. This is the Flight Service frequency. Answer (C) is incorrect. This is an FSS frequency.

14. (Refer to Figure 26 on page 167.) What does the line of latitude at area 4 measure?

    A.   The degrees of latitude east and west of the Prime Meridian.

    B.   The degrees of latitude north and south from the equator.

    C.   The degrees of latitude east and west of the line that passes through Greenwich, England.

Answer (B) is correct. *(sUASSG Chap 11)*
    DISCUSSION: Lines of latitude are parallel to the equator and used to measure degrees of latitude north (N) or south (S) of the Equator.
    Answer (A) is incorrect. Lines of longitude, not latitude, measure degrees east and west of the Prime Meridian. Answer (C) is incorrect. Lines of longitude, not latitude, measure degrees east and west of the line passing through Greenwich, England (Prime Meridian).

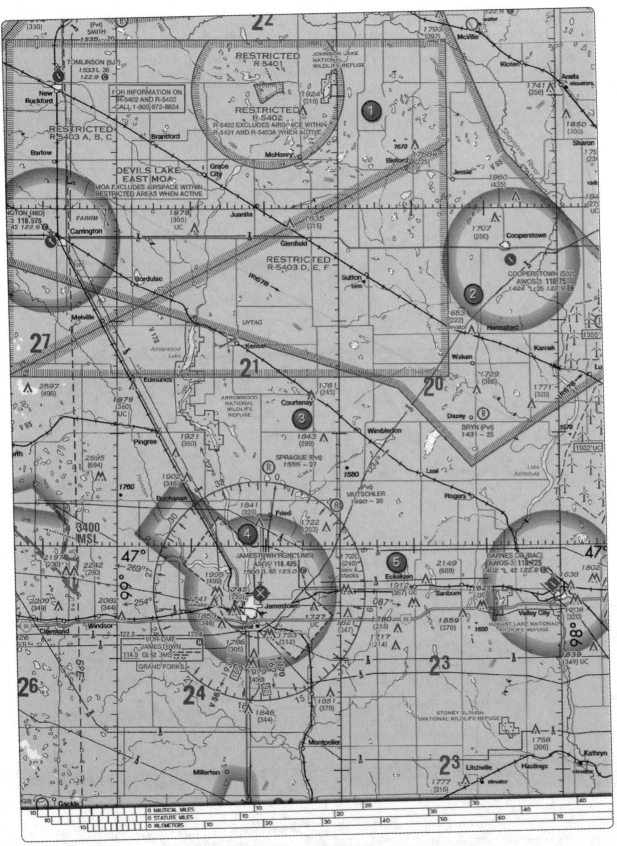

Figure 26. – Sectional Chart Excerpt.
NOTE: Chart is not to scale and should not be used for navigation. Use associated scale.

15. (Refer to Figure 78 below, and Figure 79 on page 169.) At Sioux Gateway/Col Day (N42°20.67' W96°19.42'), which frequency should be used as a Common Traffic Advisory Frequency (CTAF) to self-announce position and intentions when the control tower is closed?

    A.   122.95 MHz.

    B.   119.45 MHz.

    C.   118.7 MHz.

Answer (C) is correct. *(Chart Supplement)*
    DISCUSSION: Fig. 79 is the Chart Supplement excerpt for Sioux Gateway/Col Day Airport. Look for the section titled "Communications." On that same line, it states that the CTAF frequency is 118.7 MHz. It is also located on Fig. 78 in the Sioux Gateway Airport Data Description, indicated by a "C" surrounded by a shaded blue circle.
    Answer (A) is incorrect. This is the UNICOM frequency, not the CTAF frequency. Answer (B) is incorrect. The ATIS (Automatic Terminal Information Service) frequency is 119.45 MHz and is not the CTAF frequency.

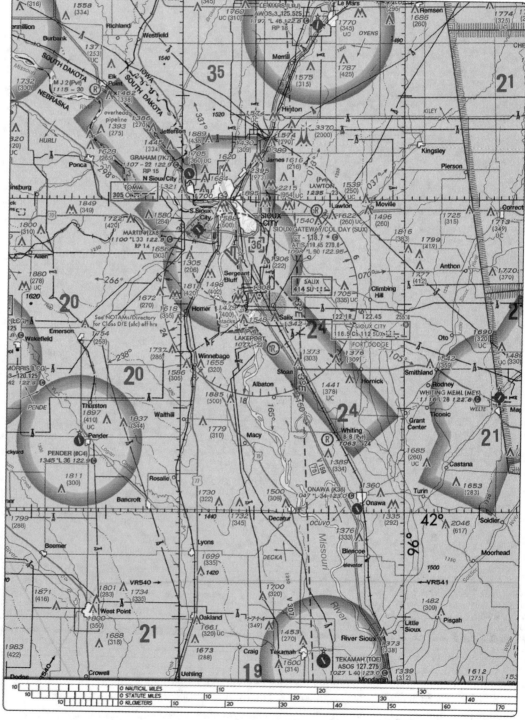

Figure 78. – Sectional Chart Excerpt.
NOTE: Chart is not to scale and should not be used for navigation. Use associated scale.

64 **IOWA**

SIOUX CITY N42°20.67′ W96°19.42′   NOTAM FILE SUX   **OMAHA**
(L) **VORTAC** 116.5   SUX   Chan 112   313 ° 4.4 NM to Sioux Gateway/Col Bud Day Fld. 1087/9E.   **HIWAS.**   **L–12I**
  VOR unusable:
    280°–292° byd 25 NM   306°–350° byd 20 NM blo 3,000′
    293°–305° byd 20 NM blo 4,500′   350°–280° byd 30 NM blo 3,000′
    293°–305° byd 35 NM
  RCO 122.45 122.1R 116.5T (FORT DODGE RADIO)

SIOUX CITY
SIOUX GATEWAY/COL BUD DAY FLD   (SUX)   6 S   UTC −6(−5DT)   N42°24.16′ W96°23.06′   **OMAHA**
  1098   B   S4   **FUEL** 100LL, 115, JET A   OX 1, 2, 3, 4   Class I, ARFF Index—See Remarks   **H–5C, L–12I**
  NOTAM FILE SUX   **IAP, AD**
  RWY 13–31: H9002X150 (CONC–GRVD)   S–100, D–120, 2S–152,
    2D–220   HIRL
    RWY 13: MALS. VASI(V4L)—GA 3.0 ° TCH 49′. Tree.
    RWY 31: MALSR. VASI(V4L)—GA 3.0 ° TCH 50′.
  RWY 17–35: H6600X150 (ASPH–PFC)   S–65, D–80, 2S–102,
    2D–130   MIRL
    RWY 17: REIL. VASI(V4R)—GA 3.0 ° TCH 50′. Trees.
    RWY 35: PAPI(P4L)—GA 3.0 ° TCH 54′. Pole.
  LAND AND HOLD SHORT OPERATIONS

LANDING	HOLD SHORT POINT	DIST AVBL
RWY 13	17–35	5400
RWY 17	13–31	5650

  ARRESTING GEAR/SYSTEM
    RWY 13 ←BAK–14 BAK–12B(B) (1392′)
              BAK–14 BAK–12B(B) (1492′) →RWY 31
  AIRPORT REMARKS: Attended continuously. PAEW 0330–1200Z ‡ during
    inclement weather Nov–Apr. AER 31–BAK–12/14 located (1492′)
    from thld. Airfield surface conditions not monitored by arpt
    management between 0600–1000Z ‡ daily. Rwy 13–BAK–12/14
    located (1392′) from thld. All A–gear avbl only during ANG flying ops. Twr has limited visibility southeast of
    ramp near ARFF bldg and northeast of Rwy 31 touchdown zone. Rwy 31 is calm wind rwy. Class I, ARFF Index
    B. ARFF Index E fire fighting equipment avbl on request. Twy F unlit, retro–reflective markers in place. Portions
    of Twy A SE of Twy B not visible by twr and is designated a non–movement area. Rwy 13–31 touchdown and
    rollout rwy visual range avbl. When twr clsd, ACTIVATE HIRL Rwy 13–31; MIRL Rwy 17–35; MALS Rwy 13;
    MALSR Rwy 31; and REIL Rwy 17—CTAF.
  WEATHER DATA SOURCES: ASOS (712) 255–6474. **HIWAS** 116.5 SUX. LAWRS.
  COMMUNICATIONS: CTAF 118.7   **ATIS** 119.45   **UNICOM** 122.95
    SIOUX CITY RCO 122.45 122.1R 116.5T (FORT DODGE RADIO)
  Ⓡ **SIOUX CITY APP/DEP CON** 124.6 (1200–0330Z ‡)
  Ⓡ **MINNEAPOLIS CENTER APP/DEP CON** 124.1 (0330–1200Z ‡)
    SIOUX CITY TOWER 118.7 (1200–0330Z ‡)   **GND CON** 121.9
  AIRSPACE: CLASS D svc 1200–0330Z ‡ other times CLASS E.
  RADIO AIDS TO NAVIGATION: NOTAM FILE SUX.
    SIOUX CITY (L) VORTAC 116.5   SUX   Chan 112   N42 °20.67′ W96°19.42′   313° 4.4 NM to fld. 1087/9E.
      HIWAS.
    NDB (MHW) 233   GAK   N42°24.49′ W96°23.16′   at fld.
    SALIX NDB (MHW/LOM) 414   SU   N42°19.65′ W96°17.43′   311° 6.1 NM to fld. Unmonitored.
    TOMMI NDB (MHW/LOM) 305   OI   N42°27.61′ W96°27.73′   128° 4.9 NM to fld. Unmonitored.
    ILS 109.3   I–SUX   Rwy 31   Class IT.   LOM SALIX NDB. ILS Unmonitored when twr clsd. Glide path
      unusable coupled approach (CPD) blo 1805′.
    ILS 111.3   I–OIQ   Rwy 13   LOM TOMMI NDB. Localizer shutdown when twr clsd.
    ASR (1200–0330Z ‡)

SNORE   N43°13.96′ W95°19.66′   NOTAM FILE SPW.   **OMAHA**
  NDB (LOM) 394   SP   121° 6.8 NM to Spencer Muni.

SOUTHEAST IOWA RGNL   (See BURLINGTON)

Figure 79. – Chart Supplements U.S. (formerly Airport/Facility Directory).

16. (Refer to Figure 25 on page 171.) (Refer to area 3.) If Dallas Executive Tower is not in operation, which frequency should be used as a Common Traffic Advisory Frequency (CTAF) to monitor airport traffic?

A.   127.25 MHz.

B.   122.95 MHz.

C.   126.35 MHz.

Answer (A) is correct. *(ACL)*

DISCUSSION: In Fig. 25, find the Dallas Executive Airport just above area 3. When the Dallas Executive tower is not in operation, the CTAF is 127.25 MHz because that frequency is marked with a C, which indicates a CTAF.

Answer (B) is incorrect. The UNICOM frequency is 122.95 MHz. Answer (C) is incorrect. The ATIS frequency is 126.35 MHz.

17. (Refer to Figure 25 on page 171.) (Refer to area 2.) The control tower frequency for Addison Airport is

A.   122.95 MHz.

B.   126.0 MHz.

C.   133.4 MHz.

Answer (B) is correct. *(ACL)*

DISCUSSION: Addison Airport (Fig. 25, area 2) control tower frequency is given as the first item in the second line of the airport data to the right of the airport symbol. The control tower (CT) frequency is 126.0 MHz.

Answer (A) is incorrect. This is the UNICOM, not control tower, frequency for Addison Airport. Answer (C) is incorrect. This is the ATIS, not control tower, frequency for Addison Airport.

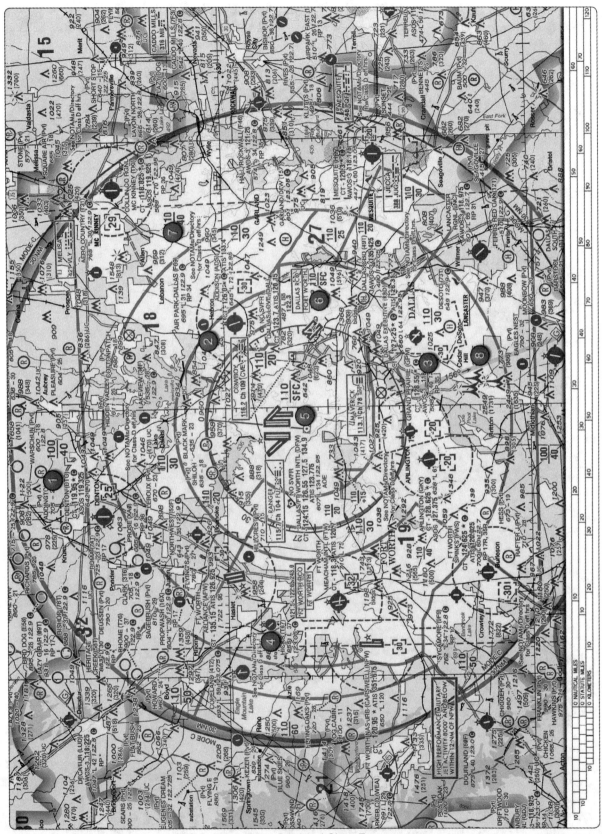

Figure 25. – Sectional Chart Excerpt.
NOTE: Chart is not to scale and should not be used for navigation. Use associated scale.

172

GLEIM® Reference Books

Pilot Handbook

- Comprehensive ground school text in outline format
- Expanded weather coverage
- Sections on flight reviews and instrument proficiency checks
- Color images and diagrams

FAR/AIM

- Expanded indexes
- Full color graphics

Aviation Weather & Weather Services

- A detailed explanation of weather
- A reorganization of
  - AC 00-6 Aviation Weather
  - AC 00-45 Aviation Weather Services
- Color graphics of weather depictions

Pilot Logbook

- Versatile and durable
- Ideal for pilots of all skill levels
- Professional quality at an affordable price
- The new standard in logbooks

GleimAviation.com
800.874.5346

STUDY UNIT SEVEN
AIRPORT OPERATIONS

(20 pages of outline)

7.1 AIRPORT OPERATIONS

1. **The applicant demonstrates understanding of the types of airports, such as towered, uncontrolled towered, heliport, and seaplane bases.**

    a. Pilots must be familiar with the operational requirements for each of the various types or classes of airspace.

        1) Situational awareness must be maintained at all times.

            a) It may be difficult to see other aircraft due to obstructions on the ground between a remote pilot and an aircraft in flight.

            b) Focusing solely on your own aircraft's flight while omitting the surrounding airspace could lead to a midair collision.

            c) Familiarity with airport operations and radio communications will help remote pilots know where to expect other aircraft to be operating.

        2) Towered airport operations.

            a) Approaching aircraft: Tower control will provide instructions to either land straight-in or to enter the pattern on either the left or right downwind leg of the runway.

            b) Departing aircraft: Tower control will provide instructions to depart straight out or turn left or right after takeoff.

                i) Monitoring communications with ground control will help advise when aircraft are taxiing to a runway and which general direction they may be departing toward.

        3) Non-towered airport operations.

            a) Approaching aircraft: Pilots self-announce their position when approaching airports and should state their intention to either land straight-in or enter the pattern on the downwind leg of the runway.

                i) Landing traffic should also announce their position on various legs of the traffic pattern, such as "base" or "final."

                ii) Listen for the mentions of "left or right traffic" to determine which side of the runway the aircraft will be using in the pattern. Different aircraft may use different types of approaches.

            b) Departing aircraft: Similar to approaching aircraft, manned aircraft pilots will self-announce their intention to takeoff and make position reports in the vicinity of the airport after departure.

2. **The applicant demonstrates understanding of ATC towers, such as ensuring the remote pilot can monitor and interpret ATC communications to improve situational awareness**

    a. To demonstrate understanding of Air Traffic Control (ATC) towers, remote pilots must be familiar with typical ATC communications.

        1) The tower controller coordinates all aircraft activity on the active runway and in the vicinity of the airport.

        2) When an aircraft is ready to takeoff, the pilot addresses the tower, identifies their call sign and registration number, and states their intentions.

3)   The tower controller may then issue a clearance for takeoff if appropriate, e.g., "Bonanza six-six-four-two-one, cleared for takeoff Runway six, left turn northbound approved." However, listen carefully to the response.

    a)   The controller may issue certain restrictions for departure, such as right turn or maintain runway heading, or you may ask for the direction of flight.

    b)   The tower may not clear the pilot due to traffic, e.g., "Bonanza six-six-four-two-one, hold short of Runway six, landing traffic."

        i)   Pilots must read back all runway hold short instructions, e.g., "Hold short of Runway six, Bonanza six-six-four-two-one."

    c)   Once a clearance for takeoff is received, pilots should acknowledge, e.g.," Bonanza six-six-four-two-one cleared for takeoff Runway six."

    d)   If there is a departure control to contact, the tower will direct pilots to that frequency when appropriate, e.g., " Bonanza six-six-four-two-one contact departure control 125.65, good day."

4)   Tower control is also used for landing. Pilots generally contact tower control 10 to 15 NM out, so the controller has time to route them to the active runway and coordinate their approach with the other traffic.

5)   Pilots will address the tower, stating who they are, where they are, and what they want.

6)   EXAMPLE: "Jacksonville Tower, Bonanza six-six-four-two-one, one-five miles southwest, landing."

b.   The Air Traffic Organization (ATO) does not have the authority to deny sUAS operations on the basis of equipage that exceeds the part 107 requirements.

1)   Because additional equipage and technologies, such as geo-fencing, have not been certified by the FAA, they need to be examined on a case-by-case basis in order for the FAA to determine their reliability and functionality.

2)   Additionally, requiring ATC to review equipage would place a burden on ATC and detract from other duties. Instead, a remote pilot who wishes to operate in controlled airspace because he or she can demonstrate mitigations through equipage may do so by applying for a waiver.

3)   ATC may impose certain restrictions and require the remote pilot to maintain two-way communications with the tower, or at least be capable of monitoring ATC communications.

3.   **The applicant demonstrates understanding of runway markings and signage.**

a.   A runway is marked in accordance with its present usage as a visual runway, nonprecision instrument runway, or precision instrument runway. Pilots can use any of these runways for takeoff and landing.

1)   A **visual runway** is used for visual flight rules (VFR) operations. Its markings include

    a)   **Designation marking.** Runway numbers and letters are determined from the approach direction. The runway number is the whole number nearest one-tenth the magnetic direction of the runway (e.g., a runway with a magnetic direction of 200° would be designated as runway 20). Letters differentiate between left (L), right (R), or center (C) parallel runways, if applicable.

        i)   For two parallel runways -- "L," "R"
        ii)   For three parallel runways -- "L," "C," "R"

b) **Centerline marking.** The runway centerline identifies the center of the runway and provides alignment guidance during takeoff and landing. The runway centerline is a dashed line.

c) **Optional markings**

   i) If the runway is used or intended to be used by international commercial transport, threshold markings are required.

   ii) If the runway is 4,000 ft. or longer and is used by jet aircraft, an aiming point marking is required.

   iii) Runway side stripes may be added if necessary.

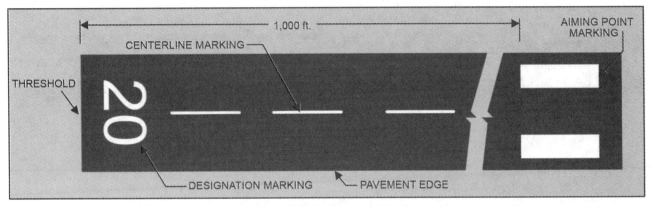

2) A **nonprecision instrument runway** is served by a nonprecision instrument approach (i.e., no electronic glide slope), and its markings include

   a) Designation marking.

   b) Centerline marking.

   c) **Threshold markings.** The runway threshold markings help you to identify the beginning of the runway that is available for landing. Threshold markings come in two configurations:

      i) Eight longitudinal stripes (four on each side of the centerline)

      ii) The number of stripes designated according to the width of the runway

   d) **Aiming point marker.** The aiming point marker serves as a visual aiming point during landing. The aiming point markings are two broad white stripes located on each side of the runway centerline approximately 1,000 ft. from the landing threshold.

   e) Optional markings -- runway side stripes.

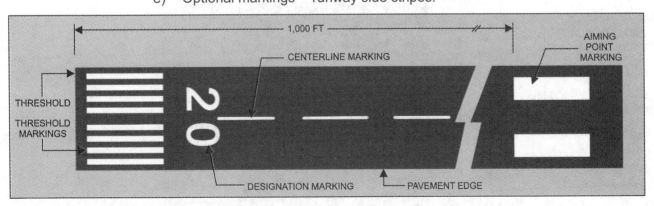

3) A **precision instrument runway** is served by a precision instrument approach, e.g., an instrument landing system (ILS). Its markings include

a) All the required markings for a nonprecision instrument runway.

b) **Touchdown zone marker.** The touchdown zone markings identify the touchdown zone for landing operations and are coded to provide distance information in 500-ft. increments.

    i) These markings consist of groups of one, two, and three rectangular bars arranged on each side of the centerline, as shown below.

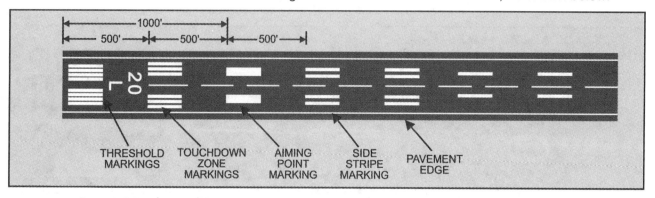

b. Additional Runway Markings.

1) **Side stripe marking.** Runway side stripes are continuous white stripes located on each side of the runway to provide a visual contrast between the runway and the abutting terrain or shoulders.

2) **Runway shoulder markings** are yellow and may be used to supplement runway side stripes to identify the runway shoulder area as shown below. This area is not intended for use by aircraft.

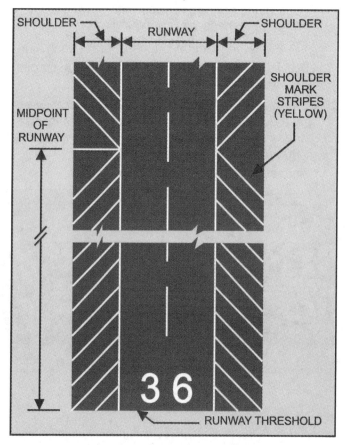

3) A **runway threshold bar** is used to mark the beginning of the runway that is available for landing when the threshold has been relocated or displaced. The threshold bar is 10 ft. wide, white, and extends across the width of the runway.

  a) A **relocated threshold** is a threshold that is temporarily relocated (due to construction, maintenance, etc.) toward the departure end of the runway.

   i) While methods for identifying the relocated threshold vary, the most common method is to use a threshold bar to mark the relocated threshold.

  b) A **displaced threshold** is a threshold that is not at the beginning of the paved runway.

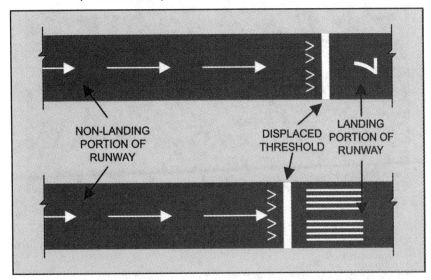

   i) The paved area before the displaced runway threshold (marked by arrows) is available for taxiing, the takeoff of aircraft, and a landing rollout from the opposite direction, but not for landing in the direction of the runway in question.

   ii) A threshold bar is located across the width of the runway at the displaced threshold.

   iii) White arrows are located along the centerline in the area between the beginning of the runway and the displaced threshold.

   iv) White arrowheads are located across the width of the runway just prior to the threshold bar.

4) **Chevrons** are used to show pavement areas (e.g., blast pads, stopways, etc.) aligned with the runway that are unusable for landing, takeoff, and taxiing. Chevrons are yellow.

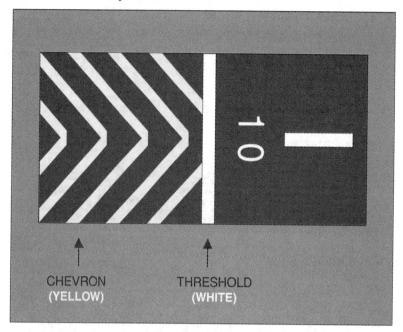

CHEVRON
(YELLOW)

THRESHOLD
(WHITE)

5) A **demarcation bar** separates a runway that has a displaced threshold from a taxiway or an area marked by chevrons that precedes the runway, as shown below. The demarcation bar is 3 ft. wide and is colored yellow since it is not on the runway.

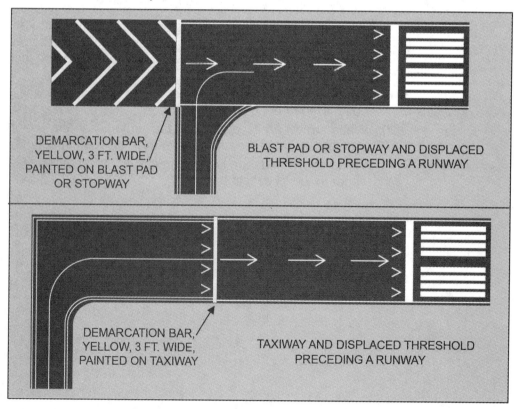

DEMARCATION BAR, YELLOW, 3 FT. WIDE, PAINTED ON BLAST PAD OR STOPWAY

BLAST PAD OR STOPWAY AND DISPLACED THRESHOLD PRECEDING A RUNWAY

DEMARCATION BAR, YELLOW, 3 FT. WIDE, PAINTED ON TAXIWAY

TAXIWAY AND DISPLACED THRESHOLD PRECEDING A RUNWAY

6) **Closed or Temporarily Closed Runway.**

a) A permanently closed runway has all runway lighting disconnected, all runway markings obliterated, and yellow crosses placed at each end of the runway and at 1,000-ft. intervals.

b) A temporarily closed runway is marked by yellow crosses placed only at each end of the runway.

i) An alternative is to place a raised lighted yellow cross at each end of the runway.

ii) A visual indication may not be present depending on the reason for the closure, the duration of the closure, airport configuration, and the existence (and operating hours) of a control tower.

c. Taxiway and Destination Signs.

1) Destination signs have black characters on a yellow background with an arrow showing the direction of the taxiing route to the destination listed. Outbound destinations commonly show directions to the take-off runways.

a) Signs I, J, and K are examples of destination signs as shown in Figure 65 on the next page.

i) Sign K designates the direction of taxiway bravo.

2) Taxiway location signs identify the taxiway on which an aircraft is currently located.

a) Location signs feature a black background with yellow lettering and do not have directional arrows.

3) Taxiway directional signs indicate the designation and direction of a taxiway.

a) When turning from one taxiway to another, a taxiway directional sign indicates the designation and direction of a taxiway leading out of the intersection.

b) Taxiway directional signs feature a yellow background with black lettering and directional arrows.

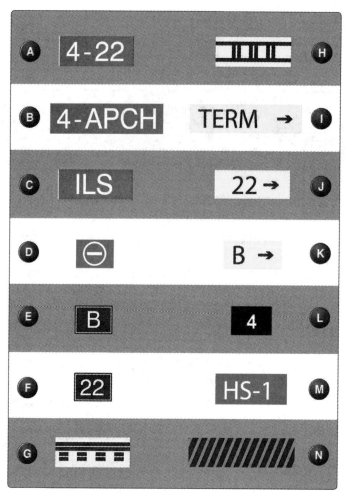

Figure 65. – U.S. Airport Signs.

4) When approaching taxiway holding lines from the side with continuous lines, the pilot should not cross the lines without an ATC clearance.

   a) Taxiway holding lines are painted across the width of the taxiway and are yellow.

5) A runway holding position sign is a mandatory instruction sign with white characters on a red background. It is located at the holding position on taxiways that intersect a runway or on runways that intersect other runways.

6) Each of the letters below corresponds to the type of sign or marking in Figure 65.

   a) Runway Holding Position Sign
   b) Holding Position Sign for a Runway Approach Area
   c) Holding Position Sign for ILS Critical Area
   d) Sign Prohibiting Aircraft Entry into an Area
   e) Taxiway Location Sign
   f) Runway Location Sign
   g) Runway Boundary Sign
   h) ILS Critical Area Boundary Sign
   i) Direction Sign for Terminal
   j) Direction Sign for Common Taxiing Route to Runway
   k) Direction Sign for Runway Exit
   l) Runway Distance Remaining Sign
   m) Hold Short-1
   n) Taxiway Ending Sign

d.   Vehicle Roadway Markings.

   1)   Vehicle roadway markings define pathways for vehicles to cross areas of the airport used by aircraft.

      a)   Vehicle roadway markings exist in two forms, as indicated by letter C in Figure 64 below.

         i)   The edge of vehicle roadway markings may be defined by a solid white line or white zipper markings.

      b)   A dashed white line separates opposite-direction vehicle traffic inside the roadway.

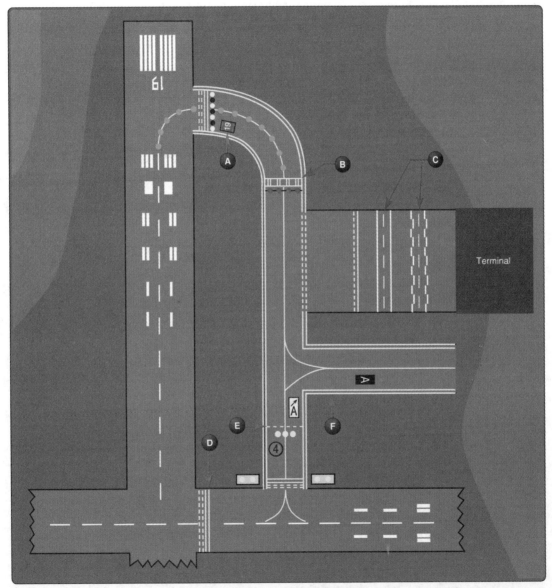

Figure 64. – Airport Markings.

   2)   Each of the letters below corresponds to the type of airport markings in Figure 64.

      a)   Holding Position Markings at Beginning of Takeoff Runway 19
      b)   ILS Critical Area Boundary Marking
      c)   Roadway Edge Stripes
      d)   Runway Holding Position Marking
      e)   Taxiway Holding Position Marker
      f)   Taxiway Boundary

e.   Beacons and Taxiway Lights.

1)   Operation of the green and white rotating beacon at an airport located in Class D airspace during the day indicates that the weather is not VFR; i.e.,

a)   The visibility is less than 3 SM or
b)   The ceiling is less than 1,000 ft.

2)   A lighted heliport may be identified by a green, yellow, and white rotating beacon.

3)   Military airports are indicated by beacons with two white flashes between each green flash.

4)   Airport taxiways are lighted with blue edge lights.

4.   **The applicant demonstrates understanding of traffic patterns used by manned aircraft pilots.**

a.   Established airport traffic patterns ensure that air traffic flows into and out of an airport in an orderly manner. You should use the basic rectangular airport traffic pattern at the recommended altitude unless modified by air traffic control (ATC) or by approved visual markings at the airport.

b.   **The Basic Rectangular Airport Traffic Pattern.**

1)   The traffic pattern altitude is usually 1,000 ft. above the elevation of the airport, unless otherwise specified in the Chart Supplement. Using a common altitude is the key to minimizing collision risk.

2)   At all airports, the direction of traffic flow is to the left, unless right turns are indicated by

a)   Visual markings (i.e., traffic pattern indicators) on the airport
b)   Control tower instructions

3)   The basic rectangular traffic pattern consists of five "legs" positioned in relation to the runway in use, as illustrated on the following page.

a)   The **departure leg** of the traffic pattern is a straight course aligned with and leading from the takeoff runway.

b)   The **crosswind leg** is horizontally perpendicular to the extended centerline of the takeoff runway. It is entered by making a 90° turn from the upwind leg.

c)   The **downwind leg** is flown parallel to the landing runway but in a direction opposite to the intended landing direction.

d)   The **base leg** is the transitional part of the traffic pattern between the downwind leg and the final approach leg.

e)   The **final approach leg** is a descending flight path starting at the completion of the base-to-final turn and extending to the point of touchdown.

4)   The **upwind leg** is commonly misunderstood to be another name for the departure leg.

a)   It is actually a separate leg of the pattern entirely.

b)   The upwind leg is used to side-step the departure leg. This may be done in the case of a go-around or aborted landing.

5) The traffic pattern

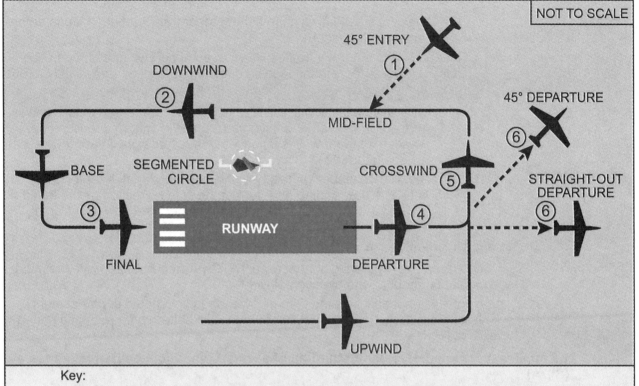

Key:

1. Enter pattern in level flight, abeam the midpoint of the runway, at pattern altitude.
2. Maintain pattern altitude until abeam approach end of the landing runway on the downwind leg.
3. Complete turn to final at least 1/4 mi. from the runway.
4. Continue straight ahead until beyond departure end of runway.
5. If remaining in the traffic pattern, commence turn to crosswind leg beyond the departure end of the runway, within 300 ft. of pattern altitude.
6. If departing the traffic pattern, continue straight out, or exit with a 45° left turn (right turn for right traffic pattern) beyond the departure end of the runway, after reaching pattern altitude.

c. **Entering a Traffic Pattern**

1) At an airport with an operating control tower, the controller will direct when and where pilots should enter the traffic pattern.

   a) Once the pilot is in the pattern, the controller may request that the pilot perform some maneuvers for better traffic spacing, including

      i) Shortening or extending the downwind leg; increasing or decreasing the aircraft's speed; or performing a 360° turn or S-turns to provide spacing ahead of the aircraft.

2) To enter the traffic pattern at an airport without an operating control tower, inbound pilots are expected to observe other aircraft already in the pattern and to conform to the traffic pattern in use.

   a) If no other aircraft are in the pattern, traffic and wind indicators on the ground must be checked to determine which runway and traffic pattern direction should be used.

      i) Overfly the airport at least 500 to 1,000 ft. above the traffic pattern altitude.

      ii) After the proper traffic pattern direction has been determined, the pilot should proceed to a point well clear of the pattern before descending to the pattern altitude.

b) When approaching an airport for landing, the pilot should enter the traffic pattern at a 45° angle to the downwind leg at the midpoint of the runway.

  i) The pilot should always be at the proper traffic pattern altitude before entering the pattern.

c) One method to enter the traffic pattern at an airport without an operating control tower is to fly in the landing direction parallel to, and slightly to one side of, the runway.

  i) Once the pilot is about 15 sec. past the departure end of the runway, turn 45° in the same direction as the traffic pattern direction (i.e., turn left if the runway is using left traffic; turn right if the runway is using right traffic).

  ii) The pilot continues on this heading for approximately 2 NM; then makes a descending 180° turn in the same direction as the traffic pattern to traffic pattern altitude, and enters the downwind leg at approximately a 45° angle at midfield.

d. **Departing a Traffic Pattern**

1) At airports with an operating control tower, ATC will generally approve the most expedient turnout for the direction of flight.

2) At airports without an operating control tower, the pilot should depart straight out or with a 45° turn in the direction of the traffic pattern after reaching pattern altitude.

5. **The applicant demonstrates understanding of security Identification Display Areas (SIDA).**

a. Security Identification Display Areas (SIDA) are limited access areas that require a badge issued in accordance with procedures in 49 CFR Part 1542. Movement through or into these areas is prohibited without proper identification being displayed. If you are unsure of the location of a SIDA, contact the airport authority for additional information. Airports that have a SIDA must have the following information available:

1) A description and map detailing boundaries and pertinent features;

2) Measures used to perform the access control functions required under 49 CFR 1542.201(b)(1);

3) Procedures to control movement within the secured area, including identification media required under 49 CFR 1542.201(b)(3); and

4) A description of the notification signs required under 49 CFR 1542.201(b)(6).

b. Pilots or passengers without proper identification that are observed entering a SIDA (ramp area) may be reported to TSA or airport security.

6. **The applicant demonstrates understanding of sources for airport data.**

a. **Longitude and Latitude**

1) Lines of longitude and latitude provide a common grid system that is the key to navigation. The location of any point on the Earth can be determined by the intersection of the lines of longitude and latitude.

a) **Lines of latitude**, or **parallels**, are imaginary circles parallel to the Equator. They are drawn as lines on charts running east and west around the world.

  i) They are used to measure degrees of latitude north (N) or south (S) of the Equator.

  ii) Angular distance from the Equator to the pole is one-fourth of a circle, or 90°.

  iii) The 48 conterminous states of the United States are located between 24° and 49°N latitude.

      b) **Lines of longitude**, or **meridians**, are drawn from the North Pole to the South Pole and are at right angles to the Equator and the parallels.

          i) The **Prime Meridian**, which passes through Greenwich, England, is used as the zero line from which measurements are made in degrees east (E) and west (W) to 180°.

          ii) The 48 conterminous states of the United States are located between 67° and 125°W longitude.

          iii) Because lines of longitude connect the poles, they mark the direction of true north and south.

  2) Any specific geographical point on Earth can thus be located by reference to its latitude and longitude.

      a) EXAMPLES: Washington, D.C., is approximately 39°N latitude, 77°W longitude, and Chicago is approximately 42°N latitude, 88°W longitude.

      b) The lines of longitude and latitude are printed on aeronautical (e.g., sectional) charts with each degree subdivided into 60 equal segments called minutes; i.e., 1/2° is equal to 30' (the ' is the symbol for min.).

          i) Each minute shown on lines of longitude equals one nautical mile, and this scale may be used to measure distances on aeronautical charts.

  3) The meridians are also useful for designating time zones.

      a) A day is defined as the time required for the Earth to make one complete revolution of 360°. Since the day is divided into 24 hr., the Earth revolves at the rate of 15° an hour.

          i) When the sun is directly above a meridian

             • It is noon at that meridian.
             • To the west of that meridian, it is forenoon.
             • To the east of that meridian, it is afternoon.

b) The standard practice is to establish a time belt for each 15° of longitude. This makes a difference of exactly 1 hr. between each belt.

i) The Continental United States has four time belts: Eastern (75°), Central (90°), Mountain (105°), and Pacific (120°).

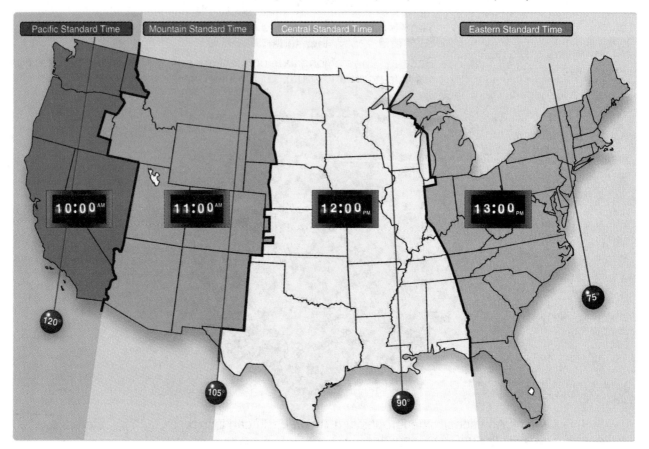

c) The actual dividing lines are somewhat irregular because communities near the boundaries often find it more convenient to use the time designations of neighboring communities or trade centers.

b. **Aeronautical charts**

1) Sectional charts are the most common charts used by pilots today.

a) The charts have a scale of 1:500,000 [1 inch = 6.86 nautical miles (NM) or approximately 8 statute miles (SM)], which allows for more detailed information to be included on the chart.

i) Sectional charts provide an abundance of information, including airport data, navigational aids, airspace, and topography.

ii) The figure on the following page is an excerpt from the legend of a sectional chart. By referring to the chart legend, a pilot can interpret most of the information on the chart.

- A pilot should also check the chart for other legend information, which includes air traffic control (ATC) frequencies and information on airspace.

iii) These charts are revised semiannually except for some areas outside the conterminous United States where they are revised annually.

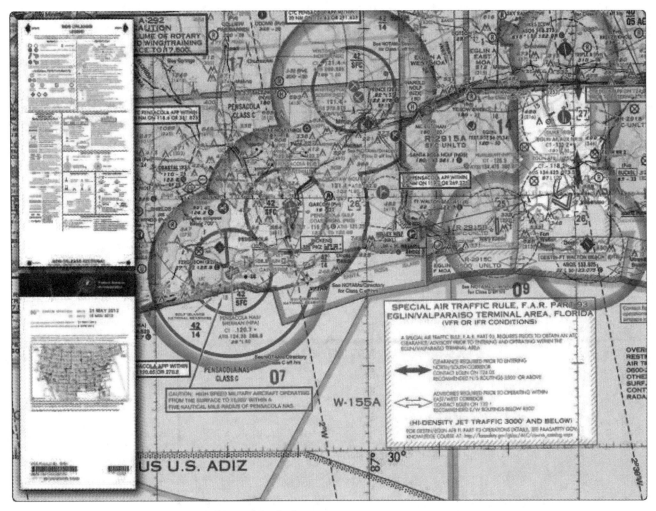

2) Sectional Chart Symbology

    a) The following information appears on the front of every sectional chart. Study it carefully! Few pilots take the time to study the whole legend because they are in a hurry to look at the chart itself.

        i) Airports

NOTE: On sectional charts, airports having control towers are illustrated in blue; all others are illustrated in magenta.

● Additional airport information

ADDITIONAL AIRPORT INFORMATION

Ⓡ   Private "(Pvt)" - Non-public use having emergency or landmark value.

◎ ◎   Military - Other than hard-surfaced. All military airports are identified by abbreviations AFB, NAS, AAF, etc. For complete airport information consult DOD FLIP.

Ⓗ	Ⓤ	⊗	Ⓕ
Heliport Selected	Unverified	Abandoned - paved having landmark value, 3000 ft. or greater	Ultralight Flight Park Selected

Services-fuel available and field tended during normal working hours depicted by use of ticks around basic airport symbol. (Normal working hours are Mon thru Fri 10:00 A.M. to 4:00 P.M. local time.) Consult A/FD for service availability at airports with hard-surfaced runways greater than 8069 ft.

☆ Rotating airport beacon in operation Sunset to Sunrise.

ii)   Airport data

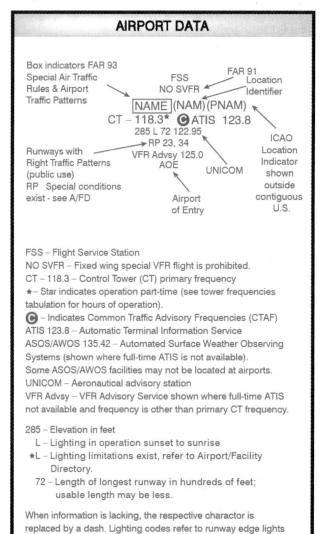

AIRPORT DATA

Box indicators FAR 93 Special Air Traffic Rules & Airport Traffic Patterns

FSS
NO SVFR

FAR 91
Location Identifier

NAME (NAM)(PNAM)

CT – 118.3* Ⓒ ATIS 123.8

285 L 72 122.95

RP 23, 34

VFR Advsy 125.0
AOE

Runways with Right Traffic Patterns (public use)
RP   Special conditions exist - see A/FD

Airport of Entry

UNICOM

ICAO Location Indicator shown outside contiguous U.S.

FSS – Flight Service Station
NO SVFR – Fixed wing special VFR flight is prohibited.
CT – 118.3 – Control Tower (CT) primary frequency
★– Star indicates operation part-time (see tower frequencies tabulation for hours of operation).
Ⓒ – Indicates Common Traffic Advisory Frequencies (CTAF)
ATIS 123.8 – Automatic Terminal Information Service
ASOS/AWOS 135.42 – Automated Surface Weather Observing Systems (shown where full-time ATIS is not available).
Some ASOS/AWOS facilities may not be located at airports.
UNICOM – Aeronautical advisory station
VFR Advsy – VFR Advisory Service shown where full-time ATIS not available and frequency is other than primary CT frequency.

285 – Elevation in feet
  L – Lighting in operation sunset to sunrise
  ★L – Lighting limitations exist, refer to Airport/Facility Directory.
    72 – Length of longest runway in hundreds of feet; usable length may be less.

When information is lacking, the respective charactor is replaced by a dash. Lighting codes refer to runway edge lights and may not represent the longest runway or full length lighting.

iii) Radio aids to navigation and communication boxes

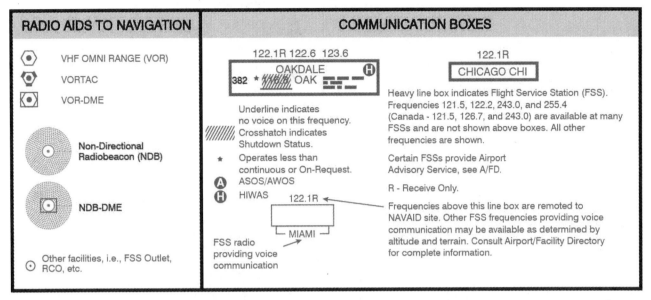

iv) Airport traffic service and airspace information

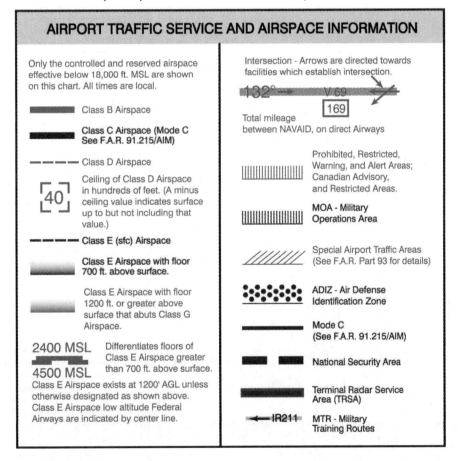

v) Obstructions

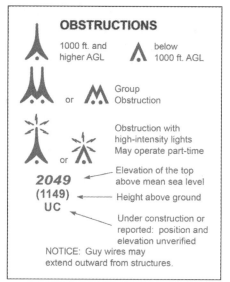

vi) Topographic information

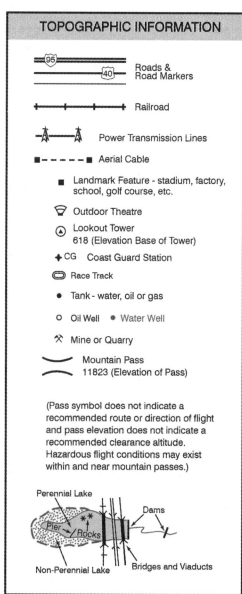

vii) Miscellaneous

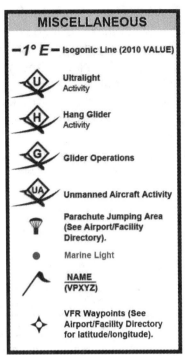

3) For information on the depiction of each class of airspace, refer to Study Unit 2.

c. **Chart Supplements**

1) Chart Supplements are a listing of data on record with the FAA on all open-to-the-public airports, seaplane bases, heliports, military facilities and selected private use airports specifically requested by the Department of Defense (DOD) for which a DOD instrument approach procedure has been published in the U.S. Terminal Procedures Publication, airport sketches, NAVAIDs, communications data, weather data sources, airspace, special notices, VFR waypoints, Airport Diagrams, and operational procedures.

   a) Seven volumes cover the conterminous United States, Puerto Rico, and the Virgin Islands.

   b) The supplements include data that cannot be readily depicted in graphic form; e.g., airport hours of operation, types of fuel available, runway data, lighting codes, etc.

   c) The supplements are designed to be used in conjunction with sectional charts and published every 56 days.

   d) The supplements also contains the Aeronautical Chart Bulletin.

      i) The purpose of the bulletin is to provide major changes, in aeronautical information, that have occurred since the last publication date of each VFR Sectional, Terminal Area, and Helicopter Route Chart listed.

d. Sectional charts can be purchased from most pilot shops and many online pilot retail stores.

   1) Digital charts are available at www.faa.gov/air_traffic/flight_info/aeronav/digital_products/.

7. **The applicant demonstrates understanding of avoiding bird and wildlife hazards and reporting collisions between aircraft and wildlife.**

   a. Many airports advise pilots of other wildlife hazards caused by large animals on the runway through the Chart Supplement U.S. and the NOTAM system.

   b. Collisions of landing and departing aircraft and animals on the runway are increasing and are not limited to rural airports.

   c. These accidents have also occurred at several major airports.

   d. Pilots should exercise extreme caution when warned of the presence of wildlife on and in the vicinity of airports.

   e. If you observe deer or other large animals in close proximity to movement areas, advise the FSS, tower, or airport management.

QUESTIONS

7.1 Airport Operations

1. The numbers 8 and 26 on the approach ends of the runway indicate that the runway is orientated approximately

  A. 008° and 026° true.

  B. 080° and 260° true.

  C. 080° and 260° magnetic.

Answer (C) is correct. *(AIM Para 2-3-3)*
  DISCUSSION: Runway numbers are determined from the approach direction. The runway number is the whole number nearest one-tenth the magnetic direction of the centerline. Thus, the numbers 8 and 26 on a runway indicate that the runway is oriented approximately 080° and 260° magnetic.
  Answer (A) is incorrect. The ending digit, not a leading zero, is dropped. Answer (B) is incorrect. Runways are numbered based on magnetic, not true, direction.

2. What is the purpose of the runway/runway hold position sign?

  A. Denotes entrance to runway from a taxiway.

  B. Denotes area protected for an aircraft approaching or departing a runway.

  C. Denotes intersecting runways.

Answer (C) is correct. *(AIM Para 2-3-8)*
  DISCUSSION: Runway/runway hold position signs are a type of mandatory instruction sign used to denote intersecting runways. These are runways that intersect and are being used for "Land, Hold Short" operations or are normally used for taxiing. These signs have a red background with white lettering. Runway/runway hold position signs are identical to the signs used for taxiway/runway intersections.
  Answer (A) is incorrect. A runway/runway hold position sign is located on a runway and denotes an intersecting runway, not the entrance to a runway from a taxiway. Answer (B) is incorrect. A runway approach area holding position sign protects an area from approaching or departing aircraft.

3. What purpose does the taxiway location sign serve?

  A. Provides general taxiing direction to named runway.

  B. Denotes entrance to runway from a taxiway.

  C. Identifies taxiway on which an aircraft is located.

Answer (C) is correct. *(AIM Para 2-3-9)*
  DISCUSSION: Taxiway location signs are used to identify a taxiway on which the aircraft is currently located. Taxiway location signs consist of a black background with a yellow inscription and yellow border.
  Answer (A) is incorrect. A runway destination sign, not a taxiway location sign, provides general taxiing information to a named runway. Answer (B) is incorrect. A runway holding position sign, not a taxiway location sign, identifies the entrance to a runway from a taxiway. Runway holding position signs consist of a red background with white inscription.

4. The recommended entry position to an airport traffic pattern is

  A. 45° to the base leg just below traffic pattern altitude.

  B. to enter 45° at the midpoint of the downwind leg at traffic pattern altitude.

  C. to cross directly over the airport at traffic pattern altitude and join the downwind leg.

Answer (B) is correct. *(AIM Para 4-3-3)*
  DISCUSSION: The recommended entry position to an airport traffic pattern is to enter 45° at the midpoint of the downwind leg at traffic pattern altitude.
  Answer (A) is incorrect. The recommended entry to an airport traffic pattern is to enter 45° at the midpoint of the downwind, not base, leg and at traffic pattern altitude, not below. Answer (C) is incorrect. The recommended entry to an airport traffic pattern is to enter 45° at the midpoint of the downwind, not to cross directly over the airport and join the downwind leg. Also, flying at traffic pattern altitude directly over an airport is an example of poor judgment in collision avoidance precautions.

5. (Refer to Figure 48 below.) Area C on the airport depicted is classified as a

A. stabilized area.

B. multiple heliport.

C. closed runway.

Answer (C) is correct. *(AIM Para 2-3-6)*
    DISCUSSION: The runway marked by the arrow C in Fig. 48 has Xs on the runway, indicating it is closed.
    Answer (A) is incorrect. Stabilized areas are designed to be load bearing but may be limited to emergency use only. Area E on the airport indicates a stabilized area. Answer (B) is incorrect. Heliports are marked by Hs, not Xs.

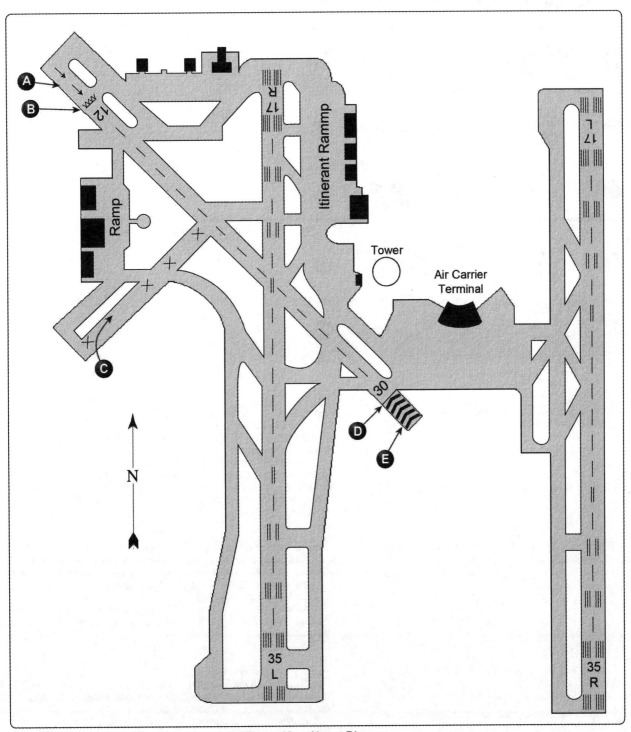

Figure 48. – Airport Diagram.

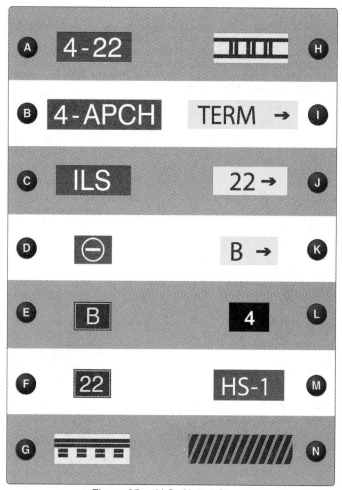

Figure 65. – U.S. Airport Signs.

6. (Refer to Figure 65 above.) Which sign is a designation and direction of an exit taxiway from a runway?

A.   J.

B.   F.

C.   K.

Answer (C) is correct. *(AIM Para 2-3-11)*
   DISCUSSION: Sign K designates the direction of taxiway B; while both J and K are destination signs, only K designates the route to a taxiway.
   Answer (A) is incorrect. Though a destination sign, Sign J designates the direction of Runway 22, not the direction of a taxiway. Answer (B) is incorrect. Sign F is a location sign indicating that the aircraft is located on Runway 22.

7. (Refer to Figure 65 above.) Which sign identifies where aircraft are prohibited from entering?

A.   D.

B.   G.

C.   B.

Answer (A) is correct. *(AIM Para 2-3-8)*
   DISCUSSION: Mandatory instruction signs have a red background with a white inscription and are used to denote an entrance to a runway or critical area and areas where an aircraft is prohibited from entering.
   Answer (B) is incorrect. "G" is a runway boundary sign. Answer (C) is incorrect. "B" is a holding position sign for a runway approach area.

8. (Refer to Figure 65 above.) (Refer to E.) This sign is a visual clue that

A.   confirms the aircraft's location to be on taxiway "B."

B.   warns the pilot of approaching taxiway "B."

C.   indicates "B" holding area is ahead.

Answer (A) is correct. *(AIM Chap 3)*
   DISCUSSION: The taxiway location sign consists of a yellow letter on a black background with a yellow border. This sign confirms the pilot is on taxiway "B."
   Answer (B) is incorrect. A direction sign with a yellow background, a black letter, and an arrow pointing to taxiway "B" would be required to warn a pilot that (s)he is approaching taxiway "B." Answer (C) is incorrect. A taxiway location sign defines a position on a taxiway, not a holding area.

9. (Refer to Figure 65 on page 194.) (Refer to F.) This sign confirms your position on

A.   runway 22.

B.   routing to runway 22.

C.   taxiway 22.

Answer (A) is correct. *(AIM Chap 2)*
   DISCUSSION: A runway location sign has a black background with a yellow inscription and a yellow border. The inscription on the sign informs the pilot (s)he is located on Runway 22.
   Answer (B) is incorrect. A direction sign with a yellow background and black inscription would be required to inform a pilot (s)he is routing to Runway 22. Answer (C) is incorrect. Only runways are numbered. Taxiways are always identified by a letter.

10. A lighted heliport may be identified by a

A.   green, yellow, and white rotating beacon.

B.   flashing yellow light.

C.   blue lighted square landing area.

Answer (A) is correct. *(AIM Para 2-1-10)*
   DISCUSSION: A lighted heliport may be identified by a green, yellow, and white rotating beacon.
   Answer (B) is incorrect. A flashing yellow light is sometimes used to help a pilot locate a lighted water airport. It is used in conjunction with the lighted water airport's white and yellow rotating beacon. Answer (C) is incorrect. A lighted heliport may be identified by a green, yellow, and white rotating beacon, not a blue lighted square landing area.

11. An airport's rotating beacon operated during daylight hours indicates

A.   there are obstructions on the airport.

B.   that weather at the airport located in Class D airspace is below basic VFR weather minimums.

C.   the Air Traffic Control tower is not in operation.

Answer (B) is correct. *(AIM Para 2-1-10)*
   DISCUSSION: Operation of the airport beacon during daylight hours often indicates that weather at the airport located in controlled airspace (e.g., Class D airspace) is below basic VFR weather minimums, i.e., less than 1,000 ft. ceiling or 3 SM visibility. Note that there is no regulatory requirement for daylight operation of an airport's rotating beacon.
   Answer (A) is incorrect. The obstructions near or on airports are usually listed in NOTAMs or the Chart Supplement as appropriate to their hazard. Answer (C) is incorrect. There is no visual signal of tower operation/non-operation.

12. A military air station can be identified by a rotating beacon that emits

A.   white and green alternating flashes.

B.   two quick, white flashes between green flashes.

C.   green, yellow, and white flashes.

Answer (B) is correct. *(AIM Para 2-1-8)*
   DISCUSSION: Lighted land airports are distinguished by white and green airport beacons. To further distinguish it as a military airport, there are two quick white flashes between each green.
   Answer (A) is incorrect. White and green alternating flashes designate a lighted civilian land airport. Answer (C) is incorrect. Green, yellow, and white flashes designate a lighted heliport.

13. Which is the correct traffic pattern departure procedure to use at a noncontrolled airport?

A.   Depart in any direction consistent with safety, after crossing the airport boundary.

B.   Make all turns to the left.

C.   Comply with any FAA traffic pattern established for the airport.

Answer (C) is correct. *(14 CFR 91.127)*
   DISCUSSION: Each person operating an airplane to or from an airport without an operating control tower shall (1) in the case of an airplane approaching to land, make all turns of that airplane to the left unless the airport displays approved light signals or visual markings indicating that turns should be made to the right, in which case the pilot shall make all turns to the right, and (2) in the case of an airplane departing the airport, comply with any FAA traffic pattern for that airport.
   Answer (A) is incorrect. The correct traffic pattern departure procedure at a noncontrolled airport is to comply with any FAA established traffic pattern, not to depart in any direction after crossing the airport boundary. Answer (B) is incorrect. The FAA may establish right- or left-hand traffic patterns, not only left-hand traffic.

14. Which statement about longitude and latitude is true?

A.   Lines of longitude are parallel to the Equator.

B.   Lines of longitude cross the Equator at right angles.

C.   The 0° line of latitude passes through Greenwich, England.

Answer (B) is correct. *(PHAK Chap 16)*
   DISCUSSION: Lines of longitude are drawn from the north pole to the south pole and cross the equator at right angles. They indicate the number of degrees east and west of the 0° line of longitude, which passes through Greenwich, England.
   Answer (A) is incorrect. Lines of latitude, not longitude, are parallel to the equator. Answer (C) is incorrect. The 0° line of longitude, not latitude, passes through Greenwich, England.

15. (Refer to Figure 26 on page 197.) (Refer to area 4.) You have been hired to inspect the tower under construction at 46.9N and 98.6W, near Jamestown Regional (JMS). What must you receive prior to flying your unmanned aircraft in this area?

    A. Authorization from the military.

    B. Authorization from ATC.

    C. Authorization from the National Park Service.

Answer (B) is correct. *(PHAK)*

DISCUSSION: There is a tower approximately 5 miles east of the Jamestown Regional airport with a height of 1,727 ft. MSL. The letters UC beneath the altitude indicate the tower is under construction. This tower is located within the boundary of a dashed magenta line, which indicated Class E controlled airspace starts at the surface. Operations in controlled airspace require prior authorization from ATC.

NOTE: Coordinates can be read as a decimal format or degrees-minutes-seconds. Similar to a clock, there are 60 seconds in a minute and 60 minutes in each degree. Therefore, 46.9N and 98.6W are the approximate decimal equivalents to 46 degrees 55 minutes and 98 degrees 33 minutes.

Answer (A) is incorrect. Operations in Class E controlled airspace require authorization from ATC, not the Military. Answer (C) is incorrect. The tower under construction is located in Class E controlled airspace, not a national park.

16. (Refer to Figure 26 on page 197.) (Refer to area 2.) What is the approximate latitude and longitude of Cooperstown Airport?

    A. 47°25'N – 98°06'W.

    B. 47°25'N – 99°54'W.

    C. 47°55'N – 98°06'W.

Answer (A) is correct. *(PHAK Chap 16)*

DISCUSSION: First locate the Cooperstown Airport on Fig. 26. It is just above 2, middle right of chart. Note that it is to the left (west) of the 98° line of longitude. The line of longitude on the left side of the chart is 99°. Thus, the longitude is a little bit more than 98°W, but not near 99°W.

With respect to latitude, note that Cooperstown Airport is just below a line of latitude that is not marked in terms of degrees. However, the next line of latitude below is 47° (see the left side of the chart, northwest of Jamestown Airport). As with longitude, there are two lines of latitude for every degree of latitude; i.e., each line is 30 min. Thus, latitude of the Cooperstown Airport is almost 47°30'N, but not quite. Accordingly, Cooperstown Airport's latitude is 47°25'N and longitude is 98°06'W.

Answer (B) is incorrect. Cooperstown is just west of the 98° line of longitude (not just east of 99°). Answer (C) is incorrect. Cooperstown is just south of the 47°30' line of latitude (not the 48°00' line).

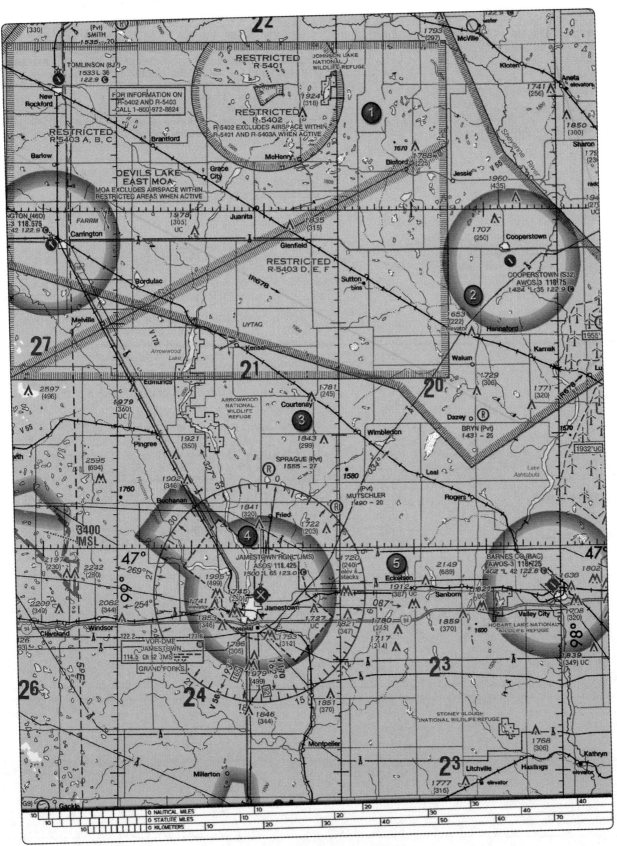

Figure 26. – Sectional Chart Excerpt.
NOTE: Chart is not to scale and should not be used for navigation. Use associated scale.

17. (Refer to Figure 21 on page 199.) What airport is located approximately 47 (degrees) 40 (minutes) N latitude and 101 (degrees) 26 (minutes) W longitude?

    A. Mercer County Regional Airport.

    B. Semchenko Airport.

    C. Garrison Airport.

Answer (C) is correct. *(Aeronautical charts)*
    DISCUSSION: You are asked to locate an airport at 47°40'00"N latitude and 101°26'00"W longitude. Referring to the chart, find the longitude (vertical) 101° W line (increases to the west) and the latitude (horizontal) 48° line (decreases to the south). The longitude line to the west of 101° is 101° 30 min. (each additional crossline is 1 min.). Find 101°26 min. by moving east four crosslines. The latitude line south of 48° is 47° 30 min. (each additional crossline is 1 min.). Find 47° 40 min. by moving north an additional 10 crosslines. These two coordinates (101°26'00"W and 47°40'00"N) intersect over Garrison Airfield.
    Answer (A) is incorrect. The coordinates for Mercer County Regional are approximately 47° 17 min. 00 sec. N latitude and 101° 35 min. 00 sec. W longitude. Answer (B) is incorrect. The coordinates for Semchenko are approximately 47° 46 min. 00 sec. N latitude and 101° 16 min. 00 sec. W longitude.

18. (Refer to Figure 21 on page 199.) (Refer to area 2.) Which airport is located at approximately 47°34'30"N latitude and 100°43'00"W longitude?

    A. Linrud.

    B. Makeeff.

    C. Johnson.

Answer (B) is correct. *(PHAK Chap 16)*
    DISCUSSION: On Fig. 21, you are asked to locate an airport at 47°34'30"N latitude and 100°43'W longitude. Note that the 101°W longitude line runs down the middle of the figure. Accordingly, the airport you are seeking is 17 min. to the east of that line.
    Each crossline is 1 min. on the latitude and longitude lines. The 48°N latitude line is approximately two-thirds of the way up the chart. The 47°30'N latitude line is about one-fourth of the way up. One-third up from 47°30'N to 48°N latitude would be 47°39'N. At this spot is Makeeff Airport.
    Answer (A) is incorrect. Linrud is north of the 48°N latitude line. Answer (C) is incorrect. Johnson is south of the 47°30'N latitude line.

19. (Refer to Figure 21 on page 199.) (Refer to area 3.) Which airport is located at approximately 47°21'N latitude and 101°01'W longitude?

    A. Underwood.

    B. Pietsch.

    C. Washburn.

Answer (C) is correct. *(PHAK Chap 16)*
    DISCUSSION: On Fig. 21, find the 48° line of latitude (2/3 up the figure). Start at the 47°30' line of latitude (the line below the 48° line) and count down nine tick marks to the 47°21'N tick mark and draw a horizontal line on the chart. Next find the 101° line of longitude and go left one tick mark and draw a vertical line. The closest airport is Washburn.
    Answer (A) is incorrect. Underwood is a city (not an airport) northwest of Washburn by about 1 in. Answer (B) is incorrect. Pietsch is north of the 48°00' latitude line.

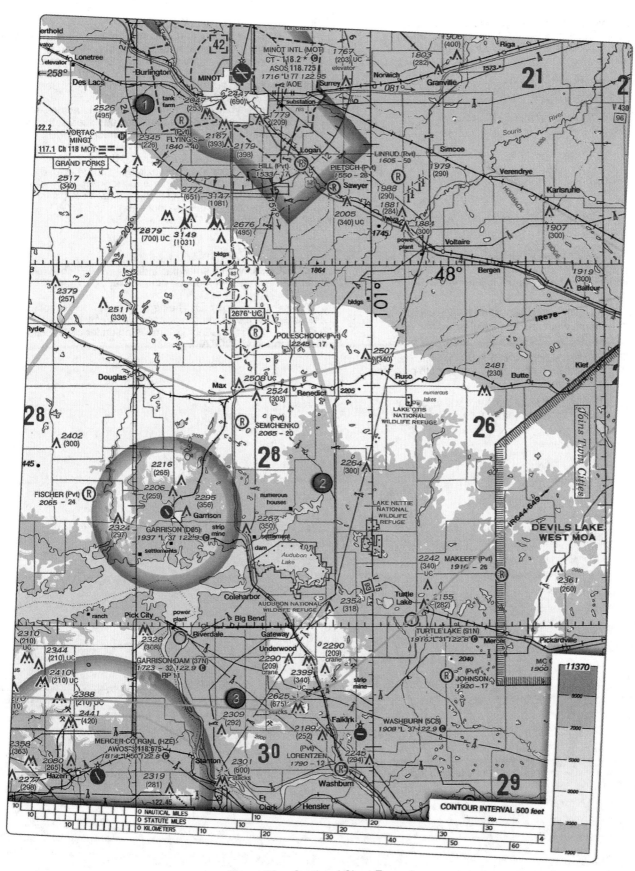

Figure 21. – Sectional Chart Excerpt.
NOTE: Chart is not to scale and should not be used for navigation. Use associated scale.

20. (Refer to Figure 20 on page 201.) (Refer to area 3.) Determine the approximate latitude and longitude of Currituck County Airport.

    A.   36°24'N – 76°01'W.

    B.   36°48'N – 76°01'W.

    C.   47°24'N – 75°58'W.

Answer (A) is correct. *(PHAK Chap 16)*
    DISCUSSION: On Fig. 20, find the Currituck County Airport, which is northeast of area 3. Note that the airport symbol is just to the west of 76° longitude (find 76° just north of Virginia Beach). There are 60 min. between the 76°W and 77°W lines of longitude, with each tick mark depicting 1 min. The airport is one tick mark to the west of the 76° line, or 76°01'W.
    The latitude is below the 30-min. latitude line across the center of the chart. See the numbered latitude lines at the top (37°) of the chart. Since each tick mark represents 1 min. of latitude, and the airport is approximately six tick marks south of the 36°30'N latitude, the airport is at 36°24'N latitude. Thus, Currituck County Airport is at approximately 36°24'N – 76°01'W.
    Answer (B) is incorrect. Currituck County Airport is south of the 36°30'N (not 37°00'N) line of latitude. Answer (C) is incorrect. Currituck County Airport is west (not east) of the 76°W line of longitude and 47°24'N is 11°N of the airport.

21. (Refer to Figure 20 on page 201.) Why would the small flag at Lake Drummond in area 2 of the sectional chart be important to a remote PIC?

    A.   The flag indicates a VFR check point for manned aircraft, and a higher volume of air traffic should be expected there.

    B.   The flag indicates a GPS check point that can be used by both manned and remote pilots for orientation.

    C.   The flag indicates that there will be a large obstruction depicted on the next printing of the chart.

Answer (A) is correct. *(PHAK Chap 16)*
    DISCUSSION: The small flag indicates a VFR checkpoint. A higher concentration of manned aircraft may be expected in the vicinity.
    Answer (B) is incorrect. The flag indicates a VFR (not a GPS) checkpoint. Answer (C) is incorrect. A new obstruction may be depicted using the letters UC, meaning under construction, or will be reported via NOTAM.

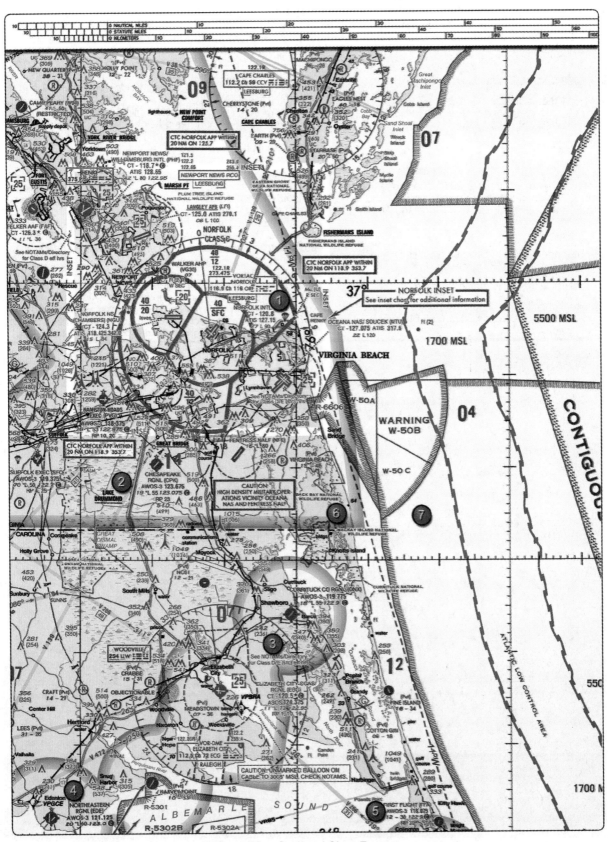

Figure 20. – Sectional Chart Excerpt.
NOTE: Chart is not to scale and should not be used for navigation. Use associated scale.

22. (Refer to Figure 23 on page 203.) (Refer to area 3.) What is the height of the lighted obstacle approximately 6 nautical miles southwest of Savannah International?

    A.   1,498 feet MSL.

    B.   1,531 feet AGL.

    C.   1,548 feet MSL.

Answer (C) is correct. *(ACL)*
    DISCUSSION: On Fig. 23, find the lighted obstacle noted by its proximity to Savannah International by being outside the surface area of the Class C airspace, which has a 5-NM radius. It is indicated by the obstacle symbol with arrows or lightning flashes extending from the tip. According to the numbers to the northeast of the symbol, the height of the obstacle is 1,548 ft. MSL or 1,534 ft. AGL.
    Answer (A) is incorrect. The unlighted tower 8 NM, not 6 NM, southwest of the airport has a height of 1,498 ft. MSL. Answer (B) is incorrect. An unlighted tower 9 NM, not 6 NM, southwest of the airport has a height of 1,531 ft. AGL.

23. (Refer to Figure 23 on page 203.) The flag symbols at Statesboro Bullock County Airport, Claxton-Evans County Airport, and Ridgeland Airport are

    A.   outer boundaries of Savannah Class C airspace.

    B.   airports with special traffic patterns.

    C.   visual checkpoints to identify position for initial callup prior to entering Savannah Class C airspace.

Answer (C) is correct. *(ACL)*
    DISCUSSION: On Fig. 23, note the flag symbols at Claxton-Evans County Airport (1 in. to the left of 2), at Statesboro Bullock County Airport (2 in. above 2), and at Ridgeland Airport (2 in. above 3). These airports are visual checkpoints to identify position for initial callup prior to entering the Savannah Class C airspace.
    Answer (A) is incorrect. They do not indicate outer boundaries of the Class C airspace. The flags are outside the Class C airspace area, the boundaries of which are marked by solid magenta lines. Answer (B) is incorrect. Airports with special traffic patterns are noted in the Chart Supplement and also by markings at the airport around the wind sock or tetrahedron.

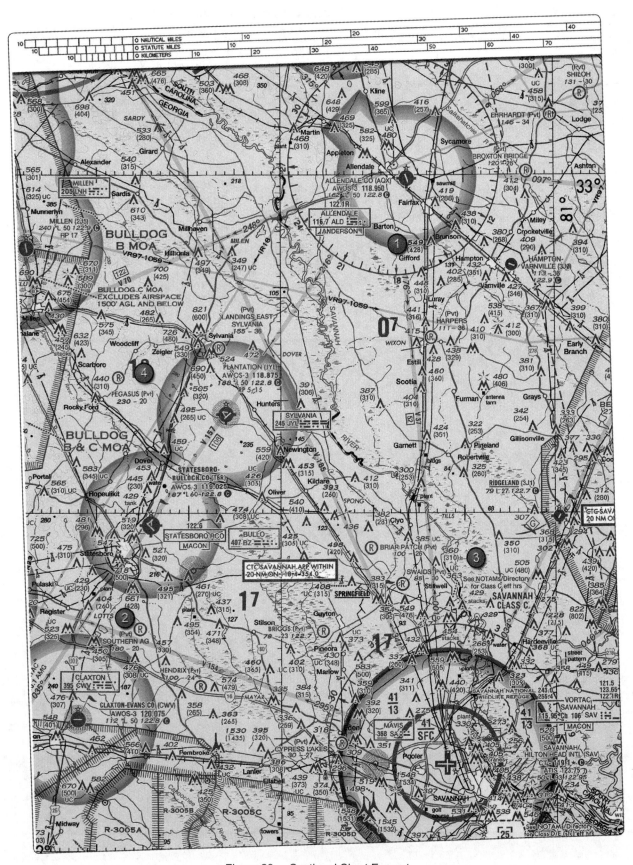

Figure 23. – Sectional Chart Excerpt.
NOTE: Chart is not to scale and should not be used for navigation. Use associated scale.

24. As standard operating practice, all inbound traffic to an airport without a control tower should continuously monitor the appropriate facility from a distance of

    A. 25 miles.

    B. 20 miles.

    C. 10 miles.

Answer (C) is correct. *(AIM Para 4-1-9)*
    DISCUSSION: As a standard operating practice, pilots of inbound traffic to an airport without a control tower should continuously monitor and communicate, as appropriate, on the designated Common Traffic Advisory Frequency (CTAF) from 10 mi. to landing.
    Answer (A) is incorrect. All inbound traffic to an airport without a control tower should continuously monitor the CTAF from a distance of 10 mi., not 25 mi. Answer (B) is incorrect. All inbound traffic to an airport without a control tower should continuously monitor the CTAF from a distance of 10 mi., not 20 mi.

25. (Refer to Figure 22 on page 205.) Weather information is available at the Coeur d'Alene (COE) Airport (area 2)

    A. at the flight service station on the field.

    B. from AWOS 3 135.075.

    C. from UNICOM (CTAF) on 122.8.

Answer (B) is correct. *(PHAK Chap 13 and Sectional Chart)*
    DISCUSSION: On the sectional chart excerpt, to the right of the airport, you will find in the information for the airport weather in the third line. It states the type of Automated Weather Observation System (AWOS) and the frequency of 135.075.
    Answer (A) is incorrect. There is no flight service station on the field. This would be found in the Chart Supplement as FSS "on arpt" in the Communications section for this airport. Answer (C) is incorrect. The UNICOM (CTAF) is the Common Traffic Advisory Frequency.

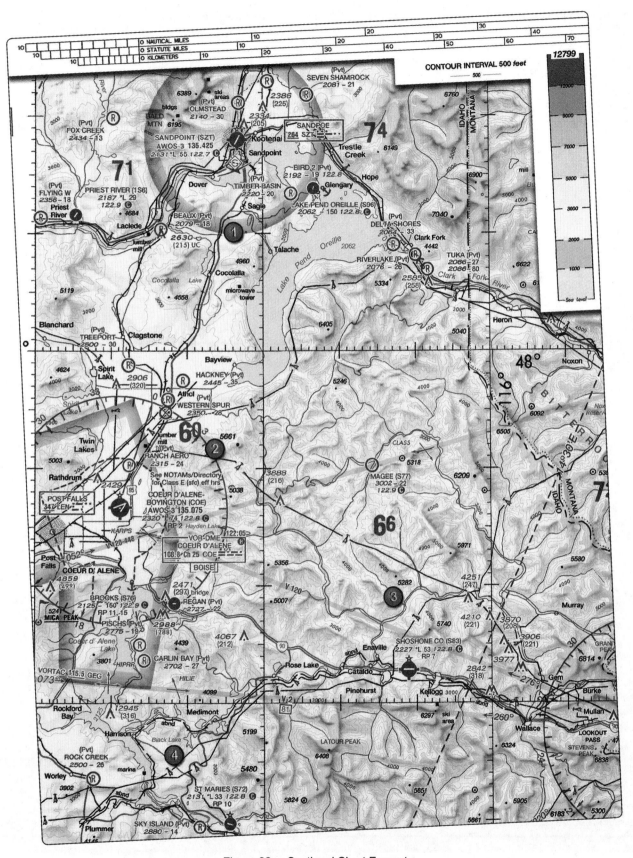

Figure 22. – Sectional Chart Excerpt.
NOTE: Chart is not to scale and should not be used for navigation. Use associated scale.

26. (Refer to Figure 52 on page 207.) Traffic patterns in effect at Lincoln Municipal are

    A. to the right on Runway 14 and Runway 32; to the left on Runway 18 and Runway 35.

    B. to the left on Runway 14 and Runway 32; to the right on Runway 18 and Runway 35.

    C. to the right on Runways 14 - 32.

Answer (B) is correct. *(Chart Supplement)*
    DISCUSSION: Fig. 52 contains the Chart Supplement excerpt for Lincoln Municipal. For this question, you need to locate the runway end data elements, i.e., Rwy 18, Rwy 14, Rwy 32, Rwy 17, Rwy 35, and Rwy 36. Traffic patterns are to the left unless right traffic is noted by the contraction "Rgt tfc." The only runways with right traffic are Rwy 18 and Rwy 35.
    Answer (A) is incorrect. Traffic patterns are to the left, not right, for Rwy 14 and Rwy 32. Traffic patterns are to the right, not left, for Rwy 18 and Rwy 35. Answer (C) is incorrect. The traffic pattern for Rwy 14 and Rwy 32 is to the left, not right.

27. (Refer to Figure 52 on page 207.) Where is Loup City Municipal located with relation to the city?

    A. Northwest approximately 4 miles.

    B. Northwest approximately 1 mile.

    C. East approximately 7 miles.

Answer (B) is correct. *(Chart Supplement)*
    DISCUSSION: Fig. 52 contains the Chart Supplement excerpt for Loup City Municipal. On the first line, the third item listed, 1 NW, means that Loup City Municipal is located approximately 1 NM northwest of the associated city.
    Answer (A) is incorrect. 4 NW is the approximate location of LNK airport to the associated city, not Loup City Municipal airport. Answer (C) is incorrect. The airport is approximately 1 NM northwest, not 7 NM east, of the associated city.

NEBRASKA 271

LINCOLN (LNK) 4 NW UTC−6(−5DT) N40°51.05′ W96°45.55′ **OMAHA**
1219 B S4 **FUEL** 100LL, JET A TPA—See Remarks ARFF Index—See Remarks H−5C, L−10I
NOTAM FILE LNK IAP, AD
RWY 18−36: H12901X200 (ASPH−CONC−GRVD) S−100, D−200,
  2S−175, 2D−400 HIRL
  RWY 18: MALSR. PAPI(P4L)—GA 3.0° TCH 55′. Rgt tfc. 0.4%
    down.
  RWY 36: MALSR. PAPI(P4L)—GA 3.0° TCH 57′.
RWY 14−32: H8649X150 (ASPH−CONC−GRVD) S−80, D−170,
  2S−175, 2D−280 MIRL
  RWY 14: REIL. VASI(V4L)—GA 3.0° TCH 48′. Thld dsplcd 363′.
  RWY 32: VASI(V4L)—GA 3.0° TCH 50′. Thld dsplcd 470′.
    Pole. 0.3% up.
RWY 17−35: H5800X100 (ASPH−CONC−AFSC) S−49, D−60
  HIRL 0.8% up S
  RWY 17: REIL. PAPI(P4L)—GA 3.0° TCH 44′.
  RWY 35: ODALS. PAPI(P4L)—GA 3.0° TCH 30′. Rgt tfc.
RUNWAY DECLARED DISTANCE INFORMATION
  RWY 14: TORA−8649 TODA−8649 ASDA−8649 LDA−8286
  RWY 17: TORA−5800 TODA−5800 ASDA−5400 LDA−5400
  RWY 18: TORA−12901 TODA−12901 ASDA−12901 LDA−12901
  RWY 32: TORA−8649 TODA−8649 ASDA−8286 LDA−7816
  RWY 35: TORA−5800 TODA−5800 ASDA−5800 LDA−5800
  RWY 36: TORA−12901 TODA−12901 ASDA−12901 LDA−12901
AIRPORT REMARKS: Attended continuously. Birds invof arpt. Rwy 18 designated calm wind rwy. Rwy 32 apch holdline
  on South A twy. TPA−2219 (1000), heavy military jet 3000 (1781). Class I, ARFF Index B. ARFF Index C level
  equipment provided. Rwy 18−36 touchdown and rollout rwy visual range avbl. When twr clsd MIRL Rwy 14−32
  preset on low ints, HIRL Rwy 18−36 and Rwy 17−35 preset on med ints, ODALS Rwy 35 operate continuously on
  med ints, MALSR Rwy 18 and Rwy 36 operate continuously and REIL Rwy 14 and Rwy 17 operate continuously
  on low ints. VASI Rwy 14 and Rwy 32, PAPI Rwy 17, Rwy 35, Rwy 18 and Rwy 36 on continuously.
WEATHER DATA SOURCES: ASOS (402) 474−9214. LLWAS
COMMUNICATIONS: CTAF 118.5 **ATIS** 118.05 **UNICOM** 122.95
  RCO 122.65 (COLUMBUS RADIO)
Ⓡ **APP/DEP CON** 124.0 (180°−359°) 124.8 (360°−179°)
  TOWER 118.5 125.7 (1130−0600Z‡) **GND CON** 121.9 **CLNC DEL** 120.7
AIRSPACE: CLASS C svc 1130−0600Z‡ ctc **APP CON** other times **CLASS E.**
RADIO AIDS TO NAVIGATION: NOTAM FILE LNK.
  (H) VORTACW 116.1 LNK Chan 108 N40°55.43′ W96°44.52′ 181° 4.4 NM to fld. 1370/9E
  POTTS NDB (MHW/LOM) 385 LN N40°44.83′ W96°45.75′ 355° 6.2 NM to fld. Unmonitored when twr clsd.
  ILS 111.1 I−OCZ Rwy 18. Class IB OM unmonitored.
  ILS 109.9 I−LNK Rwy 36 Class IA LOM POTTS NDB. MM unmonitored. LOM unmonitored when twr
    clsd.
COMM/NAV/WEATHER REMARKS: Emerg frequency 121.5 not available at twr.

LOUP CITY MUNI (ØF4) 1 NW UTC−6(−5DT) N41°17.20′ W98°59.41′ **OMAHA**
2071 B **FUEL** 100LL NOTAM FILE OLU L−10H, 12H
RWY 16−34: H3200X60 (CONC) S−12.5 MIRL
  RWY 34: Trees.
RWY 04−22: 2040X100 (TURF)
  RWY 04: Tree. **RWY 22:** Road.
AIRPORT REMARKS: Unattended. For svc call 308−745−1344/1244/0664.
COMMUNICATIONS: CTAF 122.9
RADIO AIDS TO NAVIGATION: NOTAM FILE OLU.
  WOLBACH (H) VORTAC 114.8 OBH Chan 95 N41°22.54′ W98°21.22′ 253° 29.3 NM to fld. 2010/7E.

MARTIN FLD (See SO SIOUX CITY)

Figure 52. − Chart Supplements U.S. (formerly Airport/Facility Directory).

28. The most comprehensive information on a given airport is provided by

    A. the Chart Supplements U.S. (formerly Airport Facility Directory).

    B. Notices to Airmen (NOTAMS).

    C. Terminal Area Chart (TAC).

Answer (A) is correct. *(PHAK Chap 16)*
    DISCUSSION: Chart Supplements are a listing of data on record with the FAA on all open-to-the-public airports, seaplane bases, heliports, military facilities, and selected private use airports.
    Answer (B) is incorrect. NOTAMs contain current notices to airmen that are considered essential to the safety of flight as well as supplemental data affecting other operational publications. Answer (C) is incorrect. A TAC is similar to a sectional chart, but the scale is larger. TACs provide an abundance of information in additional to airport data, such as navigational aids, airspace, and topography, but they are not the most comprehensive source for airport information.

29. (Refer to Figure 59 on page 209.) (Refer to area 2.) What kind of airport is Deshler (6D7)?

    A. A private airport with a grass runway.

    B. A public airport with a runway that is not a hard surface.

    C. An abandoned paved airport having landmark value.

Answer (B) is correct. *(AIM Chap 3)*
    DISCUSSION: According to the Sectional Chart Legend, a magenta circle with nothing indicated on the inside of the circle indicates that airport is not hard-surfaced.
    Answer (A) is incorrect. There is not a letter "R" inside the magenta circle indicating it is a private airport. Answer (C) is incorrect. There is no "X" inside the magenta circle to indicate it is an abandoned paved airport having landmark value.

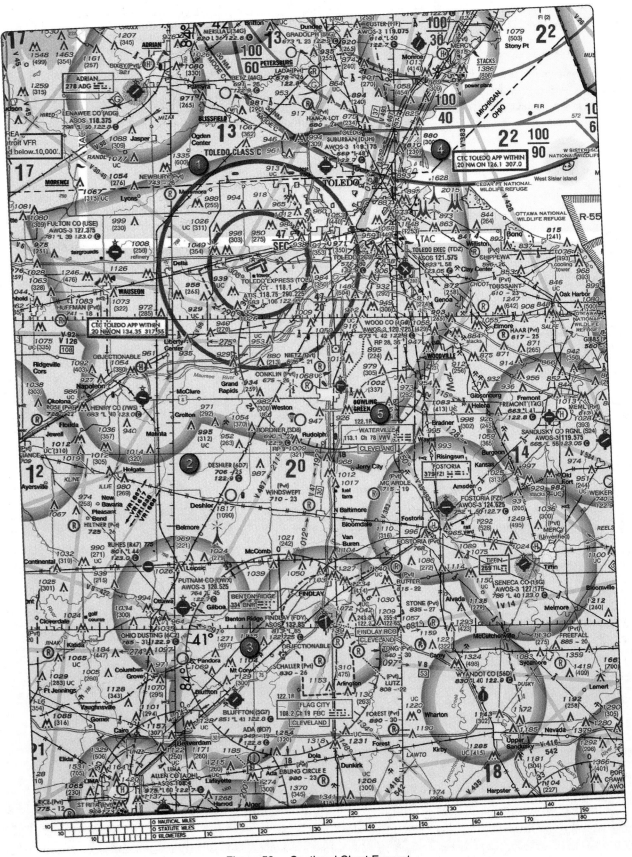

Figure 59. – Sectional Chart Excerpt.
NOTE: Chart is not to scale and should not be used for navigation. Use associated scale.

30. (Refer to Figure 71 on page 211.) (Refer to area 1.) Dubey Airport is

A. a privately owned airport restricted to use.

B. a restricted military stage field within restricted airspace.

C. an airport restricted to use by sport pilots only.

Answer (A) is correct. *(ACL)*

DISCUSSION: Dubey Airport (south of 1) is a private, i.e., nonpublic-use, airport as indicated by the term "(Pvt)" after the airport name. Private airports that are shown on the sectional charts have an emergency or landmark value. The airport symbol with the letter "R" in the center means it is a nonpublic-use airport.

Answer (B) is incorrect. Military airfields are labeled as AFB, NAS, AAF, NAAS, NAF, MCAS, or DND. Answer (C) is incorrect. Dubey is restricted by its use according to its owners and management.

31. (Refer to Figure 71 on page 211.) (Refer to area 6.) Sky Way Airport is

A. an airport restricted to use by private and recreational pilots.

B. a restricted military stage field within restricted airspace.

C. a nonpublic-use airport.

Answer (C) is correct. *(ACL)*

DISCUSSION: Sky Way Airport (west of 6) is a private, i.e., nonpublic-use, airport as indicated by the term "(Pvt)" after the airport name or the letter "R" in the center of the airport symbol. Private airports that are shown on the sectional charts have an emergency or landmark value.

Answer (A) is incorrect. Sky Way Airport (west of 6) is a private, i.e., nonpublic-use, airport as indicated by the term "(Pvt)" after the airport name or the letter "R" in the center of the airport symbol. This does not mean that only private and recreational pilots may use the airport. Answer (B) is incorrect. Military airfields are labeled as AFB, NAS, AAF, NAAS, NAF, MCAS, or DND.

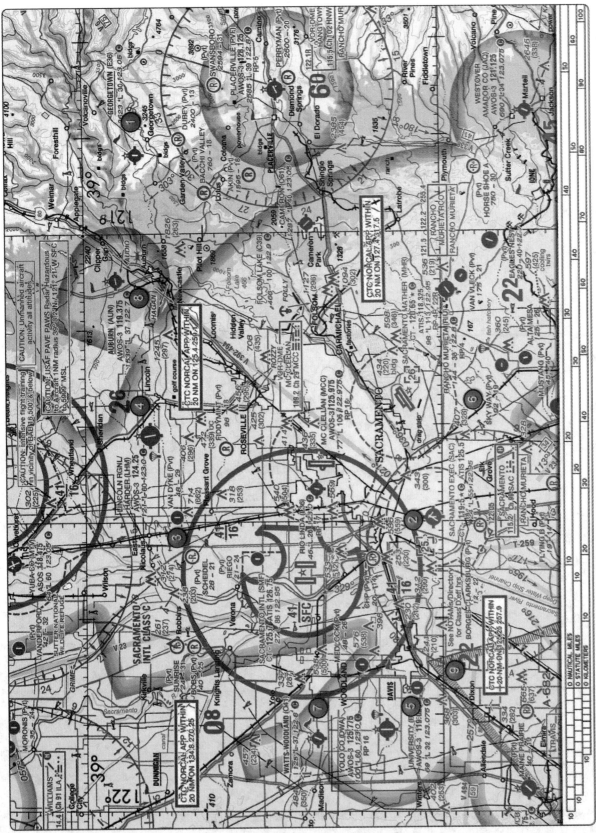

Figure 71. – Sectional Chart Excerpt.
NOTE: Chart is not to scale and should not be used for navigation. Use associated scale.

32. (Refer to Figure 64 below.) Which marking indicates a vehicle lane?

- A. A.
- B. C.
- C. E.

Answer (B) is correct. *(AIM Para 2-3-6)*
   DISCUSSION: Vehicle roadway markings define a route of travel for vehicles to cross areas intended for use by aircraft. The roadway is defined by solid white lines, with a dashed line in the middle to separate traffic traveling in opposite directions. White zipper markings may be used instead of solid white lines to define the edge of the roadway at some airports.
   Answer (A) is incorrect. This marking represents a surface painted holding position sign, not a vehicle lane. In this instance, the marking indicates the aircraft is holding short of Runway 19. Answer (C) is incorrect. This marking represents a standard taxiway holding position and is used by ATC to hold aircraft short of an intersecting taxiway.

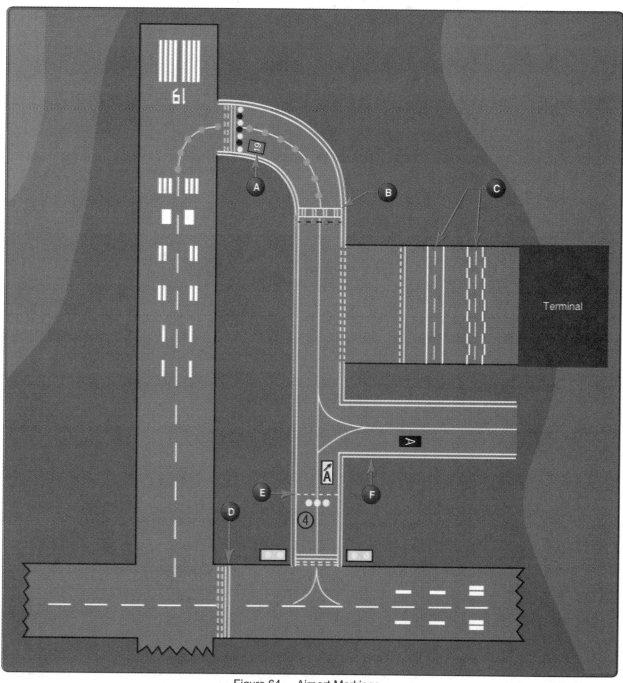

Figure 64. – Airport Markings.

33. (Refer to Legend 15 below.) What depicts a Class E airspace that begins at 700 feet AGL?

A. A dashed blue circle around an airport.

B. A solid magenta circle around an airport.

C. A magenta vignette that goes around an airport.

Answer (C) is correct. *(PHAK Chap 15)*
   DISCUSSION: Class E airspace floor begins at 700 ft. AGL. It is depicted by a magenta vignette circle or area around an airport.
   Answer (A) is incorrect. A dashed blue circle around an airport depicts a Class D airspace. Answer (B) is incorrect. A solid magenta circle going around an airport depicts Class C airspace.

DIRECTORY LEGEND   17

uncontrolled airports may contact ATC and FSS via VHF to a telephone connection to obtain an instrument clearance or close a VFR or IFR flight plan. They may also get an updated weather briefing prior to takeoff. Pilots will use four "key clicks" on the VHF radio to contact the appropriate ATC facility or six "key clicks" to contact the FSS. The GCO system is intended to be used only on the ground.
DEP CON—Departure Control. The symbol Ⓡ indicates radar departure control.
CLNC DEL—Clearance Delivery.
PRE TAXI CLNC—Pre taxi clearance.

VFR ADVSY SVC—VFR Advisory Service. Service provided by Non-Radar Approach Control.
   Advisory Service for VFR aircraft (upon a workload basis) ctc APP CON.
COMD POST—Command Post followed by the operator call sign in parenthesis.
PMSV—Pilot-to-Metro Service call sign, frequency and hours of operation, when full service is other than continuous. PMSV installations at which weather observation service is available shall be indicated, following the frequency and/or hours of operation as "Wx obsn svc 1900–0000Z‡" or "other times" may be used when no specific time is given. PMSV facilities manned by forecasters are considered "Full Service". PMSV facilities manned by weather observers are listed as "Limited Service".
OPS—Operations followed by the operator call sign in parenthesis.
CON
RANGE
FLT FLW—Flight Following
MEDIVAC
NOTE: Communication frequencies followed by the letter "X" indicate frequency available on request.

 AIRSPACE

Information concerning Class B, C, and part-time D and E surface area airspace shall be published with effective times. Class D and E surface area airspace that is continuous as established by Rulemaking Docket will not be shown.
CLASS B—Radar Sequencing and Separation Service for all aircraft in CLASS B airspace.
CLASS C—Separation between IFR and VFR aircraft and sequencing of VFR arrivals to the primary airport.
TRSA—Radar Sequencing and Separation Service for participating VFR Aircraft within a Terminal Radar Service Area.
Class C, D, and E airspace described in this publication is that airspace usually consisting of a 5 NM radius core surface area that begins at the surface and extends upward to an altitude above the airport elevation (charted in MSL for Class C and Class D). Class E surface airspace normally extends from the surface up to but not including the overlying controlled airspace.
When part-time Class C or Class D airspace defaults to Class E, the core surface area becomes Class E. This will be formatted as:
AIRSPACE: CLASS C svc "times" ctc APP CON other times CLASS E:
or
AIRSPACE: CLASS D svc "times" other times CLASS E.
When a part-time Class C, Class D or Class E surface area defaults to Class G, the core surface area becomes Class G up to, but not including, the overlying controlled airspace. Normally, the overlying controlled airspace is Class E airspace beginning at either 700' or 1200' AGL and may be determined by consulting the relevant VFR Sectional or Terminal Area Charts. This will be formatted as:
AIRSPACE: CLASS C svc "times" ctc APP CON other times CLASS G, with CLASS E 700' (or 1200') AGL & abv:
or
AIRSPACE: CLASS D svc "times" other times CLASS G with CLASS E 700' (or 1200') AGL & abv:
or
AIRSPACE: CLASS E svc "times" other times CLASS G with CLASS E 700' (or 1200') AGL & abv.
NOTE: AIRSPACE SVC "TIMES" INCLUDE ALL ASSOCIATED ARRIVAL EXTENSIONS. Surface area arrival extensions for instrument approach procedures become part of the primary core surface area. These extensions may be either Class D or Class E airspace and are effective concurrent with the times of the primary core surface area. For example, when a part-time Class C, Class D or Class E surface area defaults to Class G, the associated arrival extensions will default to Class G at the same time. When a part-time Class C or Class D surface area defaults to Class E, the arrival extensions will remain in effect as Class E airspace.
NOTE: CLASS E AIRSPACE EXTENDING UPWARD FROM 700 FEET OR MORE ABOVE THE SURFACE, DESIGNATED IN CONJUNCTION WITH AN AIRPORT WITH AN APPROVED INSTRUMENT PROCEDURE.
Class E 700' AGL (shown as magenta vignette on sectional charts) and 1200' AGL (blue vignette) areas are designated when necessary to provide controlled airspace for transitioning to/from the terminal and enroute environments. Unless otherwise specified, these 700'/1200' AGL Class E airspace areas remain in effect continuously, regardless of airport operating hours or surface area status. These transition areas should not be confused with surface areas or arrival extensions.
(See Chapter 3, AIRSPACE, in the Aeronautical Information Manual for further details)

NE, 09 FEB 20XX to 05 APR 20XX

Legend 15. – Chart Supplements U.S. (formerly Airport/Facility Directory).

STUDY UNIT EIGHT
AERONAUTICAL DECISION-MAKING AND PHYSIOLOGY

(14 pages of outline)

8.1 AERONAUTICAL DECISION-MAKING

1. **The applicant demonstrates understanding of Aeronautical Decision-Making (ADM).**

   a. **ADM** is a systematic approach to the mental process used by aircraft pilots to determine consistently the best course of action in response to a given set of circumstances.

   b. **Effective team communication**

      1) The remote PIC, person manipulating the controls, and VO must work out a method of communication, such as the use of a hand-held radio or other effective means, that would not create a distraction and allows them to understand each other. The remote PIC should evaluate which method is most appropriate for the operation and should be determined prior to flight.

   c. **Task management**

      1) Tasks very depending on the complexity of the operation. Depending upon the area of the operations, additional crewmembers may be needed to safely operate. Enough crewmembers should be utilized to ensure no one on the team becomes overloaded. Once a member of the team becomes overworked, there's a greater possibility of an incident/accident.

2. **The applicant demonstrates understanding of Crew Resource Management (CRM).**

   a. **CRM** in single-pilot or multiperson crew configurations is the effective use of all personnel and material assets available to a pilot or a flight crew.

      1) CRM emphasizes good communication and other interpersonal relationship skills.

   b. CRM is a component of ADM, where the pilot of sUAS makes effective use of all available resources: human resources, hardware, and information.

      1) Many remote pilots operating under Part 107 may use a VO, oversee other persons manipulating the controls of the small UA, or any other person who the remote PIC may interact with to ensure safe operations.

         a) Therefore, a remote PIC must be able to function in a team environment and maximize team performance.

      2) This skill set includes situational awareness, proper allocation of tasks to individuals, avoidance of work overloads in self and in others, and effectively communicating with other members of the crew, such as VOs and persons manipulating the controls of an sUAS.

3. **The applicant demonstrates understanding of situational awareness.**

    a. **Situational awareness** is pilot knowledge of where the aircraft is in regard to location, air traffic control, weather, regulations, aircraft status, and other factors that may affect flight.

    b. **Situational awareness** is the accurate perception of operational and environmental factors that affect the airplane, pilot, and passengers during a specific period of time.

        1) When situationally aware, the pilot has an overview of the total operation and is not fixed on one perceived significant factor.

        2) A pilot should maintain an awareness of the environmental conditions of the flight, such as spatial orientation of the airplane, and its relationship to terrain, traffic, weather, and airspace.

        3) To maintain situational awareness, all of the skills of aeronautical decision making should be used.

    c. **Obstacles to Maintaining Situational Awareness**

        1) Fatigue, stress, and work overload can cause a pilot to lose overall awareness of the flight situation.

        2) Complacency can be an obstacle to situational awareness by reducing a pilot's effectiveness in the cockpit.

4. **The applicant demonstrates understanding of hazardous attitudes.**

    a. **Antiauthority (*Don't tell me!*).** This attitude is found in people who do not like anyone telling them what to do. In a sense, they are saying, "No one can tell me what to do." They may be resentful of having someone tell them what to do or may regard rules, regulations, and procedures as silly or unnecessary. Of course, it is always your prerogative to question authority if you feel it is in error.

    b. **Impulsivity (*Do something quickly!*).** This is the attitude of people who frequently feel the need to do something -- anything -- immediately. They do not stop to think about what they are about to do, they do not determine the best alternative, and they do the first thing that comes to mind.

    c. **Invulnerability (*It won't happen to me.*).** Many people feel that accidents happen to others but never to them. They know accidents can happen, and they know that anyone can be affected. However, they never really feel or believe that they will be personally involved. Pilots who think this way are more likely to take chances and increase risk.

    d. **Macho (*I can do it.*).** Pilots who are always trying to prove that they are better than anyone else are thinking *I can do it -- I'll show them*. Pilots with this type of attitude will try to prove themselves by taking risks in order to impress others. While this pattern is thought to be a male characteristic, women are equally susceptible.

    e. **Resignation (*What's the use?*).** Pilots who think *What's the use?* do not see themselves as being able to make a great deal of difference in what happens to them. The pilot is apt to think that things go well due to good luck. When things go badly, the pilot may feel that someone is out to get him or her or may attribute the situation to bad luck. The pilot will leave the action to others, for better or worse. Sometimes, such pilots will even go along with unreasonable requests just to be nice.

5. **The applicant demonstrates understanding of hazard identifications and risk assessment.**

    a. **Hazard Identification.** Hazards in the sUAS and its operating environment must be identified, documented, and controlled. The analysis process used to define hazards needs to consider all components of the system, based on the equipment being used and the environment it is being operated in. The key question to ask during analysis of the sUAS and its operation is, "what if?" sUAS remote PICs are expected to exercise due diligence in identifying significant and reasonably foreseeable hazards related to their operations.

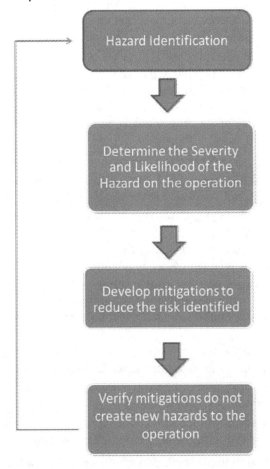

Hazard Identification and Risk Assessment Process Chart.

    b. Risk is the future impact of a hazard that is not controlled or eliminated. It can be viewed as future uncertainty created by the hazard.

c.   Risk management is the part of the decision-making process that relies on situational awareness, problem recognition, and good judgment to reduce risks associated with each flight.

    1)   The goal of risk management is to proactively identify safety-related hazards and mitigate the associated risks.

        a)   Risk management is an important component of ADM. When a pilot follows good decision-making practices, the inherent risk in a flight is reduced or even eliminated.

        b)   The ability to make good decisions is based on direct or indirect experience and education.

        c)   A remote pilot must consider risk management to prevent the final link in the accident chain.

    2)   There are four risk elements involved in decisions made during a flight: the **P**ilot in command, the **A**irplane, the en**V**ironment, and the **E**xternal pressures of the operation. You can remember these items using the PAVE checklist. In decision making, each risk element is evaluated to obtain an accurate perception of circumstances.

        a)   **Pilot.** Consider such factors as competency, condition of health, mental and emotional state, level of fatigue, and many other variables.

        b)   **Airplane.** Assess performance, equipment, or airworthiness.

        c)   **enVironment.** Consider a range of factors not related to pilot or airplane: weather, air traffic control, NAVAIDs, terrain, takeoff and landing areas, and surrounding obstacles.

        d)   **External pressures.** Assessing factors relating to pilot, airplane, and environment is largely influenced by the purpose of the operation. Decisions should be made in the context of why the flight is being made, how critical it is to maintain the schedule, and whether the trip is worth the risks.

d.   **Risk Analysis and Assessment.** The risk assessment should use a conventional breakdown of risk by its two components: severity and likelihood of occurrence.

    1)   Severity and Likelihood Criteria. Each level of severity and likelihood needs to be defined in terms that are realistic for the operational environment. This ensures each remote PIC's decision tools are relevant to their operations and operational environment, recognizing the extensive diversity that exists.

        a)   The definitions and construction of the matrix are left to the sUAS remote PIC to design. An example of severity and likelihood definitions is shown in Table 1, Sample Severity and Likelihood Criteria.

Severity of Consequences			Likelihood of Occurrence		
Severity Level	Definition	Value	Likelihood Level	Definition	Value
Catastrophic	Equipment destroyed, multiple deaths.	5	Frequent	Likely to occur many times	5
Hazardous	Large reduction in safety margins, physical distress, or a workload such that crewmembers cannot be relied upon to perform their tasks accurately or completely. Serious injury or death. Major equipment damage.	4	Occasional	Likely to occur sometimes	4
Major	Significant reduction in safety margins, reduction in the ability of crewmembers to cope with adverse operating conditions as a result of an increase in workload, or as result of conditions impairing their efficiency. Serious incident. Injury to persons.	3	Remote	Unlikely, but possible to occur	3
Minor	Nuisance. Operating limitations. Use of emergency procedures. Minor incident.	2	Improbable	Very unlikely to occur	2
Negligible	Little consequence.	1	Extremely Improbable	Almost inconceivable that the event will occur	1

Table 1. – Sample Severity and Likelihood Criteria.

2)   **Risk Acceptance.** In the development of risk assessment criteria, sUAS remote PICs are expected to develop risk acceptance procedures, including acceptance criteria and designation of authority and responsibility for risk management decision making. The acceptability of risk can be evaluated using a risk matrix. Table 2, Risk Assessment Matrix, shows three areas of acceptability. Risk matrices may be color coded; unacceptable (red), acceptable (green), and acceptable with mitigation (yellow).

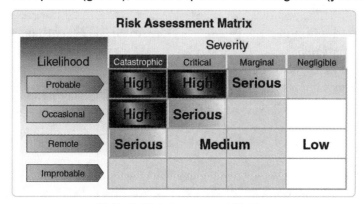

Table 2. Risk Assessment Matrix.

a)   **Unacceptable (Red).** Where combinations of severity and likelihood cause risk to fall into the red area, the risk would be assessed as unacceptable and further work would be required to design an intervention to eliminate that associated hazard or to control the factors that lead to higher risk likelihood or severity.

b)   **Acceptable (Green).** Where the assessed risk falls into the green area, it may be accepted without further action. The objective in risk management should always be to reduce risk to as low as practicable regardless of whether or not the assessment shows that it can be accepted as is.

c)   **Acceptable with Mitigation (Yellow).** Where the risk assessment falls into the yellow area, the risk may be accepted under defined conditions of mitigation.

i)   An example of this situation would be an assessment of the impact of an sUAS operation near a school yard. Scheduling the operation to take place when school is not in session could be one mitigation to prevent undue risk to the children that study and play there.

ii)   Another mitigation could be restricting people from the area of operations by placing cones or security personnel to prevent unauthorized access during the sUAS flight operation.

3)   Other Risk Assessment Tools for Flight and Operational Risk Management. Other tools can also be used for flight or operational risk assessments and can be developed by the remote PICs themselves.

a)   The key is to ensure that all potential hazards and risks are identified and appropriate actions are taken to reduce the risk to persons and property not associated with the operations.

4)   Reducing Risk. Risk analyses should concentrate not only on assigning levels of severity and likelihood, but on determining why these particular levels were selected. This is referred to as root cause analysis and is the first step in developing effective controls to reduce risk to lower levels. In many cases, simple brainstorming sessions among crewmembers is the most effective and affordable method of finding ways to reduce risk. This also has the advantage of involving people who will ultimately be required to implement the controls developed.

a) It is also very easy to get quite bogged down in trying to identify all hazards and risks. That is not the purpose of a risk assessment. The focus should be upon those hazards which pose the greatest risks. As stated earlier, by documenting and compiling these processes, a remote PIC can build an arsenal of safety practices that will add to the safety and success of future operations.

5) Sample Hazard Identification and Risk Assessment.

a) EXAMPLE: I am the remote PIC of an sUAS in the proximity of an accident scene shooting aerial footage. Much like pilots in manned aircraft must adhere to preflight action (14 CFR 91.103), I must adhere to preflight familiarization, inspection, and aircraft operations (14 CFR 107.49). Let's say that there is an obvious takeoff and landing site that I intend to use. What if, while I am operating a manned aircraft [emergency medical services (EMS) helicopter] requires use of the same area and I am not left with a suitable landing site? Furthermore, I am running low on power. If I consider this situation prior to flight, I can use the Basic Hazard Identification and Mitigation Process. Through this process, I might determine that an acceptable level of risk can be achieved by also having an alternate landing site and possibly additional sites at which I can sacrifice the UA to avoid imposing risk to people on the ground or to manned aircraft operations.

i) It is really a simple process. I must consider the hazards presented during this particular operation, determine the risk severity, and then develop a plan to lessen (or mitigate) the risk to an acceptable level.

ii) By documenting and compiling these processes, I can build an arsenal of safety practices that will add to the safety and success of future operations. Some proven methods that can help a new remote PIC along the way are discussed further in this study unit.

b) Hazard Identification. Using the Minimums (PAVE) Checklist for Risk Management, I will set personal minimums based upon my specific flight experience, health habits, and tolerance for stress, just to name a few. After identifying hazards, I will assess them with the Hazard Identification and Risk Assessment Process Chart.

i) **P**ersonal: Am I healthy for flight and what are my personal minimums based upon my experience operating this sUAS? During this step, I will often use the IMSAFE checklist in order to perform a more in-depth evaluation:

- **I**llness – Am I suffering from any illness or symptom of an illness which might affect me in flight?

- **M**edication – Am I currently taking any drugs (prescription or over-the-counter)?

- **S**tress – Am I experiencing any psychological or emotional factors which might affect my performance?

- **A**lcohol – Have I consumed alcohol within the last 8 to 24 hours?

- **F**atigue – Have I received sufficient sleep and rest in the recent past?

- **E**motion – Am I emotional due to any factor? Bereavement, arguments, hostility, stress.

ii)   **A**ircraft: Have I conducted a preflight check of my sUAS [aircraft, control station (CS), takeoff and landing equipment, etc.] and determined it to be in a condition for safe operation? Is the filming equipment properly secured to the aircraft prior to flight?

iii)   En**V**ironment: What is the weather like? Am I comfortable and experienced enough to fly in the forecast weather conditions? Have I considered all of my options and left myself an "out?" Have I determined alternative landing spots in case of an emergency?

iv)   **E**xternal Pressures: Am I stressed or anxious? Is this a flight that will cause me to be stressed or anxious? Is there pressure to complete the flight operation quickly? Am I dealing with an unhealthy safety culture? Am I being honest with myself and others about my personal operational abilities and limitations?

c)   Controlling Risk. After hazards and risks are fully understood through the preceding steps, risk controls must be designed and implemented. These may be additional or changed procedures, additional or modified equipment, the addition of VOs, or any of a number of other changes.

d)   Residual and Substitute Risk. Residual risk is the risk remaining after mitigation has been completed. Often, this is a multistep process, continuing until risk has been mitigated down to an acceptable level necessary to begin or continue operation.

i)   After these controls are designed, but before the operation begins or continues, an assessment must be made of whether the controls are likely to be effective and/or if they introduce new hazards to the operation.

ii)   The latter condition, introduction of new hazards, is referred to as substitute risk, a situation where the cure is worse than the disease.

iii)   The loop seen in Figure 1 that returns back to the top of the diagram depicts the use of the preceding hazard identification, risk analysis, and risk assessment processes to determine if the modified operation is acceptable.

e)   Starting the Operation. Once appropriate risk controls are developed and implemented, then the operation can begin.

8.2 PHYSIOLOGY

1. **The applicant demonstrates understanding of physiological considerations and their effects on safety, such as dehydration and heatstroke.**

    a. **Dehydration** is the excessive loss of water from the body, as from illness or fluid deprivation.

       1) This fluid loss can occur in any environment. Causes include hot cockpits and flight lines, high humidity, diuretic drinks (i.e., coffee, tea, cola), as well as improper attire.

    b. Some common signs and symptoms of dehydration include headache, fatigue, cramps, sleepiness, dizziness, and with severe dehydration, lethargy and coma.

       1) Heat exhaustion often accompanies dehydration. Below are the three stages of heat exhaustion, along with accompanying signs and symptoms.

          a) Heat stress (body temp., 99.5°-100° F) – reduces performance, decision-making ability, alertness, and visual capabilities.

          b) Heat exhaustion (body temp., 101°-105° F) – fatigue, nausea/vomiting, cramps, rapid breathing, and fainting.

          c) Heat stroke (body temp., >105° F) – body's heat control mechanism stops working, mental confusion, disorientation, and coma.

    c. To help prevent dehydration and heat exhaustion, you should drink two to four quarts of water every 24 hours. Or, follow the generally prescribed eight-glasses-a-day rule.

       1) Because each individual is physiologically different, this is only to be used as a guide. Your daily fluid intake should be varied to meet your individual needs depending on work conditions, environment, and individual physiology.

       2) Other useful tips on avoiding heat exhaustion are limiting your daily intake of caffeine and alcohol (both are diuretics), properly acclimating to major weather and/or climate changes, and planning ahead by carrying sufficient fluids and choosing appropriate attire for the forecast conditions.

2. **The applicant demonstrates understanding of drug and alcohol use.**

    a. **Alcohol**

       1) As little as 1 oz. of liquor, 1 bottle of beer, or 4 oz. of wine can impair flying skills.

          a) Even after your body has completely destroyed a moderate amount of alcohol, you can still be severely impaired for many hours by hangover.

          b) Alcohol also renders you much more susceptible to disorientation and hypoxia.

       2) The FARs prohibit pilots from performing cockpit duties within 8 hr. after drinking any alcoholic beverage or while under the influence of alcohol.

          a) An excellent rule is to allow at least 12 to 24 hr. "from bottle to throttle," depending on how much you drank and the severity of the residual effects.

3. **The applicant demonstrates understanding of prescription and over-the-counter medication.**

    a. Pilot performance can be seriously impaired by both prescribed and over-the-counter medications.

        1) Many medications, such as tranquilizers, sedatives, strong pain relievers, and cough-suppressant preparations, have primary effects that may impair judgment, memory, alertness, coordination, vision, and the ability to make calculations.

            a) Others, such as antihistamines, blood pressure drugs, muscle relaxants, and agents to control diarrhea and motion sickness, have side effects that may impair the same critical functions.

MOST COMMONLY EXPERIENCED SIDE EFFECTS AND INTERACTIONS OF OTC MEDICATIONS			
	MEDICATIONS	**SIDE EFFECTS**	**INTERACTIONS**
PAIN RELIEF/FEVER	**ASPIRIN** Alka-Seltzer Bayer Aspirin Bufferin	Ringing in ears, nausea, stomach ulceration, hyperventilation	Increase effect of blood thinners
	ACETAMINOPHEN Tylenol	Liver toxicity (in large doses)	
	IBUPROFEN Advil Motrin Nuprin	Upset stomach, dizziness, rash, itching	Increase effect of blood thinners
COLDS/FLU	**ANTIHISTAMINES** Actifed Dristan Benadryl Drixoral Cheracol-Plus NyQuil Chlortrimeton Sinarest Contac Sinutab Dimetapp	Sedation, dizziness, rash, impairment of coordination, upset stomach, thickening of bronchial secretions, blurring of vision	Increase sedative effects of other medications
	DECONGESTANTS Afrin Nasal Spray Sine-Aid Sudafed	Excessive stimulation, dizziness, difficulty with urination, palpitations	Aggravate high blood pressure, heart disease, and prostate problems
	COUGH SUPPRESSANTS Benylin Robitussin CF/DM Vicks Formula #44	Drowsiness, blurred vision, difficulty with urination, upset stomach	Increase sedative effects of other medications
BOWEL PREPARATIONS	**LAXATIVES** Correctol Ex-Lax	Unexpected bowel activity at altitude, rectal itching	
	ANTI-DIARRHEALS Imodium A-D Pepto-Bismol	Drowsiness, depression, blurred vision (see Aspirin)	
APPETITE SUPPRESSANTS	Acutrim Dexatrim	Excessive stimulation, dizziness, palpitations, headaches	Increase stimulatory effects of decongestants, interfere with high blood pressure medications
SLEEPING AIDS	Nytol Sominex	(Contain antihistamine) Prolonged drowsiness, blurred vision	Cause excessive drowsiness when used with alcohol
STIMULANTS	**CAFFEINE** Coffee, tea, cola, chocolate	Excessive stimulation, tremors, palpitations, headache	Interfere with high blood pressure medications

    b. The safest rule is not to fly while taking any medication, unless approved by the FAA.

    c. The table above lists the common over-the-counter medications and outlines some of their possible side effects that could affect your flying abilities. As with all drugs, side effects may vary with the individual and with changes in altitude and other flight conditions.

    d.   FAA advice on over-the-counter medications:

        1)   Read and follow label directions for use of medication.

        2)   If the label warns of side effects, do not fly until twice the recommended dosing interval has passed.

            a)   EXAMPLE: If the label says "take every 4-6 hours," you should wait at least 12 hr. before you fly.

        3)   Remember, the condition you are treating may be as disqualifying as the medication.

        4)   When in doubt, ask your AME for advice.

        5)   As a pilot, you are responsible for your own personal preflight. Be wary of any illness that requires medicine to make you feel better.

        6)   If an illness is serious enough to require medication, it is also serious enough to prevent you from flying.

        7)   Do not fly if you have a cold.

            a)   Changes in atmospheric pressures with changes in altitude could cause serious ear and sinus problems.

        8)   Avoid mixing decongestants and caffeine (contained in coffee, tea, cola, chocolate).

        9)   Beware of medications that use alcohol as a base for the ingredients.

4.   The applicant demonstrates understanding of hyperventilation.

    a.   **Hyperventilation**, which is an abnormal increase in the volume of air breathed in and out of the lungs, can occur subconsciously when you encounter a stressful situation in flight.

        1)   This abnormal breathing flushes from your lungs and blood much of the carbon dioxide your system needs to maintain the proper degree of blood acidity.

            a)   The resulting chemical imbalance in the body produces dizziness, tingling of the fingers and toes, hot and cold sensations, drowsiness, nausea, and a feeling of suffocation. Often you may react to these symptoms with even greater hyperventilation.

        2)   Incapacitation can eventually result from incoordination, disorientation, and painful muscle spasms. Finally, unconsciousness can occur.

    b.   The symptoms of hyperventilation subside within a few minutes after the rate and depth of breathing are consciously brought back under control.

        1)   The buildup of the appropriate balance of carbon dioxide in your body can be hastened by controlled breathing in and out of a paper bag held over your nose and mouth. Also, talking, singing, or counting aloud often helps.

5.   The applicant demonstrates understanding of stress and fatigue.

    a.   **Stress**

        1)   Stress from the pressures of everyday living can impair pilot performance, often in very subtle ways.

            a)   Difficulties can occupy thought processes so as to decrease alertness.
            b)   Distraction can so interfere with judgment that unwarranted risks are taken.
            c)   Stress and fatigue can be a deadly combination.

        2)   When you are under more stress than usual, you should consider delaying flight until your difficulties have been resolved.

b.   **Fatigue**

1)   Fatigue can be treacherous because it may not be apparent to you until serious errors are made.

a)   It is best described as either acute (short-term) or chronic (long-term).

2)   Acute fatigue is the everyday tiredness felt after long periods of physical or mental strain.

a)   Consequently, coordination and alertness can be reduced.

b)   Acute fatigue is prevented by adequate rest and sleep, as well as regular exercise and proper nutrition.

3)   Chronic fatigue occurs when there is not enough time for full recovery between episodes of acute fatigue.

a)   Performance continues to fall off, and judgment becomes impaired.
b)   Recovery from chronic fatigue requires a prolonged period of rest.

6.   **The applicant demonstrates understanding of factors affecting vision.**

a.   Of the body senses, vision is the most important for safe flight. It is important for you to understand your eye's construction and the effect of darkness on the eye.

1)   The **fovea** is a small, notched area that is located directly behind the lens on the retina. This area contains cones only.

a)   The fovea is where your vision is the sharpest. Thus, when you look directly at an object, the image is focused mainly on the fovea.

b)   The fovea field of vision is a conical field of only about 1°.

i)   To demonstrate how small a 1° field is, take a quarter and tape it to a flat piece of glass, such as a window. Now stand 4 1/2 ft. from the mounted quarter and close one eye. The area of your field of view covered by the quarter is a 1° field, similar to your fovea vision.

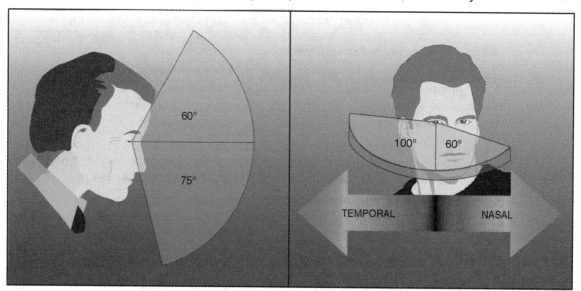

c)   The normal field of vision for each eye is about 135° vertically and about 160° horizontally, as shown above.

i)   The fovea field is the central 1° field.

d) Your visual acuity (detail) drops off rapidly outside the fovea cone.

   i) EXAMPLE: Outside of a 10° cone (centered on the fovea cone), you will see only about one-tenth of what you can see in the fovea cone. In terms of collision avoidance, an aircraft that you are capable of seeing in your fovea cone at 5,000 ft. away must be as close as 500 ft. to detect it with peripheral vision.

2) Effective scanning is accomplished with a series of short, regularly spaced eye movements that bring successive areas of the sky into the central visual field.

   a) Each eye movement should not exceed 10°.
   b) Each area should be observed for at least 1 sec. to enable detection.

3) The fact that the rods are distributed around the cones and do not lie directly behind the pupils makes **off-center viewing** (i.e., looking to one side of an object) important during night flight.

   a) During daylight, an object can be seen best by looking directly at it.

      i) As the cones become less effective as the level of light decreases, you may not be able to see an object if you look directly at it.

         • Since the cones are at the center of vision, when they stop working in the dark, a night blind spot develops at your center of vision.

   b) After some practice, you will find that you can see things more clearly at night by looking to one side of them rather than directly at them.

      i) Remember that rods do not detect objects while your eyes are moving, only during the pauses.

b. Adapting your eyes to darkness is an important aspect of night vision.

   1) When entering a dark area, the pupils of the eyes enlarge to receive as much of the available light as possible.

   2) It will take approximately 5 to 10 min. (with enough available light) for the cones to become moderately adjusted. After the adjustment, your eyes become 100 times more sensitive than they were before you entered the dark area.

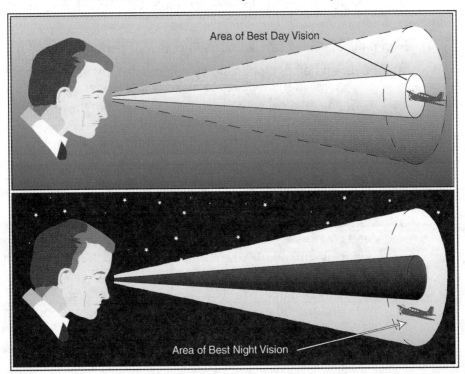

Area of Best Day Vision

Area of Best Night Vision

3) After about 30 min., the rods will be fully adjusted to darkness and become about 100,000 times more sensitive to light than they were in the lighted area.

    a) Since the rods can still function in light of 1/5,000 the intensity at which the cones cease to function, they are used for night vision.

4) The rods need more time to adjust to darkness than the cones do to bright light. Your eyes become adapted to sunlight in 10 sec., whereas they need 30 min. to adjust fully to a dark night.

5) You must consider the adaptation process before and during night flight.

    a) First, your eyes should be allowed to adapt to the low level of light, and then they must be kept adapted.

    b) Next, you must avoid exposing your eyes to any bright light which may cause temporary blindness, possibly resulting in serious consequences.

        i) Temporary blindness may result in illusions or "after images" during the time your eyes are recovering from the bright light.

c. The eyes are the first part of your body to suffer from low oxygen at altitude because the capillaries are very small and have a limited capacity to carry oxygen.

1) Night vision may be adversely affected above 5,000 ft. MSL.

    a) Fly at lower altitudes and/or use oxygen when flying at night to maximize your visual acuity.

2) Good vision depends on your physical condition. Fatigue, colds, vitamin deficiencies, alcohol, stimulants, smoking, or medication can seriously impair your vision.

    a) EXAMPLE: Smoking lowers the sensitivity of the eyes and reduces night vision by approximately 20%.

7. **The applicant demonstrates understanding of fitness for flight.**

a. **Medical Certification**

1) The FARs prohibit you from performing crewmember duties while you have a known medical condition or an aggravation of a known medical condition that would make you unable to fulfill your duties as remote pilot in command.

b. **Illness**

1) Even a minor illness can seriously impair your performance as a pilot.

    a) Fever and other distracting symptoms can impair judgment, memory, alertness, and the ability to make calculations.

    b) Also, any medication you are taking to combat these symptoms may itself decrease your performance as a pilot.

2) The safest rule is not to fly while suffering from any illness.

c. **Medication**

1) Pilot performance can be seriously impaired by both prescribed and over-the-counter medications.

    a) Many medications, such as tranquilizers, sedatives, strong pain relievers, and cough-suppressant preparations, have primary effects that may impair judgment, memory, alertness, coordination, vision, and the ability to make calculations.

        i) Others, such as antihistamines, blood pressure drugs, muscle relaxants, and agents to control diarrhea and motion sickness, have side effects that may impair the same critical functions.

2) The safest rule is not to operate aircraft while taking any medication, unless approved by the FAA.

QUESTIONS

8.1 Aeronautical Decision-Making

1. The effective use of all available resources–human, hardware, and information–prior to and during flight to ensure the successful outcome of the operation is called

A. Risk Management.

B. Crew Resource Management.

C. Safety Management System.

Answer (B) is correct. *(AC 107)*
    DISCUSSION: Crew resource management (CRM) in single-pilot or multi-person crew configurations is the effective use of all personnel and material assets available to a pilot or a flight crew.
    Answer (A) is incorrect. Risk management is the part of the decision-making process that relies on situational awareness, problem recognition, and good judgment to reduce risks associated with each flight. Answer (C) is incorrect. A safety management system is the formal, top-down, organization-wide approach to managing safety risk and assuring the effectiveness of safety-risk controls.

2. Safety is an important element for a remote pilot to consider prior to operating an unmanned aircraft system. To prevent the final "link" in the accident chain, a remote pilot must consider which methodology?

A. Crew Resource Management.

B. Safety Management System.

C. Risk Management.

Answer (C) is correct. *(ADM)*
    DISCUSSION: Risk management is the part of the decision-making process that relies on situational awareness, problem recognition, and good judgment to reduce risks associated with each flight.
    Answer (A) is incorrect. Crew resource management is the effective use of all personnel and material assets available to a pilot or a flight crew. Answer (B) is incorrect. A safety management system is the formal, top-down, organization-wide approach to managing safety risk and assuring the effectiveness of safety-risk controls.

3. Identify the hazardous attitude or characteristic a remote pilot displays while taking risks in order to impress others?

A. Impulsivity.

B. Invulnerability.

C. Macho.

Answer (C) is correct. *(PHAK Chap 2)*
    DISCUSSION: Pilots who are always trying to prove they are better than anyone else are thinking I can do it -- I'll show them. Pilots with this type of attitude will try to prove themselves by taking risks in order to impress others.
    Answer (A) is incorrect. Impulsivity is the attitude of people who frequently feel the need to do something -- anything -- immediately. Answer (B) is incorrect. Invulnerability is the attitude of people who feel that accidents happen to others but never to them.

4. You have been hired as a remote pilot by a local TV news station to film breaking news with a small UA. You expressed a safety concern and the station manager has instructed you to "fly first, ask questions later." What type of hazardous attitude does this attitude represent?

A. Machismo.

B. Invulnerability.

C. Impulsivity.

Answer (C) is correct. *(PHAK Chap 2)*
    DISCUSSION: Impulsivity (Do something quickly!) is the attitude of people who frequently feel the need to do something -- anything -- immediately. They do not stop to think about what they are about to do; they do not determine the best alternative; and they do the first thing that comes to mind.
    Answer (A) is incorrect. Pilots exhibiting the machismo attitude will try to prove themselves by taking risks in order to impress others. Answer (B) is incorrect. Pilots exhibiting the invulnerability attitude never believe that they will be personally involved in accidents.

5. When adapting crew resource management (CRM) concepts to the operation of a small UA, CRM must be integrated into

A. the flight portion only.

B. all phases of the operation.

C. the communications only.

Answer (B) is correct. *(CRM)*
    DISCUSSION: CRM is a component of ADM, where the pilot of sUAS makes effective use of all available resources: human resources, hardware, and information. CRM applies to all phases of the operation.
    Answer (A) is incorrect. CRM should be adapted to plan for all phases of the operation, not just the flight portion. Answer (C) is incorrect. CRM emphasizes good communication and other interpersonal relationship skills; however, it must be integrated into all phases of the operation.

6. A local TV station has hired a remote pilot to operate their small UA to cover news stories. The remote pilot has had multiple near misses with obstacles on the ground and two small UAS accidents. What would be a solution for the news station to improve their operating safety culture?

A. The news station should implement a policy of no more than five crashes/incidents within 6 months.

B. The news station does not need to make any changes; there are times that an accident is unavoidable.

C. The news station should recognize hazardous attitudes and situations and develop standard operating procedures that emphasize safety.

Answer (C) is correct. *(sUASSG Chap 10)*
DISCUSSION: Hazards in the sUAS and its operating environment must be identified, documented, and controlled. The analysis process used to define hazards needs to consider all components of the system, based on the equipment being used and the environment it is being operated in.
Answer (A) is incorrect. All operators should identify hazards and minimize risks. There is no quantifiable amount of accidents that is acceptable. Answer (B) is incorrect. Remote PICs are expected to exercise due diligence in identifying significant and reasonably foreseeable hazards related to their operations.

7. Risk management, as part of the aeronautical decision making (ADM) process, relies on which features to reduce the risks associated with each flight?

A. Application of stress management and risk element procedures.

B. The mental process of analyzing all information in a particular situation and making a timely decision on what action to take.

C. Situational awareness, problem recognition, and good judgment.

Answer (C) is correct. *(AC 60-22)*
DISCUSSION: Risk management is that part of the ADM process that relies on situational awareness, problem recognition, and good judgment to reduce risks associated with each flight.
Answer (A) is incorrect. Risk management relies on situational awareness, problem recognition, and good judgment, not the application of stress management and risk-element procedures, to reduce the risks associated with each flight. Answer (B) is incorrect. Judgment, not risk management, is the mental process of analyzing all information in a particular situation and making a timely decision on what action to take.

8. What is one of the neglected items when a pilot relies on short and long term memory for repetitive tasks?

A. Checklists.

B. Situational awareness.

C. Flying outside the envelope.

Answer (A) is correct. *(AC 60-22)*
DISCUSSION: Neglect of checklists, flight planning, preflight inspections, etc., indicates a pilot's unjustified reliance on his or her short- and long-term memory for repetitive flying tasks.
Answer (B) is incorrect. Situational awareness suffers when a pilot gets behind the airplane, which results in an inability to recognize deteriorating circumstances and/or misjudgment on the rate of deterioration. Answer (C) is incorrect. Flying outside the envelope occurs when the pilot believes (often in error) that the aircraft's high-performance capability meets the demands imposed by the pilot's (often overestimated) flying skills.

9. Hazardous attitudes occur to every pilot to some degree at some time. What are some of these hazardous attitudes?

A. Antiauthority, impulsivity, macho, resignation, and invulnerability.

B. Poor situational awareness, snap judgments, and lack of a decision making process.

C. Poor risk management and lack of stress management.

Answer (A) is correct. *(AC 60-22)*
DISCUSSION: The five hazardous attitudes addressed in the ADM process are antiauthority, impulsivity, invulnerability, macho, and resignation.
Answer (B) is incorrect. Poor situational awareness and snap judgments are indications of the lack of a decision-making process, not hazardous attitudes. Answer (C) is incorrect. Poor risk management and lack of stress management lead to poor ADM and are not considered hazardous attitudes.

10. In the aeronautical decision making (ADM) process, what is the first step in neutralizing a hazardous attitude?

A. Recognizing hazardous thoughts.

B. Recognizing the invulnerability of the situation.

C. Making a rational judgment.

Answer (A) is correct. *(AC 60-22)*
DISCUSSION: Hazardous attitudes, which contribute to poor pilot judgment, can be effectively counteracted by redirecting that hazardous attitude so that appropriate action can be taken. Recognition of hazardous thoughts is the first step in neutralizing them in the ADM process.
Answer (B) is incorrect. Invulnerability is a hazardous attitude. The first step in neutralizing a hazardous attitude is to recognize it. Answer (C) is incorrect. Before a rational judgment can be made, the hazardous attitude must be recognized then redirected so that appropriate action can be taken.

11. What is the antidote when a pilot has a hazardous attitude, such as "Antiauthority"?

    A. Rules do not apply in this situation.

    B. I know what I am doing.

    C. Follow the rules.

Answer (C) is correct. *(AC 60-22)*
    DISCUSSION: When you recognize a hazardous thought, you should correct it by stating the corresponding antidote. The antidote for the antiauthority ("Do not tell me!") hazardous attitude is "Follow the rules. They are usually right."
    Answer (A) is incorrect. "Rules do not apply in this situation" is an example of the antiauthority hazardous attitude, not its antidote. Answer (B) is incorrect. "I know what I'm doing" is an example of the macho hazardous attitude, not an antidote to the antiauthority attitude.

12. What is the antidote when a pilot has a hazardous attitude, such as "Impulsivity"?

    A. It could happen to me.

    B. Do it quickly to get it over with.

    C. Not so fast, think first.

Answer (C) is correct. *(AC 60-22)*
    DISCUSSION: When you recognize a hazardous thought, you should correct it by stating the corresponding antidote. The antidote for the impulsivity ("Do something quickly!") hazardous attitude is "Not so fast. Think first."
    Answer (A) is incorrect. "It could happen to me" is the antidote for the invulnerability, not impulsivity, hazardous attitude. Answer (B) is incorrect. "Do it quickly and get it over with" is an example of the impulsivity hazardous attitude, not its antidote.

13. What is the antidote when a pilot has the hazardous attitude of "Invulnerability"?

    A. It cannot be that bad.

    B. It could happen to me.

    C. It will not happen to me.

Answer (B) is correct. *(AC 60-22)*
    DISCUSSION: The antidote to counteract the attitude of invulnerability is thinking or saying, "It could happen to me."
    Answer (A) is incorrect. "It cannot be that bad" describes the hazardous macho attitude, not invulnerability. Answer (C) is incorrect. "It will not happen to me" describes the hazardous attitude of invulnerability. It is not the antidote.

14. What is the antidote when a pilot has a hazardous attitude, such as "Macho"?

    A. I can do it.

    B. Taking chances is foolish.

    C. Nothing will happen.

Answer (B) is correct. *(AC 60-22)*
    DISCUSSION: When you recognize a hazardous thought, you should correct it by stating the corresponding antidote. The antidote for the macho ("I can do it") hazardous attitude is "Taking chances is foolish."
    Answer (A) is incorrect. "I can do it" is an example of the macho hazardous attitude, not its antidote. Answer (C) is incorrect. "Nothing will happen" is an example of the invulnerability hazardous attitude, not an antidote to the macho attitude.

15. What is the antidote when a pilot has a hazardous attitude, such as "Resignation"?

    A. What is the use?

    B. Someone else is responsible.

    C. I am not helpless.

Answer (C) is correct. *(AC 60-22)*
    DISCUSSION: When you recognize a hazardous thought, you should correct it by stating the corresponding antidote. The antidote for the resignation ("What is the use?") hazardous attitude is "I am not helpless. I can make a difference."
    Answer (A) is incorrect. "What is the use?" is an example of the resignation hazardous attitude, not its antidote. Answer (B) is incorrect. "Someone else is responsible" is an example of the resignation hazardous attitude, not its antidote.

16. Who is responsible for determining whether a pilot is fit to fly for a particular flight, even though he or she holds a current medical certificate?

    A. The FAA.

    B. The medical examiner.

    C. The pilot.

Answer (C) is correct. *(AC 60-22)*
    DISCUSSION: A number of factors, from lack of sleep to illness, can reduce a pilot's fitness to make a particular flight. It is the responsibility of the pilot to determine whether (s)he is fit to make a particular flight, even though (s)he holds a current medical certificate. Additionally, 14 CFR 61.53 prohibits a pilot who possesses a current medical certificate from acting as pilot in command, or in any other capacity as a required pilot flight crewmember, while the pilot has a known medical condition or an aggravation of a known medical condition that would make the pilot unable to meet the standards for a medical certificate.
    Answer (A) is incorrect. The pilot, not the FAA, is responsible for determining whether (s)he is fit for a particular flight. Answer (B) is incorrect. The pilot, not the medical examiner, is responsible for determining whether (s)he is fit for a particular flight.

17. What is the one common factor which affects most preventable accidents?

A. Structural failure.

B. Mechanical malfunction.

C. Human error.

Answer (C) is correct. *(AC 60-22)*
DISCUSSION: Most preventable accidents, such as fuel starvation or exhaustion, VFR flight into IFR conditions leading to disorientation, and flight into known icing, have one common factor: human error. Pilots who are involved in accidents usually know what went wrong. In the interest of expediency, cost savings, or other often irrelevant factors, the wrong course of action (decision) was chosen.
Answer (A) is incorrect. Most preventable accidents have human error, not structural failure, as a common factor. Answer (B) is incorrect. Most preventable accidents have human error, not mechanical malfunction, as a common factor.

18. What antidotal phrase can help reverse the hazardous attitude of impulsivity?

A. Do it quickly to get it over with.

B. It could happen to me.

C. Not so fast, think first.

Answer (C) is correct. *(PHAK Chap 2)*
DISCUSSION: Impulsivity is the attitude of people who frequently feel the need to do something, anything, immediately. They do not stop to think about what they are about to do. They do not select the best alternative but instead do the first thing that comes to mind. They should recognize this attitude and state the antidote, "Not so fast. Think first," before taking action.
Answer (A) is incorrect. "Do it quickly to get it over with" is the hazardous attitude of impulsivity, not the antidote. Answer (B) is incorrect. "It could happen to me" is the antidote for the hazardous attitude of invulnerability.

8.2 Physiology

19. A pilot should be able to overcome the symptoms or avoid future occurrences of hyperventilation by

A. closely monitoring the flight instruments to control the airplane.

B. slowing the breathing rate, breathing into a bag, or talking aloud.

C. increasing the breathing rate in order to increase lung ventilation.

Answer (B) is correct. *(AIM Para 8-1-3)*
DISCUSSION: To recover from hyperventilation, the pilot should slow the breathing rate, breathe into a bag, or talk aloud.
Answer (A) is incorrect. Closely monitoring the flight instruments is used to overcome vertigo (spatial disorientation). Answer (C) is incorrect. Increased breathing aggravates hyperventilation.

20. Rapid or extra deep breathing while using oxygen can cause a condition known as

A. hyperventilation.

B. aerosinusitis.

C. aerotitis.

Answer (A) is correct. *(AIM Para 8-1-3)*
DISCUSSION: Hyperventilation occurs when an excessive amount of carbon dioxide is passed out of the body and too much oxygen is retained. This occurs when breathing rapidly and especially when using oxygen.
Answer (B) is incorrect. Aerosinusitis is an inflammation of the sinuses caused by changes in atmospheric pressure. Answer (C) is incorrect. Aerotitis is an inflammation of the inner ear caused by changes in atmospheric pressure.

21. When a stressful situation is encountered in flight, an abnormal increase in the volume of air breathed in and out can cause a condition known as

A. hyperventilation.

B. aerosinusitis.

C. aerotitis.

Answer (A) is correct. *(AIM Para 8-1-3)*
DISCUSSION: Hyperventilation occurs when an excessive amount of carbon dioxide is passed out of the body and too much oxygen is retained. This occurs when breathing rapidly and especially when using oxygen.
Answer (B) is incorrect. Aerosinusitis is an inflammation of the sinuses caused by changes in atmospheric pressure. Answer (C) is incorrect. Aerotitis is an inflammation of the inner ear caused by changes in atmospheric pressure.

22. Which would most likely result in hyperventilation?

A. Emotional tension, anxiety, or fear.

B. The excessive consumption of alcohol.

C. An extremely slow rate of breathing and insufficient oxygen.

Answer (A) is correct. *(AIM Para 8-1-3)*
DISCUSSION: Hyperventilation usually occurs when one becomes excited or undergoes stress, which results in an increase in one's rate of breathing.
Answer (B) is incorrect. Hyperventilation is usually caused by some type of stress, not by alcohol. Answer (C) is incorrect. The opposite is true: Hyperventilation is an extremely fast rate of breathing that produces excessive oxygen.

23. A pilot experiencing the effects of hyperventilation should be able to restore the proper carbon dioxide level in the body by

    A. slowing the breathing rate, breathing into a paper bag, or talking aloud.

    B. breathing spontaneously and deeply or gaining mental control of the situation.

    C. increasing the breathing rate in order to increase lung ventilation.

Answer (A) is correct. *(PHAK Chap 17)*
    DISCUSSION: A stressful situation can often lead to hyperventilation, which results from an increased rate and depth of respiration that leads to an abnormally low amount of carbon dioxide in the bloodstream. By slowing the breathing rate, breathing into a paper bag, or talking aloud, a pilot can overcome the effects of hyperventilation and return the carbon dioxide level in the bloodstream to normal.
    Answer (B) is incorrect. Breathing deeply further aggravates the effects of hyperventilation. Answer (C) is incorrect. Increasing the rate of breathing will further aggravate the effects of hyperventilation.

24. Why is fatigue hazardous to flight safety?

    A. The pilot hurries to get done in order to rest.

    B. Fatigue may not be apparent to a pilot until serious errors are made (an impaired pilot is a dangerous pilot).

    C. The pilot is lazy and rushes to get done quickly.

Answer (B) is correct. *(IFH Chap 3, AIM Para 8-1-1)*
    DISCUSSION: Fatigue is one of the most treacherous hazards to flight safety because it may not become apparent to a pilot until serious errors are made.
    Answer (A) is incorrect. The risk is not found in the pilot hurrying, but rather the risk is found in the diminished cognitive power that fatigue introduces to the situation, sometimes causing pilots to make serious errors before they realize how fatigued they are. Answer (C) is incorrect. The risk is not found in the pilot being lazy or rushing to complete a series of tasks, but rather the risk is found in the diminished cognitive power that fatigue introduces to the situation, sometimes causing pilots to make serious errors before they realize how fatigued they are.

25. What effect does haze have on the ability to see traffic or terrain features during flight?

    A. Haze causes the eyes to focus at infinity.

    B. The eyes tend to overwork in haze and do not detect relative movement easily.

    C. All traffic or terrain features appear to be farther away than their actual distance.

Answer (C) is correct. *(AIM Para 8-1-5)*
    DISCUSSION: Atmospheric haze can create the illusion of being at a greater distance and height from traffic or terrain than you actually are. The pilot who does not recognize this illusion will fly a lower approach.
    Answer (A) is incorrect. In haze, the eyes focus at a comfortable distance, which may be only 10 to 30 ft. outside of the cockpit. Answer (B) is incorrect. In haze, the eyes relax and tend to stare outside without focusing or looking for common visual cues.

26. Which technique should a remote pilot use to scan for traffic? A remote pilot should

    A. systematically focus on different segments of the sky for short intervals.

    B. concentrate on relative movement detected in the peripheral vision area.

    C. continuously scan the sky from right to left.

Answer (A) is correct. *(AIM Para 4-4-14)*
    DISCUSSION: Due to the fact that eyes can focus only on a narrow viewing area, effective scanning is accomplished with a series of short, regularly-spaced eye movements that bring successive areas of the sky into the central vision field.
    Answer (B) is incorrect. Detecting relative movement using peripheral vision concerns scanning for traffic at night. Answer (C) is incorrect. A pilot must continually scan successive, small portions of the sky. The eyes can focus only on a narrow viewing area and require at least 1 sec. to detect a faraway object.

27. The most effective method of scanning for other aircraft for collision avoidance during daylight hours is to use

    A. regularly spaced concentration on the 3-, 9-, and 12-o'clock positions.

    B. a series of short, regularly spaced eye movements to search each 10-degree sector.

    C. peripheral vision by scanning small sectors and utilizing off-center viewing.

Answer (B) is correct. *(AC 90-48D)*
    DISCUSSION: The most effective way to scan for other aircraft during daylight hours is to use a series of short, regularly spaced eye movements that bring successive areas of the sky into your central visual field. Each movement should not exceed 10°, and each area should be observed for at least one second to enable detection. Only a very small center area of the eye has the ability to send clear, sharply focused messages to the brain. All other areas provide less detail.
    Answer (A) is incorrect. The spacing between the positions should be 10°, not 90°. Answer (C) is incorrect. This is the recommended nighttime scanning procedure.

28. Eye movements during daytime collision avoidance scanning should

A. not exceed 10 degrees and view each sector at least 1 second.

B. be 30 degrees and view each sector at least 3 seconds.

C. use peripheral vision by scanning small sectors and utilizing off-center viewing.

Answer (A) is correct. *(AC 90-48C)*
  DISCUSSION: The most effective way to scan for other aircraft during daylight hours is to use a series of short, regularly spaced eye movements that bring successive areas of the sky into your central visual field. Each movement should not exceed 10°, and each area should be observed for at least 1 second to enable detection. Only a very small center area of the eye has the ability to send clear, sharply focused messages to the brain.
  Answer (B) is incorrect. The spacing for the scan between positions should be 10°, not 30°. Answer (C) is incorrect. At night, collision avoidance scanning must use the off-center portions of the eyes. These portions are most effective at seeing objects at night. Accordingly, peripheral vision should be used, scanning small sectors and using off-screen viewing. This is in contrast to daytime searching for air traffic when center viewing should be used.

29. Most midair collision accidents occur during

A. hazy days.

B. clear days.

C. cloudy nights.

Answer (B) is correct. *(AC 90-48D)*
  DISCUSSION: Most midair collision accidents and reported near midair collision incidents occur during good VFR weather conditions (i.e., clear days) and during the hours of daylight. This is when more aircraft are likely to be flying.
  Answer (A) is incorrect. During hazy days, fewer pilots will be flying, and those who are will be more vigilant in their scanning for other traffic. Answer (C) is incorrect. During cloudy nights, fewer pilots will be flying, and those who are will be more vigilant in their scanning for other traffic.

30. Which is true regarding the presence of alcohol within the human body?

A. A small amount of alcohol increases vision acuity.

B. Consuming an equal amount of water will increase the destruction of alcohol and alleviate a hangover.

C. Judgment and decision-making abilities can be adversely affected by even small amounts of alcohol.

Answer (C) is correct. *(PHAK Chap 17)*
  DISCUSSION: As little as 1 oz. of liquor, 1 bottle of beer, or 4 oz. of wine can impair flying skills.
  Answer (A) is incorrect. Alcohol decreases vision acuity. Answer (B) is incorrect. Time is the best method to ensure alcohol has metabolized in the body.

31. You are a remote pilot for a co-op energy service provider. You are to use your UA to inspect power lines in a remote area 15 hours away from your home office. After the drive, fatigue impacts your abilities to complete your assignment on time. Fatigue can be recognized

A. easily by an experienced pilot.

B. as being in an impaired state.

C. by an ability to overcome sleep deprivation.

Answer (B) is correct. *(PHAK Chap 2)*
  DISCUSSION: Fatigue, stress, and work overload can cause a pilot to become impaired by losing overall awareness of the flight situation.
  Answer (A) is incorrect. Fatigue is not easily recognized. It can be treacherous because it may not be apparent until serious errors are made. Answer (C) is incorrect. Fatigue is not the ability to overcome sleep deprivation. Fatigue is overcome by periods of adequate rest and sleep as well as regular exercise and proper nutrition.

STUDY UNIT NINE
EMERGENCY PROCEDURES, MAINTENANCE, AND INSPECTIONS

(7 pages of outline)

9.1 EMERGENCY PROCEDURES

1. **The applicant demonstrates understanding of emergency planning and communication.**

   a. An in-flight emergency is an unexpected and unforeseen serious occurrence or situation that requires urgent, prompt action.

      1) In case of an in-flight emergency, the remote PIC is permitted to deviate from any rule of Part 107 to the extent necessary to respond to that emergency.

      2) A remote PIC who exercises this emergency power to deviate from the rules of Part 107 is required, upon FAA request, to send a written report to the FAA explaining the deviation. Emergency action should be taken in such a way as to minimize injury or damage to property.

   b. Contingency planning should include an alternate landing/recovery site to be used in the event of an abnormal condition that requires a precautionary landing away from the original launch location.

      1) Incorporate the means of communication with ATC throughout the descent and landing (if required for the flight operation) as well as a plan for ground operations and securing/parking the aircraft on the ground. This includes the availability of control stations capable of launch/recovery, communication equipment, and an adequate power source to operate all required equipment.

      2) Take into consideration all airspace constructs and minimize risk to other aircraft by avoiding congested areas to the maximum extent possible.

2. **The applicant demonstrates understanding of the characteristics and potential hazards of lithium batteries.**

   a. Lithium-based batteries are highly flammable and capable of ignition. A battery fire could cause an in-flight emergency by causing a LOC of the sUA. Lithium battery fires can be caused when a battery short circuits, is improperly charged, is heated to extreme temperatures, is damaged as a result of a crash, is mishandled, or is simply defective. The most common type of lithium-based battery used in sUAS is Lithium-Polymer (LiPo). The remote PIC should consider following the manufacturer's recommendations, when available, to help ensure safe battery handling and usage.

      1) **Safe transportation, such as proper inspection and handling**

         a) Ensure careful storage of spare (uninstalled) lithium batteries.

         b) Prevent short circuits by placing each individual battery in the original retail packaging, a separate plastic bag, or a protective pouch or by insulating exposed terminals with tape.

         c) Do not allow spare batteries to come in contact with metal objects, such as coins, keys, or jewelry.

         d) Take steps to prevent objects from crushing, puncturing, or applying pressure on the battery.

2) **Safe charging**

    a)   Always use the proper charger/discharger for LiPo batteries.

    b)   LiPo fires are rare but can occur quickly. Use a fireproof container whenever charging, discharging, or storing LiPo batteries.

    c)   Store LiPo batteries in a safe fireproof container. Do not store them inside the aircraft or flight case.

3) **Safe usage**

    a)   LiPo batteries that are installed in an sUAS for power during the operation are not considered a hazardous material under Part 107.

    b)   However, spare (uninstalled) LiPo batteries would meet the definition of hazardous material and may not be carried on the sUAS.

    c)   LiPo batteries do not perform well in extremely cold temperatures.

        i)   Some sUAS manufacturers place limitations on the acceptable temperature operating range.

        ii)   For cold weather operations, power on the sUAS and allow the battery to warm up to normal operating temperatures prior to starting your flight mission.

4) **Risks of fires involving lithium batteries**

    a)   When preparing to conduct sUAS operations, do not use any battery with signs of damage or defect.

        i)   For example, check carefully for small nicks in the battery casing and be alert for signs of bubbling or warping during charging.

        ii)   Once the battery is installed and the sUAS takes flight, the remote PIC or ground crew may not observe a battery fire until it is too late to land the aircraft safely.

        iii)   If a battery fire occurs, follow any manufacturer guidance for response procedures.

3.   **The applicant demonstrates understanding of loss of aircraft control link and flyaways.**

    a.   **Lost Link**

        1)   Without an onboard pilot, sUAS crewmembers rely on the command and control link to operate the aircraft. For example, an uplink transmits command instructions to the aircraft, and a downlink transmits the status of the aircraft and provides situational awareness to the remote PIC or person manipulating the controls.

        2)   **Lost link** is an interruption or loss of the control link between the control station and the unmanned aircraft, preventing control of the aircraft. As a result, the unmanned aircraft performs preset lost link procedures.

            a)   Such procedures ensure that the unmanned aircraft

                i)   Remains airborne in a predictable or planned maneuver, allowing time to re-establish the communication link

                ii)   Autolands, if available, after a predetermined length of time or terminates the flight when the power source is depleted

        3)   A lost link is an abnormal situation but not an emergency. A lost link is not considered a flyaway, which is defined later in the section.

4) Follow the manufacturer's recommendations for programming lost link procedures prior to the flight.

   a) Examples of lost link procedures may include, when applicable,

      i) A route of flight that avoids flight over populated areas and
      ii) Communications procedures.

5) Plan contingency measures if recovery of the sUAS is not feasible.

   a) Contingency planning should include an alternate landing/recovery site to be used in the event of an abnormal condition that requires a precautionary landing away from the original launch location.

   b) Incorporate the means of communication with ATC throughout the descent and landing (if required for the flight operation) as well as a plan for ground operations and securing/parking the aircraft on the ground.

      i) This includes the availability of control stations capable of launch/recovery, communication equipment, and an adequate power source to operate all required equipment.

   c) Take into consideration all airspace constructs and minimize risk to other aircraft by avoiding congested areas to the maximum extent possible.

   d) **Flight termination** is the intentional and deliberate process of performing controlled flight to the ground. Flight termination may be part of lost link procedures, or it may be a contingency that you elect to use if further flight of the aircraft cannot be safely achieved or if other potential hazards exist that require immediate discontinuation of flight.

      i) Execute flight termination procedures if you have exhausted all other contingencies.

      ii) Flight termination points (FTPs), if used, or alternative contingency planning measures must

         • Be located within power-off glide distance of the aircraft during all phases of flight
         • Be based on the assumption of an unrecoverable system failure
         • Take into consideration altitude, winds, and other factors

b. **Flyaways**

   1) A flyaway begins as a lost link.

      a) As a result, the unmanned aircraft is not operating in a predicable or planned manner. However in a flyaway, the preset lost link procedures are not established or are not being executed by the unmanned aircraft, creating an emergency situation.

      b) If a flyaway occurs while operating in airspace that requires authorization, notify ATC as outlined in the authorization.

4.   **The applicant demonstrates understanding of loss of Global Positioning System (GPS) signal during flight and potential consequences.**

   a.   GPS tools can be a valuable resource for flight planning and situational awareness during sUAS operation.

   b.   However, as with manned aviation, remote PICs in sUAS operations must avoid overreliance on automation and must be prepared to operate the unmanned aircraft manually if necessary.

   1)   Prior to flight, check NOTAMs for any known GPS service disruptions in the planned location of the sUAS operation.

   2)   Make a plan of action to prevent or minimize damage in the event of equipment malfunction or failure.

   c.   Current NOTAM information and GPS service outages and status reports can be obtained from Leidos Flight Service or DUATS as described in Study Unit 3, "Aviation Weather Services."

5.   **The applicant demonstrates understanding of frequency spectrums and associated limitations.**

   a.   Frequency Spectrum (RF) Basics.

   1)   The 2.4 GHz and 5.8 GHz systems are the unlicensed band RFs that most sUAS use for the connection between the CS and the sUA.

   2)   Note the frequencies are also used for computer wireless networks and the interference can cause problems when operating an sUA in an area (e.g., dense housing and office buildings) that has many wireless signals.

   3)   LOC and flyaways are some of the reported problems with sUAS frequency implications.

   a)   To avoid frequency interference, many modern sUAS operate using a 5.8 GHz system to control the sUA and a 2.4 GHz system to transmit video and photos to the ground.

   4)   Consult the sUAS operating manual and manufacturer's recommended procedures before conducting sUAS operations.

   a)   It should be noted that both RF bands (2.4 GHz and 5.8 GHz) are considered line of sight and the command and control link between the CS and the sUA will not work properly when barriers are between the CS and the UA.

   b)   Part 107 requires the remote PIC or person manipulating the controls to be able to see the UA at all times, which should also help prevent obstructions from interfering with the line of sight frequency spectrum.

   b.   Frequency spectrum used for sUA operations are regulated by the Federal Communications Commission (FCC).

   1)   Radio transmissions, such as those used to control a UA and to downlink real-time video, must use frequency bands that are approved for use by the operating agency.

   2)   The FCC authorizes civil operations. Some operating frequencies are unlicensed and can be used freely (e.g., 900 MHz, 2.4 GHz, and 5.8 GHz) without FCC approval.

   3)   All other frequencies require a user-specific license for all civil users, except federal agencies, to be obtained from the FCC. For further information, visit www.fcc.gov/licensing-databases/licensing.

9.2 MAINTENANCE AND INSPECTION PROCEDURES

1. **The applicant demonstrates understanding of basic maintenance.**

    a. Maintenance of an sUAS includes scheduled and unscheduled overhaul, repair, inspection, modification, replacement, and system software upgrades of the sUAS and its components necessary for flight. Whenever possible, the operator should maintain the sUAS and its components in accordance with manufacturer's instructions. The aircraft manufacturer may provide the maintenance program, or, if one is not provided, the applicant may choose to develop one.

        1) Scheduled maintenance. The sUAS manufacturer may provide documentation for scheduled maintenance of the entire UA and associated system equipment.

            a) There may be components of the sUAS that are identified by the manufacturer to undergo scheduled periodic maintenance or replacement based on time-in-service limits (such as flight hours, cycles, and/or the calender days).

            b) All manufacturer-scheduled maintenance instructions should be followed in the interest of achieving the longest and safest service life of the sUAS.

            c) If there are no scheduled maintenance instructions provided by the sUAS manufacturer or component manufacturer, the operator should establish a scheduled maintenance protocol.

                i) This could be done by documenting any repair, modification, overhaul, or replacement of a system component resulting from normal flight operations, and recording the time-in-service for that component at the time of the maintenance procedure. Over time, the operator should then be able to establish a reliable maintenance schedule for the sUAS and its components.

        2) Unscheduled maintenance. During the course of a preflight inspection, the remote PIC may discover that an sUAS component is in need of servicing (such as lubrication), repair, modification, overhaul, or replacement outside of the scheduled maintenance period as a result of normal flight operations or resulting from a mishap.

            a) In addition, the sUAS manufacturer or component manufacturer may require an unscheduled system software update to correct a problem. In the event such a condition is found, the remote PIC should not conduct flight operations until the discrepancy is corrected.

2. **The applicant demonstrates understanding of preflight inspection.**

    a. Before each flight, the remote PIC must inspect the sUAS to ensure that it is in a condition for safe operation, such as inspecting for equipment damage or malfunction(s). The preflight inspection should be conducted in accordance with the sUAS manufacturer's inspection procedures when available (usually found in the manufacturer's owner or maintenance manual) and/or an inspection procedure developed by the sUAS owner or operator.

    b. Creating an inspection program. As an option, the sUAS owner or operator may wish to create an inspection program for their UAS. The person creating an inspection program for a specific sUAS may find sufficient details to assist in the development of a suitable inspection program tailored to a specific sUAS in a variety of industry programs.

    c. Scalable preflight inspection. The preflight check as part of the inspection program should include an appropriate UAS preflight inspection that is scalable to the UAS, program, and operation to be performed prior to each flight. An appropriate preflight inspection should encompass the entire system in order to determine a continued condition for safe operation prior to flight.

d.   14 CFR Part 43, Appendix D – Scope and Detail of Items (as Applicable to the Particular Aircraft) To Be Included in Annual and 100-Hour Inspections. Another option and best practice may include the applicable portions of Part 43, Appendix D as an inspection guideline correlating to the UA only. System-related equipment, such as, but not limited to, the CS, data link, payload, or support equipment, are not included in the list in Appendix D. Therefore, these items should be included in a comprehensive inspection program for the UAS.

3.   **The applicant demonstrates understanding of techniques to mitigate mechanical failures of all elements used in sUAS operations, such as the battery and/or any device(s) used to operate the sUAS.**

a.   Preflight inspection items. Even if the sUAS manufacturer has a written preflight inspection procedure, it is recommended that the remote PIC ensure that the following inspection items are incorporated into the preflight inspection procedure required by Part 107 to help the remote PIC determine that the sUAS is in a condition for safe operation.

b.   The preflight inspection should include a visual or functional check of the following items:

1)   Conditions of UAS components
2)   Airframe structure (including undercarriage), all flight control surfaces, and linkages
3)   Registration markings, for proper display and legibility
4)   Movable control surface(s), including airframe attachment point(s)
5)   Servo motor(s), including attachment point(s)
6)   Propulsion system, including powerplant(s), propeller(s), rotor(s), ducted fan(s), etc.
7)   Adequate energy supply and proper functionality of all systems (e.g., aircraft and control unit) for the intended operation
8)   Avionics, including control link transceiver, communication/navigation equipment, and antenna(s)
9)   Calibration of UAS compass prior to any flight
10) Control link transceiver, communication/navigation data link transceiver, and antenna(s)
11) Display panel, if used
12) Ground support equipment, including takeoff and landing systems
13) Control link correct functionality established between the aircraft and the CS
14) Correct movement of control surfaces using the CS
15) Onboard navigation and communication data links
16) Flight termination system, if installed
17) Fuel for correct type and quantity
18) Battery levels for the aircraft and CS
19) Secure attachment of any equipment, such as a camera
20) Communication with UAS and that UAS has acquired GPS location from at least four satellites
21) UAS propellers for any imbalance or irregular operation
22) All controller operation for heading and altitude
23) If required by flight path walkthrough, any noted obstructions that may interfere with the UAS
24) At a controlled low altitude, fly within range of any interference and recheck all controls and stability

4. **The applicant demonstrates understanding of appropriate recordkeeping.**

   a. Benefits of recordkeeping. The sUAS owners and operators may find recordkeeping to be beneficial. This could be done by documenting any repair, modification, overhaul, or replacement of a system component resulting from normal flight operations, and recording the time-in-service for that component at the time of the maintenance procedure.

   b. Over time, the operator then should be able to establish a reliable maintenance schedule for the sUAS and its components. Recordkeeping that includes a record of all periodic inspections, maintenance, preventative maintenance, repairs, and alterations performed on the sUAS could be retrievable from either hardcopy and/or electronic logbook format for future reference.

      1) This includes all components of the sUAS: sUA, CS, launch and recovery equipment, CS link equipment, payload, and any other components required to safely operate the sUAS. Recordkeeping of documented maintenance and inspection events reinforces owner/operator responsibilities for airworthiness through systematic condition for safe flight determinations.

   c. Maintenance and inspection recordkeeping provides retrievable empirical evidence of vital safety assessment data defining the condition of safety-critical systems and components supporting the decision to launch.

   d. Recordkeeping of an sUAS may provide essential safety support for commercial operators that may experience rapidly accumulated flight operational hours/cycles.

   e. Methodical maintenance and inspection data collection can prove to be very helpful in the tracking of sUAS component service life, as well as systemic component, equipage, and structural failure events.

5. **The applicant demonstrates understanding of persons that may perform maintenance on an sUAS.**

   a. Performing maintenance. In some instances, the sUAS or component manufacturer may require certain maintenance tasks be performed by the manufacturer or by a person or facility (personnel) specified by the manufacturer.

      1) It is highly recommended that the maintenance be performed in accordance with the manufacturer's instructions.

         a) However, if the operator decides not to use the manufacturer or personnel recommended by the manufacturer and is unable to perform the required maintenance, the operator should consider the expertise of maintenance personnel familiar with the specific sUAS and its components. In addition, though not required, the use of certificated maintenance providers are encouraged, which may include repair stations, holders of mechanic and repairman certificates, and persons working under the supervision of these mechanics and repairman.

      2) If the operator or other maintenance personnel are unable to repair, modify, or overhaul an sUAS or component back to its safe operational specification, then it is advisable to replace the sUAS or component with one that is in a condition for safe operation. It is important that all required maintenance be completed before each flight, preferably in accordance with the manufacturer's instructions or, in lieu of that, within known industry best practices.

QUESTIONS

9.1 Emergency Procedures

1. Damaged lithium batteries can cause

   A. an inflight fire.

   B. a change in aircraft center of gravity.

   C. increased endurance.

Answer (A) is correct. *(SAFO 10017)*
    DISCUSSION: Lithium-based batteries are highly flammable and capable of ignition. A battery fire could cause an in-flight emergency by causing an LOC of the sUA.
    Answer (B) is incorrect. Changes in center of gravity are caused by shifting weight. Answer (C) is incorrect. A damaged or short-circuited lithium battery could lose power and cause a loss of control, not increased endurance.

2. During your preflight inspection, you discover a small nick in the casing of your sUAS battery. What action should you take?

   A. Throw it away with your household trash.

   B. Use it as long as it will still hold a charge.

   C. Follow the manufacturer's guidance.

Answer (C) is correct. *(AC 107)*
    DISCUSSION: The remote PIC should consider following the manufacturer's recommendations, when available, to help ensure safe battery handling and usage.
    Answer (A) is incorrect. Small-unmanned-aircraft batteries should be properly disposed of according to the manufacturer's recommendations. Answer (B) is incorrect. Never use any battery with signs of damage or defect. You may not observe a battery fire until it is too late to land the aircraft safely.

9.2 Maintenance and Inspection Procedures

3. Under what condition should the operator of a small UA establish scheduled maintenance protocol?

   A. When the manufacturer does not provide a maintenance schedule.

   B. UAS does not need a required maintenance schedule.

   C. When the FAA requires you to, following an accident.

Answer (A) is correct. *(AC 107)*
    DISCUSSION: If there are no scheduled maintenance instructions provided by the sUAS manufacturer or component manufacturer, the operator should establish a scheduled maintenance protocol.
    Answer (B) is incorrect. The operator should maintain the sUAS and its components in accordance with manufacturer's instructions, or if one is not provided, the applicant may choose to develop one. Answer (C) is incorrect. The FAA requires a report within 10 calendar days of an accident resulting from an operation that caused injury or damage, not a scheduled maintenance protocol.

4. Scheduled maintenance should be performed in accordance with the:

   A. Contractor requirements.

   B. Manufacturer's suggested procedures.

   C. Stipulations in 14 CFR Part 43.

Answer (B) is correct. *(AC 107)*
    DISCUSSION: Whenever possible, the operator should maintain the sUAS and its components in accordance with manufacturer's instructions. The aircraft manufacturer may provide the maintenance program, or if one is not provided, the applicant may choose to develop one.
    Answer (A) is incorrect. If there are no scheduled maintenance instructions provided by the sUAS manufacturer or component manufacturer, the operator should establish a scheduled maintenance protocol. There is no requirement to follow contractor requirements. Answer (C) is incorrect. 14 CFR Part 43 is applicable to aircraft having a U.S. airworthiness certificate; foreign-registered civil aircraft used in common carriage or carriage of mail under the provisions of 14 CFR Part 121 or 135; and airframe, aircraft engines, propellers, appliances, and component parts of such aircraft.

5. According to 14 CFR Part 107, the responsibility to inspect the small unmanned aircraft system (sUAS) to ensure it is in a safe operating condition rests with the

   A. visual observer.

   B. remote Pilot in Command.

   C. owner of the sUAS.

Answer (B) is correct. *(14 CFR 107.49)*
    DISCUSSION: Before each flight, the remote PIC must inspect the sUAS to ensure that it is in a condition for safe operation, such as inspecting for equipment damage or malfunction(s).
    Answer (A) is incorrect. The remote PIC, not the visual observer, is responsible for ensuring that the sUAS is in a condition for safe operation. Answer (C) is incorrect. The remote PIC, not the owner of the sUAS, is responsible for ensuring that the sUAS is in a condition for safe operation.

6. Which of the following source of information should you consult **first** when determining what maintenance should be performed on an sUAS or its components?

   A. Local pilot best practices.

   B. 14 CFR Part 107.

   C. Manufacturer guidance.

Answer (C) is correct. *(AC 107)*

    DISCUSSION: There may be components of the sUAS that are identified by the manufacturer to undergo scheduled periodic maintenance or replacement based on time-in-service limits. All manufacturer scheduled maintenance instructions should be followed in the interest of achieving the longest and safest service life of the sUAS.

    Answer (A) is incorrect. Manufacturer guidance, not local pilot best practices, should be consulted first when determining what maintenance should be performed. Answer (B) is incorrect. 14 CFR Part 107 provides guidance and best practices on how to inspect and maintain an sUAS, which includes first consulting with the manufacturer.

7. How often is the Remote PIC required to inspect the sUAS to ensure that it is in a condition for safe operation?

   A. Annually.

   B. Monthly.

   C. Before each flight.

Answer (C) is correct. *(14 CFR 107.49)*

    DISCUSSION: Before each flight, the remote PIC must inspect the sUAS to ensure that it is in a condition for safe operation, such as inspecting for equipment damage or malfunction(s).

    Answer (A) is incorrect. A preflight inspection should be completed prior to each flight, not annually. Answer (B) is incorrect. A preflight inspection should be completed prior to each flight, not monthly.

8. During the preflight inspection who is responsible for determining the aircraft as safe for flight?

   A. The pilot in command.

   B. The owner or operator.

   C. The certificated mechanic who performed the annual inspection.

Answer (A) is correct. *(14 CFR 91.7)*

    DISCUSSION: During the preflight inspection, the pilot in command is responsible for determining whether the airplane is in condition for safe flight.

    Answer (B) is incorrect. The owner or operator is responsible for maintaining the airplane in an airworthy condition, not for determining whether the airplane is safe for flight during the preflight inspection. Answer (C) is incorrect. The pilot in command, not the mechanic who performed the annual inspection, is responsible for determining whether the airplane is safe for flight.

APPENDIX A
REMOTE PILOT PRACTICE TEST

The following 60 questions have been randomly selected from the questions in our remote pilot test bank. You will be referred to figures (charts, tables, etc.) throughout this book. Be careful not to consult the answers or answer explanations when you look for and at the figures. Topical coverage in this practice test is similar to that of the FAA pilot knowledge test. Use the correct answer listing on page 250 to grade your practice test.

NOTE: Our **FAA Test Prep Online** provides unlimited Study and Test Sessions for your personal use. See the discussion on pages 10 through 11 in the introduction of this book.

1. (Refer to Figure 8 on page 133.) Determine the pressure altitude at an airport that is 3,563 feet MSL with an altimeter setting of 29.96.

A — 3,527 feet MSL.
B — 3,556 feet MSL.
C — 3,639 feet MSL.

2. For aviation purposes, ceiling is defined as the height above the Earth's surface of the

A — lowest reported obscuration and the highest layer of clouds reported as overcast.
B — lowest broken or overcast layer or vertical visibility into an obscuration.
C — lowest layer of clouds reported as scattered, broken, or thin.

3. A blue segmented circle on a Sectional Chart depicts which class airspace?

A — Class B.
B — Class C.
C — Class D.

4. (Refer to Figure 75 on page 71.) The airspace surrounding the Gila Bend AF AUX Airport (GXF) (area 6) is classified as Class

A — B.
B — C.
C — D.

5. (Refer to Figure 26 on page 197.) (Refer to area 2.) What hazards to aircraft may exist in areas such as Devils Lake East MOA?

A — Unusual, often invisible, hazards to aircraft such as artillery firing, aerial gunnery, or guided missiles.
B — Military training activities that necessitate acrobatic or abrupt flight maneuvers.
C — High volume of pilot training or an unusual type of aerial activity.

6. (Refer to Figure 25 on page 171.) (Refer to area 3.) If Dallas Executive Tower is not in operation, which frequency should be used as a Common Traffic Advisory Frequency (CTAF) to monitor airport traffic?

A — 127.25 MHz.
B — 122.95 MHz.
C — 126.35 MHz.

7. (Refer to Figure 26 on page 197.) (Refer to area 2.) What is the approximate latitude and longitude of Cooperstown Airport?

A — 47°25'N – 98°06'W.
B — 47°25'N – 99°54'W.
C — 47°55'N – 98°06'W.

8. (Refer to Figure 21 on page 199.) (Refer to area 3.) Which airport is located at approximately 47°21'N latitude and 101°01'W longitude?

A — Underwood.
B — Pietsch.
C — Washburn.

9. (Refer to Figure 23 on page 203.) The flag symbols at Statesboro Bullock County Airport, Claxton-Evans County Airport, and Ridgeland Airport are

A — outer boundaries of Savannah Class C airspace.
B — airports with special traffic patterns.
C — visual checkpoints to identify position for initial callup prior to entering Savannah Class C airspace.

10. (Refer to Figure 19 on page 109.) The enclosed shaded area associated with the low pressure system over northern Utah is forecast to have

A — continuous snow.
B — intermittent snow.
C — continuous snow showers.

11. (Refer to Figure 15 on page 105.) During the time period from 0600Z to 0800Z, what visibility is forecast for KOKC?

A — Greater than 6 statute miles.
B — Possibly 6 statute miles.
C — Not forecasted.

12. (Refer to Figure 15 on page 105.) Between 1000Z and 1200Z the visibility at KMEM is forecast to be?

A — 1/2 statute mile.
B — 3 statute miles.
C — 6 statute miles.

13. (Refer to Figure 15 on page 105.) In the TAF from KOKC, the "FM (FROM) Group" is forecast for the hours from 1600Z to 2200Z with the wind from

A — 160° at 10 knots.
B — 180° at 10 knots.
C — 180° at 10 knots, becoming 200° at 13 knots.

14. (Refer to Figure 48 on page 193.) Area C on the airport depicted is classified as a

A — stabilized area.
B — multiple heliport.
C — closed runway.

15. Who is responsible for determining whether a pilot is fit to fly for a particular flight, even though he or she holds a current medical certificate?

A — The FAA.
B — The medical examiner.
C — The pilot.

16. (Refer to Figure 26 on page 197.) (Refer to area 4.) You have been hired to inspect the tower under construction at 46.9N and 98.6W, near Jamestown Regional (JMS). What must you receive prior to flying your unmanned aircraft in this area?

A — Authorization from the military.
B — Authorization from ATC.
C — Authorization from the National Park Service.

17. You have been hired as a remote pilot by a local TV news station to film breaking news with a small UA. You expressed a safety concern and the station manager has instructed you to "fly first, ask questions later." What type of hazardous attitude does this attitude represent?

A — Machismo.
B — Invulnerability.
C — Impulsivity.

18. What is one of the neglected items when a pilot relies on short and long term memory for repetitive tasks?

A — Checklists.
B — Situational awareness.
C — Flying outside the envelope.

19. What is the antidote when a pilot has a hazardous attitude, such as "Impulsivity"?

A — It could happen to me.
B — Do it quickly to get it over with.
C — Not so fast, think first.

20. What is the antidote when a pilot has the hazardous attitude of "Invulnerability"?

A — It cannot be that bad.
B — It could happen to me.
C — It will not happen to me.

21. According to 14 CFR Part 107, an sUAS is an unmanned aircraft system weighing

A — Less than 55 lbs.
B — 55 kg or less.
C — 55 lbs. or less.

22. What effect, if any, does high humidity have on aircraft performance?

A — It increases performance.
B — It decreases performance.
C — It has no effect on performance.

23. (Refer to Figure 65 on page 194.) (Refer to F.) This sign confirms your position on

A — runway 22.
B — routing to runway 22.
C — taxiway 22.

24. A military air station can be identified by a rotating beacon that emits

A — white and green alternating flashes.
B — two quick, white flashes between green flashes.
C — green, yellow, and white flashes.

25. (Refer to Figure 26 on page 197.) (Refer to area 2.) While monitoring the Cooperstown CTAF you hear an aircraft announce that they are midfield left downwind to RWY 13. Where would the aircraft be relative to the runway?

A — The aircraft is East.
B — The aircraft is South.
C — The aircraft is West.

26. Which is the correct traffic pattern departure procedure to use at a noncontrolled airport?

A — Depart in any direction consistent with safety, after crossing the airport boundary.
B — Make all turns to the left.
C — Comply with any FAA traffic pattern established for the airport.

27. (Refer to Figure 52 on page 207.) Traffic patterns in effect at Lincoln Municipal are

A — to the right on Runway 14 and Runway 32; to the left on Runway 18 and Runway 35.
B — to the left on Runway 14 and Runway 32; to the right on Runway 18 and Runway 35.
C — to the right on Runways 14 - 32.

28. In accordance with 14 CFR Part 107, except when within a 400' radius of a structure, at what maximum altitude can you operate sUAS?

A — 500 feet AGL.
B — 400 feet AGL.
C — 600 feet AGL.

29. When a control tower located on an airport within Class D airspace ceases operation for the day, what happens to the airspace designation?

A — The airspace designation normally will not change.
B — The airspace remains Class D airspace as long as a weather observer or automated weather system is available.
C — The airspace reverts to Class E or a combination of Class E and G airspace during the hours the tower is not in operation.

30. The term "angle of attack" is defined as the angle between the

A — chord line of the wing and the relative wind.
B — airplane's longitudinal axis and that of the air striking the airfoil.
C — airplane's center line and the relative wind.

31. An ATC radar facility issues the following advisory to a pilot flying on a heading of 360°:

"TRAFFIC 10 O'CLOCK, 2 MILES, SOUTHBOUND..."

Where should the pilot look for this traffic?

A — Northwest.
B — Northeast.
C — Southwest.

32. Which factor would tend to increase the density altitude at a given airport?

A — An increase in barometric pressure.
B — An increase in ambient temperature.
C — A decrease in relative humidity.

33. During your preflight inspection, you discover a small nick in the casing of your sUAS battery. What action should you take?

A — Throw it away with your household trash.
B — Use it as long as it will still hold a charge.
C — Follow the manufacturer's guidance.

34. A local TV station has hired a remote pilot to operate their small UA to cover news stories. The remote pilot has had multiple near misses with obstacles on the ground and two small UAS accidents. What would be a solution for the news station to improve their operating safety culture?

A — The news station should implement a policy of no more than five crashes/incidents within 6 months.
B — The news station does not need to make any changes; there are times that an accident is unavoidable.
C — The news station should recognize hazardous attitudes and situations and develop standard operating procedures that emphasize safety.

35. Why is fatigue hazardous to flight safety?

A — The pilot hurries to get done in order to rest.
B — Fatigue may not be apparent to a pilot until serious errors are made (an impaired pilot is a dangerous pilot).
C — The pilot is lazy and rushes to get done quickly.

36. In which environment is aircraft structural ice most likely to have the highest accumulation rate?

A — Cumulus clouds with below freezing temperatures.
B — Freezing drizzle.
C — Freezing rain.

37. (Refer to Figure 23 on page 64, and Legend 1 on page 65.) (Refer to area 3.) For information about glider operations at Ridgeland Airport, refer to

A — notes on the border of the chart.
B — the Chart Supplement.
C — the Notices to Airmen (NOTAM) publication.

38. (Refer to Figure 2 on page 152.) If an unmanned airplane weighs 33 pounds, what approximate weight would the airplane structure be required to support during a 30° banked turn while maintaining altitude?

A — 34 pounds.
B — 47 pounds.
C — 38 pounds.

39. What could be a consequence of operating a small unmanned aircraft above its maximum allowable weight?

A — Faster speed.
B — Shorter endurance.
C — Increased maneuverability.

40. Before each flight, the Remote PIC must ensure that

A — Objects carried on the sUAS are secure.
B — The site supervisor has approved the flight.
C — ATC has granted clearance.

41. To ensure that the unmanned aircraft center of gravity (CG) limits are not exceeded, follow the aircraft loading instructions specified in the

A — Pilot's Operating Handbook or UAS Flight Manual.
B — Aeronautical Information Manual (AIM).
C — Aircraft Weight and Balance Handbook.

42. A pilot should be able to overcome the symptoms or avoid future occurrences of hyperventilation by

A — closely monitoring the flight instruments to control the airplane.
B — slowing the breathing rate, breathing into a bag, or talking aloud.
C — increasing the breathing rate in order to increase lung ventilation.

43. You are operating a 1280 g (2.8 lb.) quadcopter for your own enjoyment. Is this sUAS operation subject to 14 CFR Part 107?

A — Yes, this sUAS operation is subject to Part 107.
B — No, this sUAS operation is not subject to Part 107.
C — Yes, all sUAS aircraft weighing over .55 lbs. are subject to Part 107.

44. Which of the following source of information should you consult **first** when determining what maintenance should be performed on an sUAS or its components?

A — Local pilot best practices.
B — 14 CFR Part 107.
C — Manufacturer guidance.

45. According to 14 CFR Part 107, the responsibility to inspect the small unmanned aircraft system (sUAS) to ensure it is in a safe operating condition rests with the

A — visual observer.
B — remote Pilot in Command.
C — owner of the sUAS.

46. A person may not act as a crewmember of a civil aircraft if alcoholic beverages have been consumed by that person within the preceding

A — 8 hours.
B — 12 hours.
C — 24 hours.

47. If there is thunderstorm activity in the vicinity of an airport at which you plan to land, which hazardous atmospheric phenomenon might be expected on the landing approach?

A — Precipitation static.
B — Wind-shear turbulence.
C — Steady rain.

48. What conditions are necessary for the formation of thunderstorms?

A — High humidity, lifting force, and unstable conditions.
B — High humidity, high temperature, and cumulus clouds.
C — Lifting force, moist air, and extensive cloud cover.

49. Thunderstorms reach their greatest intensity during the

A — mature stage.
B — downdraft stage.
C — cumulus stage.

50. Which weather phenomenon signals the beginning of the mature stage of a thunderstorm?

A — The appearance of an anvil top.
B — Precipitation beginning to fall.
C — Maximum growth rate of the clouds.

51. One weather phenomenon which will always occur when flying across a front is a change in the

A — wind direction.
B — type of precipitation.
C — stability of the air mass.

52. One of the most easily recognized discontinuities across a front is

A — a change in temperature.
B — an increase in cloud coverage.
C — an increase in relative humidity.

53. What are characteristics of unstable air?

A — Turbulence and good surface visibility.
B — Turbulence and poor surface visibility.
C — Nimbostratus clouds and good surface visibility.

54. A stable air mass is most likely to have which characteristic?

A — Showery precipitation.
B — Turbulent air.
C — Poor surface visibility.

55. What are characteristics of a moist, unstable air mass?

A — Cumuliform clouds and showery precipitation.
B — Poor visibility and smooth air.
C — Stratiform clouds and showery precipitation.

56. The amount of water vapor which air can hold depends on the

A — dewpoint.
B — air temperature.
C — stability of the air.

57. The wind at 5,000 feet AGL is southwesterly while the surface wind is southerly. This difference in direction is primarily due to

A — stronger pressure gradient at higher altitudes.
B — friction between the wind and the surface.
C — stronger Coriolis force at the surface.

58. Where does wind shear occur?

A — Only at higher altitudes.
B — Only at lower altitudes.
C — At all altitudes, in all directions.

59. Under what condition would a small UA not have to be registered before it is operated in the United States?

A — When the aircraft weighs less than .55 pounds on takeoff, including everything that is on-board or attached to the aircraft.
B — When the aircraft has a takeoff weight that is more than .55 pounds, but less than 55 pounds, not including fuel and necessary attachments.
C — All small UAS need to be registered regardless of the weight of the aircraft before, during, or after the flight.

60. According to 14 CFR Part 48, when must a person register a small UA with the Federal Aviation Administration?

A — All civilian small UAs weighing greater than .55 pounds must be registered regardless of its intended use.
B — When the small UA is used for any purpose other than as a model aircraft.
C — Only when the operator will be paid for commercial services.

PRACTICE TEST LIST OF ANSWERS

Listed below are the answers to the practice test. To the immediate right of each answer is the page number on which the question, as well as correct and incorrect answer explanations, can be found.

Q. #	Answer	Page	Q. #	Answer	Page	Q. #	Answer	Page	Q. #	Answer	Page
1.	A	132	16.	B	196	31.	A	162	46.	A	40
2.	B	105	17.	C	229	32.	B	134	47.	B	136
3.	C	60	18.	A	230	33.	C	242	48.	A	137
4.	C	70	19.	C	231	34.	C	230	49.	A	137
5.	B	68	20.	B	231	35.	B	233	50.	B	137
6.	A	170	21.	A	37	36.	C	138	51.	A	136
7.	A	196	22.	B	134	37.	B	64	52.	A	136
8.	C	198	23.	A	195	38.	C	152	53.	A	141
9.	C	202	24.	B	195	39.	B	151	54.	C	141
10.	A	108	25.	A	166	40.	A	39	55.	A	141
11.	A	104	26.	C	195	41.	A	151	56.	B	139
12.	B	104	27.	B	206	42.	B	232	57.	B	135
13.	B	104	28.	B	34	43.	B	36	58.	C	138
14.	C	193	29.	C	59	44.	C	243	59.	A	35
15.	C	231	30.	A	152	45.	B	242	60.	A	39

APPENDIX B
INTERPOLATION

The following is a tutorial based on information that has appeared in the FAA's *Pilot's Handbook of Aeronautical Knowledge*. Interpolation is required in questions found in the following subunit:
Study Unit 4, Subunit 1, "Effects of Weather on Performance" (pages 111, 131)

A. To interpolate means to compute intermediate values between a series of given values.

1. In many instances when performance is critical, an accurate determination of the performance values is the only acceptable means to enhance safe flight.

2. Guessing to determine these values should be avoided.

B. Interpolation is simple to perform if the method is understood. The following are examples of how to interpolate, or accurately determine the intermediate values, between a series of given values.

C. The numbers in column A range from 10 to 30, and the numbers in column B range from 50 to 100. Determine the intermediate numerical value in column B that would correspond with an intermediate value of 20 placed in column A.

A	B
10	50
20	X = Unknown
30	100

1. It can be visualized that 20 is halfway between 10 and 30; therefore, the corresponding value of the unknown number in column B would be halfway between 50 and 100, or 75.

D. Many interpolation problems are more difficult to visualize than the preceding example; therefore, a systematic method must be used to determine the required intermediate value. The following describes one method that can be used.

1. The numbers in column A range from 10 to 30 with intermediate values of 15, 20, and 25. Determine the intermediate numerical value in column B that would correspond with 15 in column A.

A	B
10	50
15	
20	
25	
30	100

2. First, in column A, determine the relationship of 15 to the range between 10 and 30 as follows:

$$\frac{15 - 10}{30 - 10} = \frac{5}{20} \text{ or } 1/4$$

a. It should be noted that 15 is 1/4 of the range between 10 and 30.

3.   Now determine 1/4 of the range of column B between 50 and 100 as follows:

$$100 - 50 = 50$$
$$1/4 \text{ of } 50 = 12.5$$

    a.   The answer 12.5 represents the number of units, but to arrive at the correct value, 12.5 must be added to the lower number in column B as follows:

$$50 + 12.5 = 62.5$$

4.   The interpolation has been completed and 62.5 is the actual value which is 1/4 of the range of column B.

E.   Another method of interpolation is shown below:

    1.   Using the same numbers as in the previous example, a proportion problem based on the relationship of the number can be set up.

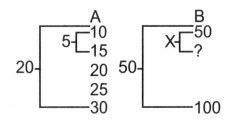

$$\text{Proportion:} \quad \frac{5}{20} = \frac{X}{50}$$
$$20X = 250$$
$$X = 12.5$$

    a.   The answer, 12.5, must be added to 50 to arrive at the actual value of 62.5.

F.   The following example illustrates the use of interpolation applied to a problem dealing with one aspect of airplane performance:

Temperature (°F)	Takeoff Distance (ft.)
70	1,173
80	1,356

    1.   If a distance of 1,173 feet is required for takeoff when the temperature is 70°F and 1,356 feet is required at 80°F, what distance is required when the temperature is 75°F? The solution to the problem can be determined as follows:

$$
\begin{array}{cc}
10\!-\!\!\begin{array}{c} 5\!-\!\!\begin{array}{l}70° \\ 75° \end{array} \\ 80° \end{array} 183\!-\!\!\begin{array}{c} X\!-\!\!\begin{array}{l}1{,}173 \\ ? \end{array} \\ 1{,}356 \end{array}
\end{array}
$$

$$\frac{5}{10} = \frac{X}{183}$$
$$10X = 915$$
$$X = 91.5$$

    a.   The answer, 91.5, must be added to 1,173 to arrive at the actual value of 1,264.5 ft.

FAA LISTING OF
LEARNING STATEMENT CODES

Reprinted below and on the following pages are all of the FAA's learning statement codes for pilots. These are the codes that will appear on your Airman Computer Test Report. See the example on page 9. Your test report will list the learning statement code of each question answered incorrectly. The statements are designed to represent the knowledge test topic areas in clear verbal terms and encourage applicants to study the entire area of identified weakness instead of merely studying a specific question area. You should discuss your test results with your CFI.

When you receive your Airman Computer Test Report, you can trace the learning statement codes listed on it to these pages to find out which topics you had difficulty with. To determine the knowledge area in which a particular question was incorrectly answered, compare the learning statement code(s) on your Airman Computer Test Report to the listing that follows. The total number of test items missed may differ from the number of learning statement codes shown on your test report because you may have missed more than one question in a certain knowledge area.

Additionally, you should trace the learning statement codes on your Airman Computer Test Report to our cross-reference listing of questions beginning on page 259. Determine which Gleim subunits you need to review.

The FAA will periodically revise the existing learning codes and add new ones. As Gleim learns about any changes, we will update our materials.

PLT001	Calculate a course intercept
PLT002	Calculate aircraft performance - airspeed
PLT003	Calculate aircraft performance - center of gravity
PLT004	Calculate aircraft performance - climb / descent / maneuvering
PLT005	Calculate aircraft performance - density altitude
PLT006	Calculate aircraft performance - glide
PLT007	Calculate aircraft performance - IAS
PLT008	Calculate aircraft performance - landing
PLT009	Calculate aircraft performance - turbine temperatures (MGT, EGT, ITT, T4, etc) / torque / horsepower
PLT010	Calculate aircraft performance - STAB TRIM
PLT011	Calculate aircraft performance - takeoff
PLT012	Calculate aircraft performance - time / speed / distance / course / fuel / wind
PLT013	Calculate crosswind / headwind components
PLT014	Calculate distance / bearing to a station
PLT015	Calculate flight performance / planning - range
PLT016	Calculate fuel - dump time / weight / volume / quantity / consumption
PLT017	Calculate L/D ratio
PLT018	Calculate load factor / stall speed / velocity / angle of attack
PLT019	Calculate pressure altitude
PLT020	Calculate turbulent air penetration
PLT021	Calculate weight and balance
PLT022	Define Aeronautical Decision Making (ADM)
PLT023	Define altitude - absolute / true / indicated / density / pressure
PLT024	Define atmospheric adiabatic process
PLT025	Define Bernoulli's principle
PLT026	Define ceiling
PLT027	Define coning
PLT028	Define crewmember
PLT029	Define critical phase of flight
PLT030	Define false lift
PLT031	Define isobars / associated winds
PLT032	Define MACH speed regimes
PLT033	Define MEA / MOCA / MRA
PLT034	Define stopway / clearway
PLT035	Define Vne / Vno
PLT036	Interpret a MACH meter reading
PLT037	Interpret a Radar Weather Report / National Convective Weather Forecast
PLT038	Interpret aircraft Power Schedule Chart
PLT039	Interpret airport landing indicator
PLT040	Interpret airspace classes - charts / diagrams
PLT041	Interpret altimeter - readings / settings
PLT042	Interpret Constant Pressure charts / Isotachs Chart
PLT043	Interpret Analysis Heights / Temperature Chart
PLT044	Interpret ATC communications / instructions / terminology
PLT045	Interpret Descent Performance Chart
PLT046	Interpret drag ratio from charts
PLT047	Interpret/Program Flight Director/FMS/ Automation - modes / operation / indications / errors
PLT048	Interpret Hovering Ceiling Chart
PLT049	Interpret ILS - charts / RMI / CDI / indications
PLT050	Interpret information on a Brake Energy Limit Chart
PLT051	Interpret information on a Convective Outlook
PLT052	Interpret information on a Departure Procedure Chart
PLT053	Interpret information on a Flight Plan
PLT054	Interpret information on a Glider Performance Graph
PLT055	Interpret information on a High Altitude Chart
PLT056	Interpret information on a Horizontal Situation Indicator (HSI)
PLT057	Interpret information on a Hot Air Balloon Performance Graph
PLT058	Interpret information on a Low Altitude Chart
PLT059	Interpret information on a METAR / SPECI report
PLT060	Interpret information on a Performance Curve Chart
PLT061	Interpret information on a PIREP
PLT062	Interpret information on a Pseudo-Adiabatic Chart / K Index / Lifted Index
PLT063	Deleted
PLT064	Interpret information on a Sectional Chart
PLT065	Interpret information on a Service Ceiling Engine Inoperative Chart

PLT066	Interpret information on a Convective Outlook Chart
PLT067	Interpret information on a SIGMET
PLT068	Interpret information on a Significant Weather Prognostic Chart
PLT069	Interpret information on a Slush/Standing Water Takeoff Chart
PLT070	Interpret information on a Stability Chart
PLT071	Interpret information on a Surface Analysis Chart
PLT072	Interpret information on a Terminal Aerodrome Forecast (TAF)
PLT073	Interpret information on a Tower Enroute Control (TEC)
PLT074	Interpret information on a Velocity/Load Factor Chart
PLT075	Interpret information on a Weather Depiction Chart
PLT076	Interpret information on a Winds and Temperatures Aloft Forecast (FB)
PLT077	Interpret information on an Airport Diagram
PLT078	Interpret information in a Chart Supplements U.S.
PLT079	Interpret information on an Airways Chart
PLT080	Interpret information on an Arrival Chart
PLT081	Interpret information on an Aviation Area Forecast (FA)
PLT082	Interpret information on an IFR Alternate Airport Minimums Chart
PLT083	Interpret information on an Instrument Approach Procedures (IAP)
PLT084	Interpret information on an Observed Winds Aloft Chart
PLT085	Interpret information on Takeoff Obstacle / Field / Climb Limit Charts
PLT086	Interpret readings on a Turn and Slip Indicator
PLT087	Interpret readings on an Aircraft Course and DME Indicator
PLT088	Interpret speed indicator readings
PLT089	Interpret Takeoff Speeds Chart
PLT090	Interpret VOR - charts / indications / CDI / NAV
PLT091	Interpret VOR / CDI - illustrations / indications / procedures
PLT092	Interpret weight and balance - diagram
PLT093	Recall administration of medical oxygen
PLT094	Recall aerodynamics - airfoil design / pressure distribution / effects of altitude
PLT095	Recall aerodynamics - longitudinal axis / lateral axis
PLT096	Recall aeromedical factors - effects of altitude
PLT097	Recall aeromedical factors - effects of carbon monoxide poisoning
PLT098	Recall aeromedical factors - fitness for flight
PLT099	Recall aeromedical factors - scanning procedures
PLT100	Recall aeronautical charts - IFR En Route Low Altitude
PLT101	Recall aeronautical charts - pilotage
PLT102	Recall aeronautical charts - terminal procedures
PLT103	Recall Aeronautical Decision Making (ADM) - hazardous attitudes
PLT104	Recall Aeronautical Decision Making (ADM) - human factors / CRM
PLT105	Recall airborne radar / thunderstorm detection equipment - use / limitations
PLT106	Recall aircraft air-cycle machine
PLT107	Recall aircraft alternator / generator system
PLT108	Recall aircraft anti-icing / deicing - methods / fluids
PLT109	Recall aircraft batteries - capacity / charging / types / storage / rating / precautions
PLT110	Recall aircraft brake system

PLT111	Recall aircraft circuitry - series / parallel
PLT112	Recall aircraft controls - proper use / techniques
PLT113	Recall aircraft design - categories / limitation factors
PLT114	Recall aircraft design - construction / function
PLT115	Recall aircraft engine - detonation/backfiring/ after firing, cause/characteristics
PLT116	Recall aircraft general knowledge / publications / AIM / navigational aids
PLT117	Recall aircraft heated windshields
PLT118	Recall aircraft instruments - gyroscopic
PLT119	Recall aircraft lighting - anti-collision / landing / navigation
PLT120	Recall aircraft limitations - turbulent air penetration
PLT121	Recall aircraft loading - computations
PLT122	Recall aircraft operations - checklist usage
PLT123	Recall aircraft performance - airspeed
PLT124	Recall aircraft performance - atmospheric effects
PLT125	Recall aircraft performance - climb / descent
PLT126	Recall aircraft performance - cold weather operations
PLT127	Recall aircraft performance - density altitude
PLT128	Recall aircraft performance - effects of icing
PLT129	Recall aircraft performance - effects of runway slope / slope landing
PLT130	Recall aircraft performance - fuel
PLT131	Recall aircraft performance - ground effect
PLT132	Recall aircraft performance - instrument markings / airspeed / definitions / indications
PLT133	Recall aircraft performance - normal climb / descent rates
PLT134	Recall aircraft performance - takeoff
PLT135	Recall aircraft pressurization - system / operation
PLT136	Recall aircraft systems - anti-icing / deicing
PLT137	Recall aircraft systems - environmental control
PLT138	Recall aircraft landing gear/tires - types / characteristics
PLT139	Recall aircraft warning systems - stall / fire / retractable gear / terrain awareness
PLT140	Recall airport operations - LAHSO
PLT141	Recall airport operations - markings / signs / lighting
PLT142	Recall airport operations - noise avoidance routes
PLT143	Recall airport operations - rescue / fire fighting vehicles and types of agents
PLT144	Recall airport operations - runway conditions
PLT145	Recall airport operations - runway lighting
PLT146	Recall airport operations - traffic pattern procedures / communication procedures
PLT147	Recall airport operations - visual glideslope indicators
PLT148	Recall airport operations lighting - MALS / ALSF / RCLS / TDZL
PLT149	Recall airport preflight / taxi operations - procedures
PLT150	Recall airport traffic patterns - entry procedures
PLT151	Recall airship - buoyancy
PLT152	Recall airship - flight characteristics / controllability
PLT153	Recall airship - flight operations
PLT154	Recall airship - ground weight-off / static / trim condition
PLT155	Recall airship - maintaining pressure
PLT156	Recall airship - maximum headway / flight at equilibrium
PLT157	Recall airship - pressure height / dampers / position
PLT158	Recall airship - pressure height / manometers
PLT159	Recall airship - pressure height / super heat / valving gas

PLT160 Recall airship - stability / control / positive superheat

PLT161 Recall airspace classes - limits / requirements / restrictions / airspeeds / equipment

PLT162 Recall airspace requirements - operations

PLT163 Recall airspace requirements - visibility / cloud clearance

PLT164 Recall airspeed - effects during a turn

PLT165 Recall altimeter - effect of temperature changes

PLT166 Recall altimeter - settings / setting procedures

PLT167 Recall altimeters - characteristics / accuracy

PLT168 Recall angle of attack - characteristics / forces / principles

PLT169 Recall antitorque system - components / functions

PLT170 Recall approach / landing / taxiing techniques

PLT171 Recall ATC - reporting

PLT172 Recall ATC - system / services

PLT173 Recall atmospheric conditions - measurements / pressure / stability

PLT174 Recall autopilot / yaw damper - components / operating principles / characteristics / failure modes

PLT175 Recall autorotation

PLT176 Recall balance tab - purpose / operation

PLT177 Recall balloon - flight operations

PLT178 Recall balloon - flight operations / gas

PLT179 Recall balloon - ground weigh-off / static equilibrium / load

PLT180 Recall balloon gas/hot air - lift / false lift / characteristics

PLT181 Recall balloon - hot air / physics

PLT182 Recall balloon - inspecting the fabric

PLT183 Recall balloon flight operations - ascent / descent

PLT184 Recall balloon flight operations - launch / landing

PLT185 Recall basic instrument flying - fundamental skills

PLT186 Recall basic instrument flying - pitch instruments

PLT187 Recall basic instrument flying - turn coordinator / turn and slip indicator

PLT188 Recall cabin atmosphere control

PLT189 Recall carburetor - effects of carburetor heat / heat control

PLT190 Recall carburetor ice - factors affecting / causing

PLT191 Recall carburetors - types / components / operating principles / characteristics

PLT192 Recall clouds - types / formation / resulting weather

PLT193 Recall cockpit voice recorder (CVR) - operating principles / characteristics / testing

PLT194 Recall collision avoidance - scanning techniques

PLT195 Recall collision avoidance - TCAS

PLT196 Recall communications - ATIS broadcasts

PLT197 Recall Coriolis effect

PLT198 Recall course / heading - effects of wind

PLT199 Recall cyclic control pressure - characteristics

PLT200 Recall dead reckoning - calculations / charts

PLT201 Recall departure procedures - ODP / SID

PLT202 Recall DME - characteristics / accuracy / indications / Arc

PLT203 Recall earth's atmosphere - layers / characteristics / solar energy

PLT204 Recall effective communication - basic elements

PLT205 Recall effects of alcohol on the body

PLT206 Recall effects of temperature - density altitude / icing

PLT207 Recall electrical system - components / operating principles / characteristics / static bonding and shielding

PLT208 Recall emergency conditions / procedures

PLT209 Deleted

PLT210 Recall engine shutdown - normal / abnormal / emergency / precautions

PLT211 Recall evaluation testing characteristics

PLT212 Recall fire extinguishing systems - components / operating principles / characteristics

PLT213 Recall flight characteristics - longitudinal stability / instability

PLT214 Recall flight characteristics - structural / wing design

PLT215 Recall flight instruments - magnetic compass

PLT216 Recall flight instruments - total energy compensators

PLT217 Recall flight maneuvers - quick stop

PLT218 Recall flight operations - common student errors

PLT219 Recall flight operations - maneuvers

PLT220 Recall flight operations - night and high altitude operations

PLT221 Recall flight operations - takeoff / landing maneuvers

PLT222 Recall flight operations - takeoff procedures

PLT223 Recall flight operations multiengine - engine inoperative procedures

PLT224 Recall flight plan - IFR

PLT225 Recall flight plan - requirements

PLT226 Recall fog - types / formation / resulting weather

PLT227 Recall FOI techniques - integrated flight instruction

PLT228 Recall FOI techniques - lesson plans

PLT229 Recall FOI techniques - professionalism

PLT230 Recall FOI techniques - responsibilities

PLT231 Recall FOI techniques / human behavior - anxiety / fear / stress

PLT232 Recall FOI techniques / human behavior - dangerous tendencies

PLT233 Recall FOI techniques / human behavior - defense mechanisms

PLT234 Recall forces acting on aircraft - 3 axis intersect

PLT235 Recall forces acting on aircraft - aerodynamics

PLT236 Recall forces acting on aircraft - airfoil / center of pressure / mean camber line

PLT237 Recall forces acting on aircraft - airspeed / air density / lift / drag

PLT238 Recall forces acting on aircraft - aspect ratio

PLT239 Recall forces acting on aircraft - buoyancy / drag / gravity / thrust

PLT240 Recall forces acting on aircraft - CG / flight characteristics

PLT241 Recall forces acting on aircraft - drag / gravity / thrust / lift

PLT242 Recall forces acting on aircraft - lift / drag / thrust / weight / stall / limitations

PLT243 Recall forces acting on aircraft - propeller / torque

PLT244 Recall forces acting on aircraft - stability / controllability

PLT245 Recall forces acting on aircraft - stalls / spins

PLT246 Recall forces acting on aircraft - steady state climb / flight

PLT247 Recall forces acting on aircraft - thrust / drag / weight / lift

PLT248 Recall forces acting on aircraft - turns

PLT249 Recall fuel - air mixture

PLT250 Recall fuel - types / characteristics / contamination / fueling / defueling / precautions

PLT251 Recall fuel characteristics / contaminants / additives

PLT252 Recall fuel dump system - components / methods

PLT253 Recall fuel system - components / operating principles / characteristics / leaks

PLT254 Recall fuel tank - components / operating principles / characteristics

PLT255   Recall fueling procedures - safety / grounding / calculating volume
PLT256   Recall glider performance - effect of loading
PLT257   Recall glider performance - speed / distance / ballast / lift / drag
PLT258   Recall ground reference maneuvers - ground track diagram
PLT259   Recall ground resonance - conditions to occur
PLT260   Recall gyroplane - aerodynamics / rotor systems
PLT261   Recall hail - characteristics / hazards
PLT262   Recall helicopter hazards - dynamic rollover / Low G / LTE
PLT263   Recall hazardous weather - fog / icing / turbulence / visibility restriction
PLT264   Recall helicopter approach - settling with power
PLT265   Recall helicopter takeoff / landing - ground resonance action required
PLT266   Recall high lift devices - characteristics / functions
PLT267   Recall hot air balloon - weight-off procedure
PLT268   Recall hovering - aircraft performance / tendencies
PLT269   Recall human behavior - defense mechanism
PLT270   Recall human behavior - social / self fulfillment / physical
PLT271   Recall human factors (ADM) - judgment
PLT272   Recall human factors - stress management
PLT273   Recall hydraulic systems - components / operating principles / characteristics
PLT274   Recall icing - formation / characteristics
PLT275   Recall ILS - indications / HSI
PLT276   Recall ILS - indications / OBS / CDI
PLT277   Recall ILS - marker beacon / indicator lights / codes
PLT278   Recall indicating systems - airspeed / angle of attack / attitude / heading / manifold pressure / synchro / EGT
PLT279   Recall Inertial/Doppler Navigation System principles / regulations / requirements / limitations
PLT280   Recall inflight illusions - causes / sources
PLT281   Recall information in a Chart Supplements U.S.
PLT282   Recall information in the certificate holder's manual
PLT283   Recall information on a Constant Pressure Analysis Chart
PLT284   Recall information on a Forecast Winds and Temperatures Aloft (FB)
PLT285   Recall information on a Height Velocity Diagram
PLT286   Recall information on a Significant Weather Prognostic Chart
PLT287   Recall information on a Surface Analysis Chart
PLT288   Recall information on a Terminal Aerodrome Forecast (TAF)
PLT289   Recall information on a Weather Depiction Chart
PLT290   Recall information on AIRMETS / SIGMETS
PLT291   Recall information on an Aviation Area Forecast (FA)
PLT292   Recall information on an Instrument Approach Procedures (IAP)
PLT293   Recall information on an Instrument Departure Procedure Chart
PLT294   Recall information on Inflight Aviation Weather Advisories
PLT295   Recall instructor techniques - obstacles / planning / activities / outcome
PLT296   Recall instrument procedures - holding / circling
PLT297   Recall instrument procedures - unusual attitude / unusual attitude recovery
PLT298   Recall instrument procedures - VFR on top
PLT300   Recall instrument/navigation system checks/ inspections - limits / tuning / identifying / logging

PLT301   Recall inversion layer - characteristics
PLT302   Recall jet stream - types / characteristics
PLT303   Recall L/D ratio
PLT304   Recall launch / aero-tow procedures
PLT305   Recall leading edge devices - types / effect / purpose / operation
PLT306   Recall learning process - levels of learning / transfer of learning / incidental learning
PLT307   Recall learning process - memory / fact / recall
PLT308   Recall learning process - laws of learning elements
PLT309   Recall load factor - angle of bank
PLT310   Recall load factor - characteristics
PLT311   Recall load factor - effect of airspeed
PLT312   Recall load factor - maneuvering / stall speed
PLT313   Recall loading – limitations / terminology
PLT314   Recall longitudinal axis - aerodynamics / center of gravity / direction of motion
PLT315   Recall Machmeter - principles / functions
PLT316   Recall meteorology - severe weather watch (WW)
PLT317   Recall microburst - characteristics / hazards
PLT318   Recall minimum fuel advisory
PLT319   Recall navigation – celestial / navigation chart / characteristics
PLT320   Recall navigation - true north / magnetic north
PLT321   Recall navigation - types of landing systems
PLT322   Recall navigation - VOR / NAV system
PLT323   Recall NOTAMS - classes / information / distribution
PLT324   Recall oil system - types / components / functions / oil specifications
PLT325   Recall operations manual - transportation of prisoner
PLT326   Recall oxygen system - components / operating principles / characteristics
PLT327   Recall oxygen system - install / inspect / repair / service / precautions / leaks
PLT328   Recall performance planning - aircraft loading
PLT329   Recall physiological factors - cabin pressure
PLT330   Recall physiological factors - cause / effects of hypoxia
PLT331   Recall physiological factors - effects of scuba diving / smoking
PLT332   Recall physiological factors - hyperventilation / stress / fatigue
PLT333   Recall physiological factors - night vision
PLT334   Recall physiological factors - spatial disorientation
PLT335   Recall pilotage - calculations
PLT337   Recall pitot-static system - components / operating principles / characteristics
PLT338   Recall pneumatic system - operation
PLT340   Recall positive exchange of flight controls
PLT341   Recall power setting - characteristics
PLT342   Recall powerplant - controlling engine temperature
PLT343   Recall powerplant - operating principles / operational characteristics / inspecting
PLT344   Recall precipitation - types / characteristics
PLT345   Recall pressure altitude
PLT346   Recall primary / secondary flight controls - types / purpose / functionality / operation
PLT347   Recall principles of flight - critical engine
PLT348   Recall principles of flight - turns
PLT349   Recall procedures for confined areas
PLT350   Recall propeller operations - constant / variable speed
PLT351   Recall propeller system - types / components / operating principles / characteristics
PLT352   Recall purpose / operation of a stabilizer
PLT353   Recall Radar Summary Chart
PLT354   Recall radio - GPS / RNAV / RAIM

PLT355	Recall radio - HSI
PLT356	Recall radio - ILS / compass locator
PLT357	Recall radio - ILS
PLT358	Recall radio - LOC / ILS
PLT359	Deleted
PLT360	Deleted
PLT361	Deleted
PLT362	Deleted
PLT363	Recall radio - VOR / VOT
PLT364	Recall radio system - license requirements / frequencies
PLT365	Recall reciprocating engine - components / operating principles / characteristics
PLT366	Recall regulations - accident / incident reporting and preserving wreckage
PLT367	Recall regulations - additional equipment/ operating requirements large transport aircraft
PLT368	Recall regulations - admission to flight deck
PLT369	Recall regulations - aerobatic flight requirements
PLT370	Recall regulations - Air Traffic Control authorization / clearances
PLT371	Recall regulations - Aircraft Category / Class
PLT372	Recall regulations - aircraft inspection / records / expiration
PLT373	Recall regulations - aircraft operating limitations
PLT374	Recall regulations - aircraft owner / operator responsibilities
PLT375	Recall regulations - aircraft return to service
PLT376	Recall regulations - airspace, other, special use / TFRS
PLT377	Recall regulations - airworthiness certificates / requirements / responsibilities
PLT378	Recall regulations - Airworthiness Directives
PLT379	Recall regulations - alternate airport requirements
PLT380	Recall regulations - alternate airport weather minima
PLT381	Recall regulations - altimeter settings
PLT382	Recall regulations - approach minima
PLT383	Recall regulations - basic flight rules
PLT384	Recall regulations - briefing of passengers
PLT385	Recall regulations - cargo in passenger compartment
PLT386	Recall regulations - certificate issuance / renewal
PLT387	Recall regulations - change of address
PLT388	Recall regulations - cockpit voice / flight data recorder(s)
PLT389	Recall regulations - commercial operation requirements / conditions / OpSpecs
PLT390	Recall regulations - communications enroute
PLT391	Recall regulations - communications failure
PLT392	Recall regulations - compliance with local regulations
PLT393	Recall regulations - controlled / restricted airspace - requirements
PLT394	Recall regulations - declaration of an emergency
PLT395	Recall regulations - definitions
PLT396	Recall regulations - departure alternate airport
PLT397	Recall regulations - destination airport visibility
PLT398	Recall regulations - dispatch
PLT399	Recall regulations - display / inspection of licenses and certificates
PLT400	Recall regulations - documents to be carried on aircraft during flight
PLT401	Recall regulations - dropping / aerial application / towing restrictions
PLT402	Recall regulations - ELT requirements
PLT403	Recall regulations - emergency deviation from regulations
PLT404	Recall regulations - emergency equipment
PLT405	Recall regulations - equipment / instrument / certificate requirements
PLT406	Recall regulations - equipment failure
PLT407	Recall regulations - experience / training requirements
PLT408	Recall regulations - fire extinguisher requirements
PLT409	Recall regulations - flight / duty time
PLT410	Recall regulations - flight engineer qualifications / privileges / responsibilities
PLT411	Recall regulations - flight instructor limitations / qualifications
PLT412	Recall regulations - flight release
PLT413	Recall regulations - fuel requirements
PLT414	Recall regulations - general right-of-way rules
PLT415	Recall regulations - IFR flying
PLT416	Recall regulations - immediate notification
PLT417	Recall regulations - individual flotation devices
PLT418	Recall regulations - instructor demonstrations / authorizations
PLT419	Recall regulations - instructor requirements / responsibilities
PLT420	Recall regulations - instrument approach procedures
PLT421	Recall regulations - instrument flight rules
PLT422	Recall regulations - intermediate airport authorizations
PLT423	Recall regulations - knowledge and skill test checks
PLT424	Recall regulations - limits on autopilot usage
PLT425	Recall regulations - maintenance reports / records / entries
PLT426	Recall regulations - maintenance requirements
PLT427	Recall regulations - medical certificate requirements / validity
PLT428	Recall regulations - minimum equipment list
PLT429	Recall regulations - minimum flight / navigation instruments
PLT430	Recall regulations - minimum safe / flight altitude
PLT431	Recall regulations - operating near other aircraft
PLT432	Recall regulations - operational control functions
PLT433	Recall regulations - operational flight plan requirements
PLT434	Recall regulations - operational procedures for a controlled airport
PLT435	Recall regulations - operational procedures for an uncontrolled airport
PLT436	Recall regulations - operations manual
PLT437	Recall regulations - overwater operations
PLT438	Recall regulations - oxygen requirements
PLT439	Recall regulations - persons authorized to perform maintenance
PLT440	Recall regulations - Pilot / Crew duties and responsibilities
PLT441	Recall regulations - pilot briefing
PLT442	Recall regulations - pilot currency requirements
PLT443	Recall regulations - pilot qualifications / privileges / responsibilities / crew complement
PLT444	Recall regulations - pilot-in-command authority / responsibility
PLT445	Recall regulations - preflight requirements
PLT446	Recall regulations - preventative maintenance
PLT447	Recall regulations - privileges / limitations of medical certificates
PLT448	Recall regulations - privileges / limitations of pilot certificates
PLT449	Recall regulations - proficiency check requirements
PLT450	Recall regulations - qualifications / duty time
PLT451	Recall regulations - ratings issued / experience requirements / limitations
PLT452	Recall regulations - re-dispatch
PLT453	Recall regulations - records retention for domestic / flag air carriers
PLT454	Recall regulations - required aircraft / equipment inspections

PLT455   Recall regulations - requirements of a flight plan release
PLT456   Recall regulations - runway requirements
PLT457   Recall regulations - student pilot endorsements / other endorsements
PLT458   Recall regulations - submission / revision of Policy and Procedure Manuals
PLT459   Recall regulations - takeoff procedures / minimums
PLT460   Recall regulations - training programs
PLT461   Recall regulations - use of aircraft lights
PLT462   Recall regulations - use of microphone / megaphone / interphone / public address system
PLT463   Recall regulations alcohol or drugs
PLT464   Recall regulations - use of safety belts / harnesses (crew member)
PLT465   Recall regulations - use of seats / safety belts / harnesses (passenger)
PLT466   Recall regulations - V speeds
PLT467   Recall regulations - visual flight rules and limitations
PLT468   Recall regulations - Visual Meteorological Conditions (VMC)
PLT469   Recall regulations - weather radar
PLT470   Recall rotor system - types / components / operating principles / characteristics
PLT471   Recall rotorcraft transmission - components / operating principles / characteristics
PLT472   Recall rotorcraft vibration - characteristics / sources
PLT473   Recall secondary flight controls - types / purpose / functionality
PLT474   Recall soaring - normal procedures
PLT475   Recall squall lines - formation / characteristics / resulting weather
PLT476   Recall stabilizer - purpose / operation
PLT477   Recall stalls - characteristics / factors / recovery / precautions
PLT478   Recall starter / ignition system - types / components / operating principles / characteristics
PLT479   Recall starter system - starting procedures
PLT480   Recall static/dynamic stability/instability - characteristics
PLT481   Recall student evaluation - learning process
PLT482   Recall student evaluation - written tests / oral quiz / critiques
PLT483   Recall supercharger - characteristics / operation
PLT484   Recall symbols - chart / navigation
PLT485   Recall taxiing / crosswind / techniques
PLT486   Recall taxiing / takeoff - techniques / procedures
PLT487   Recall teaching methods - demonstration / performance
PLT488   Recall teaching methods - group / guided discussion / lecture
PLT489   Recall teaching methods - known to unknown
PLT490   Recall teaching methods - motivation / student feelings of insecurity
PLT491   Recall teaching methods - organizing material / course of training
PLT492   Recall temperature - effects on weather formations
PLT493   Recall the dynamics of frost / ice / snow formation on an aircraft
PLT494   Recall thermals - types / characteristics / formation / locating / maneuvering / corrective actions
PLT495   Recall thunderstorms - types / characteristics / formation / hazards / precipitation static

PLT496   Recall towrope - strength / safety links / positioning
PLT497   Recall transponder - codes / operations / usage
PLT498   Recall Transportation Security Regulations
PLT499   Recall turbine engines - components / operational characteristics / associated instruments
PLT500   Recall turboprop engines - components / operational characteristics
PLT501   Recall turbulence - types / characteristics / reporting / corrective actions
PLT502   Recall universal signals - hand / light / visual
PLT503   Recall use of narcotics / drugs / intoxicating liquor
PLT504   Recall use of training aids - types / function / purpose
PLT505   Recall use of training aids - usefulness / simplicity / compatibility
PLT506   Recall V speeds - maneuvering / flap extended / gear extended / V_1, V_2, r, ne, mo, mc, mg, etc.
PLT507   Recall VOR - indications / VOR / VOT / CDI
PLT508   Recall VOR/altimeter/transponder checks - identification / tuning / identifying / logging
PLT509   Recall wake turbulence - characteristics / avoidance techniques
PLT510   Recall weather - causes / formation
PLT511   Recall weather associated with frontal activity / air masses
PLT512   Recall weather conditions - temperature / moisture / dewpoint
PLT513   Recall weather information - FAA Avcams
PLT514   Recall weather reporting systems - briefings / forecasts / reports / AWOS / ASOS
PLT515   Recall weather services - TIBS / TPC / WFO / HIWAS
PLT516   Recall winds - types / characteristics
PLT517   Recall winds associated with high / low-pressure systems
PLT518   Recall windshear - characteristics / hazards / power management
PLT519   Recall wing spoilers - purpose / operation
PLT520   Calculate density altitude
PLT521   Recall helicopter takeoff / landing – slope operations
PLT522   Recall helicopter – Pinnacle / Ridgeline operations
PLT523   Recall vortex generators – purpose / effects / aerodynamics
PLT524   Interpret / Program information on an avionics display
PLT525   Interpret table – oxygen / fuel / oil / accumulator / fire extinguisher
PLT526   Recall near midair collision report
PLT527   Recall BASIC VFR – weather minimums
PLT528   Recall regulations – small UAS operations / weight limitations
PLT529   Recall physiological factors – prescription and over-the-counter drugs
PLT530   Recall regulations – small UAS aircraft registration / display of registration
PLT531   Recall regulations – operation of multiple small UAs
PLT532   Recall operating limitations – small UAS aircraft visibility / distance from clouds
PLT533   Recall regulations – small UAS operation over humans
PLT534   Recall regulations – small UAS operational control / condition for safe operation / VLOS
PLT535   Recall regulations – hazardous operational
PLT536   Recall physiological factors – dehydration / heat stroke

CROSS-REFERENCES TO
THE FAA LEARNING STATEMENT CODES

Pages 259 through 261 contain a listing of all of the questions from our remote pilot knowledge test bank. Non-airplane questions are excluded. The questions are in FAA Learning Statement Code (LSC) sequence. To the right of each LSC, we present our study unit/question number and our answer. For example, note that in one instance below, PLT005 is cross-referenced to 4-5, which represents our Study Unit 4, question 5; the correct answer is C.

Pages 253 through 258 contain a complete listing of all the FAA Learning Statement Codes associated with all of the private pilot questions presented in this book. Use this list to identify the specific topic associated to each Learning Statement Code.

The first line of each of our answer explanations in Study Units 1 through 9 contains

1. The correct answer and
2. A reference for the answer explanation, e.g., *AFH Chap 1*. If this reference is not useful, use the following chart to identify the learning statement code to determine the specific reference appropriate for the question.

FAA Learning Code	Gleim SU/ Q. No.	Gleim Answer	FAA Learning Code	Gleim SU/ Q. No.	Gleim Answer	FAA Learning Code	Gleim SU/ Q. No.	Gleim Answer
PLT005	4-5	C	PLT064	2-16	B	PLT064	7-31	C
PLT005	4-6	C	PLT064	2-24	B	PLT068	3-24	B
PLT011	2-13	B	PLT064	2-25	C	PLT068	3-25	A
PLT019	4-3	A	PLT064	2-26	A	PLT072	3-11	A
PLT019	4-4	A	PLT064	6-8	C	PLT072	3-12	A
PLT026	3-19	B	PLT064	6-9	C	PLT072	3-13	A
PLT037	2-5	C	PLT064	6-10	B	PLT072	3-14	C
PLT040	2-4	C	PLT064	6-12	B	PLT072	3-15	B
PLT040	2-8	C	PLT064	6-13	B	PLT072	3-16	B
PLT040	2-14	C	PLT064	6-14	B	PLT072	3-17	B
PLT040	2-17	A	PLT064	6-16	A	PLT075	3-23	C
PLT040	2-19	C	PLT064	6-17	B	PLT077	7-5	C
PLT040	2-21	C	PLT064	7-14	B	PLT078	2-20	C
PLT040	2-27	B	PLT064	7-16	A	PLT078	6-15	C
PLT059	3-1	C	PLT064	7-17	C	PLT078	7-27	B
PLT059	3-2	B	PLT064	7-18	B	PLT098	8-16	C
PLT059	3-3	B	PLT064	7-19	C	PLT099	8-25	C
PLT059	3-4	A	PLT064	7-20	A	PLT101	7-15	B
PLT059	3-5	A	PLT064	7-22	C	PLT103	8-3	C
PLT064	2-6	B	PLT064	7-23	C	PLT103	8-4	C
PLT064	2-7	A	PLT064	7-29	B	PLT103	8-8	A
PLT064	2-15	B	PLT064	7-30	A	PLT103	8-9	A

FAA Learning Code	Gleim SU/ Q. No.	Gleim Answer	FAA Learning Code	Gleim SU/ Q. No.	Gleim Answer	FAA Learning Code	Gleim SU/ Q. No.	Gleim Answer
PLT103	8–10	A	PLT168	5–8	A	PLT274	4–32	C
PLT103	8–11	C	PLT168	5–9	C	PLT281	2–9	B
PLT103	8–12	C	PLT168	5–10	B	PLT281	2–11	B
PLT103	8–13	B	PLT173	4–50	A	PLT281	2–12	B
PLT103	8–14	B	PLT173	4–54	B	PLT281	7–28	A
PLT103	8–15	C	PLT173	4–55	A	PLT289	3–18	A
PLT103	8–18	C	PLT173	4–57	B	PLT289	3–22	A
PLT104	8–2	C	PLT192	4–46	B	PLT301	4–7	A
PLT104	8–5	B	PLT192	4–47	B	PLT301	4–33	C
PLT104	8–17	C	PLT192	4–48	B	PLT309	5–7	C
PLT116	1–15	A	PLT192	4–49	C	PLT310	5–3	B
PLT116	1–17	A	PLT192	4–59	B	PLT312	5–4	C
PLT116	7–25	B	PLT194	1–20	B	PLT312	5–5	B
PLT119	1–1	A	PLT194	1–27	C	PLT312	5–6	B
PLT124	4–11	B	PLT194	6–5	B	PLT313	1–31	A
PLT124	4–14	C	PLT194	6–6	A	PLT313	5–1	A
PLT124	4–58	A	PLT194	6–7	C	PLT323	2–22	B
PLT141	7–1	C	PLT194	8–26	A	PLT323	2–23	A
PLT141	7–2	C	PLT194	8–27	B	PLT323	7–3	C
PLT141	7–6	C	PLT194	8–28	A	PLT332	8–19	B
PLT141	7–7	A	PLT194	8–29	B	PLT332	8–20	A
PLT141	7–8	A	PLT196	6–1	C	PLT332	8–21	A
PLT141	7–9	A	PLT196	6–2	C	PLT332	8–22	A
PLT141	7–10	A	PLT204	6–3	A	PLT332	8–23	A
PLT141	7–11	B	PLT204	6–4	C	PLT336	1–16	C
PLT141	7–12	B	PLT205	1–21	A	PLT345	4–10	A
PLT141	7–32	B	PLT205	8–30	C	PLT351	4–8	B
PLT146	6–11	A	PLT206	4–1	A	PLT351	4–13	B
PLT150	7–4	B	PLT206	4–12	B	PLT366	1–28	C
PLT150	7–13	C	PLT208	9–1	A	PLT366	1–30	B
PLT150	7–26	B	PLT208	9–2	C	PLT370	1–43	C
PLT161	1–4	B	PLT222	8–1	B	PLT370	1–44	C
PLT161	1–5	C	PLT226	4–9	B	PLT372	1–13	A
PLT161	1–38	A	PLT226	4–42	C	PLT373	1–3	B
PLT161	2–2	B	PLT226	4–43	B	PLT373	1–9	A
PLT161	2–3	C	PLT226	4–44	A	PLT387	1–8	B
PLT161	2–10	C	PLT226	4–45	C	PLT387	1–10	A
PLT161	7–21	A	PLT271	8–6	C	PLT387	1–11	A
PLT161	7–33	C	PLT271	8–7	C	PLT387	1–22	B
PLT162	2–1	C	PLT271	8–24	B	PLT387	1–41	C
PLT163	2–18	C	PLT272	8–31	B	PLT387	1–42	C
PLT165	4–16	A	PLT274	4–31	C	PLT393	1–37	B

FAA Learning Code	Gleim SU/ Q. No.	Gleim Answer	FAA Learning Code	Gleim SU/ Q. No.	Gleim Answer
PLT393	1–39	B	PLT512	4–37	C
PLT399	1–6	B	PLT512	4–38	B
PLT399	1–12	B	PLT512	4–39	A
PLT399	1–19	B	PLT512	4–41	A
PLT401	1–34	B	PLT514	3–6	C
PLT403	1–2	C	PLT514	3–7	C
PLT426	9–4	B	PLT514	3–8	C
PLT426	9–6	C	PLT514	3–9	A
PLT435	7–24	C	PLT514	3–10	A
PLT441	1–40	A	PLT514	3–20	A
PLT442	1–18	A	PLT514	3–21	B
PLT442	1–24	B	PLT516	4–17	B
PLT442	1–25	A	PLT516	4–19	C
PLT443	1–14	A	PLT518	4–34	C
PLT443	1–23	A	PLT518	4–35	B
PLT444	1–33	B	PLT520	4–2	A
PLT444	9–8	A	PLT528	1–32	C
PLT445	9–5	B	PLT530	1–7	A
PLT445	9–7	C	PLT530	1–26	A
PLT446	9–3	A	PLT530	1–29	A
PLT454	5–2	A			
PLT463	1–35	C			
PLT463	1–36	A			
PLT475	4–24	B			
PLT493	4–40	B			
PLT494	4–18	C			
PLT495	4–23	B			
PLT495	4–25	A			
PLT495	4–26	B			
PLT495	4–27	A			
PLT495	4–28	B			
PLT495	4–29	B			
PLT495	4–30	A			
PLT511	4–20	C			
PLT511	4–21	A			
PLT511	4–22	A			
PLT511	4–51	A			
PLT511	4–52	C			
PLT511	4–53	A			
PLT511	4–56	A			
PLT512	4–15	C			
PLT512	4–36	C			

ABBREVIATIONS AND ACRONYMS IN
REMOTE PILOT FAA KNOWLEDGE TEST PREP

AAAM	Association for Advancement of Automotive Medicine
AAH	*Advanced Avionics Handbook*
AC	Advisory Circular
ACL	Aeronautical Chart Legend
ACR	Airman Certification Representative
ADM	aeronautical decision making
AFH	*Airplane Flying Handbook*
AGL	above ground level
AIM	*Aeronautical Information Manual*
AIRMET	Airmen's Meteorological Information
AIS	abbreviated injury scale
ASOS	automated surface observing system
ATC	Air Traffic Control
ATIS	Automatic Terminal Information Service
ATO	Air traffic organization
AvW	*Aviation Weather*
AWBH	*Aircraft Weight and Balance Handbook*
AWOS	automated weather observing system
AWS	*Aviation Weather Services*
AWSS	automated weather sensor system
CFI	Certificated Flight Instructor
CFR	Code of Federal Regulations
CG	center of gravity
CoA	Certificate of Authorization
CONUS	continental United States
CoW	Certificate of Waiver
CRM	crew resource management
CS	control station
CT	control tower
CTAF	Common Traffic Advisory Frequency
DOD	Department of Defense
DPE	Designated Pilot Examiner
DROTAM	drone NOTAM
DUATS	Direct User Access Terminal System
FA	area forecast
FAA	Federal Aviation Administration
FAR	Federal Aviation Regulations
FB	winds and temperatures aloft forecast
FBO	Fixed-Base Operator
FCC	Federal Communications Commission
FL	flight level
FPV	first-person view
FSDO	Flight Standards District Office
FSS	Flight Service Station
FTP	Flight termination point
GMT	Greenwich mean time
GPS	Global Positioning System
Hg	mercury
IACRA	Integrated Airmen Certification and/or Rating Application
ICAO	International Civil Aviation Organization
IFH	*Instrument Flying Handbook*
IFR	instrument flight rules

ILS	Instrument landing system
IR	instrument route
KTC	knowledge testing center
LIDAR	Light detection and ranging
LiPO	lithium-polymer
LOC	loss of control
mb	millibar
METAR	aviation routine weather report
MOA	Military Operations Area
MSL	mean sea level
MTR	Military Training Route
MVFR	marginal VFR
NAS	National Airspace System
NEXRAD	Next generation radar
NM	nautical mile
NOTAM	notice to airmen
NSA	national security area
NTSB	National Transportation Safety Board Regulations
PAVE	Pilot, Aircraft, enVironment, External Pressures
PHAK	*Pilot's Handbook of Aeronautical Knowledge*
PIC	pilot in command
PIREP	Pilot Weather Report
PROG	Short-range surface prognostic charts
RPIC	remote PIC
RVR	Runway visible range
SAA	Special Activity Airspace
SFC	surface
SIDA	security identification display area
SIGMET	SIgnificant Meteorological Information
SIGWX	Low-level significant weather charts
SM	statute mile
sUA	small unmanned aircraft
sUAS	small unmanned aircraft system
TAF	terminal aerodrome forecast
TFR	temporary flight restriction
TRSA	terminal radar service area
TSA	Transportation Security Administration
UA	unmanned aircraft
UAS	unmanned aircraft system
UAV	unmanned aerial vehicle
UNICOM	Aeronautical advisory communications station
USC	United States Code
UTC	Coordinated Universal Time
VFR	visual flight rules
VHF	very high frequency
VLOS	visual line of sight
VO	visual observer
VOR	Victor airways or Federal airways
VR	visual route
Z	Zulu or UTC time

AUTHORS' RECOMMENDATIONS

AIRCRAFT OWNERS AND PILOTS ASSOCIATION (AOPA)

AOPA is the largest, most influential aviation association in the world, with two thirds of all pilots in the United States as members. AOPA's most important contribution to the world's most accessible, safest, least expensive, friendliest, easiest-to-use general aviation environment is their lobbying on our behalf at the federal, state, and local levels. AOPA also provides legal services, advice, and other assistance to the aviation community.

We recommend that you become an AOPA member to get the most out of AOPA's resources. To join, call 1-800-USA-AOPA or visit the AOPA website at www.aopa.org.

ASSOCIATION FOR UNMANNED VEHICLE SYSTEMS INTERNATIONAL (AUVSI)

The AUVSI is the world's largest organization devoted exclusively to advancing the unmanned systems and robotics industries. AUVSI provides their members with a unified voice in advocacy for policies and regulations that encourage growth and innovation. It educates the public and media on the safe and beneficial uses of unmanned systems and enables market growth by offering its members custom resources that can help them realize their full industry potential. AUVSI's Remote Pilots Council also provides local networking for certificated remote pilots and a forum for feedback to the FAA.

Learn more about AUVSI at www.auvsi.org/membership.

ACADEMY OF MODEL AERONAUTICS (AMA)

The AMA is the world's largest model aviation association, representing a membership of more than 195,000 people from every walk of life, income level, and age group. The purpose of this self-supporting, non-profit organization is to promote the development of model aviation as a recognized sport and recreation activity. They are the official national body for model aviation in the United States.

The AMA sanctions more than 2,000 model competitions throughout the country each year, and certifies official model flying records on a national and international level. It organizes the annual National Aeromodeling Championships, the world's largest model airplane competition. The AMA is the chartering organization for more than 2,500 model airplane clubs across the country, offering its chartered clubs official contest sanction, insurance, and assistance in acquiring and maintaining flying sites.

Membership is open to anyone interested in model aviation. Consider joining the AMA today at www.modelaircraft.org.

INDEX OF LEGENDS AND FIGURES

INDEX